Janet Leigh

Janet Leigh

A Biography

MICHELANGELO CAPUA

McFarland & Company, Inc., Publishers
Jefferson, North Carolina, and London

To Walter Federico Salazar

Photographs are from the collection of the
author unless credited otherwise.

LIBRARY OF CONGRESS CATALOGUING-IN-PUBLICATION DATA

Capua, Michelangelo, 1966–
    Janet Leigh : a biography / Michelangelo Capua.
        p.   cm.
    Includes bibliographical references and index.

    ISBN 978-0-7864-7022-8
    softcover : acid free paper ∞

    1. Leigh, Janet.   2. Motion picture actors and actresses —
United States — Biography.   I. Title.
    PN2287.L35C37 2013
    791.4302'8092—dc23
    [B]   2013000004

BRITISH LIBRARY CATALOGUING DATA ARE AVAILABLE

On the cover: Janet Leigh, publicity photograph, 1953
(author's collection); filmstrip © 2013 Shutterstock

Manufactured in the United States of America

*McFarland & Company, Inc., Publishers
    Box 611, Jefferson, North Carolina 28640
    www.mcfarlandpub.com*

Table of Contents

Preface

A few years ago on a cross-country train ride in Italy, I watched a film titled *Holiday Affair* on DVD starring Robert Mitchum. Suddenly I found myself hypnotized by the breathtaking presence of Mitchum's female co-star — a stunning blond with delicately modeled features, whom I recognized shortly after as Janet Leigh.

I knew very little about this actress, except that she had been married to Tony Curtis and her daughter was Jamie Lee Curtis, and she had starred in Alfred Hitchcock's *Psycho* and in Orson Welles' *Touch of Evil*.

I quickly researched her life and career and found out she had written her own autobiography in 1985. Yet, in contrast to her ex-husband, no other book had been published on this underrated star whose talent and exquisite beauty graced more than 50 films over a period of 50 years.

Soon I realized what a beautiful, compassionate and gracious woman Jeanette Helen Morrison (Janet Leigh's real name) was, and what an amazing and fulfilling life she had.

She earned a Golden Globe and an Academy Award nomination, appeared on many TV shows, published four books, volunteered for numerous charitable organizations, was an active political campaigner for the Democratic Party and raised two beautiful daughters.

It all began as a true Cinderella story when she was discovered by MGM silver screen diva Norman Shearer. Janet was first cast in roles that enhanced her qualities as a fresh-faced ingénue. Later she starred in four movies that became instant classics: *Touch of Evil, Psycho, The Manchurian Candidate* and *Bye Bye Birdie*.

Her marriage to dreamboat Tony Curtis was celebrated as a Hollywood fairy tale. "Remarkable" was the word that fellow actress and Leigh's good friend, Debbie Reynolds, used to describe that magical yet turbulent union.

> Sometimes two people really clicked. Tony Curtis and Janet Leigh met one day.... Janet was something to behold; beautiful as well as talented. Not jealous, not vindictive, not a bitch, not boring; she's a guileless, dear, terrific lady. Tony was a big, macho, Rambo-type guy; stunning, with gorgeous blue eyes and an ego on steroids. But he took one look at her and it was like the Fourth of July tripled.
>
> Janet had the world trying to get her, but Tony wanted her and she didn't have a prayer. It was physical; it was sexual. It was like dynamite. He got her and married her.

Janet Leigh was unbelievably loved by almost everyone, especially in the entertainment business. As a crewmember said once to her daughter Jamie Lee, Janet was the only person he ever worked with for which no one had said anything unpleasant about her character. She was always smiling and ready to help someone in difficulties.

Janet always downplayed her achievements, yet she felt a great responsibility toward her fans, whom she tried to make happy by being approachable and available all the time. She once said:

> We hold people's dreams in our hands. We should keep the old image of Hollywood alive. Every time I go to a black tie function I always wear something spectacular. People come to me and say, "You look just like a movie star." And I say, "Well, isn't that what we're supposed to be?"

Sadly, she was not given enough chances during her career to demonstrate her incredible talent, probably because she did not receive the critical acclaim she deserved. Yet she was always genuinely grateful for her amazing life. The invaluable and often concealed humanitarian aid to the underprivileged she gave throughout the years brought her the most satisfaction.

In Hollywood, the land of dreams, Janet Leigh managed to stay real. "Jeanette Helen Morrison is who I am. That's the reality," she liked to repeat.

> Janet Leigh is who I am working, and that's my profession. I think that possibly trouble happens with some of our stars who do claw their way up; once they get there, it's almost as if they feel that the profession becomes the reality of their life, and to me it didn't — for me, the reality was my life. Does that make any sense?

I have benefited from the help of many individuals and institutions, and from the assistance and support of friends, without whom the completion of this project would have been impossible. I would like to thank Yaakov Perry; Beatrice Nadalutti; the helpful staff of the British Film Institute in London; the staff of Bobst Library, New York University; the staff of New York Public Library for the Performing Arts at Lincoln Center; Museum of Television and Radio, New York; the staff of the British Library's Humanity Reading Room,

St. Pancras, London; Trish Richards, special collections assistant, University of the Pacific Library, Stockton, California; and Jerry Ohlinger's Movie Material Store, New York.

Finally I offer my immense gratitude to my editor and dear friend, Stuart Williams.

1

Jeanette Helen Morrison

She's beautiful, but the chances of anything coming of all this are so terribly slight. — Norma Shearer

At the beginning of the twentieth century, hardworking couple John B. and Kate Reeb Morrison settled with their four sons in Hornitos, California. Life was very hard for the Morrisons, who struggled to make a decent living to feed their big family.

By the time their youngest child, Frederick Robert, was seven, Kate had developed an incurable cataract and soon became blind. The family moved a few miles southwest to the little town of Merced where work opportunities seemed more favorable. John found employment at a railway company, and the four boys did odd jobs to help their parents pay the bills.

After his older brothers married and moved away from home, young Fred opted to stay in Merced where he met Helen Lita Westergaard, a pretty, spirited daughter of Danish immigrants. The young couple quickly tied the knot after a few months of dating. For William and Lita Coffee Westergaard, their daughter Helen's marriage to Fred was most likely a welcomed one. Helen was, in fact, the second of six children William supported with his modest salary as a ditch digger.

Helen discovered she was pregnant a few weeks after their wedding. On July 6, 1927, she gave birth to a healthy, beautiful girl. Writing as Mrs. Fred Morrison, Helen described the circumstances connected to the happy event twenty-two years later in an article for *Photoplay*:

> Fred and I ... were awaiting our long-overdue first baby and we still didn't have a name for her. *Her.* That was the way I always spoke of the baby from the very first day I knew she was coming. My handsome young husband and I had been married a little over a year and he indulged me in everything. Fred got as close to an argument then as he ever does.

"Look Helen," he said, "We ought to consider a few boys' names, anyhow."

"I just can't," I answered, stubbornly. "She's simply got to be a girl with your nose and my eyes."

"Okay, hon," Fred said. "She's a girl!"

Two days later, she actually was, and she did have my eyes and Fred's nose and wavy hair. The next thing I noticed after taking all that in was the doctor asking me her name. "Jeanette," I said, for no reason at all....[1]

From the start, Jeanette was a good baby. At the end of 1929 the Great Depression took hold of the American economy, and Fred Morrison, like millions of Americans, struggled to find a permanent job. In spite of her family's destitution, those were happy times for little Jeanette, who grew in a caring and loving environment.

After being employed in various local factories, Fred Morrison moved his family to Stockton — "a hot cattle town," as Helen used to call it — sixty miles away from Merced. Hired by Grover Grider, Fred worked for some time as an electrical store salesman at ten dollars a week salary. On such a modest income the family was barely able to survive, let alone be able to afford its own house. Jeanette's parents tried to save money for her future college education — a dream they both had, but could never fulfill. Since her birth, Jeanette became the center of their world. Fred and Helen were very protective of their only child, spoiling her as much as they could afford. Still, the Morrisons were often able to scrape some money together to at least make their Jeanette happy. One Christmas Jeanette wished for a pair of key roller-skates, and, true to form, they did not hesitate to make some sacrifices to get them for her.

Jeanette's first childhood memories were from around age four and connected to her excitement of visiting her Westergaard grandparents' house for Christmas. It was there where she could finally play with her favorite cousin, on whom she had her first crush. She remembered the thrill the whole family felt on that same festive occasion when her mother and five uncles and aunts presented her grandparents with a washing machine that they had all chipped in to buy.

Jeanette was also very close to the Morrisons' grandparents and would spend several weeks there during the summers. Despite belonging to an extended family with many cousins, Jeanette missed the presence of a sibling, someone to spend time with at home while her parents were still at work. She began to get lost in a world of her own, avidly reading books, listening to the radio or watching movies. Cinema was a perfect, inexpensive babysitter, especially on the weekend when she could watch a double-bill with one ticket. With little Jeanette "parked" in a safe, fun place, Fred and Helen had the

opportunity to have a little time for themselves. Once the show was over she would
run home and meticulously tell all about
what she had watched. Spencer Tracy,
Katharine Hepburn, and Judy Garland
were her favorite stars.

"I just loved the movies," Janet revealed years later. "I lived for the movies: I
travelled all over the world, I wore beautiful
gowns. It was the dream world of everyone's
life ... there was no other form of visual
entertainment. Yet I never thought that I'd
be in it."[2]

Jeanette attended Weber Grammar
School, where she was a precocious student,
excelling in math under Fred's tutelage.

"She was really an eager beaver," explained Helen. "I don't know just when she

Janet Leigh at age 6 (1933).

first learned to swim or dance or any of that. It seems to me she always knew.
As a matter of fact, she loved everything except housework, though she'd do
it. And cooking she never did have much chance to learn about ... both her
father and I worked, so we arranged for her to go to a boarding house for a
hot meal at lunch time."[3]

As she grew older, her parents were very proud of her beauty and of her
good character. However, this did not stop them from being very protective — especially Helen, who was obsessed with the idea that Jeanette might
fall ill. The anxious mother was always trying to get her daughter into coats,
boots and hats, and Jeanette was always resisting. After washing her hair,
Helen would insist Jeanette wear two hats, fearing she would catch a cold.

When she was around nine, Jeanette was invited to a birthday party.
Helen, as usual, before picking out her daughter's clothes, washed her hair
and made her wear a little cap to pull down over her head, and topping this
with a wide-brimmed hat. This was a frustrating imposition which embarrassed Jeanette in front of the other kids. Later on, when her daughter became
a movie star and would be all done up, ready to go to a party, Fred would
joke with his daughter: "Be sure and wear your two hats."

When Jeanette was ready to graduate from grammar school, Helen
wanted to get her a very special graduation dress but could only afford $7.95
on her meager budget. The two walked all over Stockton trying to find a
pretty outfit at that price. They kept seeing beautiful dresses all over town,

but at more expensive prices. While Helen was trying to figure out how she could possibly afford a more expensive one, Janet balked, saying that if they could not find a dress at $7.95 she would not graduate. They finally found a lovely dress, and she proudly attended her graduation ceremony.

Fred and Helen considered her daughter very talented because she was good at singing, having a pleasant voice. They saw her as a sort of child prodigy. Helen, in fact, later claimed that Jeanette always wanted to be a singer. "She came by that ambition naturally," said Helen. "Fred sang in the Presbyterian Church choir, where Janet went to Sunday school. We really did have a hard time making ends meet, but since Janet had such a clear, sweet voice, we did manage voice and piano lessons for her."[4]

Fred's boss, Grover Grider, was a drum major in the Stockton marching band. Grider offered ten-year-old Jeanette a place in the band along with his younger son, as a miniature drum girl and boy in an upcoming march. After a short period of training, Jeanette quickly learned her routines and made her first public appearance in a local parade. The band was so impressed with her skills that they wanted to reward her with a gift. Jeanette asked for a raincoat, which she received together with a hat and an umbrella.

As her daughter was growing older, Helen began to live the life she never had for herself, such as completing her education and developing a talent. Eventually, Jeanette felt the onerous responsibility for living a life of "two people."

At age twelve Jeanette entered Stockton High School, where she was accepted in one of the school musical groups and also participated in the Young People's Christian Endeavor at the local Presbyterian Church. During that time she met Richard "Dick" Doane, a very handsome boy whose family had recently moved to Stockton. They first met in church, and later they discovered they were to be classmates in the eighth grade. They platonically dated for over a year. Later, when the Second World War started, Dick was one of the first boys from Stockton to enlist. To Janet this gesture was very romantic, even though she was devastated at the idea of losing him. She wrote him long letters while he was in camp. When he left, Helen, as she later admitted, drew a sigh of relief, afraid Jeanette would have otherwise married him.

When Grandpa Morrison was hospitalized with terminal cancer, Fred, Helen and Jeanette packed up and moved back to Merced and into the Morrisons' house. That Christmas season also brought the tragedy of Pearl Harbor.

For the first time Janet worked at the local dime store during the holidays, but by the time summer vacation came, Stockton's College of the Pacific was packed with young boys in uniform. So Jeanette took a new job in another local shop. While Helen and Fred, who had found a job in a nearby market, were grateful for the extra income her daughter was bringing home, they were not too happy about her contact with so many men. The store was, in fact, a haberdashery, and Jeanette worked in the military department where the cadets were always swarming. Some of them would ask her out, but Helen did not allow her to date men much older than her fifteen-year-old daughter. Regardless, Helen's fears were realized when, only few months later, Jeanette met a nineteen-year-old student, John Kenneth "Kenny" Carlyle. Kenny was a handsome young man who gave her great comfort when her grandfather died. Eventually they fell deeply and madly in love. However, when Fred decided that it was time to go back to Stockton where better job opportunities were available, Janet was devastated by the idea of losing her friends and leaving Kenny.

At the beginning, the Morrisons stayed in a cheap motel in Stockton. Jeanette was very depressed, and when she received an invitation by letter to spend two weeks with a girlfriend in Merced, Helen and Fred gave her permission to go. In Merced her friends came up with the idea that, in order to make her stay permanently in Merced, she should marry Kenny. With the Carlyles' blessings, Jeanette and Kenny drove to Reno, where she had to lie about her age in order to be legally married. When they returned to Merced they found Fred and Helen at the Carlyles' waiting for her. Silently they took her by the arm, put her in the car and drove her away from Kenny, who was stunned and unable to react. Four months later the whole "mistake" was annulled. Despite several attempts on his part, Jeanette never saw her Kenny again. The news of her short marriage and its annulment was kept hush-hush to prevent any scandal in their small town. Dick Doane was a very supportive friend during that dark moment in her life, even though he never knew the real reason for Jeanette's depression. Slowly, when school started back and all her regular activities resumed, Jeanette was able to return to her normal life. Yet for years to come she would live in fear that her secret would come back to haunt her.

Being extremely smart and a hard-working student, Jeanette graduated from high school in three and a half years. In September 1943, at only sixteen years old, she enrolled at the College of the Pacific in Stockton to study music and psychology. Her parents' dream had come true. The education denied them because of their young marriage was now possible for their beloved daughter. During her free time Jeanette would work at the college information desk or would rehearse with the a capella choir she joined.

During the summer semester of 1944 Jeanette, now living at the Alpha

Theta Tau sorority house, met Stanley Reames. Stan was a good-looking, tall, young Navy man, studying radiology under the V-12 program for training reserve officers at the nearby Officers Training School. He was also forming an orchestra for the student body at the College of the Pacific and needed a vocalist. When he heard that Jeanette was a singer, he asked to meet her for an audition. Stan listened, looked her over carefully and decided right then that the beautiful blond creature with those big brown eyes and a pleasant voice was going to be his singer. But after they started dating, he changed his mind. "Not my girl," he said. "Too public!"[5]

Dating Stan, who was sort of glamorous at school because of his band's popularity, was wonderful for Jeanette. It was on the porch of the sorority house where he first kissed her, and on the same porch where they secretly became engaged. From the very beginning, Fred and Helen approved of their daughter's relationship with Stan. When the time came for the young couple to announce their engagement, Jeanette's parents did not object to the decision.

Jeanette and Stan were married on October 5, 1945, in the Morris Chapel at the College of the Pacific. The bride wore a lovely white long dress with a finger-tip veil. Her best friend, Maggie Shepherd, was her bridesmaid. Helen wept from the moment Fred walked her daughter up the aisle right down to the last peal of the organ. After an intimate reception at the sorority house, the newlyweds drove down the coast toward Los Angeles for a ten-day honeymoon. When they returned to Stockton, Mrs. Stanley Reames learned of her parents' plan to move out of Stockton. Fred had taken an offer to be assistant desk clerk at the Sugar Bowl Sky Lodge in Soda Springs, California, where Helen later worked as a waitress in the dining room. They had never seen snow, so the offer seemed an exciting, congenial, and well paid proposition, which could have provided them with a pleasant place to live and new people to be around.

Fred and Helen promised Jeanette and Stan a trip to Sugar Bowl later that year as a Christmas present. By the time the holiday approached, Jeanette surely needed a vacation. In order to keep up with their expenses, the Reameses had taken in two uniformed college boys as boarders. Jeanette took care of the house, cleaning, washing and cooking, while at the same time trying to keep up with her studies. When Christmas finally came, the couple joined Fred and Helen at Sugar Bowl. They had a wonderful, unforgettable week playing out in the snow all day and enjoying a healthy lifestyle in the mountains. One day, wearing an old flying jacket over a little ski suit, her hair blowing in the wind, Janet stood laughing at the club photographer, who took a shot of her. He planned to print it in the lodge album they had for guests. Jeanette couldn't know at the time how that photograph would soon change her life forever.

The following year the Reameses planned to move to Los Angeles where Stan hoped to become part of a famous band. Jeanette was against the idea, having only one year left to earn her degree. It was not an easy decision to make and caused a lot of anguish between husband and wife. While she wanted to complete her education and look for a stable job, Stan, who did not enjoy his studies, felt he was ready to pursue his dreams in the music industry, and Los Angeles was the place to be. During spring break of 1947, before agreeing to sell their car and move out of Stockton, Jeanette and Stan once again visited Helen and Fred at the Sugar Bowl Ski Lodge. This time it was not as fun as the previous holiday. Jeanette was concerned about her husband's choice, which seemed very unrealistic and quite frightening — especially moneywise. Moreover, the idea of giving up college after all the sacrifices her family had made for her did not feel right. She expected advice from her parents, which did not come. They were disappointed in her leaving college, yet they also thought that her place was to be with her husband.

During Jeanette and Stan's stay, Fred mentioned to Jeanette that actress Norma Shearer and her husband Marty Arrougé had been guests at the lodge for several weeks. Jeanette was excited at the idea her parents had met one of her favorite movie stars. She was also surprised to learn that the actress had noticed her in a photograph. From this point there are several versions of the story that led to Jeanette's ticket to Hollywood. Her own, reported in her autobiography, has it that Shearer and Arrougé noticed the photograph on Fred's desk and liked it so much that they took it home with them. Her version claimed that later they asked for additional snapshots, which Fred sent, taken during Jeanette's second holiday at the lodge.

A second version, reported by Helen in the article she wrote for *Photoplay*, has Shearer and her husband "looking through the album and [seeing] the picture of Janet. Miss Shearer asked who she was and when I said my daughter, she asked if she could borrow the picture for a few days. She said she wanted to take the photograph to Hollywood and show it to M.G.M., but she cautioned us not to mention it to Janet. 'She's beautiful,' Miss Shearer said, 'but the chances of anything coming of all this are so terribly slight.'"[6]

A third version, similar to the latter and reported by a Shearer's biographer, has Shearer ordering an enlargement of the picture after noticing Jeanette's striking beauty in the hotel's souvenir album. Regardless of how it happened, it took almost six months before something incredible — what all the magazines would later call a "Cinderella story" — shook Jeanette's life. In the meantime, the Reameses moved, as planned, to Los Angeles. They rented a seven-dollar-a-week room in the crummy Harvey Hotel on Santa Monica Boulevard. While Stan was auditioning all over the city for a band to work with, Jeanette stayed in their squalid room most of the time, keeping house and trying to make it more livable. It was a grim period — Stan could not find a job, as the era of big bands was coming to an end — and the couple was often broke.

Unexpectedly, a letter forwarded from Stockton, addressed to Miss Jeanette Morrison, was delivered to the Harvey Hotel. It was a request from MCA, one the most prominent talent agencies, to call them up as soon as possible to make an appointment for a possible representation. At first Jeanette thought it was a joke or a mistake. But after she nervously phoned the MCA Beverly Hills office of Levis Green, who had signed the letter, and made an appointment the following day, she realized that nobody had made an error.

She was equally stunned afterwards when she learned of the events leading to Green's letter. It was at a dinner at Romanoff's with agent Charles Feldman and MGM executives Eddie Mannix and Benny Thau that Norma Shearer had shown one of the photographs Fred had sent her. Shearer had waited until the gentlemen had finished their dessert and were enjoying their cigars. Then, much in the manner of a proud lady displaying her prized jewels, she produced the photograph. The men were not particularly impressed; however, to not displease the star, they passed on the picture to Lew Wasserman, head of MCA. Wasserman subsequently, along with a stack of other photos of potential new faces, passed it on to Green, head of the new talent department, who looked at Jeanette's beautiful, fresh young face and agreed with Shearer's hunch that it was worth a follow-up.

With the help of some members in Stan's band, Jeanette chose the dress and make-up to wear to the meeting. She only had 30 cents in her pocket and spent it on a little flower to place in her hair. The following morning when she walked into Green's office, the executive took a quick look at her and told her he wanted her to look like she appeared in the photograph he had of her — with no make-up and with her hair down. He also promised to take her the next day to the talent department of MGM. Jeanette left MCA's offices and ran home, nearly in tears. She took a ten-dollar bill her parents had sent her for her birthday and bought a simple pink dress for her second meeting with Green. Green was happy to drive her in his big car to the office of Lucille Ryman, head of the talent department at MGM. Jeanette was gently questioned about her personal and professional background. At the end of the interview she was told by Ryman that MGM had offered her a seven-year exclusive standard contract at $50 per week, with the option to revise it periodically. Jeanette was ecstatic, as she was ushered to the office of the drama coach Lillian Burns, who immediately gave her a scene to work on from Mervyn LeRoy's *Thirty Seconds Over Tokyo* in which a wife says goodbye to her husband, leaving for a dangerous mission.

The next day Jeanette nervously entered Burns' office, and the drama coach noticed immediately how tense she was in reading the assigned part. Without commenting on her acting, Burns explained that the studio wanted to bring her along very slowly and dismissed her after telling her to wait for a call. Jeanette was devastated, as she thought she had made a terrible impression on Burns and would never be called again. Nonetheless, the following Monday she was asked to return to MGM. Upon her arrival Burns asked Jeanette to wait in one of her offices. An executive producer, who had a fixation with singing actresses, had insisted that Beverly Tyler read for the part. Tyler, a young actress who had just made her first film, *The Green Years* (1946), was very determined to get the part of Lissy Anne McBean for the upcoming film *The Romance of Rosy Ridge*, opposite Van Johnson, MGM's most popular leading man.

While Jeanette was waiting in one room, Tyler, who was in costume for the picture, read for the part after being introduced by Burns to the film director and the producer. As soon as she was finished, Burns went into the other room to Jeanette and brought her a copy of that same scene, spending half an hour explaining the script and the part. She asked Jeanette if she could come back the following day to read the lines, specifying that it was not necessary for her to memorize them. Burns saw instantly that Jeanette would be perfect for that role. Jeanette came back and read the scene for Burns, who immediately called Jack Cummings, the producer, who brought along the director, Roy Rowland. They all sat in Burns' office, and suddenly, after Jeanette had read the scene once again in front of the two men, Cummings' eyes popped open. He immediately took Jeanette to wardrobe and outfitted her, then shot some silent color tests. The following day Jeanette received a phone call from Harry Friedman, who was her assigned agent at MCA. He instructed her to be ready to go to MGM's stage 10 to make a screen test with Selena Royle, who played the mother in the film. It was quite a difficult scene, in which Janet had to make a quick transition from laughing happily to tears. Royle had previously done the same test with Beverly Tyler, still considered first choice by the film's executive producer. Ten days later both tests were shown to Louis B. Mayer in the presence of Burns, Cummings and Rowland. After the lights were turned on in the screening room the president of MGM said only one line: "Give it to the new girl!" He did not know Jeanette's name or who she was, but his decision was final and indisputable. Janet remembered how she learned about the news

> I had a lesson with Miss Burns, and I was waiting in the little anteroom — her office was in the back — and I was early. I was always early. It was just fun to sit there and watch people come in and out. And I had to go to the ladies room, so

I went, and I'm washing my hands and I hear somebody pounding on the door. It's Harry Friedman, my agent. He said, "Jeanette, are you in here? Jeanette? Jeanette?" I said, "Harry, what are you doing? I'm in the ladies room." He burst in the door, got my hand, ran back to Lillian's office, and the door's open and Lillian's there, and Jack Cummings is there and Ray Rowland is there and Harry dragged me into the room and sits me down, and says, "You've got the picture!" ... I started to cry. I've goose bumps right now. I'll never forget it as long as I live.... The first thing they did was to bring me to wardrobe. And after I got back from wardrobe I went to Miss Burns' office and I called my husband, Stan, at my aunt's house, and then I called Mom and Dad. That's when Stan and I lived in the back of their garage. It was their laundry room, but was big enough so that we could get a bed in there.... I just said, "I'm going to be in a movie."[7]

"It was her smile that did it," Roy Rowland remarked afterwards.[8]

Without delay Jeanette completed the fittings of all her costumes. She was, in fact, told to be ready within two weeks to go on location at a Santa Cruz mountain site for a three-month shoot. She suddenly became visibly nervous and began to cry, thinking she could not afford the transportation and living expenses on location. She was completely naïve and did not know anything about the film industry.

An early publicity shot.

"Thank you," she said to the MGM executives when they explained to her that all the expenses were going to be paid by the production, "but it would be months before I could repay you and I can't be under that sort of obligation." They finally got it across to her that the studio always paid such costs.[9]

Years later Jeanette learned that Mr. Mayer found Beverly Tyler "too sophisticated for the rustic girl. Roy loved [my] test but told Van he was taking a gamble because of my inexperience, I was not told until years later that a trained actress was waiting back at the studio in case I faltered."[10]

The entire thing seemed like a dream to Jeanette, who just a couple of months earlier was standing in line to see Van Johnson's latest film. Now he was her leading man. On their first meeting, Jeanette had butterflies in her stomach and stayed silent while standing in front of Johnson. Her movie idol quickly congratulated her for a wonderful screen test.

She received the same reaction a couple of days later when she met Mr. Mayer in his office. The president of MGM gracefully welcomed her to the big MGM family, wishing her a great and long-lasting career. Jeanette, who felt very intimidated by her new mega-boss, politely thanked him but was unable to pronounce any other word.

When Norma Shearer was told of Jeanette's casting as the female romantic lead in *The Romance of Rosy Ridge*, she promptly went to the studio to personally congratulate her. It was the first time the star and her "discovery" had met. Shearer kindly agreed to pose for some publicity stills with Van Johnson and Jeanette, who waved the famous photograph Shearer had shown to the MGM executives in her hand. When the photo session was over, Jeanette was told that her name had to be changed. First, the studio suggested that Reames could be easily mispronounced by fans, so they opted to keep the Morrison. But Van Johnson came up with a better name. He shortened Jeanette to Janet, and since *The Romance of Rosy Ridge* was set during the Civil War, he thought of General Lee, but spelled it Leigh. At first Jeanette was baffled by sharing her new last name with Vivien Leigh, who was an established star, but Johnson convinced her that he had no problem sharing his own first name with actor Van Heflin. How could she ever disagree with her favorite film star and idol of millions of fans? That day Jeanette Helen Morrison Reames walked out of the MGM studios with a new name: Janet Leigh. A few days later, on August 22, 1946, the *New York Times* published a short article entirely dedicated to Hollywood's new leading actress, titled "Girl's First Screen Role Is Opposite Van Johnson."

HOLLYWOOD. Calif., Aug 21— Janet Leigh, 19-year-old newcomer to the screen, was named today by Metro-Goldwyn-Mayer for the leading feminine role opposite Van Johnson in "The Romance of Rosy Ridge." Miss Leigh, who has no theatrical experience at all, according to the studio, was discovered by Norma Shearer in Stockton, Calif., and was brought to the studio on Miss Shearer's advice.

The Metro publicity department regards Miss Leigh as the first legitimate example of a Hollywood Cinderella fable to appear in many years, since her first assignment is a leading role in a major picture and much fanfare will accompany her screen debut. She will play an Ozark mountain girl in "Rosy Ridge," which

With Van Johnson in Roy Rowland's *The Romance of Rosy Ridge* (1947).

has been adapted from a MacKinlay Kantor short story of the post–Civil War period.[11]

At the end of August, at nineteen years old and without any acting experience, Janet Leigh was ready to leave for Santa Cruz, California, to film *The Romance of Rosy Ridge*, playing opposite Van Johnson, the highest paid actor in Hollywood. Before saying good-bye, Stan promised to visit her soon. A car picked her up and took her to the station where the MGM crew boarded a train. She traveled overnight in the company of Ruth Rowland, the director's wife. In Santa Cruz the cast and part of the crew was lodged in a nice hotel overlooking a pier and an amusement park.

Janet soon became a favorite with the production crew. "Everyone was so kind on the set," she said in one of her first interviews. "Mr. Johnson gave me heaps of acting tips."[12] She added:

> I could not have gotten through without the support of Van and the crew. I was on my own a few months now without the grooming I always thought I needed. I washed out my clothes every day because I didn't know the wardrobe mistress did that. I stayed by my trailer and knitted furiously between takes to prevent myself from fretting. I remember Thomas Michell [who played the role of her

father] kept telling me to tone down and even said, "Stop acting because the camera will not be on you in this scene."[13]

Despite her naïveté, Janet was never scared or nervous. "It was such a fairy story," she said, "it was almost unreal. I didn't know that they had scheduled some of the harder scenes, so that if I hadn't cut it they would have replaced me just like that. But I didn't know that. I didn't know the workings of anything."[14]

Van Johnson later commented, "I've acted with a lot of girls but I've never known a newcomer to do as well as Janet Leigh."[15] Janet confessed that she learned from him

With second husband Stanley Reames at an MGM film premiere (1947) (Ken Galente collection).

how to handle herself on a set. Once during a scene she accidentally blocked him from the camera's view. When the take was over, Janet panicked, knowing that she had made a terrible mistake. "Honey, don't worry about that," Johnson calmly told her. "The camera will find me. If not, we'll do it again."[16]

The atmosphere on and off the set was extremely relaxed. Often various members of the crew cooked for the group in Johnson's hotel suite, since he could not go to a restaurant without running into hordes of fans. "We were a unified, happy family, working toward our mutual goal," Janet recalled. Johnson became her favorite leading man. He eventually made three films with her. Every day at dawn, studio limousines transported the cast from their hotel to the set, which was based on a farm where they all worked. Janet pitched hay, hauled water, gathered the wheat and learned the art of milking a cow. Her hands and nails broke soon enough to give her the authentic look of a farm girl, yet she never complained. Often fans were lined around the fence of the farm to catch a glimpse of the shoot, hoping to get Van Johnson's autograph.

When an elevator operator at the hotel asked Janet for her autograph, she was so pleased — it being the first request for her signature — that she suggested the boy give her his autograph in return.

The production stopped only for a few days when Johnson ran into poison oak during a chase scene. In October the cast and crew moved to Sonora, near Yosemite National Park, where location work was to be completed. Stan arrived on location, and even took a temporary job with the company to spend more time closer to Janet.

Apparently he was also on the set when she received her first screen kiss — from Johnson. "It doesn't seem right to have anyone else kiss me; I'm glad you are here," she supposedly told Stan, who gave his approval.[17] However, many years later Janet revealed that her marriage was already on the rocks, specifying, "It was broken up before we even got married."[18]

The shooting then moved to an MGM sound stage. The Reameses were then living over a garage, sharing a house with one of Janet's aunts in Glendale. The production decided to put them up temporarily in a Santa Monica hotel to ease Janet's daily commute to the studio. In the meantime, Fred and Helen had left Sugar Bowl to settle in Los Angeles. To save money, Janet and Stan decided to share a house in the San Fernando Valley with the Morrisons. It was not a wise decision. Stan, who was out of work, was constantly reminded by his in-laws that he was living off Janet's salary, creating an atmosphere of great tension within the family.

2

Cinderella in Hollywood

The only good thing about *Words and Music* was they had Janet Leigh play my wife. And I found *that* highly acceptable. — Richard Rodgers

The Romance of Rosy Ridge was completed in early December and released in September 1947. There was much talk that the film was assured of some Academy Award nominations, but the circumstances which followed its release made it impossible. Screenwriter Lester Cole, a member of the American Communist Party, was cited for contempt and blacklisted after he refused to answer questions before the House Committee on Un-American Activities. *Rosy Ridge* was critically acclaimed, but it was a disappointment at the box office. Nevertheless, Janet received very enthusiastic reviews.

Thomas M. Pryor of the *New York Times* wrote, "Janet Leigh is as fresh and pretty as a daisy in the spring. This is Miss Leigh's first picture and it must be said that she is a welcome addition to the ranks of leading ladies. Time and a few more pictures will tell the full extent of her talent, for in *The Romance of Rosy Ridge*, Metro-Goldwyn-Mayer has carefully avoided making heavy demands upon Miss Leigh."[1]

Two weeks before the completion of *Rosy Ridge* Janet was invited by CBS radio to take part in a broadcast of a popular series called *The Cresta Blanca Hollywood Players*. The episode was "All Through the House" and the cast included four major Hollywood stars — Gregory Peck, Gene Kelly, John Garfield and Joseph Cotten. Janet played the part of a young girl who brings peace to three feuding brothers just as the New Year begins. The first rehearsal reading was a nightmare for Janet. She was extremely tense and stumbled several times over her lines. Things improved only after her four partners helped her relax. On Christmas Eve, in front of a live CBS radio studio audience, Janet gave an impeccable performance, broadcast live all over the country.

Fred and Helen finally moved into a new house, while Janet and Stan rented a tiny apartment in Beverly Hills. It was the only way to save what was left of the relationship between her husband and her parents, which had deteriorated into an unbearable situation.

Despite the unpleasant situation at home, Janet was still excited by her first premiere, her first car, and a dog she picked up from the pound. She was thrilled when she received an invitation to her first Hollywood party, thrown by the famous tycoon Atwater Kent. While Stan had to rent a seven-dollar dinner jacket (since his tuxedo had moth holes), Janet borrowed her outfit from Evie Wynn, Van Johnson's wife. Wynn kindly lent her a pretty skirt, matched with an elegant blouse and a valuable brooch. That night she felt like Cinderella going to the Royal Ball. She was so excited that Van Johnson told Walter Pidgeon, "I have never seen anyone enjoying anything quite so wholeheartedly as Janet did. She had stars in her eyes all evening. It was a pleasure to watch her."[2]

Only four months went by and Janet, still coached by Lillian Burns, was cast in her second film, *If Winter Comes*. "They needed a young girl who gets pregnant, kills herself and then everyone blames Walter Pidgeon, so they looked at their list of people and they thought I would be right for it," she candidly explained on how she got the part.[3]

If Winter Comes was based on A.S.M. Hutchinson's melodramatic novel about the vicious consequences of gossip in a small English village. It was a remake of a 1923 silent film directed by Harry F. Millarde and starring Percy Marmont. British director Victor Saville, who had made two of Vivien Leigh's early films, was asked by MGM to direct it. It featured an almost all–British cast, which included Angela Lansbury, Dame May Whitty, Hugh French, Hughie Green and Deborah Kerr (in her second picture in Hollywood). In her autobiography, Janet revealed that Saville was not aware of her actual heritage until late in the shoot. The studio hired a personal language

With Angela Lansbury (left) and Deborah Kerr (center) in *If Winter Comes* (1947).

coach to teach her an English accent so that her speech would sound believably British.[4]

Angela Lansbury, then 22 years old, wanted Janet's touching but difficult role of Effie, the waif-like village girl fallen on hard times. Effie ultimately hurried the destruction of a professor offering help. Lansbury, however, was forced by Saville to play Mabel, the bitter 35-year-old wife of the 50-year-old Walter Pidgeon. Although very disgruntled, Lansbury accepted the role.

On the first day of production, Pidgeon (a Canadian-born actor with a solid background on the British stage) was impressed by Janet's natural talent. "Her acting was so sensitive I was totally unprepared, that in my amazement I hardly remembered my lines!" commented Pidgeon. "Janet is astonishing."

In an article for *Silver Screen* he mentioned a curious episode involving Janet's outstanding performance:

> Victor Saville ... and I were running rushes of scenes done during our initial day's work, scenes in which Janet Leigh and I had appeared. At their end Vic turned to me and said, most flatteringly, I must admit:
> "My dear Mr. Pidgeon, I've never seen an actor do a better job."
> "My dear Mr. Saville," I countered, "would you mind running those rushes again so I may see *myself*?" I had *not* seen myself, quite truthfully. I had been watching Janet in those scenes, and that is the first time within my memory that ever has happened — one actor distracting another so completely by artistic achievement that the other hasn't seen his own work.... Seeing those first rushes I was totally oblivious of my own performance. I just watched Janet, her acting was so compelling. Janet Leigh is one of the greatest natural actresses I had encountered in my entire career. She has wonderful eyes which reflect her every mood. She has great sincerity in her work. She can walk off with honors in just about every scene.[5]

Janet also recalled how she carefully observed her colleague in order to learn more about acting, "I did my first scene with Walter Pidgeon and he seemed so low-keyed but the camera caught everything he was trying to achieve."[6]

The shooting of *If Winter Comes* finished in the late summer of 1947, just in time for Janet to run to the set of her next film, *Hills of Home*. MGM shelved the release of *Winter* until the following summer, when it was met by mixed reviews and poor box office sales.

Janet left for the Sonora Pass in the California High Sierras, which were used as the backdrop of a supposedly Scottish setting. *Hills of Home* was a Lassie film which reunited the most famous dog in Hollywood with Edmund Gwenn, who had appeared in the successful *Lassie Come Home* (1943). This new film was a sentimental tale of an old Scottish doctor who teaches Lassie, rescued from a cruel master, to overcome his fear of water. The cast also included Donald Crisp and Tom Drake, on whom Janet had a little teenage crush.

During the entire shooting Janet was lucky to receive coaching from Lillian Burns, who came on location with her. Fred Wilcox was, in fact, not a strong director; he gave little real guidance to his actors, who were left on their own. Still, Janet was able to manage herself pretty well, giving a convincing performance as the young Margit Mitchell.

After three weeks on location the production was transferred to MGM studios. This was now a convenient location for Janet, since she and Stan had moved into a small apartment just three blocks away.

Although the reviews of *Hills of Home* were solid and the sales good, the picture did nothing to enhance Janet's career.

An article titled "Cinderella Herself. Or How Janet Leigh Got to Be a Movie Star Without Even Half Trying" appeared that summer in the *New York Times*. Morgan Hudgins ran the story of the lucky events that led to Janet's discovery. The editor compared her, like many others already had, to the fairy tale heroine. The piece included a funny anecdote which showed that even a girl portrayed as naïve and innocent had a shrewd side:

> There's a strong possibility that the name of Janet Leigh may some day be every bit as famous as that of the woman who discovered her. But Janet herself is taking no chances. The other day, while driving down Wilshire Boulevard, her car was forced to the curb by a persistent driver, who stepped over and presented her with his card. It revealed he was a casting executive of the Twentieth Century–Fox studios. He had, he said, been trailing her for blocks. Would she care to sign a contract with his studio? Janet admits she felt great pride when she announced she is already an actress — under contract.
>
> "However," she says seriously, "I took the card. You never know in Hollywood!"[7]

Janet was ecstatic to learn that she had been cast as Dorothy Feiner Rodgers, the wife of the composer Richard Rodgers, in *Words and Music*. The film was based on the life and songs of Rodgers and lyricist Lorenz "Larry" Hart.

Rodgers and his attorneys were known for carefully supervising all the productions, live or filmed, in which the composer was involved. However, for this MGM project, Rodgers, who did not want to be in Hollywood, asked producer Arthur Freed to hire his brother-in-law, Ben Feiner, Jr., on his behalf. Feiner became an associate producer of the project and got involved in the casting process. The part of Rodgers was given to Tom Drake, with whom Janet had just finished *Hills of Home*. Mickey Rooney was awarded the role of Larry Hart. Slowly the project was transformed, for commercial reasons,

As Dorothy Feiner Rodgers in *Words and Music* (1948).

in an all-star revue presented in lavish Technicolor. The lives of Rodgers and Hart were tied together with musical numbers depicted as staged theatrical performances featuring the most popular singers and dancers. Judy Garland, Lena Horne, June Allyson, Gene Kelly, Cyd Charisse, Mel Torme, Perry Como and many others were all cast in the picture. The true story of Hart's self-destructive behavior, linked with alcoholism and closeted homosexuality, could never have been filmed in those times. However, the portrayal of both artists looked ludicrous.

Janet was very tense when she was introduced to Richard and Dorothy Rodgers. She commented,

> Just the idea of meeting them and playing a live person made me shake. To prepare I read about Mrs. Rodgers, I tried to find out the kind of person that she was: what schools she went to, her favorite sports, who her friends were, whether she liked Twinkies or cupcakes. All the things that help you create a real-life character. Usually, when you play a role you manufacture all these things yourself, but Dorothy Rodgers was a living person. And a very elegant and charming one.[8]

Janet was particularly excited the time she had to work in a scene with Judy Garland, one of her favorite stars. "[She] gave me goose bumps. Although I didn't know it then, Judy was going through a bad period and she'd often be very late. Mickey Rooney, who was in the scenes with Judy, was the soul of patience with her, no matter what time she'd show up. Arthur Freed, our producer, would finally lead her onto the set like a queen, which she was, really. Once she started she was sensational."[9]

Words and Music was released in December 1948 and was an instant hit. Nonetheless, Richard Rodgers was unhappy with the final product, as he publicly commented:

> The most terrible lies have been all those Hollywood musicals, which purport to be the life story of people like Gershwin, or Porter, or Kern. They give no insight whatsoever into the working patterns of the men they're supposedly about. They did it to Larry Hart and me. The only good thing about *Words and Music* was they had Janet Leigh play my wife. And I found *that* highly acceptable.[10]

Through Lillian Burns, who was still tutoring her with daily acting lessons, Janet met actor Barry Nelson. A handsome man ten years her senior, Nelson was making a film called *Undercover Maisie* (1947). He and Janet started to spend a lot of time together, rehearsing scenes from famous plays and discussing acting techniques. At the same time Janet's marriage was slowly disintegrating. Stan was frustrated that his musical aspirations had remained unfulfilled, and that he was making a living doing a job he disliked. Moreover, his wife's popularity and career on a constant rise was probably too much for his pride.

Meanwhile, Janet and Barry's professional friendship was getting stronger every day. This was encouraged by the studio, who, to promote their names, made sure they appeared together at many social events.

Janet's next film was *Act of Violence*, directed by Fred Zinnemann and co-starring Van Heflin, Robert Ryan and Mary Astor. The picture was originally announced in 1947 as an independent production starring Howard Duff. Subsequently, in 1948, Hellinger Productions–SRO Releasing announced the film was to star Gregory Peck and Humphrey Bogart. Eventually MGM took over, and once again the cast changed. *Act of Violence* was based on a suspenseful script by Robert Richards from a story by Collier Young. It was a thrilling cat-and-mouse tale of revenge exacted by an American ex-soldier, a handicapped survivor of a World War II Nazi prison camp. After years of searching, and still filled with resentment, the veteran discovered the whereabouts of the only other survivor, who had betrayed him and many other members of his squadron in order to save himself. The traitor, now a builder respected by his family and friends, suddenly fears retaliation by his former comrade.

"On *Act of Violence*," commented Janet, "I got my first test as an actress. It was an enormously difficult part.... I kept flubbing lines."[11] Working with Heflin and Ryan was a great privilege. The two leading men were very supportive of her, who was, after all (and as Zinnemann called her in his autobiography), "a charming newcomer"[12] and "a marvelous" actress.[13]

At that time Zinnemann's seven-year contract with MGM was almost up, and he had no intention of renewing it. He was a talented director who had made dramatic pictures, which was not in the MGM style. He was used to drama focused on reality, which the studio did not appreciate. *Act of Violence* was, in fact, filmed with a documentary style technique. For two days and three nights the director toured the downtown area of Los Angeles on foot, accompanied by cinematographer Robert Surtees. The director studied the city streets, alleys, doorways, saloons, empty store fronts and street lights. Zinnemann wanted to find the perfect locations for a more accurate and realistic approach, and raise his picture to a level above the typical MGM family product. "We were very fortunate ... that the leading woman's role was played by Janet Leigh," commented Surtees, "a young, beautiful girl who photographs well without diffusion and who can take any kind of a key light."[14] Janet's relationship with Zinnemann was harmonious, despite the fact she was feeling very tired because she was looping (inserting dialogue) for *Words and Music*, doing wardrobe fittings for *Little Women* (which was in pre-production), and rehearsing for her next picture (*The Red Danube*).

"One day," she explained in an interview, "I walked in and Mr. Zinnemann said, 'I know the demands on you, Janet, but this is basic, this is your performance and it takes precedence. You must give me a performance!' He could see it in my eyes — I wasn't concentrating. After that, he worked very closely with me and everything went well. I learned a great deal on this one."[15]

The *New York Times* critic Bosley Crowther detected the chemistry between the director and his leading lady. In his review of *Act of Violence* he wrote, "Mr. Zinnemann has also extracted a tortured performance from Janet Leigh as the fearful, confused and disillusioned wife of the haunted man."[16]

One day, on a break from filming *Act of Violence*, Janet was approached at the studios by Mervyn LeRoy. After he warmly saluted her, the director said, "Janet, I want you to know that you are going to play Meg in *Little Women!*" "It struck me like a thunderbolt," she later commented.[17] The idea of being part of a classic she had read when she was a little girl was wonderful.

Little Women had been one of the favorite books of LeRoy's daughter

Linda. The director persuaded Louis B. Mayer to buy the rights from David O. Selznick. Selznick had even built some sets for his production, which MGM bought along with the rights. LeRoy's production was the third version of Louisa May Alcott's classic to appear on screen. In 1919 Paramount had released a silent version, and in 1933 Selznick produced an RKO adaptation directed by George Cukor, and starring Joan Bennett as Amy, Jean Parker as Beth, Frances Dee as Meg and Katharine Hepburn as Jo. For years Selznick himself had planned to produce a color remake with his wife Jennifer Jones as Jo, and a cast that included Rhonda Fleming, Anna Revere and Charles Coburn. Costumes and set tests were completed; however, the production shut down after three weeks of filming due to a combination of post–World War II cutbacks within the industry and the threat of craft worker strikes. Selznick abandoned the project altogether, selling the rights to MGM. Mervyn LeRoy, who had produced *The Wizard of Oz*, spent almost a year in preparation, sparing no expense to recreate the nostalgic world of the March family during the Civil War. June Allyson was cast as the tomboy Jo, Elizabeth Taylor as the vain Amy, Margaret O'Brien as the sensitive Beth and Janet as the intelligent Meg. Once everything was ready, filming was postponed until June because MGM had three other color films scheduled for an earlier release.

"On the set everybody got along swimmingly," wrote LeRoy in his autobiography. "I've really never had any major temperament problems on any of my sets."[18] Mary Astor, who played Marmie March, the mother of the four girls, had a different opinion, saying that the girls all giggled and chatted all the time and made a game of every scene. Janet admitted that on the set they did a lot of different and dumb things:

> I'll never forget the time when Peter Lawford blew a line (he had problems in perfectly pronouncing the word porcupine) and it struck us funny. Every time we would get to this line we would just start giggling and couldn't stop. We couldn't get through the scene. We had to shut down and Mervyn said, "Oh my gosh, everybody just go away."[19]
> June Allyson, Elizabeth Taylor, Margaret O'Brien and myself really did assume the aura of four sisters and had a ball.... Mr. LeRoy was great. He put up with us and still managed to turn out one of the most beautiful films I was ever in.[20]

The four co-stars enjoyed eating at the studio commissary together, as June Allyson remembered. "All the 'sisters' would troop down together in our nightclothes or hoopskirts to get our nourishment — Elizabeth Taylor, Janet Leigh, Margaret O'Brien and me. Much of our talk revolved about Papa Mayer."[21] Janet remembered Dean Martin and Jerry Lewis visiting the set. At that time Lewis was secretly seeing June Allyson's friend Gloria DeHaven, a big band singer who had worked with Allyson in *Best Foot Forward*, and who was married to the actor John Payne.

LeRoy finished shooting in September 1948, and *Little Women* opened at New York's Radio City Music Hall in April 1949 as the MGM Easter Attraction. For the first time in her career — after six films in two years — Janet's name was listed above the title, giving her the status of an established star. The picture proved very successful for MGM, winning two Oscars (for Art Direction and Set Decoration) the following year, as well as being nominated for Best Color Cinematography. Most reviews were favorable, although some critics preferred the Selznick version.

In July 1948, while she was filming *Little Women*, Janet and

With Elizabeth Taylor on the set of *Little Women* (1948).

Stan finally divorced. Stan had borrowed money from his parents and from the government as a GI loan. When they separated, since Janet was the only one who had an income, she assumed the entire government debt. She moved back with her parents in a rented house in the San Fernando Valley. Janet was the only one in the family making money, however; the salary was managed by Fred, who eventually found a job. Janet remembered a funny anecdote about that time when she was living back with her parents. Although she was a twenty-one-year-old, she was still very naïve and emotionally dependent on her family:

> I was in a store doing a photo shoot and I saw this sweater. It had a little trim of fur around the collar. And I thought, oh, I'd love to have that. I think it was sixty dollars, which at the time was a lot. So [celebrity Hollywood columnist] Hedda Hopper was at the store, and I called Dad and said, "Daddy, can I afford this sweater?" And her jaw dropped. She said, "I never heard of that in my life." And every time I ever saw her after that, she would say, "I don't believe you."[22]

To celebrate the wrap-up of *Little Women*, Janet attended a party at Mervyn Leroy's home with Barry Nelson, who she was now officially dating. Wearing a beautiful strapless gown with her hair fashionably styled, Janet looked particularly stunning that evening. She was unaware a man was observing her from the sidelines, until LeRoy told her that there was someone he wanted her to meet. He took Barry and Janet into his library and introduced them to Howard Hughes. One of the richest men in the world, a business magnate with many interests and investments, Hughes was also a film producer-director who controlled the struggling RKO studio. Janet knew who he was; however, she was rather disappointed by his bizarre look and odd manners. They made small talk, and she quickly forgot about that strange man who was twice her age.

At the end of the year Janet was cast to play June Forsyte in another period drama, *That Forsyte Woman*. Based on the novel *The Forsyte Saga* by John Galsworthy, the production hired a first-rate cast, including Errol Flynn, Greer Garson, Walter Pidgeon and Robert Young. The film's director, Compton Bennet, who had recently triumphed with *The Seventh Veil*, was very nervous about having two major stars — Flynn and Garson — in the same film. However, his fears were quickly assuaged. On the set, in fact, Flynn was on his very best behavior. He refrained from drinking or taking any drugs, and became an instant friend of Garson's. Janet, who was herself intimidated by the presence of the two great co-stars, admitted to have misjudged them — especially Garson, who she thought would be serious and uptight. However, she quickly changed that notion when Miss Garson told her to call her Greer. During the shooting, Janet witnessed many pranks Flynn and Garson played on each other. "For one scene where she was ironing a dress," Janet recalled, "Greer was then supposed to walk to a closet and open it. Which she did — and there stood Errol in his BVDs."[23] The sudden sight of her co-star in his underwear made Garson scream wildly and almost faint. However, on the last day of filming, she got even. During a scene where she was in a carriage with him, Garson attached a battery-operated device to the door handle so that Flynn received an electric shock when he touched it.

The picture was completed at the end of February 1949 and premiered in New York at Radio City Music Hall the following November, following the release of two other films Janet had made afterwards. *That Forsyte Woman* grossed over $3,697,000, but the expensive cost of the lavish production resulted in a loss of over half a million dollars. Despite her secondary role, Janet delivered a particularly fine performance which was noticed by many reviewers.

Janet was still dating Barry Nelson when he was cast in the play *Light*

Up the Sky by Moss Hart. The tryouts started in Boston, followed by the official opening on Broadway. Janet, who was madly in love, asked MGM for three weeks off before starting her new film and left for Boston with Nelson's mother to watch Barry on stage. It was Janet's first time on a plane and her first trip out of California, except for that brief night in Reno when she got married. After Boston she followed the company to Philadelphia and New York. It was a fantastic trip, which gave her the opportunity to observe closely how acting on stage was different than on camera. She also visited many fascinating historical sites she had only read about. Those three weeks with Barry were magical, yet in an article she wrote for *Photoplay*, Janet stated that before going back home, Nelson told her that he wanted her to have other dates. "He said that he loved me very much and believed I felt the same. 'But I don't believe,' he said, grinning at me, 'that you are ready to settle down again, quite yet.'"[24] She was disappointed, but slowly she began to realize that he was right. "I wanted to do different things, go dancing, go to parties, night clubs, the theater, play a little, flirt a little, have the kind of fun I'd never had."[25]

As soon as she returned home she began rehearsing for *The Red Danube*, directed by George Sidney, who also happened to be Lillian Burns' husband. Originally titled *Storm Over Vienna*, *The Red Danube* was based on Bruce Marshall's best-selling novel *Vespers in Vienna*. Its story concerned a British colonel and his junior officer, whose job is to repatriate Russian citizens in post–World War II Vienna. The young officer falls in love with a beautiful ballet dancer, who turns out to be a Russian citizen so terrified of being deported to her native country that she ultimately commits suicide. The picture benefited from a very impressive cast, which included Walter Pidgeon, Peter Lawford, Angela Lansbury and Ethel Barrymore.

The role of the Russian ballerina, Maria Buhlen, was very demanding. Janet had to learn how to speak with a German accent, taking daily classes with an Austrian actress. She also studied classical ballet with famous MGM chorographer Alex Romero.

"I began studying dancing six months before we began to shoot," she revealed. "When we finally got to it, I didn't do the leaps but I did go *en pointe*. And this is something you are supposed to start doing at six years of age. It was agony — so painful — just to get *en pointe*, but I got so I even did a turn."[26]

In addition to ballet and accent lessons, Janet was still taking acting classes with Lillian Burns. The director's wife also helped Peter Lawford on the set to call up the proper emotions by tapping her own feelings about the Holocaust.

With Ethel Barrymore, Peter Lawford and Walter Pidgeon in *The Red Danube* (1948).

Janet noticed that Lawford wasn't comfortable communicating strong emotions, and she referred to an incident that sheds some light on his limitations as an actor in an interview:

> During the scene when I jump out of the window, I got very emotional. It was a very difficult scene for me. I was really overwrought — I had burst into tears and I couldn't turn it off after the cameras stopped rolling. Peter said, "Now Janet, what's that all about?" It was like he was saying, "Just do it and forget it. This is only a movie!" But, I couldn't turn it off that quickly. I guess it was his British inwardness, that reserve, where you don't show your emotions that readily. Maybe he didn't feel as comfortable in a dramatic situation as other people. He was more comfortable playing the sophisticated or the playboy.[27]

Despite being one of Janet's favorite films, *The Red Danube* flopped at the box office on its release in December 1949, losing almost a million dollars. It received mostly negative reviews, with nearly every critic pointing out, intentionally or not, the film's anti-communist message. Sidney himself said that he had tried and failed to emulate Carol Reed's 1949 classic *The Third Man*, which was also set in post-war Vienna.[28]

To strengthen the picture's poor box-office performance, MGM sent Janet, Peter Lawford and Walter Pidgeon on a ten-city promotional tour. Sometimes the trio went together to a city, sometimes they split up. Janet visited Pittsburgh, New York and Boston. Peter Lawford brought a friend, Joe Naar, along on the tour. In an interview for Lawford's biography, Naar affirmed that Peter was dating Janet at the time. "I was still in college and it was all new to me and I didn't know anything about anything.... Before the movie opened, they would get up on stage and ... Peter with Janet would do some sort of show."[29]

Regarding that period, Janet later commented, "We had a great time. Those days were a lot of fun."[30]

That year MGM suffered a considerable drop-off in success due to the introduction of television and changing public tastes. To control costs, Louis B. Mayer hired writer and producer Dore Schary as production chief. Schary, who was 20 years Mayer's junior, immediately changed the studio policy, ordering a new approach in making pictures. Schary focused on reality and a hard-hitting kind of documentary style with a message, in contrast with Mayer's taste for "wholesome" family films that had been an MGM trademark for years. In the spirit of this new guideline, Janet was cast in a medical drama called *The Doctor and the Girl*, opposite Glenn Ford. Screenwriter Theodore Reeves based the script on *Bodies and Souls*, a current bestseller by Maxence van der Meersch. The story is of a young ambitious doctor who has to choose between assured success and fame, thanks to his father, a wealthy Park Avenue physician, or working out his own career the hard way among the poor. MGM borrowed the director Curtis Bernhardt from Warner Bros. and Glenn Ford from Columbia Pictures. Bernhardt decided to follow the gritty realistic flavor Schary sought, avoiding asking local authorities permission to shoot on location on New York's streets.

"Robert Planck was the photographer," remembered Bernardt in an interview. "We had to use a hidden camera.... We had a car built where we could ride together on the rear-end with the camera. And we shot some scenes, on 42nd Street I think, from the inside of a milk parlor. We shot through the window outside and people couldn't tell we were putting them on film."[31] Glenn Ford was sent ahead to look at the Bellevue Hospital, Columbia Presbyterian and all the other locations planned for the shoot.

Filming started at the end of October. Janet—who played a young patient romancing the doctor—and Ford had a perfect chemistry, both on and off the set. The director took advantage of the situation and encouraged the two to improvise whenever they felt it was appropriate, giving more credibility to their characters.

With Glenn Ford in *The Doctor and the Girl* (1949).

"Janet was a lovely girl and so easy to work with," Ford commented. "I was impressed with how quickly she had learned her craft. So many girls were discovered because of their looks, but it took real ability, brain and ambition to turn that break into a lasting career, as Janet did."[32] *The Doctor and the Girl* wrapped up shooting on December 13, 1948. Before leaving the set for the last time, Janet gave Ford a copy of the same photograph Norma Shearer had used to promote her. Janet inscribed it: "To one of the nicest people I've met in the career this picture started." The film opened nationwide the following September, garnering only mild interest with the public, despite generally good reviews. Janet's performance was praised by *Variety* as "excellent."[33]

Since their meeting at Melvyn LeRoy's party, Howard Hughes had become obsessed with Janet. He persisted in unwanted attentions, following her to restaurants or clubs when she went on dates with other men, seating himself close by, and staring the entire time. The first manipulation Hughes tried to make in Janet's life was to offer Barry Nelson, through RKO, a part in a film in South America for a tremendous amount of money. He wanted Barry out of the way; however, Nelson had already committed to a play on

Broadway. Hughes later tricked Janet into taking a brief plane ride (Hughes had a particular passion for airplanes), but she felt only anger and fright about the whole experience. She did not find his obsession amusing. Hughes' manipulative behavior manifested once again when he learned that Janet was dating the heir to the Loew's theatrical fortune, Arthur Loew, Jr., and tried to discredit him. As Janet recalled:

> He called me in and said, "I just want you to see this." He hands me these papers, and I said, "What is this?" He says, "Well, I have ways of getting hold of this kind of information. And I want you to know what kind of person you're going out with." I said, "Stop this. Just stop it." I said, "Why can't you be like a human being and if you want to go out with me ask me out like a person, like a man?" And he said he didn't like to do that. I think he was afraid of rejection, and so he said, "All right, will you go out with me?" I said no. And then I said—I thought. "Oh, this will fix it"—I said, "OK, I'll go out with you with my mother and father."[34]

Surprisingly, Hughes agreed. The following evening Janet, Fred and Helen had dinner with the magnate at the Sportsman's Lodge. "The three of them had a wonderful time," recalled Janet. "And I was bored to tears. I mean, it was fun because I saw Mom and Dad were having a good time."[35]

Hughes carried on with his bizarre behavior of courting Janet, who was very distraught, especially after Bennie Thau, vice president of MGM, called her into his office and said, "Janet, I have wonderful news, RKO is going to borrow you for three pictures. You'll be working with Robert Mitchum and John Wayne. It's a tremendous opportunity for you."[36] The opportunity was mostly for the studio, which was going to make a fortune on the loan-out. Janet tried to explain Hughes' intimidating behavior and all the things that had been happening, and being afraid of what could happen if she worked for his studio. Recalled Janet:

> Thau just said, "Now, honey, we're sure there's nothing to worry about. This is a business situation, nothing more. There's no funny business. We're talking about a lot of money at stake here. So you go and do as we say." And I must have still looked nervous because he added, "Look, I'm a phone call away if anything goes wrong." And that was all they wanted to hear about that.[37]

A few weeks later MGM publicly announced the news as the *New York Times* wrote: "Janet Leigh Gets 2 RKO Film Leads." (She was actually borrowed for three pictures.) The article indicated that Janet was borrowed by RKO for an undisclosed amount to play the leading feminine roles in *Christmas Gift*, opposite Robert Mitchum, and *Jet Pilot*, opposite John Wayne. The production of the first film was scheduled to start on July 11, while the second had been planned to start as soon as *Christmas Gift* was completed.[38]

When she arrived at the RKO studios on an early morning in the summer of 1949, Janet was as nervous as when she went through the gates of MGM three years earlier. However, she immediately relaxed when director Don Hartman put her at ease.

"It was a very happy set and we did good work," Janet later revealed. *Christmas Gift* was planned to try out a new image of Robert Mitchum, giving him the opportunity to play in a romantic comedy. The picture, released as *Holiday Affair*, was based on *The Man Who Played Santa Claus*, a novelette by John D. Weaver. The story was centered on the romance that developed after a brush in a department store between Connie, a young widow with a child, and shop assistant Steve, who loses his job thanks to her.

> Although I wasn't thrilled about having to do it, *Holiday Affair* turned out to be another I loved.... [It] proved a delightful film. It's become a Christmas staple on TV. And I enjoyed working with Bob Mitchum and Wendell Corey — I *think*. Bob was such a free soul. Much of the time, I didn't know what to make of him. He was funny and so relaxed he sometimes seemed in danger of falling over. But he was always professional. Both he and Wendell Corey would try to shock me; they knew a patsy when they saw one. Like when Bob was required to kiss me like I'd never been kissed before! During the big Christmas dinner scene, Bob

and Wendell each put a hand on my leg. Oh, they never followed through on any of this, they just liked to tease their victim.[39]

Janet also admitted to having learned a lot from Mitchum, as well as from Gordon Gebert, a young actor who was playing her son. In one scene he started playing with his breakfast cereal. Janet stopped delivering her lines, since this activity was not in the script. Hartman told her it was a mistake because Gebert was behaving naturally and she should have improvised, staying in character. After that she never stopped a take again.

With Robert Mitchum in *Holiday Affair* (1949).

Years later, talking about Janet, Robert Mitchum described her as "an honest woman with great dignity and no artifice at all."[40]

Although Bob Hartman had complete freedom in shooting the film, Howard Hughes had the final say regarding Janet's wardrobe, makeup and hair. He also supervised the ad campaign, promising the potential audience more than the picture intended to deliver. An image of Mitchum staring at Janet and commenting "Baby, you're just what I want for Christmas" seemed better suited to a sex comedy. A second campaign changed the line to: "When Mitchum kisses 'em, they hear bells ... wedding bells!" *Holiday Affair* was completed on September 2 and released to theaters by Thanksgiving. Critics were generally favorable, but the box-office return was very modest.

Janet's second film for Hughes was *Jet Pilot*, which she used to call "Sex Pilot." Hughes aimed to produce an ambitious epic, a modern *Hell's Angels*, the picture which had skyrocketed him to glory in the early '30s. He selected many directors who each had to shoot a test sequence. Janet stated that it was the one who made her look sexiest who won the assignment. Eventually, Joseph von Sternberg was the chosen one, after he photographed Janet in his test with her hair dripping wet and a skimpy towel wrapped around her. Von Sternberg signed a two-picture contract with RKO, with the blessing of screenwriter-producer Jules Furthman, one of Hughes' most creative executives. Furthman, in fact, had suggested von Sternberg to the magnate. Von Sternberg was noted for his sensitive Marlene Dietrich films of the '30s, but at the time was on an eight-year hiatus from the screen (his last film was *The Shanghai Gesture* made in 1941).

Production on *Jet Pilot* began in December 1949, with John Wayne cast as the hero. Cary Grant was Hughes' first choice for the role, but the British actor was already committed to another project. The silly script was written by Furthman, who also produced. The story involved a romance between a U.S. Army Air Corps colonel and a Russian jet pilot, played by Janet, who lands at an Alaskan air base with the story she has come to seek political asylum. The director was instructed by Furthman and Hughes to follow the script faithfully, with dramatic preference given to many flying sequences. Von Sternberg accepted the restrictions, recognizing immediately Hughes' own objectives: Janet and a collection of new jet-planes. Nonetheless, von Sternberg's methods were described by many on the set as "tyrannical" and "inhuman."

"He was a very difficult man," Janet recalled. "I am an easy-going person but he had the most quietly infuriating way of saying something.... I didn't particularly like him."[41] Though von Sternberg finished shooting in seven weeks, the cast was brought in months later for additional scenes. Hughes was dissatisfied with the result. Director Nicholas Ray was then brought in to shoot more scenes, and Furthman's script was further diluted.

Remembered Janet:

> It was an unhappy picture that dragged on and on. I thought my role totally ridiculous. There was no way I could be a convincing Russian spy. Von Sternberg had to do everything and he was precise in what he wanted. He had Duke Wayne doing things crazy for a big man. In one bit I floor the Duke with a chop. And he was so sarcastic about Wayne's acting ability that the Duke once ran after him. But he photographed me lovingly. Mr. Hughes fell in love with those aerial shots but the Navy would come out with a new plane and he'd start reshooting again.[42]

Three years had gone by since Janet had finished filming on *Jet Pilot* when Dore Schary received a call from Hughes asking him to permit her to return to RKO for additional work. However, Janet was busy shooting another picture and was unable to do it.

Seven years in total elapsed between the start of shooting and the release of *Jet Pilot* in September 1957. It became Hughes' obsession, as he commissioned new aerial footage, reediting and retakes because both aircraft and fashion were becoming hopelessly dated through his procrastination. When in 1955 he sold RKO studios with all his films, he bought back the rights to *Jet Pilot* a few months later and personally tried to edit its 150,000 feet of film — about 25 hours. The original version was eight hours long, as he could not decide how to cut it. Finally when it opened in the theaters through a Universal Pictures release (at just 112 minutes), the film had to be re-processed for widescreen projection. It was a moderate commercial success but received terrible reviews. It was quickly withdrawn from release and privately held by Hughes. *Jet Pilot* cost Hughes $4 million and was the last film the magnate ever produced.

While shooting *Jet Pilot*, Janet was asked by the cosmetic company Max Factor to sit for a commercial portrait as "the girl back home." The portrait was an ideal type of photo a girl would send to her dearest boyfriend — particularly if he was in the armed forces and away from home. Janet patiently sat still for a very long photographic session, though only basic make-up was applied to her face. The only corrective make-up necessary was the extension of her eyebrow arch and the cover of a tiny scar above her upper lip from when she had chicken pox.

By 1950 Janet had made eleven pictures as one of the most popular young actresses in Hollywood. The fan magazines portrayed her as if she were living the life of a real movie star, filling their pages with photographs of her at every movie premiere on the arms of the most eligible bachelors in town, like

Arthur Loew, Jr., and Lex Barker. Her salary, which MGM was increasing in proportion to her success, finally gave her the opportunity to extinguish the government debt her former husband Stan had run up in 1946. At the end of January she also made a down payment on a house for herself and her parents. It was a two-bedroom apartment located in Beverly Hills, which was fully described in *Photoplay*:

With John Wayne in *Jet Pilot* (1957).

> Janet's bedroom is maple, with baby blue curtains and a blue satin spread. She's meticulously neat. Her closets and drawers always are in perfect order. She has no maid. Her mother launders her lingerie. You find only one picture of Janet in the apartment, a scene from *The Red Danube*, in which she is seen as a nun. This hangs on her bedroom wall. The top of her chest-of-drawers is covered with photographs, however, of Arthur Loew, her steady boy friend, and his sister's three children, Other unidentified snapshots (all men) are stuck in the mirror of her dressing table.[43]

It is curious to read in the same article that Janet did not like to take tub baths but preferred to shower — a habit she drastically changed a decade later after shooting *Psycho*.

That same month Janet was presented the key to the city by the mayor of Stockton. It was a moving celebration, with many different events scheduled in recognition of her popularity. In spite of her rising success, as she confessed years later, Janet kept feeling a deep sense of guilt which made her think that her fame was undeserved. She was still haunted by her actions in relation to her first marriage:

> I was very young. [W]hen I was fourteen, I ran off and eloped. And I was obviously made to feel that I was really a terrible person, a worthless person, a bad, bad, bad person. And I was. I mean, I did something very wrong. And I think that the effect of that, the reaction to that, is a major major reason — as well as the other reasons — why I never felt I deserve it.

She always kept inside herself a sort of underlying insecurity, which she explained was caused by the fact she was discovered. "I didn't go through the struggle of knocking on doors, of doing auditions and everything, because I never went through all that, I always felt I was just so lucky. So I worked very hard. I really wanted to do my best because this industry had given me so much, and I was really grateful."[44]

Two Tickets to Broadway was Janet's final film for Howard Hughes and RKO. For the first time in her career she was asked to dance and sing. Her preparation for the role of Nancy Peterson, a young naïve small-town girl who leaves her family and friends to make it in show business in New York, took almost seven months of intensive rehearsals. Her training averaged three to four hours a day on dance technique, and an hour each day on vocal lessons with Harriet Lee on a sound stage Hughes had rented at MGM (since he never set foot on his own RKO lot, fearing it would bring him bad luck). At Janet's suggestion, Hughes hired chorographers Marge and Gower Champion. The rehearsals went very slow. After three weeks and the completion of half a number, the film's director, James V. Kern, informed the chorographers that Hughes wanted to see how Janet was progressing. The following day the magnate visited the sound stage for a few minutes and left, approving of what he saw. However, after six months the script was still unfinished, and the leading man, as well as the three supporting female dancers, remained uncast. The Champions were recalled by MGM to work for another project to which they had previously committed. Hughes became upset and, after a quarrel, let them go.

"We kept rehearsing and rehearsing," Janet recalled. "Marge and Gower had to go. I said, 'Look, I'm leaving too. We either get this show on the road or else. I'm not going to stay here for the rest of my life rehearsing.'"

Janet did leave when MGM asked her to play in an episode of *It's a Big Country*. Only a few weeks later Hughes announced that Busby Berkeley would be the new choreographer of *Two Tickets to Broadway*, with Tony Martin as the leading man and Ann Miller, Gloria DeHaven and Barbara Lawrence as the supporting dancers.[45]

Janet resumed her singing and dancing training sessions, managing to perform impeccably in front of the cameras for her five musical numbers. Commenting about her dancing, she later admitted, "I couldn't do the intricate ballet moves. That takes years to learn, I always had a good sense of rhythm and could catch on quickly ... the real leaping is for the ballerina."[46]

During the filming of "The Merry Bird" number she fell and twisted an ankle. She had to finish the dance wearing a bandage that was covered by Technicolor makeup. However, she spent many agonizing hours sobbing in her dressing room because of the pain. Despite the little accident, Berkeley had flattering words for her: "The intensive training and her natural dancing and singing talents put her among the screen's musical stars. I include her on the all-time list of greats from among the more than fifty stars I had directed."

On the set, Janet, who had recently broken up with Arthur Loew, met dancer Bobby Sheerer, who was appointed her male partner in all her dancing rehearsals. The two started dating until Hughes found out and sent him away to work on another job in Las Vegas. *Two Tickets to Broadway* premiered in the fall of 1951, achieving respectable critical and box-office acclaim.

It's a Big Country was released the same month as *Two Tickets to Broadway*. *Big Country* was originally composed of nine different episodes, which became eight after one was cut in the final editing. They all conveyed unrelated stories that examined various aspects of American life and the glory of being an American citizen, each having a different author, director, cameraman, composer and cast. Dore Schary, who wrote the story outline and personally sponsored the project, with Robert Sisk as producer, insisted on complete freedom of selection in regard to casting the stars. Fredric March and Ethel Barrymore were borrowed from their studios to play alongside other MGM contract stars, like Van Johnson, Gene Kelly, William Powell, George Murphy, Gary Cooper and Janet. The directors included Richard Thorpe, John Sturges, Charles Vidor, William A. Wellman and Don Hartman.

It took only a few shooting days for Janet to complete her work in the episode called "Rosika, the Rose." She played the part of a Hungarian American shopkeeper's daughter who falls in love with a Greek American soda jerk, played by Gene Kelly. The segment was scripted by Isobel Lennart from a story by Claudia Cranston and directed by Charles Vidor. Janet was very excited to play opposite Kelly, who did not dance but applied due dedication to his small role. *It's a Big Country* was dismissed by many critics as a propaganda film with no attempt to mask it. The use of so many stars and so many talented directors in such small vignettes was considered a big waste of talents. The picture was destined to quickly disappear from the theaters after its release.

3

Tony

It just devastated me to look at this woman. — Tony Curtis

One evening, while she was still shooting *Jet Pilot* at RKO, Janet agreed to go to a party at a restaurant located across the street from the studio. Lucy's was a hangout for people in the film industry, including top movie stars.

"The gathering was in full swing when we arrived," recalled Janet in her autobiography.

> Shoulder-to-shoulder people, photographers jostling for position. At one point I was introduced to a devastatingly handsome young man — beautiful really — with black unruly hair, large sensitive eyes fringed by long dark lashes, a full sensuous mouth — and an irresistible personality. His name was Tony Curtis. During our brief encounter I found out he was under contract to Universal Pictures, came from New York, had done a couple of minor roles and was about to start a picture that he hoped would be his big break. We were soon pulled in different directions by our respective representatives. But I didn't forget him.[1]

In his autobiography, Curtis described in his own words how that meeting changed his life:

> I walked into a cocktail party at RKO, and there she was. Up to that point, I hadn't known too much about her. I don't remember seeing too many of her films. She'd just come from the set of *Jet Pilot*, a movie she was making with John Wayne for Howard Hughes, and Hughes was hot in pursuit. He was very interested in Janet. I looked over, and there was Hughes talking with Janet, hovering in the corner.... I started to go over toward them, and he kind of stepped aside and walked away. I didn't know what that meant.... I didn't really care what it meant, or what he thought. All I cared about was Janet Leigh. That blond hair was done up in two cinnamon-roll buns on each side of her head, like earphones, with a part in the center. Her face was exquisite — and those beautiful bosoms and tiny waist. It just devastated me to look at this woman. She had an incredible figure, and there was sweetness about her that I found most appealing.

She was wearing a silk blouse, and it was very hard not to be aroused by her — not just me but every guy there. I noticed how everybody responded to her, and I said, "I want her, I want her to be mine." And toward that aim I was dedicated.[2]

That night Curtis was very persistent with Janet, and when he asked her for her number, for some reason she gave it to him. A few days later the telephone rang in Janet's house, and the unmistakable voice of Cary Grant asked her if she would do him the honor of having dinner with him the following Saturday. Janet was baffled. She had met Grant at the studios, but he had not shown any interest in her. Then she suddenly remembered that she had just read an article that week about how Tony Curtis did a great imitation of Cary Grant. She answered promptly, declining the invitation, explaining she had a previous engagement ... with Tony Curtis.

The couple started dating, and Janet learned more about Bernard "Bernie" Schwartz (Curtis' real name) and his background. He was born in the Bronx on June 3, 1925, one of three sons of Emanuel Schwartz and Helen Klein. His parents were Hungarian Jewish immigrants. He had two brothers; one of them, Julie, had been run over by a truck. His parents were so poor that they could not afford to feed them and for a while placed him in an orphanage. Curtis later enlisted in the Navy, where he learned the Cary Grant accent on a submarine while endlessly watching *Gunga Din*. After his discharge he studied acting at the New School in Manhattan and was discovered by Joyce Selznick, a talent agent, casting director and niece of producer David O. Selznick. Tony told Janet that he had recently moved to Hollywood with his family to a small apartment in the Valley. He was placed under contract with Universal Pictures and

Tony Curtis and Janet Leigh in a publicity shot from the early '50s.

changed his name into Anthony Curtis, which he later shortened to Tony Curtis. He had played some small parts and was waiting for his breakout role.

Tony patiently began courting Janet, despite Howard Hughes's advances toward her. As Janet explained:

> When we were doing some retakes of *Jet Pilot* at George Air Force Base, Tony tried to call me. We were shooting about five or six o'clock, and we saw this plane going around.... It was Hughes. He landed, and he insisted that Jules Furthman, the producer, and Joseph von Sternberg, the director, and John Wayne and I go to dinner. I wouldn't have gone if it had been just me, but since they were all there, I didn't have much choice. I had said no to him a lot of times before. So we didn't get back from dinner until midnight or so, and Tony had called, and he was upset that I wasn't in. Normally, when I was shooting, I would have been in bed at nine-thirty or ten o'clock. Tony kept pretty close tabs on me in those days and so did Hughes. But something in my deportment that night must have convinced Howard to give up. I never heard from him again.[3]

In October Tony and Janet appeared together at the premiere of the film *Harvey* at the Carthay Circle Theatre in Hollywood. Commenting about that first public event together, Tony recalled how Janet was helpful to him:

> She really amazes me. No matter what happens, she always seems to know how to handle the situation. Like the night of the *Harvey* premiere.... I felt my knees turning into jelly. When the fans in the bleachers screamed out our names — that finished me! "I'm going to die, Janet," I gasped. Then I felt a small, quiet hand in mine. It squeezed encouragingly.
> "No, you are not going to die," she barely whispered. "The fans love you and want to see you. Let's go over and talk to them."
> I felt so useless, so inadequate standing there.... How glad I am I had this experience in the beginning, and because of Janet, I'll know what to do in the future.[4]

Tony admired Janet greatly and wanted her to admire him back. He also felt a sense of security when he was in her company. Janet was better educated and a more established star than he was. She was perfectly capable of handling any public situation impeccably. Her great sense of humor was another quality he loved about her, as he revealed in an article he wrote for *Photoplay* in February 1951:

> Like one night when I was fussing about and fuming, trying to decide where I could take her to have a real wonderful time. When I first arrived in Hollywood, I arrived with a Bronx accent. I worked hard to lose it [Curtis, actually, never lost his accent, for which he was often criticized and mocked by the media], but occasionally, when I get excited, it comes creeping back. Finally I stopped pacing the floor, turned to Janet and groaned, "I give up. I can't think of a place. I'm dead." Those wonderful warm eyes began to sparkle. Stealing my Bronx line, she quietly answered. "Why, Tony? It doesn't matter where we go. After all. I'm

witcha." You see what I mean. That girl can really handle herself. I guess I'm *wit* her too — all the way.[5]

By Christmas 1950 the couple had been dating for four months. It was their first Christmas together, and Janet planned to make it memorable, giving a party at her parents' house. Tony saw a Christmas tree all trimmed with lights and ornaments for the first time. He loved it so much that Janet suggested they buy one for his family, who had welcomed her as a daughter. The Schwartzes loved that unusual gift for a Jewish family and put it in their living room, topped with a bright Star of David.

That month Janet and Tony made their first public appearance as an official couple at the touring show *Ice Follies of 1950.* The response of the fans and the reporters outside the show was overwhelming. Everybody was struck by their beauty. Soon every magazine in Hollywood was trying to snap a photograph of the dashing young stars together.

Nineteen fifty-one was a very busy year for Janet, who started shooting a new movie titled *Strictly Dishonorable* in early January. The film was based

Ezio Pinza, Janet Leigh and Millard Mitchell in *Strictly Dishonorable* (1951).

on a funny play by Preston Sturges, in which a passionate opera star gets involved in a romantic mix-up with a young Southern girl. The opera singer-turned-actor Ezio Pinza, who was still enjoying the success of his performance in Broadway's *South Pacific*, was cast as the male lead. The production was entirely shot in an MGM studio. It was completed in March and was released the following July, receiving mild critical and audience acclaim.

Over a year later Janet accepted a part in a *Lux Radio Theatre* broadcast of the film, in which Fernando Lamas took over Pinza's role. Often Tony would visit the set, having lunch with Janet or taking walks with her to the other sets.

"Our relationship was very hot, very physical in those early years," revealed Curtis years later. "That was a major part of it — the actual touching and holding. We both needed each other physically, and we were a perfect match."[6]

As soon as the shooting of *Strictly Dishonorable* was completed, Janet traveled to Pittsburgh to make *Angels in the Outfield* with Paul Douglas. It was directed and produced by Clarence Brown, whose previous pictures included big hits such as *National Velvet* and *The Yearling*.

Angels in the Outfield was a charming comedy about baseball, angels, little girls, and nuns. The movie was based on an original story written by a Jesuit priest, Father R.F. Grady of the University of Scranton, using the pen name of Richard Colin. Along with Janet and Paul Douglas, nine-year-old Donna Corcoran made her film debut after a nationwide search (not unlike the search, instigated by Brown for the role of the young Jody in *The Yearling*). Most of *Angels in the Outfield* was shot on location to add authentic color and atmosphere to the story, which included scenes at Forbes Field, home of the Pittsburgh Pirates, the baseball team managed by the Douglas character. During the filming of a scene on the field, Janet, who had the role of a sports journalist, got her high heel stuck in the mud. Ralph Kiner, the most popular player of the team, picked her up and carried her off the field. The reporters on the set made a big fuss out of it and published a few articles about a romance between the two celebrities. When Tony visited Janet in Pittsburgh and read the stories a few days later, he became very disturbed by them. Janet was able to calm his jealousy by explaining that it was just publicity and that her heart belonged only to him. Another bit of pure fabrication was Janet's liaison with Joe DiMaggio, who made a cameo appearance in the film.

Angels in the Outfield was reasonably successful when it was released in the fall of 1951. It became one of President Eisenhower's favorite pictures. He was so crazy about it that one of his staff members claimed that the president had watched it thirty-eight times, wearing out three copies of the film. Once

With Paul Douglas in *Angels in the Outfield* (1951).

the president told director Clarence Brown, "I could see it one hundred times, but my friends are getting sick of it!"

The movie was renamed *Angels and the Pirates* for the British market, since baseball was considered wholly American, with a limited appeal to British audiences.

When the picture was completed in early May, Janet was reunited with Tony for two weeks. While he was doing an extensive nationwide promotion for *The Prince Who Was a Thief*—his first film as protagonist—Janet was expected to be in New York for publicity. She was accompanied by Patti Lewis, the wife of Tony's best friend, comedian Jerry Lewis, who was playing a gig at the Copacabana. While Tony was in the middle of his tour, he decided to get married. He called Janet and proposed over the phone. She accepted enthusiastically and started to arrange their wedding. The following day, while she was having lunch with her New York publicity team and personal friends, Dorothy Day and John Springer (MGM and RKO representatives, respectively), Janet asked them to help her to arrange a very private wedding ceremony. She quickly discovered that the only nearby state without a lengthy waiting period was Connecticut. Through Don Prince, RKO's New York publicity director, a waiver of the five-day waiting period, as the law required at that time, was arranged.

The following Saturday, Janet drove with Springer to Greenwich, Connecticut, took the blood test, signed the marriage license and met with Neil Welty, the judge who would perform the ceremony. Springer introduced her by her legal name, Jeanette Morrison Neame, and she applied for a marriage license with Bernard Schwartz. Nobody noticed her, except for a woman who looked at her sharply as she entered the license bureau, saying, "Aren't you Vivien Leigh?" The marriage remained a secret as she returned to her hotel in New York. Tony called her from Chicago, and she explained that all the formalities were almost completed. Only his presence was needed to legally comply with all the requirements before the ceremony. The following days Janet tried to stay calm, working on her publicity assignments. She only shared the news with her closest friends Jerry and Patti Lewis, Gower and Marge Champion, and Robert Sterling and Anne Jeffreys. Toward the end of the week she told RKO and MGM publicity, while Tony told Universal-International. They made their plans to announce jointly their union immediately after it happened.

Finally, Tony arrived in New York on the day of his twenty-sixth birthday and the day before the wedding. Although they lodged in separate hotels, Tony and Janet spent the entire day together at a Giants baseball game.

That evening, when Tony returned to his hotel, Jerry Lewis, who was to be his best man, tried to dissuade him from getting married, claiming that tying the knot with Janet would kill his career. Tony ignored his friend's advice. Then later, the head of Universal, Leonard Goldstein, called him and told him the same thing, maintaining that if he really wanted to get married he should have done it with Piper Laurie, his co-star in many films and a

A swimsuit publicity shot (1951).

rising star at Universal. In her memoir, Laurie revealed that when Universal learned of Tony and Janet's wedding plans, the studio was not opposed but suggested that it would be better if they postponed their marriage until the promotional tour covering all the major openings of *The Prince Who Was a Thief* was over, insinuating that their marriage would invalidate the movie. Laurie was outraged by the studio's request and spoke out strongly to Goldstein on behalf of the couple.[7]

In his autobiography, Tony affirmed that Janet received the same pressure from MGM and from her father, who was her manager. Fred Morrison was afraid of losing profits on his daughter if her career suddenly stalled. Angry and confused, Tony called Janet, contemplating the potential mistake they were about to make. Upset, she hung up. It took another hour-long phone call to apologize and patch things up.

Finally, on Monday, June 4, 1951, traveling in two different cars, the couple was Greenwich bound. In Janet's car, Paula Stone, Tommy Farrell, Mack David and John Springer tried to keep her calm by singing parodies of popular songs. Once they arrived in Connecticut, Tony, having traveled with Dorothy Day, Robert Sterling and Joe Abeles, had to take care of his end of the formalities that Janet had completed the week before. The bride and the guests waited at the Pickwick Arms hotel, where Judge John Knox was ready to begin the ceremony. RKO had everything perfectly set up by their Greenwich theater managers, including the reception, complete with a wedding cake. With Tony and the Judge in place, and the guests assembled, everything was ready — except for the missing best man and matron of honor. A call from New York announced that Jerry and Patti Lewis had overslept, but they were on their way.

They arrived just an hour later, and the short ceremony commenced. Janet was wearing a simple, pale aqua short-sleeved and straight-skirted linen dress with matching shoes and hat. She was very tense, as she later revealed. "My hand was in Tony's. I saw nothing, I heard nothing, thought of nothing except the words the judge was saying. Then it was over. For a moment, everyone was very solemn. Patti Lewis was crying. Jerry Lewis changed all that."[8] The comedian, swept away by the spirit of the occasion, suddenly kissed the bride passionately.

After the luncheon, the newlyweds drove back to New York alone, stopping in the Bronx to tell the news to an old aunt of Tony's. Back at the hotel, Janet and Tony discovered that the news had preceded them. The room was filled with reporters and photographers, and the first congratulatory telegrams, and calls to Mr. and Mrs. Tony Curtis, were coming from all over the country. That night a wedding dinner had been organized at Danny's Highway, a trendy New York restaurant. The owner had invited all the couple's friends, including Dean and Jeannie Martin, Robert Sterling, Anne Jeffreys, Cyd Charisse, Gloria DeHaven and Vic Damone. During the dinner all the lights suddenly went out, and the room was lit only by the candles on a wedding cake that was being wheeled in. And through the room came the Five De Marco Sisters singing "I Love You Truly." They were soon joined by Dean Martin, Jerry Lewis, Frankie Laine and Perry Como, all singing love songs. The group later

With Richard Anderson (right) and Peter Lawford (left) in *Just This Once* **(1952).**

moved to the Copacabana nightclub, but Tony and Janet stayed just long enough to put in an appearance. The next afternoon RKO gave the newlyweds an "official" wedding reception at the plush Versailles. It was the first party given by the studio, which included many from the cast of *Two Tickets to Broadway.* The following days Janet and Tony kept on with their previously scheduled publicity assignments, during which she shot her first *Life* magazine cover, photographed by Philippe Halsman. At night they were able to be by themselves, join their friends, go to a Broadway show or just take long walks through Central Park. When the week was over, Tony returned to his long personal appearance tour across the country, while Janet went back to Hollywood to start a new picture. They postponed their honeymoon, which happened in Paris few months later.

As the press reported two months earlier, Janet had agreed to play opposite Peter Lawford and Richard Anderson in *Just This Once*, a comedy about a young woman lawyer who is appointed guardian of a trust for a spendthrift man own age. Sidney Sheldon had written the screenplay based on a magazine story by Max Trell, which MGM had bought earlier that year. Janet and Lawford were on their third film together, and Don Weis, the young director appointed by MGM, was able to catch their perfect on-set chemistry.

After Tony completed his tour, the couple moved into a furnished, modern one-bedroom apartment in Westwood, in the same building where Elizabeth Taylor was living. Besides their personal belongings (Tony had a closet with forty-three shirts), they brought to the small apartment only a TV, which was Jerry Lewis' wedding gift. Tony affirmed that in those early days as newlyweds he realized how compulsively neat and organized Janet was. The house was impeccable at all times, with the laundry always ironed, folded and put away. She would use shelf liner in all the drawers and cupboards. Janet possessed what many years later her daughter Jamie Lee defined as "a powerful drive for immaculate order and control."[9]

"Nothing could be out of place when she was around," Tony remembered. "Whenever she had to travel somewhere I would marvel at how she was able to fit so many items into one suitcase, every item fitting snugly into its compartment; and she always knew exactly where everything was!"[10]

Janet, who personally wrote thank you notes to all her fans throughout her life, already had new checks and stationery personalized, with "Mrs. Anthony Curtis" on it. Jerry Lewis described Janet as "an excellent organizer … always meticulous about social engagements and appointments…. Janet will never make a promise unless she knows that she can keep it. She is never without her 'little black book' in which she notes all her appointments and lists her daily expenditures for such items as stamps, gasoline, tips, taxi fares and cosmetics. This, she will inform you seriously, is 'for income taxes purposes.'"[11]

Janet and Tony spent much of their free time at Jerry and Patti Lewis' house on Amalfi Drive, swimming in the pool, eating barbecued food, or playing card games or charades. Often Janet would go cycling or shopping with Pat, leaving Tony and Jerry building boat or airplane models. One evening Tony started complaining to Lewis about the sort of parts he was getting at Universal, expressing his desire to break away from the silly pretty-boy roles.

"Tell you what," Jerry told him. "I'll write a funny part for you and we'll make a movie right here." The following week the comedian bought a sixteen-millimeter sound camera, five hundred rolls of film, dolly tracks and professional lighting equipment. Then he put together a parody of Paramount's hit *Sunset Blvd.*, which he called *Fairfax Avenue*, transforming the elegance of Wilder's classic into a middle-class Jewish neighborhood around the Los Angeles Farmer's Market. Later he sent out a shooting call for eight o'clock on a Saturday morning at his house. Tony was cast as the screenwriter-gigolo Yaakov Popowitz, based on William Holden's character, Janet as a spoof of Gloria Swanson's role, while Lewis himself played Erich von Stroheim. The film also featured Jeff Chandler, Vince Edwards, Shelley Winters and others in their circle of friends. It became one of the many "home movies" produced under the fictitious company name Gae-Ron Productions, named after Lewis' children Gary and Ronnie.

Another production Lewis co-wrote that included Janet and Tony was *How to Smuggle a Hernia Across the Border*. It was a funny story inspired by Dean Martin's wartime personal problems with a hernia.

"A lot of us would gather there and make these funny movies," Janet recalled. "And we would then all go and have dinner, and we would go back and continue our shoot the next day. They were funny and quite wonderful. We just had great fun in doing it."[12]

"Jerry's second movie was what he called 'the psychological story of a guy who thought he was his own sister,'" Janet remembered. "His third picture would have been sensational, too, only he forgot to turn on the sound track."[13]

Lewis became very serious about those projects, writing and directing mostly spoofs of famous productions: *A Streetcar Named Repulsive*, with Janet doing Vivien Leigh and Lewis doing Brando; *The Re-Enforcer*, a short pastiche of Humphrey Bogart's 1951 mob movie *The Enforcer*, with Dean Martin appearing as a mobster named Joe Lasagna and Janet as his moll; *Watch on the Lime*, a spoof of Lillian Hellman's *Watch on the Rhine*; *Come Back, Little Shiksa*; and many others.

To promote Tony's career, Janet started to appear with her husband in several photo spreads in the fan magazines. Suddenly their faces were on the covers of all the major movie magazines. Tony, who became an idol for the so-called "bobby soxer" fans, received tons of mail every day.

Scaramouche was Janet's next picture. Thirty years earlier, writer Rafael Sabatini made the name of Scaramouche famous thanks to his bestselling novel. Two years later MGM produced a silent film version of the book, emphasizing the hero's adventures during the first years of the French Revolution. Since Hollywood was going through a swashbuckler genre renaissance with films such as *The Three Musketeers*, *The Prisoner of Zenda* and *Ivanhoe*, MGM intended to make a new musical version starring Gene Kelly — fresh from the success of *The Three Musketeers* — with the idea of staging the sword fights like dance numbers in a musical. Later the idea of a musical was abandoned, and a remake of the film was announced in January 1951, to star Elizabeth Taylor, Ava Gardner and Stuart Granger. Taylor and Gardner turned down the roles, with Janet and Eleanor Parker replacing them. The preparation before shooting was very hard for many involved. Janet had to take riding lessons, learning to ride a horse wearing a long skirt similar to the lavish period costumes created for the production. Stewart Granger, in the role originally conceived for Errol Flynn, had long, exhausting, fencing training with European champion Jean Heremans. At first the British actor was announced by the studio to play two roles, Scaramouche and the villain Marquis de Maynes; however, this idea was dropped and Mel Ferrer was cast as the villain. *Scaramouche* reunited Janet with director George Sidney, producer Carey Wilson, and actor Robert Coote, who all worked together in *The Red Danube*. Shooting was not easy for Sidney. Granger was not a very skilled fencer, and all his duel scenes needed several retakes because he kept dropping his sword. One afternoon, Granger's wife, actress Jean Simmons, was visiting the set, whereupon the short-tempered actor picked up the weapon and threw it, just missing his wife's head. Sidney reportedly even used a metronome during the filming of the fencing scenes to give them more rhythm. Nonetheless, much of the effectiveness of the film was provided by Lillian Burns, the director's wife and Janet's first drama coach. According to leaks from the set, after shooting was completed, Burns, dissatisfied with the quality of the sound recording, took it upon herself to reassemble almost the entire cast and personally direct them in the undetectable looping, or dubbing, of about 90 percent of the film.[14]

Enacting the secondary but key role of Aline de Gavrillac, Janet looked especially charming in her powdered wigs. Her stunning beauty was enhanced by the brilliant Technicolor photography of pioneer cinematographer Charles Rosher. Her presence in *Scaramouche* was important for her career, since the film, in spite of mixed reviews, was a tremendous audience-pleasing swashbuckler that benefited from MGM's lavish sets and costumes, and contained the most spectacular six-and-half-minute swordplay sequence ever brought to the screen. The picture was such a box-office hit that it paved the way for a series of MGM adventure films,

As Aline de Gavrillac in *Scaramouche* (1952).

including *Ivanhoe* and *Knights of the Round Table*.

Six months after their wedding, Janet and Tony were presented with the opportunity of having their honeymoon in Europe — all expenses paid. The dream offer came from a charity show scheduled in London and organized by the Variety Club to benefit the National Playing Fields Association, of which his Royal Highness the Duke of Edinburgh was then the president. After the event in England, the European trip included several stops at military bases in Germany and France, including Paris, where the couple hoped to spend some time by themselves. The trip to London by plane was long and the days before them were frantic, although Janet and Tony managed to do some sightseeing. On December 10, 1951, the huge auditorium of the London Coliseum theater was crowded and filled with Scotland Yard policemen, when Princess Elizabeth and the Duke of Edinburgh visited the theater to attend a midnight matinee performance of the variety program. A series of well-known local and international artists were introduced on stage to perform for a deserving cause. Noël Coward, Frank Sinatra, Ava Gardner, Orson Welles, Rhonda Fleming, Max Wall, and Janet and Tony were among the many artists who appeared in the show. Janet was extremely tense at the idea of performing in front of royalty. She had rehearsed for weeks an amusing musical sketch with Tony, and a medley of popular tunes written by Jimmy McHughs to perform solo. She panicked when she realized there were no makeup artists to help her, and she had to rely on Tony's experience from his drama workshop to be made up.

The show also included a ballet by the Sadler's Wells Company and some extracts from the musical *Kiss Me, Kate*. The finale consisted of a performance of the bands of the Grenadier Guards and the Royal Marines that brought all the artists on stage together to be presented to Princess Elizabeth, who warmly shook her royal hand with Janet's and Tony's. It was a huge success, which allowed the Club to raise a great amount of money for the National Playing Fields Association.

The trip continued across Germany, where MGM had scheduled a couple of press receptions for Janet, since some of her films had been released recently to German theaters. The journey was not an altogether happy experience for Tony, who was extremely shaken by an emergency landing of an air force plane bound for Frankfurt. He subsequently developed such a fear of flying that for years he was unable to board a plane. Moreover, Tony was very suspicious of all the Germans, always thinking of the Holocaust and particularly of a close cousin who had been killed at Buchenwald. At the end of the German trip there was a party given in their honor. The evening was uneventful until the very end when someone, through an interpreter, asked Tony if his last name was really Curtis. He replied clearly, raising his voice so that everyone in the room could hear him, "My name is Bernard Schwartz and I am a Jew." Everybody remained silent as Tony took Janet's arm and left.[15]

After a long and exhausting overnight journey by train, the couple arrived in Paris, staying in a luxurious suite at the elegant George V Hotel. In the City of Lights they were able to finally experience the flavor of a real honeymoon. Their obligations with their studios were, in fact, very limited, and the couple enjoyed all the romantic attractions the city could offer to the two young newlyweds. It was Janet's first Christmas away from her family and out of the country. That day she felt a bit homesick after talking with her family on the phone, but quickly regained her happy spirit after they invited to their suite a group of American celebrities who happened to be in town. They dined and exchanged gifts, and just before midnight Janet and Tony took a long walk on the Left Bank where they found a little church where they attended a service. Later they went back to the hotel in the rain, sharing coins with whomever they met in the street. The following day the couple finally returned to America.

4

A Darling Couple

I think to be tolerant means you love someone not in spite of, but because of, his faults. — Janet Leigh

Janet returned to work at the end of January 1952. For the first time in her career she was dissatisfied with the picture she was scheduled to make. She disliked the script, which she found silly and uninteresting. Her strong sense of duty and her loyalty toward MGM kept her from turning down the part. The picture was *Fearless Fagan.* Based on a true story reported in *Life* magazine in 1951, *Fearless Fagan* was about a young circus trouper who secretly reported to the U.S. Army with his pet lion in tow. Janet's part was Abby Ames, a famous film star who discovers the secret when she visits the Army post to entertain the troops.

The film's producer, Eddie Knopf, approached Stanley Donen to direct it. The director accepted "only out of a sense of responsibility," as he later admitted. "What I wanted to do with the picture, but couldn't," said Donen, "was to have the movie star in the story be a really big movie star, like Deborah Kerr. This way it would have seemed more like a dream when the lion falls in love with her."[1] Instead of Kerr, Janet was cast in the role.

"What gave me a lift," said Janet, "was that Stanley was so heavily associated with musicals, and here I was doing a song for him." The song, the only one in the film, was "What Do You Think I Am?" by Hugh Martin and Ralph Blane. "What impressed me about Stanley was his attitude. He didn't want to do the film. He knew I didn't, either. So the first day of shooting he said to me, 'Aw, let's just go for it.' It was certainly a lot better than our pouting about it."[2]

Before filming began, Janet, along with her co-star Carleton Carpenter, spent considerable time at George Emerson's animal compound on the MGM lot for a "getting acquainted session" with the four-year-old 400-pound lion

Fagan. On the set she found herself working for the third time with co-star Richard Anderson, who had played the suitor who lost her to Peter Lawford in *Just This Once*, and a patriot of the downtrodden in *Scaramouche*. In *Fagan*, Anderson was the captain of the company in the Army camp where the lion Fagan was hidden.

The inexpensive production was meant to cash in on Universal's popular *Francis the Talking Mule* series. Despite Donen's reluctance to be associated with the picture, *Fearless Fagan* proved a big charmer with both critics and audiences. Janet received a flattering mention in *The Hollywood Reporter*'s review: "Janet Leigh supplies the feminine charm in most satisfactory fashion, also getting over several hearty laughs with some delicate comedy touches."

In March a successful screen test with James Stewart under Anthony Mann's direction provided Janet the only female role in MGM's *Naked Spur*. One of the film's screenwriters, Harold Jack Bloom, wanted his then-girlfriend, actress Anne Bancroft, to play the part, but she was under contract to 20th Century–Fox. MGM insisted on giving that role to one of its own contract

With Carleton Carpenter in *Fearless Fagan* (1952).

players. Janet had to make a test to see if she looked believable as the love interest of Stewart's character, who was nearly twenty years her senior — older than her own father. The screen test was successful. Later, Janet admitted that she never thought about the age difference because Stewart put her at ease immediately.

The Western was entirely shot on location in the magnificent San Juan Mountains of Southern Colorado. Principal photography took place between May 21 and July 10. The fine cast, which also included Robert Ryan, Ralph Meeker and Millard Mitchell, stayed at El Rancho Encantado, a rural lodge a few miles away from the small town of Durango. Janet brought along Tony, while James Stewart brought his wife Gloria, and Robert Ryan and Millard Mitchell had wives and children with them. The large company got along perfectly, and at the beginning of June they all celebrated Janet and Tony's first anniversary with a small party.

To look the part of wild Lina Patch, Janet cut her hair. Said Janet,

> It turned out to be a fantastic break for me because I was the only girl. Mann knew were to place the camera but he gave me little direction. I was fighting a lot for my life, and the co-stars Bob Ryan and Jimmy Stewart had this knack of not seeming to act much anyway. Jimmy would tell me to talk more slowly, and he stayed back until I completed my reaction shots, although the other stars I've known would have left for the day."[3]

Stewart's simultaneous sensitivity and self-confidence on the set highly impressed Janet, who observed:

> The contrast is startling really. You'll see him at breakfast or something ... and he'll be this enormously shy guy. But then once the lights and camera go, he would erupt with this strength that seems to come from nowhere.... Any take with him was like starting out from one place, and knowing where you wanted to arrive. It was a very secure trip. He was confident and he made me confident.[4]

Despite Mann's reputation for being uncommunicative, Janet liked working with him; his reputation for working with feelings more than with words challenged her to improve her concentration in expressing her inner emotions. She also felt that the contrasting acting styles of her four co-stars made the tensions between the characters more authentic. Interviewed for a biography on James Stewart, Janet claimed:

> It was a very macho shoot, with me practically the only woman there off-camera as much as on camera. Fortunately, I was something of a tomboy, as was my character. But then there was also the very noticeable differences among the men — and these things fed into the story of the differences among the characters. Meeker was from The Actors Studio, for instance, Ryan was as much of a nice guy off screen as Jimmy was, but he was more stage and not nearly so shy.

Mitchell was old-school theater. Isolated like we were, I think the tensions that developed among the personalities and even in just acting techniques fit the tensions among the characters perfectly.[5]

Janet's excellent performance, a mix of childish tenacity, fragile pugnacity and false ingenuousness, was not lost on the reviewers when the movie opened in New York on March 25, 1953. Despite its low-budget, *The Naked Spur* became one of the top-grossing films of 1953. It was highly praised by the critics, who defined it as a psychological Western, a sharp study of human nature with all its characters illustrative of different passions. Some observers considered the film to be one of the best Westerns ever made, especially for Mann's masterful direction and William C. Mellor's striking Technicolor photography.

In the summer of 1952 Janet was again cast opposite Van Johnson, this time in a mildly amusing comedy titled *Confidentially Connie*. Janet played the new wife of a Maine college professor, played by Johnson, who was too poor to afford meat. The couple have a falling out with Johnson's father, a big Texan rancher, over Johnson's choice of profession and want no help from home. Janet was thrilled at being reunited once again with her favorite screen partner. "Van and I worked so well together," she said. "He was such a natural actor and never seemed to be acting, although in our conversations he played himself down. I loved working with him."[6] Following its release in March 1953, *Daily Variety* reported that the Meat Association of American protested the film, claiming that it held butchers and their organizations up to ridicule. Calling *Confidentially Connie* an "attack" on the meat industry, the Institute asked MGM to withdraw the film from distribution and ordered one of its members to cancel promotional tie-ins with a local theater. In spite of being a minor MGM production, *Confidentially Connie* was well received by critics and audiences (meat-packers excepted).

A few weeks later a wonderful opportunity knocked at Janet and Tony's door when producer George Pal decided to make a film based on the life of famous magician Harry Houdini — a project he had had in mind for a long time. Pal had gained his initial fame through his *Puppetoons*, the photographing of real puppets through stop-motion camera work. The successful idea brought him to Paramount, who offered him a contract. He produced four movies for the studio, three of them in the science-fiction genre. All were major box-office hits: *Destination Moon*, *When the Worlds Collide* and *The War of the Worlds*. For his new project he thought that having the perfect Hollywood couple, Janet and Tony, together onscreen for the first time would be a very clever idea. MGM was not very happy about loaning Janet to Paramount, but she was so enthusiastic at the thought of making a film with her

With parents Fred and Helen Morrison on the *Houdini* set at Paramount in 1952.

husband that the studio eventually relented. As she had done in the past, Janet put Tony's interests ahead of her own, and when MGM insisted that she should have first billing because she was a more established star than him, she told her agent, MCA head Lew Wasserman, that she would always take second billing to her husband and that this was not negotiable. While both MGM and Universal made a lot of money by loaning their stars to Paramount, Tony and Janet received their regular salaries. To prove his great interest in the project, Tony reported to Paramount a full month before he was on salary, and spent five hours a day learning sleight-of-hand and illusions from magician George Boston. Pal also hired mentalist Joe Dunninger as technical advisor. Upon her death, Houdini's wife had willed nearly 300 of her late husband's tricks to Dunninger. As a result, he knew more about the great magician's methods than anyone alive. They both were constantly on the set to teach Tony and Janet some of the magic and escape tricks. A rivalry sprang up between Boston and Dunninger and each tried to outdo the other in magic. Visiting guests on the set were often treated to a show between camera set-ups.

Celebrities like director Billy Wilder and actor Yul Brynner came to watch Tony perform tricks and ended up watching his teachers competing with each other. George Boston spent four months training Tony before shooting started. At the beginning, Tony made it clear that had no interest in doing the picture unless he could perform the tricks himself. In addition to his long studio hours, he spent another four hours at home each night perfecting his tricks. In later years he would entertain his co-stars on movie sets by showing them simple but intriguing card tricks learned during that time of hard training.

The film's director, George Marshall, was a charming man. He was able to create a relaxed environment for his stars, but he loved pranks. Once, during the rehearsal of a very serious scene, he poured a bucket of water on Janet and Tony, who started crying with laughter.

Years later Janet revealed, "When Tony levitated me, there were no cuts, and there were no cuts during some other tricks — they were done 'legit.' When it came to the escape scenes, the roping and chaining and all, those scenes had to be fixed because Tony wasn't Houdini, he didn't have the ability to contort his body or manipulate the locks like Houdini did."[7] For this reason *Houdini* took more than eight weeks to complete. Cameraman Ernest Laszlo, in fact, kept his camera focused on Tony continuously, with no breaks and no cuts to close-ups. This, though it took a great deal of extra time and trouble, was done to convince the most skeptical of Curtis' adeptness, and also to make the character he portrayed completely credible.

During the shooting Tony tripped on a cable and tore the ligaments in his right knee. He recovered relatively quickly, although with careful viewing, his limping is noticeable in some scenes.

Janet loved working for Paramount, a studio much smaller than MGM and very family oriented. Everyone knew each other, and they would ride bicycles to move around. In pre-production, *Houdini* was scheduled to be shot in black-and-white. When Janet had her first fitting of some of the 58 costume changes (which ranged from the high-style creations of the early 1900s to the glamorous tights she wore when assisting her husband in his magic acts) with Edith Head, who was in charge of the wardrobe, the legendary costume designer called George Pal over to the fitting room to explain that the dresses were too beautiful and colorful — they would be wasted in a black-and-white production. Pal nodded and calmly said that the studio had just approved making *Houdini* in color.

In preparation for the role of Wilhelmina Beatrice "Bess" Houdini, Janet read many books about the life history of the famed magician. The picture picked up the story of Harry Houdini, born Erich Weiss of Appleton, Wisconsin, at the age of 21, taking him from his early struggles — his wife at his side — to the ultimate triumphs all over the world and his tragic premature death. Because of the presence of Tony and Janet as a team, Pal wisely had the script focus more on Houdini's fictionalized, extraordinary magic acts than on the man himself. Janet revealed that the story could not depict the actual event involving Houdini's death (a student punched him, rupturing his appendix) since the student's family was still alive and ready to sue Paramount.[8]

Houdini premiered on July 2, 1953. Most of the critics did not appreciate the historical inaccuracy and the lack of realistic aging of the main characters. Nonetheless, the success was huge, with a more-than-satisfactory financial return for the relatively small production investment. In December, a few weeks after *Houdini* was completed, the Hollywood Women's Press Club assigned the annual Golden Apple Awards to Janet and Tony as the most press-cooperative stars of the year. To mark the end of the shooting, Tony gave Janet a cute black poodle as a gift. They called the pup Houdina, and the dog and the couple became inseparable.

Janet's next film was once again with a different studio. *Walking My Baby Back Home*, originally titled *Nothing but the Blues*, was produced by Universal. It marked Universal's first musical since 1948. It was an unpretentious musical comedy starring Donald O'Connor and Buddy Hackett (in his first big-screen experience), which included a collection of popular tunes and dance numbers. Janet sang almost all her own songs but with a couple of exceptions — she was dubbed in higher keys by Paula Kelly of the Modernaires.

Said Janet:

> In *Walking My Baby Back Home*, everything was done to make me feel capable of being a good enough dancer to co-star with Donnie, as we all call him. This was only my third attempt at dancing in a picture, and here I was to do difficult numbers with one of the best dancers in the world! Fortunately Donnie must have realized it was going to be an ordeal for me to learn some of the routines. He suggested Louis Da Pron should coach me and Betty Scott, his assistant, was to teach me the steps. Louis is Donnie's personal coach and assistant. He purposely chose routines that he knew would be effective, yet not too difficult for me to master. Not once did Donnie show the flicker of a frown when I missed steps. He and Betty worked long and patiently until *they* "put my best foot forward." I had hurt my ankle during rehearsal and was in considerable pain. After that Donnie would purposely call rest times when I knew he was not tired; he was giving me a chance to rest.[9]

One day Tony visited the set with Harry Belafonte, and a photographer snapped a photograph of the black actor and Tony, with Janet in the middle, her arms slung around Tony and Belafonte's shoulders. The image appeared on the cover of the July 1953 issue of *Ebony* magazine. It was the first time that white and black Hollywood stars appeared together on the cover of an

American magazine. Sadly, after its publication, Janet reported receiving a small quantity of hate mail. When *Walking My Baby Back Home* was released the following December, it was received with mixed reviews and scarce crowd attendance, forcing Universal to take it out of theaters.

When they were not working, Janet and Tony continued to have a busy social life. One of her closest friends was actor and later popular TV host Merv Griffin, whom they invited to a costume party at Jerry Lewis' home. Griffin brought as a date Marilyn Erskin, who had been briefly married to director Stanley Kramer. Tony and Janet decided to cross-dress: Janet wearing one of his best suits, Tony with a blonde curly wig. Griffin and Erskin also decided to dress up as drag versions of Shirley Booth and Burt Lancaster in *Come Back, Little Sheba.* On the way to the party, Janet, who drove the car, was pulled over by a cop, who was stunned after seeing the four of them out of the vehicle. Since both Tony and Janet had left their drivers' licenses at home, it was very difficult for the policeman to believe they were who they were. But Tony did his impersonation of Cary Grant, and the policeman was finally convinced. By the next day the story was already on everyone's lips in Hollywood.

That same year Janet and Tony moved to a new apartment, a large penthouse in West Hollywood. She furnished it with comfortable lounge chairs, warm rugs and colorful vases of flowers. Janet loved clothes, and her wardrobe was so full she had to also use her old one at her parents' house. Despite their salaries, the couple still could not afford to buy their own home yet, but they were saving and planning to buy one in the near future.

Again Janet was loaned by MGM to 20th Century–Fox, this time to make *Prince Valiant.* Fox paid Metro a lot more than she was getting, but she thought that it was right because it still gave her the opportunity to earn $1500 a week. Tony was eager to star once again opposite his wife in another picture. Fox assigned Henry Hathaway to direct, but the part was eventually offered to a promising twenty-three-year-old actor named Robert Wagner.

Prince Valiant was an adaptation of Harold R. Foster's beautifully drawn color comic strip, which had already been popular for 17 years. The comic was printed every Sunday in a range of American newspapers and gradually acquired a nationwide following of millions of readers. It was enjoyed not only for its exciting storylines but also for its finely-detailed and meticulously researched drawings. Foster visited England to do first-hand research on castles and other settings he would use for the strip. When 20th Century–Fox announced that they were going to make a film version of *Prince Valiant*, thousand of fans of the strip wrote in urging that no changes be made to Foster's characters or story. The script was written with the order to stick as close as possible to the original. For this reason the production traveled to England to look at locations that were later shot by a second unit in the spring of 1953. Long shots employed stand-ins for the principal cast members, and these were later matched with the rest of the filming, shot in CinemaScope (making this the first movie ever to be filmed using this new widescreen technique) at 20th Century–Fox Studios in Beverly Hills. The picture had a budget of $3,000,000; most of it was spent on building a massive castle made of wood and plaster (later it had to be burned down, as required in the story), and on the payroll and the feeding of thousands of extras, stunt men, stand-ins, technicians, artisans and firemen.

Janet's character, Princess Aleta, required long daily make-up and hair sessions, which she shared not only with actress Debra Paget but also with Robert Wagner, who was required to wear a Dutch Boy hairstyle wig. The rest of the cast included stars like James Mason and Sterling Hayden. The atmosphere on the set was not always very pleasant, as Mason remembered years later it in his memoir: "The film was loaded with action scenes which tended to roughen Hathaway's temper. His vocal cords took a lot of punishment, as did the ever-present cigar. There was every kind of work for a regiment of stunt men who did not always take kindly to Hathaway's urgings."[10]

The director's difficult behavior often clashed with Wagner's lack of experience. However, the young actor, whose role was extremely demanding, never rose to Hathaway's provocations. The director would constantly insist that Wagner raise his voice when delivering his lines.

Janet was often by his side, and soon Wagner became a lifelong, faithful friend. Wagner stayed at her side when she divorced Tony years later, condemning the way her husband had behaved with her.

A few weeks before shooting *Prince Valiant*, Janet discovered she was pregnant. The baby she and Tony had long hoped for so earnestly was finally about to come. Tony was about to leave for Hawaii, where he was to star in *Beachhead*. Janet was able to sail with Tony and stay in Honolulu for a few days before she reported to the *Valiant* set. Aboard the *Lurline*, a Princess Line ship, they met Van Johnson and his wife Evie. The two couples spent most of the time together enjoying each other's company tremendously. In her autobiography, Janet maintains that onboard she told Tony she was going to have a baby in February. He was thrilled and ready to share the wonderful news with the entire world, but they later agreed to wait a bit longer before doing so. Then when Janet flew back to Hollywood she told both their families, who were ecstatic. Nevertheless, on July 8, two weeks after her return from Hawaii, she started to feel strangely queasy and sleepless. She was rushed to St. John Hospital, where she had a miscarriage. Tony learned of the sad news over the phone but was unable to return to California because of his commitment to the picture. He wrote her a long, moving letter. In his recently published memoirs, Tony affirms that while in Hawaii he received a phone call saying that Janet had had a miscarriage. She was in the hospital and wanted him to fly back. But at this point Tony's and Janet's recollections diverge.

"The news of the miscarriage was devastating," wrote Tony, "and not just for the obvious reason. I hadn't even known Janet was pregnant! As I thought about it, my insecurity and my overactive imagination started wreaking havoc. Why hadn't she told me she was pregnant? It was possible that she herself hadn't known, but I couldn't help but wonder if she was keeping it secret for some reason of her own." Curtis also stated that the marriage was not going well at that time, maintaining, "Neither Janet nor I was the best of spouses, so we'd gotten pretty distant.... I couldn't believe how flimsy our relationship had become, but I stayed in."[11]

The two versions are very contradictory. Janet's seems the more plausible, since it corresponds with a detailed article published in October 1953.[12] The reasons behind Tony's report remain unknown. Michael Munn's claims that Tony's memory in his old age became distorted, and maybe the schizophrenia he was later diagnosed with played a part in his version of the story.[13]

Working on the set of *Prince Valiant* was not very easy for Janet after the sad event, yet her strong character allowed her to go on. Her reunion with Tony after he returned from Hawaii was very emotional. He immediately ran onto the set where she was in the middle of shooting a pivotal scene, wearing a long blonde wig. He stared at her and told her she looked like an angel, like an ethereal creature. Moved by his words but able to refrain from crying, Janet laughed instead and hugged him fervently. They quickly left the set, locking themselves in her dressing room for many hours.

Prince Valiant was completed in September 1953 and was given a spectacular premiere at Grauman's Chinese Theatre in Hollywood the following spring. The expensive production was expected to make Wagner a star, but instead it received bad reviews that criticized his wooden performance and the banal script, written in modern dialogue, disappointing legions of fans of the original comic strip.

Rumors that Janet's marriage was on the rocks appeared in many tabloids, which reported false stories of the couple arguing in public and of their alleged criticism of the paparazzi's crazy behavior toward them. Years later Janet replied in retaliation, "The marriage lasted longer than the marriages of those who said it could not last."[14]

In addition, the twosome's overexposure became a source of several

unjustifiable attacks from the likes
of columnist Hedda Hopper, who
defined them as "publicity mad
exhibitionists, ambitious, tiresome
and crude."

The gossip became so persistent that Janet wrote a long article
titled "The Real Facts about Tony
and Me," which appeared in the
magazine *Silver Screen*: "Tony and
I feel that some recent stories about
us have been unfair and misleading
and I'd like to take this opportunity to answer our critics and, I
hope to correct some false impres-
sions...." With her polite but firm
words, Janet clarified the truth
about the false allegations recently
made about her marriage with
Tony and their behavior in public.
Husband and wife were, in fact,
still deeply in love.

Tony Curtis and Janet Leigh in a publicity
shot from the early '50s.

Janet was thrilled when she learned that she had been cast by Jerry Lewis
and Dean Martin in *Living It Up*. The duo had decided to produce through
York Productions, the pair's production company, an updated version of the
1937 classic screwball comedy *Nothing Sacred*, in which a cynical reporter
hears about a dying small-town girl's last wish to visit New York and takes
advantage of the tragic story.

After reading the script, however, Janet did not feel right for the part,
which had been modeled on Fredric March's original characterization. She
felt she would not be believable, since the new film version would be characterized by an inversion of genders of the main roles. Lewis, in fact, would
play the Carole Lombard role of the girl (in this case a boy), Janet the reporter,
and Dean the role of the doctor and conspirator. Being unsure about her role,
Janet asked the director, Norman Taurog, to make some minor changes to
the script. She became more relaxed on the set, where the atmosphere was
very similar to when she was making home movies in Lewis' backyard.

"They clowned around and such," she remembered, "but that was part
of their charm, and they executed very well. So it was great fun, but it was
still very professional." She also noticed that

there wasn't much of socializing with the two families. At that point we knew Jerry better than we knew Dean. Dean and Jeanne came to the premieres and everything. We knew them and liked them. It wasn't like there was a problem. It's just that he sort of had his group and Jerry had his group and all of that. I don't know why they didn't socialize. Maybe they felt that when they were on the road together they saw enough of each other and when they were home they should sort of have their own lives.[15]

Janet adored Dean and got along with Taurog, who really "understood comedy and knew his people. He allowed Jerry and Dean to have their heads, when that served the purpose. But he also reined them in when that was necessary. He didn't lose sight of the balance."[16]

Rosemary Clooney was making *White Christmas* with Bing Crosby when she met Janet at the studio. "We had a lot in common," she later said, "having watched movies all day on Saturdays as kids, and we were both newly married. Janet was very much like me — cast in the same wholesome image."[17]

Living It Up opened the following July. Janet, Dean and Jerry traveled to Atlantic City for its premiere and a long weekend of celebration. The municipality celebrated the event, proclaiming July 15 "Martin-Lewis Day." They first appeared on the NBC *Today* show from the Boardwalk, then drove

With **Dean Martin** (left) and **Jerry Lewis** in *Living It Up* (1954).

in an open convertible Cadillac across town to appear on a stage, greeting a crowd of more than fifteen thousand that gathered outside the theater where the film was shown. At midnight a private show and party with a huge cake made for the occasion was held at the 500 Club, where Lewis and Martin had debuted eight years earlier. The film was an instant box-office hit and became one of the most successful made by the dynamic duo.

For the second time in their careers Janet and Tony appeared together on the screen — in *The Black Shield of Falworth*. The picture was produced by Melville Tucker and Robert Arthur, from a screenplay by Oscar Brodney, who based his work on Howard Pyke's novel *Men of Iron*. It was Universal's first film in CinemaScope, and the studio was trying to use a larger and wider picture to fight the new competition they were facing from television. *The Black Shield of Falworth* was a romantic, swashbuckling costume melodrama set in the knighthood days of England during the reign of Henry IV, in which Tony played Myles, a hot-headed peasant who really was the son of the Earl of Falworth. Myles would later discover his true identity after training to become a squire. Janet played Lady Anne, a lady-in-waiting who becomes the object of Myles' attentions. Rudolph Maté was the director, with whom Tony had previously worked in his debut film, *The Price Who Was a Thief*. Maté suffered from a muscular tick that caused him to shake his head back and forth, as if expressing his disapproval (even when he was pleased by the performance of his actors). Tony wasn't aware of this condition and often felt insecure about his work. When he found out about the director's affliction, he warned Janet, who learned not to worry. While Tony's role involved a lot of action, Janet's was more static. Between takes she would read fan mail and note the answers her assistant should have made. When the waiting time would stretch for hours, she would become impatient and go horseback riding to cool off.

The cast of *The Black Shield of Falworth* included Barbara Rush, an old friend of Janet's, Craig Hill (as her squire-suitor) and David Farrar in the role of the villain. Despite the relatively large budget, the production apparently neglected the screenplay and characterizations to concentrate more on the technicality of the widescreen process that the CinemaScope format required. During the entire shoot Janet and Tony lived in their bungalow dressing room at Universal studio to avoid the early commute required by the long hours of makeup sessions before appearing in front of the camera. According to Tony, his marriage continued to have problems, which were noticed by Barbara Rush, who discreetly asked him if all was well between Janet and him. He confirmed the tension, saying that his wife was not feeling well. Janet, however, never mentioned having conjugal problems at that time — neither in any of her interviews or in her book.

The Black Shield of Falworth was a box-office hit. Still, many of the reviewers joked about Tony's thick New York accent. *Time* wrote, "He is possibly one of the few belted knights in history to say 'mayhap' with a Brooklyn accent." Janet explained that her husband, who had a very insecure and sensitive personality, did not take those criticisms lightly. "To have it singled out must be painful, but he never complained about it to me."[18]

After the completion of *The Black Shield of Falworth*, Janet felt that MGM had grown stale for her. She felt it was time to move on to better opportunities and did not renew her contract with the studio. "I felt I had paid off my debt in full," explained Janet. "True, the studio had built me up and given me a wide variety of movies to learn my craft. But the studio, too, had changed and men like Mr. Mayer were no longer there. I felt I'd have a better chance out on my own and when I talked to Mr. Thau I cried and he cried and he said I was doing the right thing."[19] It was not an easy choice; Janet was scared because she did not know if anyone else would want her if she was not under contract with MGM. But her agents told her they had already received offers from two other studios for a non-exclusive deal. Finally Janet won her release, although only after she promised MGM to make one last picture with them. A few days later she signed a non-exclusive four-picture, five-year deal with Universal-International, Tony's studio, and a non-exclusive contract with Columbia for five films over a period of seven years.

Rogue Cop was Janet's first picture of 1954 and her last with MGM. She was directed by Roy Rowland, who had helmed her debut in *The Romance of Rosy Ridge*. The movie, originally titled *Kelvaney*, was among the few film noir projects produced by Metro. It portrayed the aspects of a cop's life, his struggle between good and evil, realistically detailed by screenwriter Sydney Boehm, who based the story on the bestselling novel by William P. McGivern. Robert Taylor was rightly cast as the dishonest police detective who finally turns on the mobsters after they kill his brother, a decent cop, whose girlfriend was played by Janet. Filming went along at an even pace, and Janet hit it off perfectly with Taylor, who she called "a true gentleman." George Raft, who had been the king of gangster films in the '30s and '40s, was offered by Dore Schary a supporting role as the mobster boss; while Steve Forrest, the real younger brother of Dana Andrews, popular star of many film noirs, was cast as the good cop. *Rogue Cop* opened in New York the following September to mixed reviews, staying in theaters for only two weeks.

"KING AND QUEEN OF HEARTS," "SPOIL THE BRUTE!," "LOVE THOSE IN-LAWS," "HOW TONY AND JANET SAVED THEIR LOVE," "THE SECRET LIFE OF JANET LEIGH," "JANET LEIGH'S MARRIAGE SECRETS," "TONY'S DAYS DECISION," "OUR RULES FOR ROMANCE," "WE MAKE

EVERY TRIP A HONEYMOON," "WHEN LOVE IS ENOUGH." Those were some of the titles echoed in the press during 1954, focusing mostly on Janet and Tony's matrimonial life. It seemed that the fans had to be constantly reassured that the dream marriage of Hollywood's darling couple was not in danger, despite persistent rumors. In one of those articles Janet was quoted saying:

> I think Tony and I have always been honest with each other in our marriage. Honesty is one of the surest foundations for a secure marital relationship. Arguments need never develop into major hassles if love and tolerance are used. Without love, of course, there is no marriage … but when there is love there is tolerance. And I think to be tolerant means you love someone not in spite of, but because of, his faults. I have never made any issues about little annoying habits that Tony might have. He does have some, of course. Everyone does…. Forgiveness is the most important thing.[20]

In contrast, Tony in his biography bluntly admitted that they indeed were having problems at this time, explaining that it did not take long before their differences, that seemed so exciting at first, started to create friction between them. He accused Janet of bossing him around. "I was the naïve one in the relationship. I had never been married before but for Janet I was husband number three — and she had been only twenty-three years old!"[21]

That same year the Curtises moved for the third time in three years, into a spacious house on Coldwater Canyon Drive in Beverly Hills. They barely had time to settle in before Tony left for Boston to shoot a new film. Janet followed him for a few weeks but later returned to Hollywood, where she was expected to rehearse for her first film with Columbia Pictures: *My Sister Eileen*. The picture was originally based on a series of popular *New Yorker* stories written in the late '30s by Ruth McKenney about two sisters from Ohio and their adventures in the then-bohemian Greenwich Village in New York. In 1940 the series was turned into a hit comedy on Broadway called *My Sister Eileen*, later presented on television starring Rosalind Russell. Then in 1953 a musical version titled *Wonderful Town*, featuring Leonard Bernstein's music, with a book and lyrics by Betty Comden and Adolph Green, opened on Broadway, becoming an instant hit and lasting more than 500 performances. In 1941 Columbia Pictures had bought the film rights to the *Eileen* play, which was finally put into pre-production in 1954.

Harry Cohn, president of Columbia Pictures, asked Richard Quine, who had written a screenplay with Blake Edwards, to direct the picture. Cohn also signed a young choreographer named Bob Fosse, fresh from his success on Broadway with the musical *The Pajama Game*. Janet was cast in the title role of Eileen, the young beautiful sister who gets all the boys' attention. However, she had to badger Cohn for weeks to get that part, even though she had a contract with Columbia. She even agreed to work for two months without salary to get the routines right.

"I thought it was a marvelous opportunity for me," Janet revealed years later. "But Cohn had seen those corny costume melodramas Tony and I had been doing, and it took a test to bring me around."[22]

The other two stars in the film were Betty Garrett, who played the intelligent Ruth (a part originally intended for Judy Holliday), and Jack Lemmon, playing the magazine editor who falls for her.

Fosse had a supporting role as Frank Lippincott, one of Eileen's admirers. The choreographer was not very pleased about having to wear a hairpiece during the entire shoot. Fosse sometimes tried to replace it with a hat, and often had the dancers put one on in his routines.

Janet and Fosse worked together for eight weeks before principal photography began. At their first meeting she feared he would be arrogant, but instead she found him "sensitive, gentle and patient." She told him about her limited dancing experience of only two musicals, and expressed her need of help more with her style than with moving. After just three weeks of work she suddenly felt confident enough to ask him to teach her actual steps he had created for the film.

"When I did something right," she recalled, "he was so proud of me. He really made you feel good."[23] The shooting began under difficult circumstances, since a $6,000,000 lawsuit was filed against the studio by Joseph A. Fields and Jerome Chodorov, authors of the original stage and screen versions of *My Sister Eileen*. The writers claimed that Cohen had violated the 1941 contract, which clearly stated that Columbia did not have any rights to produce a sequel to the story, allowing only for a remake. According to the authors, Blake Edwards and Richard Quine's screenplay did not constitute a remake. According to Fields and Chodorov, the original 1942 production was dramatic, and Columbia's was a musical. They also felt the characters were changed and eliminated, and participated in new and different events. Moreover, the story was substantially different.

Despite the complex legal battle, Janet was thrilled to be part of that production. She got along well with her co-stars, particularly Jack Lemmon, who used to entertain the cast and crew with his piano-playing between takes (he sang in the film for the first time onscreen). Of Lemmon, Janet said:

No one had realized how wonderful he was yet. You could tell in working with him, though — although most of the scenes were with Betty. You could see what was inside. It took a little time for what was to get out. When I was with him, it didn't show through yet. I certainly didn't know the extent of his brilliance. I did know there was something more than anyone had seen yet.[24]

Bob Fosse (left), Janet Leigh, Betty Garrett and Tommy Rall in *My Sister Eileen* (1955).

In 1988, more than 40 years later, Janet appeared at a tribute organized by the American Film Institute to celebrate Lemmon's career, reminiscing about her experience with her great colleague.

My Sister Eileen took more than five months to make, but because the dancing numbers were shot first, part of the cast, including Lemmon, came on the set only at the very end. This was not Janet's case, who worked almost the entire time. Fosse was always very professional and no friendlier with her than with anyone else on the set; however, when they worked alone, he occasionally would flirt, taking her in his arms and kissing her. Janet knew he was married, although his wife never appeared on the set during the shoot. Both Bobby and I knew, even without talking about it," she confessed years later, "that an affair would have happened if we let it. There was that much electricity between us."[25]

Tony found a letter addressed to Janet from Fosse in which the choreographer said he could not wait to see her again and nothing more. Curtis became very jealous (despite his own secret affairs) but decided not to confront her, being afraid she could divorce him. Instead he went on a one-week sex binge at *Playboy* owner Hugh Hefner's home in Chicago. He and Hefner had met in 1950 while Janet was filming *Jet Pilot*.

Janet's friendship with Bob Fosse lasted throughout their lives. The following year the choreographer invited Janet, who was in New York for a movie junket, to watch the dance auditions for his new musical *Damn Yankees*. Fosse told her that choosing a handful of dancers out of hundreds was for him the hardest task in putting a show together. When he died in September 1987 she was cited in his will, along with a group of other celebrities, who were each left $378.79 for a dinner in a nice restaurant.

My Sister Eileen opened successfully in August 1955, displaying Janet's lovely dancing and singing talents, which were praised unanimously by the critics. Richard Quine worked very hard to have songs and ballets written and performed as dialogue extensions of the story action. He wanted to avoid having numbers cut from the European prints of the film, which was common practice at the time, particularly with musicals. Non–English-speaking audiences, in fact, often found it tedious to watch too many musical performances they could not understand.

5

Scenes from a Marriage

Husband came first, then everything.— Janet Leigh

Despite their immense popularity, Janet and Tony were almost shunned in certain circles in Hollywood. They were both very social, Janet even more so than her husband At their parties her friends consistently outnumbered Tony's. She was a very gracious host, and her social networking was very helpful to both of them. Still, they were stunned that they were not welcome at certain places. Said Curtis:

> We were so fucking popular. We were so famous. We had everything, [Janet] and I. When we got married, when we hit, and those magazines carried us, right after us were Eddie Fisher and Debbie Reynolds.... [However], there was so much envy in this town. I could feel it, I could see it.[1]

Tony explained that at that time he did not have any social grace, which occasionally led to the criticism and ostracizing of the couple. Janet taught him all the basic rules of etiquette and social *savoir fair*, but when he forgot to apply them, she would become embarrassed first, then furious and later critical of his behavior in public. Tony's lack of sophistication was the subject of many of the couple's arguments.

In November 1954, Janet and Tony appeared together for the first time on television as guests on Ed Murrow's *Person to Person* show. They were filmed in their Beverly Hills home, showing their house to the audience while being interviewed from New York. They represented the perfect example of the ideal couple in Hollywood.

In late March 1955 Janet starred in the Warner Bros. movie *Pete Kelley's Blues*. She played Ivy Conrad, a socialite who fell for a broke cornet-playing musician in a Kansas City speakeasy during the Roaring Twenties. The picture was inspired by a 1951 NBC radio show of the same name created by Richard

L. Breen, starring Jack Webb, in which Dick Cathcart led the Matlock jazz group. When Webb decided to star in, produce and direct a film based on the show, he asked Cathcart to dub his cornet playing. Webb, who had achieved fame for his role as Sergeant Joe Friday in the radio and TV series *Dragnet*, created an interesting film noir atmosphere for this film, in which the dialogue was inspired by *Pat Novak for Hire*— another radio series starring Webb.

Along with Janet, Webb assembled an amazing group of talents: Edmond O'Brien, Lee Marvin, Peggy Lee and Martin Milner. In addition, Ella Fitzgerald had a small role as a nightclub owner, and magnificently sang the theme for the picture and one other song. Jayne Mansfield, in her second film experience, was given a bit part as a sexy redheaded cigarette girl. Peggy Lee, who played an alcoholic mobster's moll, sang most of the movie's songs, all old standards. She later received an Academy Award nomination for Best Supporting Actress. Janet, whose character many critics compared to an F. Scott Fitzgerald heroine, sang "I'm Gonna Meet My Sweetie Now," but she was strangely dubbed. For a dance hall scene, Webb hired more than 200 extras to dance popular dances of the twenties. The picture was completed in mid–May 1955.

On July 27, 1955, *Pete Kelly's Blues* had its world premiere via a special gala event in San Antonio, Texas, followed by its official opening in New York three weeks later. The picture was surprisingly successful, grossing more than $5,000,000. In conjunction with the nationwide film opening, Webb planned a one-month tour to determine whether there was interest in creating a spin-off TV series, which he produced four years later for NBC.

While she was working on *Pete Kelly's Blues*, Janet received a tempting offer from Rodgers and Hammerstein to star in their upcoming Broadway musical *Pipe Dream*. During one of her trips to New York, she had been asked by Richard Rodgers, who greatly admired her, to casually audition for the female lead. She nervously did, and a few weeks later she learned by telegram the exciting news. Tony, however, dissuaded her from accepting because they would have been separated for more than six months. Since "husband came first, then everything" was Janet's philosophy of life — even her career — she turned down the offer. *Pipe Dream* was not a hit; coincidentally, she never again had another opportunity like that in her career.

In July 1955, Janet accepted a role in *Safari*, a British production to be shot first at the MGM studios at Elstree outside London, and afterwards on location in Kenya. The opportunity came simultaneously with an offer for Tony to play opposite Burt Lancaster and Gina Lollobrigida in Carol Reed's *Trapeze*, which was scheduled to be made in Paris that summer. Janet decided to take along her mother, whose marriage was going through a difficult time. After a brief stop in New York at the Sherry Netherland Hotel, Janet and Helen arrived in London, where they stayed in a luxurious suite at the Savoy Hotel. Columbia Pictures had arranged an immediate costume fitting and a meeting with *Safari*'s producer, "Cubby" Broccoli, and director Terence Young. Later surrounded by reporters, she met her co-stars Victor Mature (the only other American in the film), Roland Culver and John Justine, for the first time. While in London, Janet attended three concerts with her mother. They were at the opening night of Rosemary Clooney, saw Guy Mitchell at the Palladium, and attended the closing night performance of Marlene Dietrich at the Café de Paris.

As agreed with Tony, every Friday afternoon Janet flew to Paris to be with him; Tony had traveled to France by boat. Their time together was very enjoyable, as evidenced by a series of beautiful photos taken by the American photographer Milton Green on assignment for *Look* magazine. Tony was not very happy with Janet's decision to make *Safari*, being afraid that the six week separation might cause irreparable damage to their marriage. But Janet was very determined to go ahead with her plan. She loved to work, and she grabbed at the opportunity in Africa. After four weeks of shooting in the studio, the crew was ready to go on location for six weeks. Tony flew to London to spend three days with Janet before her departure for Kenya. Together they went to a party hosted by Rex Harrison and Marlene Dietrich. On August 30, 1955, Janet boarded a plane with her mother, stopping in Rome and in Cairo before finally landing in Nairobi, Kenya.

Safari's screenplay, written by Anthony Veiller, was based on a story by Robert Buckner. The picture was an adventure-melodrama set in the Mau Mau country and centered on the activities of a white hunter, Victor Mature, whose son has been killed by the Mau Mau. He agrees to lead a safari for wealthy but eccentric Brit Richard Culver, accompanied by his fiancée, played by Janet. The hunter will succeed with his hunt on all counts, avenging his son's death and winning the girl.

The crew established a base camp in Archers Post by a natural pool. Cameraman Ronnie Maasz described Janet as a very warm and friendly person. Usually at the end of the day crew and cast members would take a swim to wash away the grime of the day before dusting themselves with DDT powder to ward off fleas and mosquitoes. Remembered Maasz:

> The pool itself was not more than five feet deep. So after a swim up and down its length or so, it was customary to lean against the bank chatting to whoever happened to be there. I was doing exactly that when Janet happened by and also leaned against the side. After a couple of minutes of idle chatter I suddenly felt a

A dramatic moment from *Safari* (1956).

hand "touch me up." Janet smiled sweetly and swam away. Hello! I thought. Could it be that the leading lady fancied me? This vanity was quickly dispelled as I now observed her talking to one of the sound boys on the other side. He suddenly gave a compulsive start and looked hard at Janet as once again she swam away. I hastened across and consulted. He had had the same experience. What was going on? We both watched as she next joined our assistant director. Again, the same thing. Just then a spluttering Vic Mature surfaced hard by, and both he and Janet collapsed with laughter. It had been a put-up job between them.[2]

Although the atmosphere was relaxed among the cast and the crew members, Janet felt very lonely, terribly missing Tony, who wrote her a few times and even called when they were in proximity of a telephone, despite the frustratingly bad connection. Off the set, Janet spent most of her time in the company of Juma, a little boy from Zanzibar who played the small role of Odongo.

Shooting on location was an adventure itself. Since the picture was photographed in CinemaScope and Technicolor, it required a lot of bulky equipment, which was shipped several weeks earlier and had to be constantly inspected and cleaned. One time, after the equipment was loaded on the trucks to be carried to the designated location, the convoy ran into a terrible rain storm. After digging out cars and trucks from the mud, it arrived at the camp to find out that the site had been flooded out. In addition, the plane carrying the film wardrobe and props crashed in Khartoum, and everything had to be replaced. While Janet, Helen and the rest of the cast stayed in a tented camp, Victor Mature opted for a primitive hotel seventy miles away at Nanyuki, but he promptly retuned the next day after his room was blown up by a crude bomb planted outside the door. Later on, the second unit was attacked by Mau Mau, then a production manager had the cash box and some liquor stolen from his tent, and even Janet was robbed of a few items. Soon after filming began, Terence Young suffered from heat exhaustion that brought on fever. (The barometer, in fact, often indicated a temperature around 112 degrees.) Yet he insisted on carrying on. Even Janet nearly fainted in a scene because of the strong sun. Soon, almost every member of the unit suffered from dysentery. During a scene shot by a river, Janet, whose cheerful endurance was admired by everyone on the set, accidentally plunged into the water and swallowed some. She fell ill with a stomach bug that caused her cramps and strong dysentery. She flew to Nairobi to see a doctor, who gave her only temporary relief. Later, when she returned to London, she visited a specialist in tropical diseases who told her the bug was gone but had permanently weakened her stomach, leaving her with gastrointestinal disorders connected to a kidney infection.

"Vic Mature was such a scaredy cat," said Janet about her co-star. It was an accurate description, later confirmed by a funny anecdote reported by the Irish actor Liam Redmond. One of the first scenes Mature had to shoot took place in a piranha and crocodile–infested stream in which he had to rescue Janet, who was paddling a canoe supposedly heading toward a dangerous waterfall. Redmond described the situation when Terry Young took Vic Mature down to the riverbank:

> Young explained, "You'll paddle your canoe towards the camera and then, as you pass by…"
> "Forget it."
> "What does that mean?"
> "It means forget it, colonel! I'm not paddling any goddamn canoe. That's not a river, that's a croc city!"

Liam explained that Young enlisted the support of his technical adviser, a big-game hunter in khaki shorts, who said, "There is no problem, Mr. Mature. Crocs can't abide noise. We'll just raise a bit of hell with the drums and they'll make themselves scarce for half a mile." Mature wasn't biting:

"Forget it, will you? There's no way I'm putting a thin canoe between my arse and the jaw of a goddamn crocodile."

"Look, sir, I'll camp here all night and fire off my elephant gun every hour. By morning there won't be a single croc between here and Nairobi."

"Well now, I'll tell you what's wrong with that idea," said Mature, turning away. "One of those fuckers might be deaf!"[3]

Finally he agreed to play the scene after some natives fired shots up and down the river banks to scare the crocodiles off. It took Mature just one take to get Janet out of the water at an incredible speed. In contrast, Janet undertook many dangerous scenes when she discovered her stunt double was pregnant.

On October 5, 1955, the shooting was over, and Janet flew back to Paris to see Tony.

Safari premiered at the Empire Theatre on Leicester Square in London on April 6, 1956, and, in Janet's own words, it was "a stinker."

The Curtises missed each other during that period of separation, although Tony coped with the long distance very differently from his wife. He moved from an apartment, provided by the production of *Trapeze*, to the luxurious George V Hotel in order to be closer to other members of the troupe. On the days he could not handle his solitude he sought out the company of French girls, who, as he admitted, only served to keep his mind off his loneliness. When finally husband and wife were reunited in Paris, they moved to a different apartment at the Elysées Park Hotel, a few steps from the Champs Elysées. While Tony was busy filming, mostly at the Billancourt Studios, Janet did some promotion for her upcoming films in France.

To celebrate her return from Africa, Tony surprised her with a homecoming present — a Messerschmitt, a three-wheeled, two-seater micro-car. Their midget vehicle attracted a lot of attention as they were photographed in it while happily driving by the Arc de Triomphe.

On November 18, after having previously consulted a physician at the American Hospital in Paris, Janet received a positive pregnancy test result. Tony was ecstatic. Together they planned to keep the news quiet, but, despite their efforts, it quickly spread to both sides of the Atlantic, making headlines all over the world.

On Thanksgiving Day, after entertaining some troops at a military base in Versailles, Janet began a period of strict rest. Tony, who had just completed *Trapeze*, bought a Mercedes and planned to drive across France. The trip was very long but exciting. They stopped in Provence, then went on to the French Riviera before crossing the border into Italy, making stops in Genoa, Florence and finally Rome. In the Italian capital they were constantly chased by paparazzi while they visited historical monuments, shopped, or ate. Finally, on December 11, they returned to Genoa where they boarded the ocean liner *Cristoforo Colombo*, which took them back home via Cannes, Naples and Gibraltar. The boat finally docked in New York just five days before Christmas. The Curtises took a train to Los Angeles, however, after learning that their home had been burglarized.

Nineteen fifty-six marked a new year and a new home. After so many years of living in rented houses, Tony and Janet bought their first home. To pay many of the expenses, they both signed to appear separately in a couple of TV shows. A five-month-pregnant Janet taped a *Rosemary Clooney's Show* episode, which aired after the baby was born. A year later she starred in an episode of *Schlitz Playhouse of the Stars* called "Carriage from Britain."

Their new home was a large country-style house located in Beverly Hills, with four bedrooms and a swimming pool. "We are not rushing into furnishing," said Janet to Louella Parsons, who broke the news. Tony, who was more interested in Janet's pregnancy than discussing the nursery's decoration, changed the subject, saying, "If the baby is a boy, we plan to name him Joshua. It's a Biblical name and it goes so well with Curtis."[4]

Just a couple of weeks earlier Janet had been rushed to the hospital with painful symptoms associated with a threatened miscarriage. Luckily it was only a severe kidney condition that was quickly treated without jeopardizing the baby. After a few days at St. John's Hospital in Santa Monica, Janet returned to her new home, where she was ordered by Dr. Sarah Pearl to rest until the baby's delivery date.

Since she was forced to rest, Janet began to dedicate much of her time to a Hollywood all-volunteer charity called SHARE (Share Happily and Reap Endlessly). The charity helped developmentally disabled, abused and neglected children. It was one of the several non-profit organizations that she committed herself to for her entire life. Along with a group of brave women, every May she would help put together a charity show using her talent, along with many of her friends, to benefit the Exceptional Children's Foundation.

Janet also continued to sketch a line of dresses. She had, in fact, received an offer a few months earlier from a manufacturer of inexpensive clothes to endorse one of their lines. Many of her female fans would ask in their letters for advice on how to dress. Janet kindly shared her own shopping advice. Determined to do more then lend her name, she started learning about production and designed a small group of very basic, simple and elegant dresses. She modeled the clothes, which also appeared in a spread in *Life* magazine and on several TV shows, to promote them. The line was an instant hit, but the partnership did not last very long due to the unprofessional behavior of the manufacturer.

On June 17, at 9 P.M., Janet arrived once again at the hospital with labor pains, ready for the baby to come. She was accompanied by Tony and by *Look* photographer Bob Vose, who took photographs of the happy event. The first to be alerted by telephone were Rosemary Clooney and her husband, actor José Ferrer, who joined Tony, nervously sweating in the waiting room. Clooney, who was eight months pregnant herself, tried to distract him with card games. Arriving later were Jackie and Jerry Gershwin, old friends of the couple and the future godmother and godfather of the baby. Finally, at 2:14 P.M., Janet gave birth to a beautiful, healthy girl with Tony's deep blue eyes: Kelly Lee.

Janet explained the choice of that name many years later. "At that time we didn't know ahead of time if it would be a girl or a boy, so when I was pregnant with Kelly, my best friend, Jackie Gershwin, said, 'Why don't you call the baby Kelly, so if it's a girl, it works, and if it's a boy, it works?'"[5] She followed the same pattern two years later, naming her second daughter Jamie Lee.

Becoming a mother changed Janet's priorities. From now on, Kelly's well being would always come first. The birth of their daughter also transformed the Curtises' marriage.

> "If we had an argument," said Tony in an interview given five months later, "the important thing was who was going to win and who was going to lose. Usually both of us were too stubborn to give in."
>
> "And too proud," Janet added. "Now, since the baby, we have an easiness, a closeness that we never had before."
>
> "It's strange," Tony said, "but we are more considerate of each other without really trying to be."
>
> "Suddenly," Janet added, "it's not just my pride and my wishes fighting Tony's pride and Tony's wishes. It's both of us thinking about someone else."[6]

Janet also became more tolerant and more patient about untidiness. When she returned home from the hospital, the house was in the middle of major remodeling, with only the nursery completed. Pipes and conduits were sprawled across the floors, with electricians and plumbers loudly moving around all over the house. Janet found the disturbance less important than it used to be. She was annoyed, but would retire to Kelly's room and leave the strain and the tension behind her — something that she previously would not have been able to do.

Tony went immediately back to work on *Mister Cory*, a new film by Universal. Husband and wife formed the Curtleigh Productions company, merging their business affairs. For the first months Janet put her job on hold to fully dedicate herself to Kelly, with the help of a nanny.

In February 1957, when Kelly was seven months old, Janet took her to New York, where Tony was shooting *The Sweet Smell of Success*. She was also expected at the Republic Studio to star in "Carriage from Britain," a 30-minute teleplay episode of *Schlitz Playhouse of the Stars*. It was a light comedy in which she played a young mother obsessed with keeping one step ahead of the neighbors by acquiring a baby carriage like the one Prince Charles had. Her character imports one from England, but in the process, she becomes involved with some smugglers.

On her last day rehearsing a scene in which a burglar tries to steal the valuable English pram, she came down the stairs, jumped on the intruder's back, and fought him. While they twirled around, actor Jesse White fell on her, breaking her left arm. Janet was unaware of the break at first, but could not move her arm. She also hit her head, losing consciousness for a minute. Later, x-rays confirmed a fracture of her ulna bone. Still, she finished the shoot, with the help of some painkillers and a taped arm, which she later had cast.

6

Orson Welles

Working with Orson is like being inside a seed and seeing it sprouted and developed into a full tree. — Janet Leigh

"DEAR JANET,
SO GLAD YOU ARE GOING TO BE IN MY PICTURE
LOOKING FORWARD TO WORKING WITH YOU
REGARDS
ORSON WELLES"

This telegram was waiting at home for Janet one night after dining out with Tony. She was so excited that she immediately contacted her agent, who told her that nothing had been signed, since a script was not even ready. Janet did not want to hear anything else, saying that she would have done anything to work with Welles, who she had met with Tony at a benefit gala in London years earlier.

Universal had bought the film rights to Whit Masterson's mystery novel *Badge of Evil*, published in the spring of 1956. The screen adaptation, by young writer Paul Monash, had remained on the shelf for months, until December 1956, when Albert Zugsmith, a Columbia producer, received a memo from a Universal studio executive recommending Charlton Heston as the leading man for the project. Zugsmith resurrected the script and sent it to Heston, who liked it but wanted to be sure that the project had a good director attached to it. The name of Orson Welles was mentioned as a potential co-star; however, Heston, as claimed in his autobiography, suggested Welles as the potential director. Zugsmith, on the other hand, claimed that Welles told him he wanted to make a film and asked him to give him a script, any script. The producer handed him *Badge of Evil*, which Welles agreed to make only if they let him re-write it, which he did in only seventeen days.

Welles' version of the story of how he came onboard is also different; he maintained that he refused to act in the picture because he disliked the script. But after Columbia lied to Heston, assuring him that Welles was attached to the project, Heston accepted the part immediately. Later the producers called Welles back and offered him the director's chair, which he accepted on the condition he could rewrite what he found to be a ridiculous script. He created a totally new story, which was very loosely based on Masterson's original novel, and called it *Touch of Evil*. For Welles this was his first film in America since 1948's *Macbeth*. He agreed to a fee of $150,000 for his acting talents, but would write and direct for free.

Charlton Heston claimed that the casting of Janet was imposed by Universal because the studio thought she was solid at the box office; however, Welles did not object to that choice. He also filled the picture with unbilled cameos of many famous actors including Marlene Dietrich (who was so excited to play the role of a Mexican gypsy that she brought her own costumes and wig, taken from Paramount costume department), Joseph Cotten as a coroner, Mercedes McCambridge, as a butch gang leader biker, Keenan Wynn as a lawyer, and Zsa Zsa Gabor as the owner of a strip club. The presence of these celebrities was a shock to the studio executives, who never knew they had agreed to work for union scale and without credit.

After Columbia assessed a budget of $895,000, Welles moved into one of Zugsmith's offices on the Universal lot. Three-quarters of the picture was shot at night on location in Venice Beach in a run-down and decayed area.

Janet worried that her broken arm would be a problem for Welles. She had the cast set at a 135-degree angle instead of the normal 90-degree angle in order to more easily hide it from the camera. "I put a coat on it and went to see Orson. He said, 'I heard you broke your arm.' I said, 'Well, I did.' And showed him. He said, 'Oh, no problem.' So I played the whole picture with a broken arm."[1] For some of the scenes in which Janet appeared in a nightgown and the arm could not be hidden, the cast was sawed open, and she took it off just before they were ready to shoot.

On the Sunday before filming started, Welles invited some of the cast to his small apartment for an informal rehearsal of the first day of shooting. Janet played American Susan Vargas on a honeymoon with her husband, Heston, a Mexican government official. They clashed with a ruthless, twisted Mexican cop, Welles, who has framed a young man for murder. At the rehearsal Janet was impressed by the amazing sense of improvisation Welles had.

For the first days of the shooting, Universal sent studio "spies" to the set to watch over Welles and report on his progress. He was aware of being scrutinized and worked furiously on his first scene, finishing it at an extraordinary speed. By the end of his second day he had completed eleven pages of the script.

As Janet recalled:

> At first Orson was a good boy. He shot two weeks of material on studio sets in two days and then he got permission for location work at Venice. He fell in love with the nighttime atmosphere there, and we'd shoot all night and sleep in the day. He let me do the part the way I saw her but would go on for forty or so takes. Then we'd stop while he filmed these marvelous vignettes with friends like Marlene Dietrich.[2]

Welles suffered some injuries when, while location scouting one evening, he fell into a canal, spraining his arm, wrist, and ankle, and bruising his face, thereby forcing him to wear a splint while off-camera. The director created a role (the motel night clerk) for Dennis Weaver, whose TV show *Gunsmoke* was Welles' favorite. The director and the actor forged a sexually repressed

character which later inspired Alfred Hitchcock's character of Norman Bates in *Psycho*. Some claimed that Hitchcock also borrowed certain sexual characteristics of the Susan Vargas character to delineate the role of Marion Crane, who Janet would portray two years later.

One of the most terrifying sequences in *Touch of Evil* took place in an abandoned motel used by bums as a shelter. Janet remembers it as "insidiously frightening. I really did become hysterical. It was a real motel room in a deserted place. In the scene where I am screaming to attract attention in the street there was a vicious old drunk in the next room who threatened me, and I was petrified to go out on the balcony."[3]

With Charlton Heston in *Touch of Evil* (1958).

Charlton "Chuck" Heston found it very pleasant working

with Janet. "She was very good, in spite of breaking her arm," he said. "She wore the lightest possible cast for filming, discarding the sling during takes. A gutsy lady."[4]

In an interview with Peter Bogdanovich, Welles was asked, "How was Janet Leigh?" Welles replied:

> Wonderful. I gave her a very rough time, because she had to change her hairdo back and forth all the time, not knowing why. In the motel sequence we were shooting forty or fifty setups a day, and she never knew where she was in the plot. I just said, "The hair down. The hair up. Go to the window—and don't ask me why." You know, and she was going, because we made it very quickly."[5]

Problems came at the end of June when shooting was completed and *Touch of Evil* was edited. Because of its complex narrative structure, which Universal executives considered fragmented and confused, a re-cut of the film was ordered, and original editor Virgil Vogel was replaced with Aaron Stell. Welles was in Mexico working on his next project and was completely unaware that his film had been re-edited. Moreover, the studio demanded additional shooting to fix the non-sequential story line. Janet and Heston opposed that idea, but for contractual reasons they could not refuse to return to the set for a day and do some bits that bridged scenes, which were directed by Harry Keller, a television director under contract with Universal.

Commenting on those new setups, Heston said, "I don't know if any of them made the film better, or worse, I've never met anyone who could even pick one out of the final cut—I can only identify one or two of them myself."[6]

Despite the new edit, the studio was worried about the public response to what they still considered a fragmented and unconventional style. *Touch of Evil* was released at the bottom of a double bill in May 1958. Welles balked, saying that the augmented version was not any longer than his, and was devastated when the returns proved unimpressive. The film did not have much promotional support from Universal and was poorly received throughout the country, flopping at the box office. Nevertheless, when *Touch of Evil* opened in Europe it was hailed as a work of art, winning top prizes at the Brussels Film Festival. In Paris, due to enthusiastic reviews in influential film magazines, the picture played for an entire winter and quickly acquired the status of a cult movie. In 1998 a newly-edited 111-minute restored version of *Touch of Evil* was released. It was a reconstructed director's cut that incorporated soundtrack and editing changes requested by Welles in a 58-page memo to Universal, written in December 1957 after the studio had shot the additional scene and re-edited his film. The new version was scheduled to be screened at the Cannes Film Festival in May 1998 at a special event. However, the screening was canceled at the last moment after Beatrice Welles, the director's daughter, threatened the Festival with legal action. Universal and October Films, which was to distribute the picture, decided to withdraw it while their lawyers tackled the dispute. Beatrice Welles objected to the way the film was restored, even though Universal made great efforts to re-edit it according to Orson Welles' stated wishes. Janet, who was invited to the event, was saddened by the news.

"The original is still good, but it wasn't exactly the picture that Orson had created. When I saw this, I cried. It was the essence of Orson Welles. I saw again his passion. I just feel sad that people gathered here are not going to be able to share the excitement."[7]

The legal issue was eventually solved, and *Touch of Evil* had a limited but successful theatrical re-release.

During the shooting of *Touch of Evil* the relationship between Janet and Tony was a rollercoaster ride. One moment they were the perfect couple, and the next they argued incessantly. One of the main points of argument between Janet and Tony was be his easy way of spending money — buying a new car, a new record player or fancy clothes — while Janet would always try to save money. A new Mercedes, a new poodle (named Mercy; Houdina was given to Tony's parents) and time with a psychologist were just a few of the things Tony bought for himself and his family that year, after the success of *Trapeze* finally made him a star with a new star salary.

In September 1956 producer Jerry Bresler, along with director Richard Fleischer and art director Harper Goff, traveled to Norway and France to scout locations for an adaptation of the bestselling book *The Viking*, written by Edison Marshall. Behind the ambitious project was Kirk Douglas, who had had in his mind for very long time the idea to produce and star in a film set in the days of the Vikings. With his own production company, Bryna Productions, and the assistance of Bresler, Douglas was able to make the film, which was simply called *The Viking* (later an "s" was added to the title), the story of two lusty rivals, Einar and Eric, who are unaware that they are half-brothers, vying to win the heart of Princess Morgana.

For the part of Eric, Douglas had in mind Charlton Heston, but the actor turned down the script. Douglas cast Tony, with a $150,000 salary, along with Janet as the leading lady, at $60,000. She was the only one in the cast to have some Scandinavian blood. Husband and wife accepted it with enthusiasm, and they also agreed to partially coproduce the film with their Curtleigh production company. Douglas thought that all the English characters had to be played by British actors, while the Vikings should only be portrayed by Americans. He cast Ernest Borgnine as his father, although the actor was one-and-a-half months *younger* than him. He also offered a bonus to anybody in the cast who would grow a beard before they started shooting.

On May 1957 the Curtises were ready to move to Europe, where they planned to stay at least five months. The first stop was London, where Janet hired a nanny to take care of thirteen-month-old Kelly. Later, with the rest of the cast, they traveled across Scandinavia, where they were treated warmly. They stopped in Copenhagen, Stockholm, Oslo, Bergen and finally at the Hardanger fjord, where a full-size vessel had been built to Douglas' specifications. He had, in fact, consulted some historians to have the ship made as authentic as possible. Yet, fed up by continual disagreements, he personally went to the Oslo Viking Museum, measured the Gokstand ship, and gave the specifications to shipbuilders Askwik & Son, who created an exact replica.

The Vikings had a projected budget of $2.5 million, which subsequently increased when Douglas decided to lease the rights to an entire fjord, the Maurangerfjord, where a Viking village was constructed on a rock in the middle of it and populated by many local extras. When Janet arrived for the first time at the village, she was welcomed by a sign on the side of the hill which read, "Welcome Janet," in addition to a dressing room especially built for her. The cast and the crew were housed on two ships moored at the fjord and were shuttled back and forth by a fleet of seventeen small boats. To row the Viking vessels, the production hired oarsmen from all over Scandinavia. Although the living conditions were difficult, everybody seemed to get along fine, as Ernest Borgnine recalled:

> Janet Leigh was a sweetheart. Her main trouble ... was sleeping at night because she had her infant, Kelly Curtis, with her. In fact, sleep was a problem for all of us, because it was sunshine all the time up there. They had black-out curtains in all our rooms."[8]

In fact, Kelly Curtis made her screen debut, along with Douglas' son Peter, as babies in a Viking village.

Kirk Douglas recalled a

With Kirk Douglas in *The Vikings* (1958).

funny strip act performed by

Janet, as a sort of reverse birthday present. Douglas was throwing a thirtieth party for her onboard the *Brand VI*, anchored in the fjord. The funny and chaste striptease occurred after members of the company staged a farcical show titled *My Fair Viking* in the ship's dining room. Douglas, Borgnine and Tony played little vignettes, and in one, Janet, cheered by the happy audience, began to take off her clothes, revealing a hot bikini.

Unfortunately, the weather often proved to be a problem. Out of sixty shooting days, forty-nine were rainy and dark. Producer Bresler was so exasperated that he lost 15 pounds while on the rain-lashed location. A further weight loss–inducing problem arose when some of the rushes were lost between Norway and France, and a large portion of recorded dialogue was spoiled by the rain. A large tent was put up, under which the cast could take shelter from the rain. They would patiently wait there and then run out to shoot a scene as soon the weather conditions improved, and then run back under cover. Thirty-five extra days in Norway cost the production almost $1 million.

Janet described Fleischer's direction as very visual but also passionate in the intimate scenes. "He directed quietly," she said. "If we were moving in the right direction toward what the scene needed in pace and emotion, he would let us do it the way we tended to, naturally, in rehearsal. But also out of his quietness came those monumental action scenes, which took a tremendous amount of directing."[9]

Finally the crew left the fjord and moved to the coast of Brittany, where scenes of the English castle were shot. The French weather was as bad as that in Norway and each day of delay cost Douglas $45,000. In spite of the severe weather conditions, cinematographer Jack Cardiff superbly captured the breathtaking panoramas and the authentically reproduced sets in the lavish color of Technirama and Technicolor. Interiors for *The Vikings* were shot at the Geiselgasteig Studios in Munich, where the cast resided for more than two months. In Germany, Janet was afflicted by a severe case of flu. Luckily she was helped by Kirk Douglas' wife Anne, who spoke perfect German and called the doctors. Janet was ordered to rest for more than two weeks, and Douglas was able to change Janet's schedule to accommodate her recuperation.

During the entire trip Janet recorded everything of interest in a diary, something she did every time she was away from home. Many years later this habit turned out to be very helpful when she wrote her autobiography. At the end of every week the pages were typed up, mimeographed and sent to friends and her press agent in Hollywood, who gave some of the entries to columnists. Janet made sure, though, that very personal facts were excluded from the diary, including any fights she might have had with Tony.

The final cost of *The Vikings* was $3.5 million — $1 million over budget. The overruns could have been greater except that bankrolling United Artists insisted on some rewriting that eliminated some costly location shooting.

The Vikings had one of the most expensive publicity and marketing campaigns of the 1950s. The production sent Viking dagger letter openers to reviewers, and had seven Viking vessels sent from Bergen to New York. To celebrate the opening on two New York screens, a 261-foot replica of a Norse ship was hoisted onto the marquee of the theater — at a cost of more than $100,000. A huge billboard advertising the film appeared in Times Square. At the New York premiere on June 11, 1958, Janet, Tony, Kirk Douglas and Ernest Borgnine greeted their fans from the boat. The picture was a blockbuster, grossing more than $7 million domestically and $13 million worldwide, ranking number five at the American box office that year. Kirk Douglas was estimated to have earned in excess of $2 million, while Janet and Tony also received a smaller percentage of the profits, since their production company was involved.

Some critics found Janet's performance cold and unemotional as Princess Morgana. Many speculated that her indifference was caused by her ongoing problems with Tony. In reality, they had no major fights during the making of *The Vikings*, yet things were far from going well. Tony admitted that he would have preferred to work with any other actress than his wife because he felt that his marriage had become an inescapable trap. Ironically, while they were still in Germany finishing up *The Vikings*, Universal-International announced that they would co-star in the comedy *The Perfect Furlough*.

After a brief stop in Paris, the Curtises sailed back home, where they kept a very busy social life among lots of friends, including Frank Sinatra, Lauren Bacall, Dean Martin and Sammy Davis, Jr. Janet loved to party, and it was at one of her parties she threw in the fall of 1957 that her close friend Sammy Davis, Jr., met actress Kim Novak. The singer had noticed her in the audience at a concert he had given at Chez Paree in Chicago a few months earlier; however, he had not been officially introduced to her. When he learned that Novak had been invited to Janet and Tony's party, he attended the event with the idea of casually meeting her. That night at Janet's house, Novak and Davis began a secret affair which later scandalized the entire Hollywood community, which was not ready for a white American female star to publicly date a black man. The relationship was strongly opposed by Columbia Studios president Harry Cohn, Novak's boss, who did everything to separate the couple, eventually succeeding. Nevertheless, Janet and Tony allowed the couple to use their guest house for their romantic encounters.

In an interview given in January 1958 while shooting *The Perfect*

With Tony Curtis in *The Perfect Furlough* (1958).

Furlough, Janet revealed that the picture would be the last time she would co-star with Tony on the screen for at least three years. She explained that the value of appearing as a twosome had been "used up," and that teaming up could handicap their individual careers. "We've never been a team like Marge and Gower Champion," she said. "And it could be a handicap for an actor to appear with his wife all the time.... We want to avoid being known as a team."[10]

The Perfect Furlough was a comedy based on a screenplay by Stanley Shapiro, who won an Academy Award the following year for *Pillow Talk*. Directed by Blake Edwards, who had worked with Tony on *Mister Cory* two years earlier, the picture was all shot at Universal Studios, where a characteristic Paris street was constructed on the Little Europe back lot. Footage of the principal monuments of Paris was filmed by a second unit on location and used as a backdrop, with doubles standing in for the stars in long shots. Janet, who had a new, short haircut, noticed that her double had long blonde hair. The production asked her to wear a wig, but she refused and convinced Edwards to accept her hairdo, a more appropriate look for her role as army psychologist Lieutenant Vicki Loren. The mildly funny plot revolved around an Arctic army base where frustration and boredom have set in. To raise morale, a female Pentagon psychologist suggests the army select one of the men from the base (played by Tony) to enjoy a dream holiday in Paris together with a famous movie star of his choice.

Elaine Stritch, Keenan Wynn, Linda Cristal and future teen idol Troy Donahue were cast in supporting roles. Janet was happy to work with Edwards, who was an old friend and fostered a relaxed atmosphere during the entire shoot.

"It was a kind of a milestone for me," Edwards said about *Furlough.* "I got the feeling of comedy. Everything seemed to work. It didn't have any great screenplay, we shot it in thirty days, and I look at it now and I say how could I have done some of those things? But, all in all, in its own strange way, it is one of my favorite films."[11]

The studio promoted *The Perfect Furlough* through an unusual advertising campaign that described the picture as incredibly funny, guaranteeing the audience exactly 287 laughs — certified in an audience test by Sindlinger & Co., Inc., Research Division, from Ridley Park, Pennsylvania. Oddly re-titled *Strictly for Pleasure* for the British market, the picture performed fairly well and earned a Golden Globe nomination as Best Motion Picture Comedy in 1959.

A few weeks later Janet found out she was pregnant again. Tony's reaction was ambivalent: "[It]was good news, but it made me feel even more trapped in my marriage."[12]

After *Sweet Smell of Success* and *The Vikings* in 1957, Curtleigh Productions got involved in one of Tony's most successful films, *The Defiant Ones.* While he was occupied all day on the set, co-starring with Sidney Poitier, Janet attended a few events to promote the recently released *The Vikings.* She also kept busy moving to a new home only a few blocks away from the previous house. The new larger home had quarters for a cook, two maids and a secretary. Despite her schedule, Janet tried to rest as much as possible to avoid pregnancy complications.

On August 24, returning from a party at the Santa Monica beach house of Peter Lawford at 1 A.M., Janet and Tony were involved in a three-car traffic accident. Their car, carrying Dean and Jeanne Martin, and songwriter Sammy Cahn with his wife Gloria, was struck by a vehicle driven by Donald Seddon. The jealous drunk man thought he saw his wife riding in the company of a man in an auto in front of the Curtises' vehicle and tried to force it to the curb, bouncing instead into their car. Frank Sinatra, who was following them in his convertible, with Ernie Kovacs and his wife Edie Adams, called an ambulance from his car radio-telephone to arrange immediate treatment for Janet, who was six months pregnant.

Gloria Cahn recalled, "We were going slowly, because Janet was nervous about cars after an accident she had 10 days ago. She was just rocked a little to one side and fell against Sammy. We got her out of the car and over to a bus stop seat by the side of the road, and then Frank Sinatra came up."[13]

Visibly shaken, Janet was taken to the UCLA Medical Center, where she was examined, sedated and released, apparently with no consequences from the accident. Following the crash, Tony was so stressed over Janet's condition that he was given tranquilizers. Just ten days earlier Janet had indeed had another minor car accident on the way to pick up her mother on a rainy day. Her car was hit from the rear while she was waiting at a traffic light. The driver apologized, explaining that the brakes did not hold on the slippery road. Although she did not suffered any injuries, her family doctor was called to check that her baby was fine.

That same summer Tony was cast in Billy Wilder's comedy masterpiece *Some Like It Hot*, starring Jack Lemmon and Marilyn Monroe. Part of the film was shot on location in San Diego at the Hotel Del Coronado in Coronado Beach. In September, Janet, with Kelly and her babysitter, visited the set for two weeks, staying at the luxurious hotel. She was unaware that Tony was having an affair with Marilyn and had a very pleasant holiday, having gained weight and refusing to be photographed in her swimsuit by the many photographers on the set. In 2009 Tony wrote a behind-the-scenes book about *Some Like It Hot* in which he claimed that Marilyn Monroe, who was married to playwright Arthur Miller at the time, became pregnant with his child and was willing to marry him. But three months later she had a miscarriage. Tony suspected that the baby had been aborted on Miller's orders. Curtis never mentioned those events in either of his two autobiographies. Many doubt the credibility of the story, since on many other occasions he has contradicted himself in reporting facts about his personal life. He also claimed that, despite Janet's pregnancy with his second child, the news of Monroe's presumed abortion made him fall into a depression that later contributed to the break-up of his marriage.

On November 22, 1958, Jamie Lee Curtis was born at Cedars-Sinai Hospital, just three days after Tony's father suddenly died of a heart attack. The happy event helped cheer the family, still saddened by the tragic departure of Emanuel Schwartz.

After Jamie's birth the magazines could not get enough pictures of America's ideal family. Janet expressed very clear ideas about how to raise her girls, as she explained in an interview that tried to portray her family as one of the happiest in Hollywood:

I want what my children want. The time will never come when I'll say to them, "Look what I gave up for you — I gave up my career, just to see that you were brought up properly!" No, I'll never say it because *I* brought them into this world and they don't owe me anything! That's why Tony and I have friends. And that's why the children will have friends, too. Because children always have friends, whether the parents like it or not, no matter how selfishly some parents hug their children to their breasts, refusing to believe that some day the little bird will grow up and fly away to make its own way in the world. That's what Tony and I both mean when we say we want what our children want, even to the extent of choosing their own church affiliation when they are old enough to decide for themselves which religion they prefer.[14]

The joy of a new baby did not improve their sinking relationship, however. Regardless of the disagreeable situation, Janet later admitted, "Tony was a very good father while we were married, very good, he really participated, was a part of their lives, especially Kelly who had us alone before Jamie."[15]

The following spring, despite their shaky marital situation, Janet and Tony agreed to appear one more time onscreen as husband and wife in another comedy. Lew Wasserman, president of MCA, offered Columbia Pictures the rights to Norman Krasna's second-rate play *Who Was That Lady I Saw You With?* for $350,000. It was to be made into a film with a cast consisting of the Curtises and Dean Martin. Krasna was a longtime MCA client, and it mattered very little that the play had closed on Broadway almost as quickly as it opened, since the confirmed presence of three solid stars would have been enough to guarantee a hit for the studio. In August 1959, eight months after Jamie's birth, Janet was back on a set in better shape than she was before.

"I gained only 10 pounds while I was pregnant," she said to a journalist, continuing:

> That's the secret. Most women are afraid they'll ruin their figures by having babies. Well, it's not what a girl does after the baby arrives. It's a matter of staying in condition while they're expecting. I was careful of my diet and ate very little salt. After my daughter Jamie was born I started playing tennis, and within three weeks I could wear all my clothes. Fortunately, I'm so active around the house I didn't have to take exercises.[16]

Who Was That Lady? was a screwball comedy about a college professor, played by Tony, whose wife (Janet) catches him kissing a blonde. To stop her from divorcing him, the man asks for help from a friend, Dean Martin, who invents a crazy story that they are FBI agents trying to pierce the defenses of a beautiful spy. The original play on which the film was based had opened on Broadway in March 1958 with Peter Lind Hayes, Mary Healy and Ray Walston in the star roles.

George Sidney directed the film in only twenty-seven days. "I have never had so much fun on a picture," he said, "but the finished result never seemed to me quite to make it. It's almost a very good farce indeed, but there's something wrong. Too little real feeling, too much real feeling…. I don't know. But it was a real ball to do."[17]

Janet had a blast working again under Sidney's direction and with Dean Martin, who had become one of her closest friends. Janet, Tony, Dean and the crew worked for six days on a flooded set that portrayed a basement of the Empire State Building for one of the last scenes of the film. There were more than 10,000 gallons of water in a huge tank on Columbia's stage 9, and the "tidal wave" that hit them at the climax was a real flash flood of 6,000 gallons tripped from huge tanks. When the sequence was over, the stars celebrated by tossing the director into the tank.

One day after lunch the trio disappeared. They were expected on the set to shoot a major scene, but nobody could find them. They were discovered half an hour later trapped in an elevator between floors in the dressing room building.

Also during the shoot, Janet narrowly escaped serious injury. One scene called for her to toss a bucket of water on Tony and run away. She slipped on the wet floor and fell on an iron grating, sustaining bruises, a cut to her knee and a wrenched leg. After emergency treatment on the set, she forged on, completing the day's work.

One day the set was visited by Groucho Marx, who Sidney enlisted to make the trailer for the film.

Who Was That Lady? and its cast both received generally positive reviews, with the picture reaching number nineteen at the box office for 1960. It grossed over $3 million.

Cue magazine wrote: "Tony Curtis and Janet Leigh [are] at the top of their form," while *Harrison's Report* called Janet Leigh "superb as the bubbly, effervescent wife who complicates the impersonation by becoming overenthusiastic about it."[18]

In conjunction with the opening of *Who Was That Lady?* Janet became the sponsor of Lux Toilet Soap, a product she had previously promoted when she starred in *Walking My Baby Back Home.*

7

Shower Time

I have no intention of taking a shower ever again. — Janet Leigh

In November 1957, when Janet had just came back from Europe after shooting *The Vikings*, a man named Ed Gein was arrested in Plainfield, Wisconsin. He was accused of murdering two women after brutally torturing them. Geln turned the skulls of his victims into bowls, and their skin into seat covers and lamp shades. For twelve years he had preserved his deceased mother's bedroom fully intact. At the trial, Gein was found to be legally insane and sent to a mental hospital, where he died of cancer in 1984. The incredible story of Gein and his psychotic personality inspired Robert Bloch to write a book called *Psycho*, published in 1959 by Simon and Schuster.

Peggy Robertson, Alfred Hitchcock's personal assistant, mentioned the book to the British director. After reading it, Hitchcock was so fascinated by the subject that he decided to make it into a film, acquiring the rights for $9,000. Paramount Pictures immediately opposed the idea, considering the content too strong for a mainstream picture. Believing in his project, Hitchcock chose to personally finance 60 percent of it. For budgetary reasons he opted to shoot in black and white (Anthony Perkins claimed that Hitchcock was a great fan of Henri-Georges Cluzot's 1955 French thriller *Les Diaboliques*, and this was why he decided to shoot in black and white) at MCA's Revue Studios on the Universal Pictures lot — the same location where the episodes of the series *Alfred Hitchcock Presents* were made. He used his regular TV crew, including cameraman John L. Russell and assistant director Hilton A. Green. Initially the script was assigned to James P. Canavaugh, author of some episodes of the series, but his final work did not convince Hitchcock, who hired Joseph Stefano, a screenwriter whose brilliant abilities immediately won over the director. In the fall of 1959 Stefano completed the script, which, for

With Alfred Hitchcock on the set of *Psycho* (1960).

secrecy reasons, was called "Production #9401." In October Hitchcock sent a copy of Bloch's novel to Janet, assuring her that her character, Mary Crane (later changed to Marion Crane to avoid conflict with an actual Mary Crane found listed in the Phoenix phone directory), would be improved in the final screenplay. Janet, who had met Hitchcock and his wife Alma socially, was thrilled by the offer and read the novel in one day.

Janet was Hitchcock's first choice for the role of secretary Marion Crane. Even though many actresses were discussed for the part, including Eva Marie Saint, Marta Hyer, Hope Lange, Piper Laurie, Shirley Jones and Lana Turner, she was the first and only one to receive a specific offer. For the leading role of Norman Bates, Hitchcock cast Anthony Perkins. Stefano, who had recently seen the actor on stage on Broadway in the drama *Look Homeward, Angel*, agreed with the director's perfect choice. Anthony "Tony" Perkins was at the peak of his career. He had starred in two successful Broadway productions, *Tea and Sympathy* and *Look Homeward, Angel*, and had appeared in several films, including the hits *Fear Strikes Out* and *On the Beach*. In 1957 he had received an Oscar nomination as Best Supporting Actor for William Wyler's *Friendly Persuasion*.

"Hitchcock agreed that it was a gamble," commented Perkins years later. "He had no idea of the real possible success of the picture, but he suggested that I give it a try anyway."[1] To play Norman Bates and Mother, Perkins accepted a mere $40,000 salary, since he owed one last film to Paramount to complete his contractual obligations.

On October 28, 1959, Janet signed her contract to portray Marion Crane for just $25,000 for three weeks of work. She later admitted she would have done it for nothing.

Janet revealed in a book she co-authored, *Behind the Scenes of Psycho*, Hitchcock's reasons for casting her as Marion Crane. She quoted the director as saying:

> I hired you because you are a talented actress. You are free to do whatever you wish with the role of Marion. I won't interfere unless you are having trouble and require my guidance. Or, if you are taking too big a slice of my pie [overacting] or if you are not taking enough of a slice of my pie. But there is one rule on the set — my camera is absolute. I tell the story through that lens, so I need you to move when my camera moves, stop when my camera stops. I'm confident you'll be able to find your motivation to justify the motion. Should you have difficulty, however, I will be happy to work with you. But I will not change the timing of my camera."[2]

In his book on *Psycho*, author Stephen Rebello claimed that Hitchcock chose Janet because "he wanted a name actress because of the shock value, but he also wanted someone who could actually look like she came from Phoenix. I mean, Lana Turner might not be able to look like someone from there. He wanted a vulnerability, a softness."[3] And Janet seemed to fill the bill perfectly.

For the part of Sam Loomis, Marion's boyfriend, a number of hunky leading men were considered, but Hitchcock picked handsome John Gavin, who he had seen in Douglas Sirk's *Imitation of Life*, to play opposite Lana Turner. To complete the cast, Vera Miles and Martin Balsam were chosen for the secondary roles of Marion's sister Lila and private detective Milton Arbogast.

Before filming started, Hitchcock asked Janet to see an optometrist for a fitting of special contact lenses to wear for the final close-ups of the shower scene. Since six weeks were required for her eyes to adjust to those lenses, Hitchcock gave up the idea. Regarding clothes, the director gave *carte blanche* to costume designer Helen Colvig to decide with Janet the type of clothing Marion would wear. He only insisted that they should be bought in a store

With Anthony Perkins on the set of *Psycho* (1960).

where a secretary would normally shop. Colvig and Janet went to a popular affordable boutique in Beverly Hills and bought two simple, solid-color, shirt-waist dresses in cotton and jersey off the rack. In addition, two sets of underwear were also purchased over the counter — a white bra and half-slip for the opening bedroom scene with Gavin, and a black one worn by Marion at the Bates motel.

During preproduction, "Hitchcock violated all Hollywood cardinals of publicity by deliberately concealing the title, permitting only a few short news releases to reach columnists and trade papers," wrote the *New York Times* in a piece on the secrecy surrounded the making of *Psycho*.[4]

The picture was announced to the press simply as "Hitchcock's new shocker," with no story synopsis released. "Wimpy" (a name borrowed from second-unit cameraman Rex Wimpy) was the moniker used for the film in all in-house communications. One rumor persisted that Hitchcock bought up all available copies of the Robert Bloch novel in a monopolistic shopping spree calculated to insure secrecy.

Slowly, Janet started to create inside herself Marion's character, giving her a personal dimension by shaping in her mind what type of woman she was and what past she had. She was able to brilliantly make the character hers, someone with whom the audience would identify when she is murdered half-way through the film. This great achievement was accomplished thanks to the acting training delivered by Lillian Burns, who was the first to help her understand her roles when Janet started at MGM.

Principal photography began on November 30, 1959, on a closed set. The cast was not involved in any extensive rehearsals except for camera moves. From the beginning the ambience on the set was extremely relaxed. Hitchcock had already done major preparation work before anybody walked on the set. The picture was also partially storyboarded by Saul Bass, who designed the titles; therefore the director knew exactly how to position and move the camera. The first scene Janet shot was with Tony Perkins at the exterior of the motel Bates. The second sequence she filmed proved to be more challenging. It was the picture's opening scene, in which she appeared in her white bra in a dingy hotel room with a bare-chested John Gavin after their presumed love-making. According to Janet, Hitchcock did not feel, in the beginning, that the scene was passionate enough. He felt that Gavin was not as sexually aroused as he should be, so he let the sequence last longer, asking for extra takes. Then he pulled Janet to the side and said, "Can you do something? It's not quite there." Janet had the feeling that the director wanted her to touch her co-star. She replied, "I don't know, I'll do what I can, within reason." It finally seemed to work after she just put a little more into it than she had before to get him a little "hot and bothered."[5]

Between shots Janet would sit and talk with Hitchcock, who loved making her laugh with his jokes and gags. Then suddenly the assistant director would appear saying they were ready to shoot again and she had to regain the concentration she had lost while having a good time with him. Hitchcock intentionally wanted to keep the tone on the set from becoming heavy and gloomy because of the nature of the film's subject, but he still liked maintaining a sense of unpredictability, accepting a few changes and suggestions from cast members like Tony Perkins and Martin Balsam. He also "tested" some of the prototypes of the mummified body of Norman Bates' mother, created by the special effects department, by putting them in Janet's dressing room while she was away. Based on the degree of her terrified reaction, he decided which one to use. Despite the scary moments she experienced, Janet appreciated Hitchcock's black humor.

One of the most powerful and frightening scenes in *Psycho* takes place in a shower, with Janet being murdered by what seems to be an old woman (later revealed to be Norman Bates impersonating his dead mother). It took six days to shoot. Filming on the sequence began on December 17, right in the middle of the Christmas holidays. Hitchcock personally shot the entire scene as storyboarded from different angles by Saul Bass. Six days standing in running water, even at a comfortable temperature, proved to be very hard on Janet. Yet the main problem was nudity. Janet had nothing against it; however, for a star at that time it was inconceivable to show her body. She also believed that imagination was much stronger than what you can see, and of course she was right. To avoid troubles, Paramount made a whole torso out of rubber for Hitchcock. When one plunged a knife into it, blood would spurt from it. Still, the director did not use it, considering it too simple and artificial.

Colvig designed a flesh-colored bikini made of moleskin, a soft, almost felt-like fabric on the outside, with adhesive on the inside. After several takes the adhesive melted under the heat of the water. Since Hitchcock had a special scaffold built for that particular scene, all the technicians on it got a peak at Janet's breasts when the wardrobe malfunction occurred. The director hired professional model Marli Renfro to use for the shots in which Janet's breasts and derriere would be glimpsed.

There is still some controversy about the use of Renfro in the final scene. Janet maintained that only her own body appears in the scene. She explained that the nude model was only used to see how much of the body the camera would see at various angles and also to test what intensity level of water would look best onscreen. In Janet's opinion, Hitchcock deliberately hired the model "to plant the seed in people's minds that this picture had nudity"—a subtle way to manipulate the audience before the film even opened.[6]

Renfro claims instead:

> I was right there on the set the entire time the shower scene was shot. Janet was modestly dressed when I saw her perform. She wore a bathing suit that is straight across the top and is a full suit to her butt. The color is light tan/skin color with a sheen to it. You'll notice that the camera, when shooting Janet, never strays too far below her collar bone.... If you do not see Janet's face, it's me — hands, feet, legs, back, belly button, back of head, etc.... Even if Janet did try to do the shower scene wearing a moleskin later, which I have a hard time believing, all those scenes wound up on the editor's floor, with the only ones she did in front of me ending up in the final cut of the movie.[7]

Renfro also affirmed that she worked an additional two hours on the scene after Janet went home, shooting what was later shown onscreen. In an interview with Peter Bogdanovich, Hitchcock gave yet a third version: "All you see of Janet Leigh is her hands, her shoulders and the head. The rest is the model."[8]

When the scene was run back and forth on the Moviola, Alma Hitchcock, who had been an experienced film editor in her youth, spotted a glitch her husband and his crew had overlooked. Janet, staring in a fixed-eye close-up on the bathroom floor, had gulped air (although she later recalled it was a blink or a breath). The director took out those frames, replacing them with another shot of the showerhead. Then he had the shot of Janet's eye enlarged so that it transitioned perfectly into the bathtub drain consuming its spiraling water and blood (effectively supplied by dark chocolate syrup).

For the shower sequence, between seventy-one and seventy-eight setups were used in just forty-five seconds, each one lasting not more than three seconds. Though the knife never touches the body, the sequence leaves the onscreen impression that the blade repeatedly penetrated Marion Crane's body. The shower scene became the most memorable moment in the film and later a part of cinematic history.

By the end of December Janet had completed her scenes, of which only one was shot on location (at a used car lot located a few miles north of the Universal Studios). After a Christmas break shooting was resumed and completed by February 1, only nine days over schedule.

With the editing process completed, Hitchcock showed the picture to the Production Code office to receive the green light on the final cut. He had already made some minor changes and cuts to the dialogue, as requested when the script was sent to the office for revision. A group of censors who attended a first screening claimed to have seen nudity in the shower scene, while others did not. Hitchcock promised to fix it and showed it to them again a couple of weeks later — without having made any changes. The half that had seen nudity now did not see it, while the other half now *did*. He was able to convince them that sometimes things are in their imagination, and eventually he got away with leaving the sequence intact.

In early June, when the final editing and the musical score for *Psycho* were complete, Hitchcock invited the Curtises, Robert Bloch, Lew Wasserman and some of the technical crew with their wives to a private screening. When the screening was over and the lights were switched back on, Janet was "stupefied and electrified." She had not seen the dailies or a rough cut, and the impact of the complete film was very powerful.

Before the film's release, Hitchcock disclosed to the media only basic information regarding *Psycho*'s plot, mentioning a violent bathroom scene but no other details. Queried by the press about possible censorship problems with the shower scene, Hitchcock answered, "Men do kill nude women, you know."[9] The director personally shot and starred in a brilliant trailer in which he toured the set, illustrating where the events of the gruesome story took place but without showing any actual film footage.

To avoid spoiling the surprise factor, the cast did very little promotion for the film. Without the benefit of reviews, *Psycho* premiered in New York on June 16, 1960, at the DeMille and Baronet theaters, followed by a nationwide release. No critic was allowed to see the film before its opening, and a strict "no one ... but no one will be admitted to the theater after the film began" policy was enforced. The reviews were mixed, with some critics dismissing the picture as a gimmick horror movie. But the audience went wild, and *Psycho* was a smash hit, breaking all box-office records all over the world. It grossed $9 million in the United States and another $6 million overseas. Because of its small budget, it also became the most profitable film of the year. In Europe the movie was hailed as a masterpiece (despite England's X rating), and Janet's popularity skyrocketed.

Psycho generated controversy everywhere. Walk-outs, boycotts, phone calls and letters of protest, and talks of banning the film were reported daily in the press. People feared taking a shower after watching what everybody considered the most terrifying movie ever made. Afterward, in all her interviews, Janet admitted that prior to *Psycho* she was a relatively normal bather, but since then she had stopped taking showers:

> I have absolutely no intention of taking a shower again. It just made me feel uncomfortable, the fact of not being able to see, of being closed in by the curtain. Even in a tub I have to position myself so I'm facing the door. If there is no other way to bathe, I leave the bathroom door open, and the shower stall door open, so I have a perfect clear view.[10]

Although Janet was murdered a third of the way through the film, the impact on the audience of her performance was so shocking and powerful that she would be identified with this picture forevermore. Similarly, Anthony Perkins became firmly associated with the film, and more so with the Norman Bates character. He was typecast for the rest of his career, and starred in *Psycho II, III* and *IV*.

While *Psycho* was terrorizing America, Janet and Tony made an amusing cameo appearance in the comedy *Pepe*, directed by George Sidney. With a $5 million budget, *Pepe* was produced by Columbia on a six-month shooting schedule. Six weeks were spent on location in Mexico, and the movie was filmed in five languages simultaneously. Thirty-five guest stars appeared in it, including Edward G. Robinson, Cesar Romero, Shirley Jones, Greer Garson, Jimmy Durante, Debbie Reynolds, Sammy Davis, Jr., Bing Crosby, Jack Lemmon, Maurice Chevalier, Zsa Zsa Gabor, Judy Garland, Frank Sinatra, and Kim Novak. The movie was an attempt to launch the Mexican actor Cantiflas as a major star in Hollywood. Like all the guest stars appearing in *Pepe*, Janet had a wonderful time in shooting two of the most hilarious scenes in the film, which were a spoof of her two recent movies. In the first one she lounges in bed while talking on the phone to Tony, beckoning him to return to their bungalow (clearly inspired to *Touch of Evil*'s famous scene in the motel when she beckons Charlton Heston to return to the room). In the second scene, Pepe, played by Cantiflas, accidentally interrupts her (while humming "My Darling Clementine") in a bubble bath homage to *Psycho*'s shower scene. *Pepe* marked Janet and Tony's sixth and final joint effort onscreen. Despite being panned by the critics, the picture did fairly decent box-office business, receiving three Golden Globe nominations and seven Academy Award nominations. For her funny cameo in *Pepe*, Janet won the Laurel Award for Top Female Comedy Performance, given by the *Motion Picture Exhibitor* magazine of the American and Canadian film buyers in 1961.

During the summer, Janet, Kelly and Jamie Lee joined Tony on location in Arizona where he was shooting *The Outsider*. When they later traveled to the Marine Corps Base Camp Pendleton in Southern California, Warren Cowan, her PR man, visited her to convince her to make a bid for an Oscar nomination for *Psycho*. Janet was doubtful but finally agreed to make a bid for Best Supporting Actress after a meeting with Lew Wasserman once she returned home.

On September 7, 1960, in response to her close friend Patricia Kennedy Lawford's request, Janet opened her home to women supporters of the presidential Democratic candidate, John F. Kennedy. In July the Curtises had attended the Democratic National Convention in Los Angeles, becoming active supporters. Although she expected five hundred guests, two thousand women participated in the fund-raising luncheon, many of whom, it was assumed, only wanted to visit Janet and Tony Curtis' home. The entertainment was provided by Frank Sinatra, Dean Martin and Sammy Davis, Jr. The event was a terrific success, and Janet was elected deputy registrar for the upcoming elections. She started traveling around the West Coast to promote voter registration.

Along with Tony, Frank Sinatra and Peter Lawford, Janet joined Kennedy at the Governor's Ball at the Newark Armory in New Jersey — an event which attracted nearly 100,000 democratic supporters.

The night of the election the Curtises watched the results at home, along with other Hollywood stars and movie people. That evening their house served as a "clearinghouse" for Hollywood Democrats all around the country who had worked for Kennedy. Calls came in from celebrities from all over the country, but the final results were only confirmed the morning after.

At the end of October, while *Psycho* was still playing in theaters across America, Janet was threatened with rape and murder by a real-life psycho. A neatly typewritten letter sent from Chicago put her in a state of shock and fear. She turned it over to the police, who placed a guard at her home. The FBI and postal authorities joined the investigation, trying to trace the letter. Despite additional protection by local police, Janet hired private detectives to guard their home at night, since Tony was away on a film assignment.

Interviewed by the press, Janet said, "I'm used to getting weird letters. But this thing seemed to go a lot beyond the usual crank. It's got me jumping at every little sound."

Eventually, two offenders were located — two men the Bureau had been aware of for some time. Yet Janet remained very nervous, and on a trip to New York a few days later, while she was waiting for Tony to come back from the set, she heard a strange sound in her hotel room by the window. At 4 A.M. she leaped from bed and called the front desk for help. She crouched in a corner, arming herself with a cane she was using because of a recent foot injury. A few minutes later a house detective arrived to help her. Recalled Janet:

> He opened the window. Outside was a sheer, 12-story drop with absolutely no place for anyone to hide. It was all in my mind. But that was enough. I couldn't sleep the rest of the night. About 6 A.M., Tony arrived and sneaked in to surprise me while I was in the shower. When the bathroom door swung open, I was too scared to scream.[11]

Weird mail, strange phone calls and even recording tapes continued to arrive for years to come, forcing Janet to change her telephone number frequently.

On January 19, 1961, Janet and Tony flew to Washington to attend Kennedy's Inaugural Ball Gala, along with many other Hollywood celebrities, such as Milton Berle, Gene Kelly, Fredric March, and others. Afterwards they spent a relaxing weekend in Palm Beach, Florida, with some members of the Kennedy family.

The exciting news of Janet's Academy Award nomination for Best Supporting Actress arrived on February, 27 1967, while she was at their recently-bought house in Palm Springs. Janet was overjoyed to learn that *Psycho* had obtained three other nominations: Alfred Hitchcock for Best Director; Joseph Hurley, Robert Clatworthy, and George Milo for Best Art Direction–Set Decoration (Black and White); and John L. Russell for Best Cinematography. Her thoughts went to Anthony Perkins, who had hoped to be included, but was not. Perkins sent her two warm telegrams of congratulations. Hitchcock received a wire from Janet and Tony saying, "If this is what it's like to be *Psycho*, like to be like this all the time. Congratulations on your nomination and good luck."

Another moment of great happiness came when three weeks later, on

March 16, at a formal dinner at the Beverly Hilton Hotel, Janet was awarded with a Golden Globe for Best Supporting Actress by the Foreign Press. She was so tense that in her short speech she forgot to thank Alfred Hitchcock and Anthony Perkins.

Nevertheless, the 32nd Academy Award Ceremony, held at Santa Monica Civic Auditorium on April 17, was not meant to be her night. After co-presenting with Tony the Best Documentary Award, she lost the Oscar to Shirley Jones for *Elmer Gantry*. Yet she had to rise above her great disappointment and, like a true professional, perform the singing number "Triplets" from the musical *A Band Wagon* with Tony and Danny Kaye. That night her displeasure was greater when Alfred Hitchcock lost (his fifth and last nomination) to Billy Wilder for *The Apartment*.

8

Hard Times

I've always thought that Janet Leigh was one of the most beautiful women ever in films.— John Frankenheimer

"If it was going to be a dirty picture I didn't want any part of it. But the way it has been written, there's no concentration on sex," Janet commented with the press about her next starring role — in *The Chapman Report* for 20th Century–Fox. "José Ferrer is the director and he has good taste. It is now a story of people — sort of a modern version of *The Women* in reverse. Frustrated women rather than over-privileged."[1]

Janet was eager to play the character of Naomi Shields, a woman of loose morals in the controversial adaptation of the best-selling novel by Irving Wallace. The novel was inspired by the Kinsey Report on the sexual habits of suburban women. She was interested in acting in a part similar to the role she had in *Psycho* that was miles away from being typed as Hollywood's longtime girl next door. But just weeks before pre-production was to begin, the movie's producer, Darryl F. Zanuck, who was having financial problems with two big productions — *Cleopatra* and *The Longest Day* — offered the project to Warner Bros. Warners replaced the film's planned cast and crew with their own, and Claire Bloom took Janet's role, with George Cukor replacing director José Ferrer.

In his autobiography, Tony Curtis maintained that Janet never enjoyed media attention, and when the pressure of new fame, brought to her by *Psycho*, increased, she started to drink. According to Curtis, drinking made her a different person — one he did not like and tried to avoid whenever he had the opportunity:

> Her love affair with the bottle was poisoning her life and our marriage. I wasn't sure exactly what she was going through. Perhaps she was having a midlife crisis; after all, she had married me when she was very young. These days her career

was going well, and her roles were getting better and better, but the bigger she became, the more discontent she was.[2]

Janet acknowledged her marital difficulties with a more balanced approach, never blaming only her husband alone. At that particular time, most of the arguments they were having as a couple were related to money issues. Tony, in fact, was trying to overcome an inferiority complex towards his fellows Hollywood colleagues, whom he loved to impress with his extravagant lifestyle. He bought a $24,000 convertible Rolls-Royce which he showed off in a photographic spread in *Life* magazine, enraging Janet, who was worried about their financial situation. Nevertheless, in June they threw a lavish party to celebrate their 10th wedding anniversary. In front of 250 guests they behaved like the happiest couple. Those who were close to them knew that tensions between them had been mounting for months.

Tension was also running very high between Janet's parents. Fred Morrison was experiencing strong financial difficulties, and his relationship with his wife was very strained. On Sunday, August 6, the Morrisons showed up unannounced at Janet's house. Fred had lost a big sum of money and was in desperate need of a loan. Janet agreed, but Tony objected to it. A terrible fight ensued among the four, and nothing was resolved. The following day Janet left alone for Monte Carlo, where, on Saturday, August 12, she attended Princess Grace of Monaco's International Red Cross Ball. Before leaving she quarreled once again with Tony, but they made peace over the telephone. During the gala, after an outstanding musical performance by Sammy Davis, Jr., Janet suddenly ran into the ladies' room and broke down, hyperventilating and sobbing inconsolably, apparently for no real reason. A few hours later, when she was back at the hotel, she received a call from Tony, who told her that her father had committed suicide.

According to the press and to Janet's memoir, fifty-two-year-old Fred Morrison was found dead in his Beverly Hills insurance office with a half-emptied bottle of sleeping pills and a note nearby. The body was on a sofa, discovered by a business associate with whom he had an appointment. The Beverly Hills police chief confirmed the death as a suicide with the media, but declined to reveal the content of the note due to its "rough" nature. He only specified that it was directed to his wife Helen and it was not complimentary, insinuating that there had been some domestic problems. Helen told the police that she had seen her husband for the last time when he left their West Los Angeles home after a spat.

Tony's version of the story is once again completely different and very questionable, considering its diversion from the police reports. He claimed that Helen had called him because she was unable to reach her husband at the office after trying for several hours. She asked him to go and check on him. Tony, after calling the police, drove to Fred's office where he found him dead, slumped over his typewriter. He did not see any pills or a weapon, but he found a note that read: "I hope you're satisfied, you bitch." He stuck it in his pocket and called Helen and explained her husband was dead, without mentioning the note. Five minutes later the police arrived on the scene. Both stories confirm that the vitriolic note was kept away from Helen, who never knew of its existence.

Fred's death was a great shock for Janet. She immediately returned home to attend the funeral, which was held three days later. A great sense of guilt would resurface every time she thought of him, having the idea she could have done something to prevent his suicide and save his life. Her mother was devastated by the loss, as Janet revealed years later. "My mom started her suicide the day daddy died. She just stopped living."[3]

A few weeks later Janet decided to accompany Tony on a trip to Argentina, where he was set to star in the Harold Hect production of *Taras Bulba* opposite Yul Brynner. The trip was very long, since Tony refused to take a plane. They took a boat from Miami to Santos, Brazil, followed by a car ride to San Paulo. Then, Janet with the girls, their nanny and her personal secretary, flew to Buenos Aires while Tony took a train. In Argentina Janet made several personal appearances on behalf of the United States Information Service's "People to People" program at the personal request of her friend, Attorney General Robert Kennedy.

Later they moved to the small town of Salta in Northwestern Argentina, where the production company had rented a small cottage, with a butler, a maid, a driver and security, next door to Yul Brynner and his wife Doris. The Argentinean move was an unpleasant one. Janet contracted food poisoning and fell while horseback riding, Kelly had measles, Jamie Lee broke her clavicle while playing in a park, and Tony developed a throat infection. After six weeks, Janet returned to California, stopping for a week in Rio and Brasilia to do some extra work for the USIS. With only two weeks of work to go, Tony was left alone with the Brynners and his seventeen-year-old German co-star, Christine Kaufmann. The first week of December, after leaving the girls with the nanny at home, Janet flew to New York to introduce Eleanor Roosevelt at a ceremony held at Madison Square Garden. She also waited in New York for Tony's arrival from South America. He was expected in the Big Apple to do some publicity for *The Outsider* before returning to Hollywood to complete *Taras Bulba* at Universal.

When the Curtises reunited, Tony behaved very strangely, acting cold and distant with Janet. She could not understand his odd behavior until rumors about an affair with Kaufmann started to spread. In the beginning she thought it was a little flirtation blown out of proportion by the press, who had indiscreetly chronicled the romance burning between Tony and his young German co-star. Yet Janet decided to confront her husband by showing up at the studio and asking him to introduce her to Kaufmann. He firmly refused, and within a few days he moved out of their house.

When the news broke, Janet told a reporter, "That's perfectly ridiculous. Maybe Tony did take her out to dinner and see her in New York, but that certainly was not the reason for our break-up. Our differences had been growing for a long time."[4] The press unanimously condemned Tony's infidelity and blamed Kaufmann for the break-up.

Helping Janet overcome the heartache of her marital problems was Frank Sinatra's offer to play a supporting role in the political thriller *The Manchurian Candidate*. The film was based on Richard Condon's 1959 best-selling novel about some American soldiers brainwashed in Korea by a Chinese psychiatrist and programmed to assassinate a presidential candidate in order to replace him with a communist puppet. Janet had read the book a year earlier while on a plane chartered for President Kennedy's inauguration ball. "It bothered me so," she revealed in an interview.

I got so mad that I threw the book across the plane! I had the same reaction reading *From Here to Eternity*—when Prewitt got killed in that book. I was so upset that I threw the book. And as I said, that happened again with *The Manchurian Candidate*. And Frank Sinatra was in the plane! I had no idea that Frank was going to do the picture or that I was going to be in it! All I knew was that I had a very strong reaction to that novel.[5]

Director John Frankenheimer and screenwriter George Axelrod bought the film rights for $75,000. They later found out that almost every studio in Hollywood had turned it down,

With Frank Sinatra in a publicity shot for *The Manchurian Candidate* (1962).

and some actors, like Robert Mitchum, had been approached unsuccessfully. Axelrod heard that Sinatra was interested in it after Kennedy told him that Condon was one of his favorite authors. When a commitment from Sinatra was secured, Axelrod and Frankenheimer proposed the project to Arthur Krim, the United Artists studio boss, who was also the Democratic Party's national finance chairman. The studio head was skeptical about producing it until Kennedy, on Sinatra's request, called him and convinced him to make the picture.

Laurence Harvey and Angela Lansbury were cast in the leading roles, although Sinatra's first choices were Tony Curtis and Lucille Ball. He agreed to hire the two British stars after seeing a screen test with Harvey and watching Lansbury in Frankenheimer's last movie, *All That Falls*. Sinatra chose Janet to portray Rose Chaney, a small but intense role that she later defined as one of the most difficult parts she ever played. She accepted it immediately, without hesitation, explaining to *The New York Times*, "[It was] a good part with fine comic undertones. Now that I've graduated from ingénues, my roles are a lot more interesting."[6]

Shooting began in March 1962. The very first scene to be filmed involved Sinatra and Janet meeting for the first time on a train. Just before going to the set Janet had lunch with the director. Frankenheimer said to her, "You have twenty seconds to grab the audience, because they don't know who you are: Are you a red herring? Are you for real? Are you crazy? Are you planted? Are you what?"[7]

About that scene on the train, Janet would later comment, "I had to make an impact right away, the audience had to know, when I'm making these ridiculous non sequitur remarks, what I was trying to do. It was a very hard thing to do and I was very pleased. For the kind of role that it was, I was very happy with it."[8]

Those "ridiculous non sequitur remarks," as she called them, was a dialogue taken verbatim from Condon's novel. The sequence was completed in only three hours, thanks to the extraordinary chemistry the two stars showed in front of the camera. On the set Janet would observe Sinatra to see how he worked. She noticed that he would start off fresh but get bored quickly. So she rehearsed alone first, with Frankenheimer watching, and then Sinatra would join and complete it in one take.

Another long, difficult scene in a taxi with Sinatra, in which she had to talk incessantly, was also completed in only one take. When she asked the director if they would have to do it again, Frankenheimer told her that it was unnecessary because the first was perfect. Janet enjoyed tremendously working with Frankenheimer, who was, according to her, "a strong dynamic director." He was so dynamic that he completed the film in thirty-nine days.

Sinatra was so satisfied after watching the picture at a private screening that he called it the best film he ever made. Contrary to the star's prediction, *The Manchurian Candidate* received a mixed reaction from the press. Many critics found it incomprehensible and too ahead of its time. Frankenheimer blamed United Artists for not promoting it adequately. The picture cost $3 million but only attracted a small audience. Failing to recuperate its initial investment, the film was quickly withdrawn from theaters.

Janet received a very flattering mention in *Variety*:

A pleasant surprise is Janet Leigh as a sweet, swinging N.Y. career girl. The actress only has two or three scenes, but they count. One especially, on a ... train on which she picks up a semi-hysterical Sinatra, registers as one of the great love scenes since Bogart and Bacall first tossed non-sequiturs at one another in *To Have and Have Not*.[9]

For her astonishing performance as a ruthless, scheming mother, Angela Lansbury won a Golden Globe and scored an Academy Award nomination for Best Supporting Actress.

The Manchurian Candidate turned out to be one of President Kennedy's favorite films. Sinatra arranged a special print for him, delivering it at the same time of its theatrical release in October 1962. Sadly, almost like a prophecy fulfilled, Kennedy was assassinated thirteen months later. Some distributors wanted to exploit the tragedy and have the movie re-released, but United Artists refused.

Due to a dispute with United Artists over profit participation, *The Manchurian Candidate* was interred in Sinatra's vault, where, except for 16-mm rentals and a few TV airings, it remained for twenty-six years. Finally, in 1988, the picture was re-released in six major American cities after a special screening at the New York Film Festival, "going from failure to classic without passing through success," as Axelrod pointed out.

Jamie Lee Curtis revealed in an interview that her mother, on the day she shot *Manchurian Candidate*'s memorable scene on the train, found out that Tony had left her. "My mother persevered through it all and survived," Jamie Lee sadly said. "I'm not sure my sister and I did. There was no Demi and Bruce [Demi Moore–Bruce Willis] amicable divorce or joint family vacations for us. No love was left between them."[10]

The fairy tale was over after ten-and-a-half years of marriage. Janet suffered public embarrassment when Tony left her for a 17-year-old replacement, but this act was only the final push given to a marriage destined for divorce.

Many years later, in talking about her divorce, Janet stated:

One of the things that I think was a big block for your father and myself in our marriage was that when we achieved the heights we did, it was almost like he didn't want to know about Bernie Schwartz any more. He became Tony Curtis, and I think what started to bother me was that I married Bernie Schwartz and we weren't approaching things the same way we had before.[11]

After completing her work on *The Manchurian Candidate*, Janet was invited to appear at the Mar del Plata International Film Festival in Argentina. A few days before her departure, while in New York, she was found unconscious on the bathroom floor of her suite at the Sherry Netherland Hotel. Janet had been to a show, followed by a late dinner at Danny's Highway, with her personal physician, Dr. Richard Bachrach, his wife Beryl, Joe Warren, and her press agent Marilyn Reiss. During the meal she took two tranquilizers with some coffee, which made her feel drowsy. Later the Bachrachs took her back to her suite, where she excused herself and went into the bathroom. After quite a while, when she did not come out, they became concerned and went in and found her lying on the floor, moaning. She had slipped on a bath mat, falling and banging her head on the sink or the tub. Dr. Bachrach immediately summoned an ambulance. On a stretcher, wrapped in blankets, Janet was taken to the Le Roy Hospital, where she was diagnosed with a slight concussion, a swollen jaw and a very black eye. Five hours later, when she regained consciousness, her first words were an apology to her friends for the trouble caused by her clumsiness.

The following day, when the news created a media frenzy, she joked with the press, saying, "None of my friends were surprised. They all know I have three left feet." She was ordered to rest at the hospital for a couple of days, forcing her to cancel her appearance at the Argentinean festival. Reporters reached Tony with the news in Hollywood. He immediately called the hospital and later, when Janet was discharged, sent her some flowers, like many other close friends and colleagues did from all over the world. To the journalist who asked him about their recent split, he commented sadly, "An accident doesn't solve our problem. After the accident we still have the problem."[12]

Speculation about the accident ran wildly in gossip columns, but Janet was very good in explaining to the media the real facts. To celebrate her hospital release, a gala dinner was given at Sardi's by Joe Warren before her return to Hollywood, where she was expected to star in her next film

A week prior to her fall, Janet was notified that the District Court of Appeals of California had dismissed a libel suit filed by Kenneth Carlisle, her first husband, against her, the magazine *Motion Picture* and its distributor. Carlisle had sought $1 million for libel and invasion of privacy because the fan magazine had published a piece in December 1960 entitled "I Was a Child Bride at 14!" under Janet's byline. The article identified Carlisle merely as "a dark boy we'll call John." Carlisle had stepped forward and identified himself, confirming the story of their brief runaway marriage, and then sued.

Janet was extremely surprised when she learned about the legal action from Kenneth, whom she had not had contact with since she was fourteen. She had given that interview in good faith, as a sort of catharsis of a burdensome secret she had hidden for years and that now nobody seemed to care about. By no means had Janet any intention of being offensive toward her former husband, who claimed that, even if she had used his Christian name instead of John, her statements in the article would have caused people who knew him to believe he was "a tramp, a vagabond, a depraved and predatory male, who had conspired, abducted and exploited a fourteen-year-old girl." Finally, after more than a year, to Janet's great relief, Judge Gregory P. Mauhart tossed the case out of court.

While in New York shooting *The Manchurian Candidate*, Janet saw the musical *Bye Bye Birdie*, which had successfully opened on Broadway in March 1960. It eventually ran for 607 performances, winning a Tony Award. *Bye Bye Birdie* was a satire inspired by the commotion that exploded in December 1957 when Elvis Presley was drafted into the U.S. Army. Janet loved the show and accepted George Sidney's offer to star in the film adaptation produced by Columbia Pictures. The cast included Dick Van Dyke, Maureen Stapleton, Bobby Rydell, Paul Lynde and Ann-Margret. Real-life teen idol James Darren was first announced to play Birdie, but the part ultimately went to the unknown Jesse Pearson.

For the role of Rosie De Leon, Janet agreed to wear a short brunette wig, out of deference to the Spanish heritage of her character, played on stage by Chita Rivera. Janet asked chorographer Onna White to rehearse the routines of her four musical numbers for six weeks before the actual shooting began. The training was hard. In rehearsal she suffered a mild concussion and a scarred shin, and the arduous workouts cost her 12 pounds.

"At times I would go home and flop on the bed from exhaustion," she told *Life* magazine, which put her on the cover for the second time. "At other times I just wished that I'd never started the whole bloody thing.... I'll do another musical, maybe in 40 years!"[13]

Despite the sacrifices, Janet enjoyed being Rosie DeLeon:

I suppose at one time or another, we've all wanted to be somebody else. As an actress I fulfill this desire with each picture I do, because the role I play is always quite different from the real me. But, up until now, like Cinderella, I turn back into Janet Leigh at the end of the day's filming. Not so in my present film *Bye Bye Birdie* at Columbia. And why not? All because of a black wig. I play the role of Rosie DeLeon, Spanish secretary and girlfriend of Dick Van Dyke. Now, with my blonde hair I don't exactly look Latin, but by wearing a black wig — *Vive la difference*. And that's where the fun comes in.

People just don't recognize me and I'm fascinated by watching their reactions when they finally realized who I am. I should carry around a candid camera to catch some of the expressions. They're priceless. This doesn't only apply to my co-workers on the set. For you see, I've taken to wearing my black wig out evenings, with wonderful results. At restaurants, people I know very well will pass right by my table, saying hello to the party I happen to be with, but only giving me a perfunctory nod. Invariably comes the sudden pause, a double take, and bingo! They recognize me.

At parties, when I first enter, there are the "who's the strange girl crashing the party" looks. I'm the woman for several minutes until the dawn of recognition breaks over the assembly. Dates calling for me who have not seen me as the "other" Janet Leigh, will ask me, when they come into the house, to tell Janet that so and so is here.

At the first dress rehearsal a funny episode took place on the set when Janet showed up wearing the black wig, which she had never put on during the weeks of rehearsals. Upon arriving, she found the assistant director frantically looking for her. He finally approached her and asked her if she had seen Janet Leigh, telling her that the set was closed to visitors. She was very amused at seeing him blush when she revealed her identity.

A second incident happened a few days later, during the filming of a musical number, when a very old columnist friend of hers dropped in. After greeting the producer and the director profusely, he waved hello to Dick Van Dyke and passed by Janet without a nod. Janet called after him, he turned around, smiled, started to move off, and then whispered, "Janet, that's you!" Janet liked to joke that after wearing the black wig for so long on the set, when she showed up as her natural blonde self, some people did not recognize the real Janet.

During filming, Janet and her co-stars, Dick Van Dyke and Maureen Stapleton, were displeased that George Sidney expanded the teenager roles at the expense of their three characters. In fact, the director increased Ann-Margret's songs from two to six. Sidney had developed an intense infatuation with the twenty-one-year-old actress, whom he had spotted dancing at the Sands in Las Vegas the previous New Year's Eve.

Van Dyke described Janet as "a real doll, lots of fun on and off the camera, and a warm, generous woman who had my entire family over to her house many times." He added:

> All of us adored her. She wasn't much of a dancer, though you wouldn't have known from the way choreographer Anna [sic] White worked with her individually and the two of us together. A Broadway veteran, White figured out our capabilities and made sure we looked good. But Janet's limitations in that area

might have diminished her standing with the film's director, George Sidney, who was, quite obviously, enamored with the movie's young star, Ann-Margret. Then again, even if Janet had moved like Ginger Rogers, it's likely that Sidney would still have been fixated on the very talented redhead.[14]

"A lot of what you see onscreen with Ann-Margret was shot on a Sunday, after the movie [concluded principal photography]," Janet recalled. "I didn't know anything until I saw the preview, from which I ran out of the theater in hysterics."[15]

Bye Bye Birdie opened at Radio City Music Hall in April 1963, receiving mixed to positive reviews. Audiences adored it so much that it ranked among 1963's ten most successful movies, with its soundtrack topping the record chart.

9

Living and Loving

Janet Leigh is another example of goodness I found in Hollywood.—
Martha Hyer

In spite of great difficulties, Janet focused positively on dealing with the situation of her broken marriage. She began slowly to collect the pieces of her personal life. Her priority was to seek out the professional guidance of a psychiatrist to help Kelly and Jamie cope with the divorce and separation from their father. She wanted to make sure that her daughters would not be badly affected by the events. Concentrating with great strength on the well-being of the girls, Janet was able to regroup. Unexpectedly, great comfort came from meeting someone special in her life.

On a Sunday off from filming *Bye Bye Birdie*, Dean Martin's wife Jeanne and his agent Mort Viner invited a depressed Janet to play tennis at the house of Robert "Bob" Brandt, who Janet had casually met before at the Martins' home. This time the invitation was a sort of "blind date," since her friends were playing matchmakers. Brandt was a thirty-five-year-old successful stockbroker, so strappingly handsome that he easily could have been a movie star. He had been divorced for two years and was living in Beverly Hills in a big house with a swimming pool and tennis court. It was *un coup de foudre*. Janet was immediately smitten, not only by Bob's dark, healthy, sexy look but also by his masculine yet gentle manners. After the tennis match he took her back home on his motorbike and called the following day to invite her out to dinner. They got to know each other further, discovering many interests in common. Shortly, the two became inseparable.

In July Janet rented a house by the beach so that Kelly and Jamie could spend the summer by the sea. She introduced Bob to them, and the two girls immediately loved him and enjoyed spending their time with him.

Brandt was a very private person and not used to the spotlight. He was very patient with Janet's celebrity status and the sudden intrusion on his privacy by the paparazzi when he was in her company. The first time they officially appeared together — on the red carpet at a movie premiere — they were assaulted by a wild mob of photographers clamoring to get a view of Janet's handsome, mysterious date.

On July 11, 1962, Janet won an interlocutory decree of divorce from Tony, who was in Germany and did not appear at the hearing. He did not contest the divorce, agreeing to split the assets, pay child support and obtain no restrictions on visiting rights. When Janet walked out of the court house, photographs showed she was in tears.

Three months later, while they were together painting a redwood bench white, Brandt proposed. She accepted impulsively, but afterwards had a few doubts about marrying someone she had known for only six months. Her major concern was once again for her daughters. She sought advice from her children's psychiatrist who approved the possibility of a new male presence in the family. However, he suggested they tell Kelly and Jamie Lee that their "daddy" was still their father, but that now they would have a new family unit with Bob as head of the household.

On September 7 Janet took a red-eye to New York to attend the premiere of *The Manchurian Candidate*. On the 13th she flew, in the company of her lawyer, to Juarez, Mexico, to obtain an immediate divorce from Tony. Rather than wait a full year for the divorce to become finalized under American law, she preferred a quick decree. Before leaving, Janet gave the news to Tony, who was surprised but did not object, signing a waiver since he was planning to marry Christine Kaufmann. On the 14th Jeanette Morrison was once again single. The media broke the news about the divorce and speculated about an imminent wedding, but they had no clue it was to be the next day.

Before getting married, Janet asked Bob if he wanted her to quit acting. He told her that it was part of her life, and even if he had some adjustments to make, they agreed that she would fit pictures in around her family's schedule.

A private ceremony was organized by Jeanne Martin at the Sands in Las Vegas, where Dean Martin had an engagement. Wearing an elegant pink Jax wedding suit and a headband to hold her hair, Janet looked radiantly stunning. After her split with Tony, she had grown painfully thin, and her face took on a strained, tight look. By the wedding, she had gained back seven pounds, and appeared fantastic and healthy. The ceremony was presided over by U.S. district judge David Zenoff on the patio of the Martins' suite, which was filled with flowers and fourteen guests. The evening continued with a private dinner where other friends joined the happy couple. Then they all attended

Dean Martin's show, which ended with the surprising appearance of a tall wedding cake. Martin asked the newlyweds to join him onstage, inviting the audience to welcome them. Janet and Bob cut the cake, made a toast with champagne and kissed, sharing their beautiful union on a magical night in front of many strangers.

Talking with Louella Parsons after the wedding, Janet said,

> At the moment we have two homes. Every night we have an early dinner with Jamie and Kelly at my house. Then, after the girls are tucked into bed, we go up to Bob's place, just a couple of miles away, and spend the night. He bought the old Norma Talmadge estate, complete with swimming pool and tennis court, and being a bachelor at the time, the mansion was too big for him, so he sold it and just kept the pool, court and a small pool house where he lived. Now he's adding rooms, and as soon as the remodeling is finished, the girls and I will move in with him."[1]

A few weeks after their wedding, Janet and Bob took their first trip together abroad. The opportunity came when Natalie Wood, an old friend of Janet's, asked her to go to Argentina to accept an award on her behalf. After discussing it with Bob, Janet agreed and joined Anthony Perkins, Karl Malden and director David Miller as representatives of the State Department on a goodwill trip. The journey was a very enjoyable experience. At the beginning, Bob felt a bit awkward among the celebrities but later thought he got along very well with everybody, particularly Anthony Perkins. In their spare time, Janet, Bob and Perkins would often play long and complicated word games. After Buenos Aires, the group traveled to the small town of Cuiaba, Brazil, where Janet and Tony appeared live on a local TV show — on which Bob was mistaken for the actor George Maharis, whose series *Route 66* was very popular in Brazil. Janet and Perkins could only laugh while Bob was embarrassed and left speechless by all the questions the host asked him.

While filming *Bye Bye Birdie*, Janet had received a visit from her old friend Blake Edwards. Janet's new look with her black wig inspired him to write the part of Madame Clouseau in his new film *The Pink Panther* especially for her. Now that Edwards was ready to shoot the film, Janet decided to turned it down, not wanting to be away from Bob on location in Europe for six months.

Yet when producer Hal Wallis offered her a leading role in *Wives and Lovers*, scheduled to be filmed at Paramount Studios, she accepted without hesitation, eager to be reunited with Van Johnson, her first and favorite co-star. The comedy, a typical story of suburban married life, was originally intended as a vehicle for Shirley MacLaine, who was under contract to Wallis at the time. However, a legal dispute caused the deal with MacLaine to fall through. Janet was called in to replace her under John Rich's direction. The cast included Shelley Winters, Ray Walston and Martha Hyer. On January 23, 1963, Janet arrived at Paramount Studios for pre-production services. The enthusiasm of working in a funny comedy together with Johnson, as husband and wife, produced a perfect chemistry between the two co-stars. For the first four or five days of shooting, the production rolled on quickly and smoothly. TV director John Rich, who was helming his first film, recalled how much he loved directing Janet and Johnson: "Both of these popular stars were gems to work with. I enjoyed both their professional approach to the work and their friendship, particularly Janet's, which endured until the day she passed away."[2]

After the first week the production was almost a day ahead of schedule, and Wallis was extremely satisfied after he viewed the dailies. In fact, he was so satisfied with Janet's performance that he announced he had signed her to a five-year contract. In contrast, when Shelley Winters arrived on the set, she proceeded to make filming a nightmare. She would show up without learning her lines, often needing more than a dozen takes for one scene.

"Her work was so enervating," recalled Rich, "that Janet Leigh and Van Johnson each came to me separately, asking me not to print a scene in which they appeared exhausted, just because she had managed to get one take correctly. I promised them I would do my utmost to protect them from her shenanigans."[3]

If Winters and Rich became antagonists during the making of the movie, the rest of the cast got along splendidly with everybody.

Martha Hyer, who was married to Wallis, described Janet as "another example of goodness I found in Hollywood. She has had her share of triumph and tragedy, but she is always enthusiastic, kind to everyone, and a pleasure to work with. Just before a scene was shot, she'd go off by herself and quietly repeat a simple prayer: 'Life is the showing forth of the very Self of God.' She said it helped set her head straight."[4]

Wives and Lovers received a lukewarm reception from critics, who found the plot dated and far from witty. Needless to say, the film bombed at the box office.

Janet had a busy year in 1963, not only on the set of *Wives and Lovers*, but on the construction site of Bob's home, which they had decided to enlarge. Renovating the house took almost a year because the project involved an extra 5,000 square feet around the small original house. The original building had to be leveled to the ground and a new one built from scratch.

Janet enjoyed decorating the house that was slowly taking shape, working closely with the architects. However, after many months of delays she started

With Van Johnson and Martha Hyer in *Wives and Lovers* (1963).

to feel frustrated and exhausted. "We've been living in a very small house, waiting, and it's been miserable," she explained in an interview. "I wish we were out in a tent with sleeping bags. It would be camping out in a much more comfortable manner than we've been doing."[5]

In July the Mannequins of Los Angeles named Janet the "Best Dressed Woman of the Year," following a poll of fashion editors across the country. The following month, during a trip to New York with Bob, Janet was robbed of all her jewels and a wallet containing $80, personal cards and her driver's license. The Brandts were staying at the Regency Hotel, and upon their return after watching a Broadway play, they noticed that in their suite Janet's jewel case was empty and all her jewels were missing. The police were called. Eventually the thief was caught, and a ring was recovered.

That year Janet was also involved in many philanthropic activities, mostly projects for children. Besides volunteering for SHARE, helping to put on the annual show to raise money, she joined, along with actress Ruth Warwick, Drop Out Anonymous, a local organization which dealt with illiterate kids who drop out of school. Moreover, she found the time to raise funds for the Cedars of Lebanon Hospital, working hard at the premiere of Stanley Kramer's *It's a Mad, Mad, Mad, Mad World*, and to attend a benefit in San Francisco for Girls' Town of Italy, an organization that helped girls from 14 to 16 become governesses trained by an American nun.

In December Bob took Janet, with Kelly and Jamie Lee (now aged 7 and 5), to ski in Aspen, Colorado. It was Janet's first experience with skiing since the year Norma Shearer discovered her photograph at the resort where her parents were working. Thanks to Bob, who had a passion for skiing, Janet and the girls learned quickly and enjoyed the frequent skiing trips during the winter season. Before leaving for Colorado, Janet appeared on TV as a guest on the *Bob Hope Special*, performing a funny sketch together with Hope in which she played the double role of his wife and his girlfriend. It was one of several appearances she made that year on a variety of TV shows, like *The Tonight Show Starring Johnny Carson*, *Talent Scouts*, *Password* and *Celebrity Tennis*. In the latter she played doubles with actor Pedro Gonzales; Janet and Gonzales were beaten in an entertaining match by Rhonda Fleming and Pancho Segura at Dean Martin's estate in Beverly Hills.

The first time singer Andy Williams invited Janet to perform live on his opening show, broadcast by NBC, she was comfortably sitting with Bob at her favorite hangout, Dominick's in West Hollywood, having a drink. Caught in a weak moment, she accepted. However, the following morning she had panicky second thoughts. She called her agent, but he told her that she could not get out of it after having given her word. She was scared to death to do TV variety shows, but, supported by her professionalism, she did it and loved it. Afterwards, in an interview she explained her initial fright:

It's because they're done like live shows on tape and straight through. I've been brought up in movies where somebody yells "Cut!" and you do it all over again. Movies are so comfortable. But on TV there's a certain momentum and fervor. The excitement starts building. It catches you and exhilarates you and it mounts and mounts! That's why I get scared.[6]

She enjoyed her solo dancing performance on *The Andy Williams Show* so much that she returned a year later to do a solo number, and a song and a dance with the host.

Right after Christmas the press announced that Janet would have played a flight attendant in the upcoming comedy *Boeing Boeing*, produced by Hal Wallis for Paramount, but that when she learned that Tony was also attached to the project she bowed out.

In early spring 1964 President Lyndon Johnson named Janet to the National Advisory Council for the Peace Corps. Honored by the title, she toured university campuses and small communities, working also as a deputy registrar for voters in the upcoming elections. Adding more prestige to her political activism, she was also appointed to the State Recreation Commission by California governor Edmund Gerald "Pat" Brown.

Yet the most flattering proposition came in March while she was in Aspen on a family ski trip. She was unexpectedly reached by an urgent phone call from the president's office. After praising her work for USIS, President Johnson asked her to serve as Ambassador to Finland. Before giving her answer, she nervously considered it for twenty-four hours. Although she was very flattered by the proposal, she felt that it was too early in her marriage to contemplate separation, since Bob could not afford to leave his business for a year. She declined the offer. Nevertheless, her choice did not stop her from being a faithful activist for the Democratic party, participating in several events — like a popular rally she attended that same year as a guest speaker at the Goldwyn Studios, along with Gregory Peck, Henry Fonda and Eddie Fisher. The event attracted more than 1,000 women who bought an entrance ticket to hear them speak.

In October Janet had her first TV movie role in over seven years — in the episode "Murder in the First" on the *Bob Hope Chrysler Theatre* on NBC. The episode was directed by Sydney Pollack and co-starred Bobby Darrin.

It was United Artists Television that offered Janet her own TV show, originally called *The Janet Leigh Show*. The project was financed by the General Foods Corporation, which was considering a steady sponsorship of the series. Janet was cast as a young widow, Maggie Mulligan, who worked as a political cartoonist for a newspaper. The pilot was written and produced by Don McGuire, who re-titled the show *This Is Maggie Mulligan* and then changed it to *Meet Maggie Mulligan*, which was scheduled to air in 1965. The show was acquired by CBS but got lost in an executive shakeup of the network.

"I never did quite understand what happened to it," said Janet with great disappointment. "But the sponsor liked it and so did I. In fact, I thought it was pretty good. Recently we discussed another series project, but it never got beyond the talking stage."

A sexy publicity shot for *Kid Rodelo* (1966).

Meet Maggie Mulligan was never shown on TV. Two years later, *According to Janet*, a similar project written by Leonard Gershe, also failed to take off.

In June 1965 Janet traveled to Spain to shoot *Kid Rodelo*, a low-budget Western based on a novel by Louis L'Amour. The prolific author had not yet completed the book when some Spanish producers acquired the film rights, with the intention of making a picture in Spain with American actors.

Richard Carlson, who had also helmed a previous picture based on a L'Amour book, was called to direct the film. The picture chronicled the quest of Kid Rodelo, an ex-con looking for a fortune in stolen gold, as well as to get even with his double-crossing former partners. Don Murray, a star in decline, played the title role, while Broderick Crawford, a former Oscar-winner now battling alcoholism, played the villain. Janet had the role of Nora, Rodelo's love interest.

To contain costs, the picture was shot in black and white, using locations around Madrid as a Mexican backdrop. Later the crew moved to Alicante for some desert and beach scenery. Janet traveled with the girls and stayed at the Hotel Carlton in Alicante. Her presence caused a sensation among the locals, who were not accustomed to having an American star of her caliber in town. The relaxed Spanish atmosphere was spoiled when the cast learned that actress Judy Holliday had died of cancer at age 43. Janet, with Don Murray, Broderick Crawford and other members of the film company, had met in the lounge of their hotel for what was to be an enjoyable evening, when an American tourist approached their table and told them the tragic news. Crawford, who had worked with Holliday in *Born Yesterday*, left the party in tears, while Janet and Murray, who knew the actress socially, were so saddened that they retired to their rooms.

Kid Rodelo was released in the Unites States in January 1966. It stayed in the theaters for only two weeks after being panned by reviewers and ignored by filmgoers.

Definitely more successful was Janet's return to Hollywood on the set of *Harper*, joining a group of excellent stars, including Lauren Bacall, Robert Wagner, Julie Harris, Shelley Winters, Pamela Tiffin and Arthur Hill. The picture was helmed by Paul Newman.

Harper was based on Ross MacDonald's *The Moving Target*, the first of a series of mystery novels featuring private detective Lew Archer. The screenplay was masterfully adapted by William Goldman, who had been hired by independent producers Jerry Gershwin and Elliot Kastner. Frank Sinatra was the first choice for the role of Archer, but he turned it down, only to play private eye Tony Rome a year later.

The producers opted for Paul Newman, who was in Paris shooting *Lady L.* The star showed interest in the part on the condition that some changes were made to the script. First, the name of his character, Lew Archer, would be switched to Lew Harper, since he thought that titles like *The Hustler* and *Hud*— beginning with an H — brought him luck. Once Newman signed the contract, a cast of major actors was chosen for small roles. Janet knew Newman socially and respected him highly, especially for the great support he had given to the Democratic Party. When she was offered the small role she was pleased to finally have an opportunity to work with him.

Harper, a fairly stylish high-budget production, was filmed in the summer of 1965. Janet played Susan Harper, Newman's estranged wife, who wants to divorce him. Although she only had four scenes, she admitted to being mesmerized by him. "When Paul looks at you with those eyes of his," she said, "he commands you to look at him and listen. He makes you respond to him. That's the basis of his sex appeal."[7]

The *Harper* shoot went along very smoothly. Newman, who modeled his performance on both Humphrey Bogart and Robert Kennedy, was always professional and polite with his co-workers, never acting like a star. All Janet's scenes were shot in about a week at the Warner Bros. studios in Burbank. The crew included Newman's older brother, Arthur Newman, Jr., hired as a unit manager; and the cast included Paul's first wife, Jackie Witte Newman, in a small role, billed as Jacqueline de Wit.

Harper was released on February 23, 1966, becoming one of the biggest commercial successes of the mid-sixties. The critics hailed Newman's performance, which he reprised in *The Drowning Pool* in 1975.

Janet was praised as "excellent" by the *New York Times*, while *The Hollywood Reporter* wrote, "Janet Leigh has never had a better role, and she demonstrates ability not always realized."

Another pleasant surprise befell Janet that fall when she learned through her agent that Jerry Lewis had requested her as the female lead in his upcoming picture *Three on a Couch*, which was about to be filmed by Columbia Pictures.

Lewis had proposed the project to Paramount, the studio he had worked with for sixteen years, but the production company refused to let him make it with their money. He decided instead to produce and direct it himself, moving to Columbia Pictures.

Janet had not seen much of Lewis since she and Tony had left his circle in the late '50s after it had become crowded by too many people only interested in exploiting his celebrity status. Janet was pleased to work with her old friend Jerry, who cast her as his romantic interest, a psychiatrist specializing in the romantic traumas of young women. She told a Lewis biographer:

> He had matured and grown so. He was one of the best directors I've ever worked with. I'm not saying *the* best director, but he's definitely at the top. Really, he was wonderful. It was the first time I'd ever seen an instant replay used on the set. And it was wonderful — you didn't get the full scope, but you could see if the scene worked or not, so you would know whether to do it again.[8]

Janet was impressed by the sobriety Lewis had organized on the set, where she found the environment professional and relaxed and very different from the wild atmosphere she had experienced with him and Martin while making *Living It Up*.

Directing and starring in *Three on a Couch* was a great challenge for Lewis. He had to work very hard to adjust himself to be a comedian (playing four different roles) and a director on a script which was not his own material but was co-written by two screenwriters, and adapted from a story by two different authors. In fact, it took him several takes before he could let loose in front of the camera, but he succeeded brilliantly with the limited plot structure. His guidance and assistance on the set was remembered by Janet as outstanding and helpful.

Columbia Pictures launched a large promotional campaign for the picture, with newspaper contests and advertising gimmicks emphasizing the number 3, as in *Three on a Couch*. Jerry Lewis appeared on numerous national talks show just before the film went into general release in June 1966. In spite of lukewarm reviews, domestically *Three on a Couch* grossed over $2.5 million, turning a fair profit for Lewis, who had personally invested in the project.

Not as successful as her two last films was Janet's participation in *An American Dream*, a Warner Bros. production of Norman Mailer's novel that was both extravagantly praised and damned by critics. The one-million-dollar adaptation featured an interesting cast, sumptuous sets, and a skilled cinematographer, yet the picture turned out to be a trivial, second-class melodrama.

An American Dream (released in the United Kingdom as *See You in Hell, Darling*) had a bizarre, unbelievable script. Janet played a gangster's wife who becomes romantically involved with a successful TV commentator caught up in his wife's death. Her presence, along with professionals such as Eleanor Parker and Stuart Whitman, did not rescue the production from being disastrously received by the press. Oddly, "A Time for Love," the film's theme song, written by Johnny Mandel and Paul Francis Webster, received an Academy Award nomination for Best Original Song. Janet sang it in one scene, voiced by Jackie Ward.

In all her interviews Janet would stress that she was first a wife and mother, and then an actress, working only if it did not interfere with her family life. After divorcing Tony, her priorities had suddenly changed, and her career did not matter as it used to. She was now in her early '40s and at a difficult age for an actress, as she looked too old for many roles and too young for mature ones. Yet she was still receiving a lot of job offers, especially from television. A different casting call came from the NBC network when she was offered a role in a long episode of *The Man from U.N.C.L.E.* The

With Stuart Whitman in *An American Dream* (1966).

show was a popular TV series that followed the adventures of two secrets agents, played by Robert Vaughn and David McCallum, who worked for a fictitious secret international espionage and law-enforcement agency called U.N.C.L.E.

The episode, called "The Concrete Overcoat Affair," was divided into two parts and aired on November 25, 1966, and December 2, 1966. Janet was Miss Diketon, the sexy private secretary/killer of Louis Strago, played by Jack Palance. Strago was a liquor magnate who uses his business to cover an illegal operation connected to a criminal mastermind ready to alter the course of the Gulf Stream.

MGM, which partially produced the show, combined the two episodes into a full-length film titled *The Spy in the Green Hat* for a theatrical release in Europe. Minimal changes were made to the original episodes — only the addition of some short scenes considered too violent or too sexy to be shown on an American TV network but just right for European audiences. Janet's character had some lines which made it clear she enjoyed inflicting and receiving pain. Those lines were carefully censored for the TV version but appeared in the European movie. Playing a sexy, cartoonish villain was for Janet a new, fun experience, breaking the mold of the nice girl image.

Though reducing her Hollywood filmmaking activity, Janet felt she might have better recognition abroad. So she accepted a part in *Grand Slam*. The film was an Italo-Spanish-German co-production in English, and shot in Spain, New York, London, Rome and Rio de Janeiro, with an international cast, including veteran Edward G. Robinson, Klaus Kinski and Adolfo Celi. *Grand Slam* was a heist thriller in the tradition of films like Stanley Kubrick's *The Killing, Ocean's Eleven* and *Topkapi*. The title referred to a "Grand Slam 70," a sophisticated, ultra-sensitive security system protecting a vault in a Brazilian bank containing ten million dollars worth of diamonds targeted by a gang selected by a retired history professor, played by Robinson. Janet was the bank president's secretary seduced by one of the gang members in order to get the key to the vault. Janet flew to Rio de Janeiro, where she hit it off immediately with Italian director Giuliano Montaldo.

"Every time she comes to my mind, I think of her first as a friend and then as a movie star," Montaldo said about Janet.

> When she showed up on *Grand Slam*'s set she was a mega-star. She was the actress of the famous shower scene in *Psycho*. We all asked her about Hitchcock and his film and she would talk about it very humbly. She was a very sweet lady and extremely flexible professionally. She came from Hollywood where everything was precise and organized ... ours was an Italian crew and the way of working was completely different. However, she adjusted herself to it perfectly fine. In Rio de Janeiro we had to shoot a scene in the lobby of a building which was the headquarters of a government office, maybe a ministry. As usual we did not have any permit to film and it was impossible to obtain one in a short time. I suggested "to steal" the scene. We hid the camera in a car parked on the other side of the street and I asked Janet to get into the building, as an ordinary citizen, thinking of an excuse in case she would be stopped. She got so excited like a young girl about to steal from the jam jar. We shot the sequence with great anxiety, because I wanted to do it in one take in order not to embarrass Janet. But she had so much fun in doing it that after the first take she came to me and said cheerfully, "It was so much fun, let's do it one more time!"[9]

Shown in Europe in late 1967, *Grand Slam* was successfully released in three different lengths under three different titles (in Italy as *Ad ogni costo*, in Germany as *Top Job* and in Spain as *Diamantes a Go-Go*). In the U.S. the picture opened in a limited release in February 1968, receiving decent reviews. *New York Times* critic Howard Thomson praised Janet's interpretation as "the picture's best and lowest-keyed performance."[10] Yet the box-office results were less than satisfactory.

With Edward G. Robinson in *Grand Slam* (1967).

In the latter half of 1967 Janet accepted an offer from Paramount to star in an underwater family comedy called *Hello Down There*. She was glad to work with two dear long-time friends, Roddy McDowall and Merv Griffin (the latter's role was originally intended for Jackie Gleason). The picture was based on a story by Ivan Tors, who produced many TV series about marine adventures shot at his Florida-based studio. *Hello Down There* was a light '60s comedy about a family living in a futuristic underwater house off the coast of Florida built by Tony Randall, who played the role of an architect married to Janet and who had two teenage kids.

At the end of October Janet traveled to Hollywood, Florida, with Kelly and Jamie Lee to work on location. A few days after the beginning of the shoot, her hotel suite was burglarized while she was having dinner with her kids. Ten thousand dollars worth of valuables were stolen, including a full black mink, a grey mink stole, a fox stole and a jewel case with her daughters' watches. "At home we have Great Danes to protect us against burglars," said Janet, still in a state of shock, and remembering when she was robbed four years earlier in New York.

"I thought the picture was fun. I don't see anything wrong with a family film, and I like it," Janet commented about the movie, which was coldly received. "Tony Randall is always good and I think it was Richard Dreyfuss's first picture. Every time we see each other, it's *Glub, Glub*." (Dreyfuss played a member of a rock band and "Glub, Glub" refers to one of their songs.)

Once *Hello Down There* was completed, Janet returned home just in time to pack again and spend Christmas on a ski trip with her family.

A few weeks later she was back on the road, destination Grinon, a little town in Spain, to star in *Honeymoon with a Stranger*, a TV movie produced by the ABC network that reunited her with Rossano Brazzi, her Italian co-star in *Little Women*, after twenty years. The children traveled with her to Spain, where Jamie Lee, at age 7, made her screen debut in a crowd scene of the film. Just before the segment was filmed, Jamie whispered to her mother, "I'm going to stay close to you so I get a close-up." They were prophetic words, since eight years later she would make her official debut in TV, marking the beginning of a very successful career as an actress.

Janet continued to be a dedicated parent, allowing nothing to interfere with her being with her family. She would arrive on location with boxes of school books and would hire tutors throughout Europe to provide the girls the best education they could get. A press release for *Honeymoon with a Stranger* quoted Janet as saying:

> The children and I have a very deep relationship. They come to me with all their problems, I live a very stimulating life, and I think that attitude has given me a greater awareness and an ability to talk to them intelligently about sex, dope, politics, and all the other things that are driving a wedge between parents and children. I've never compromised family for career, but my children realize that my profession is very important to me. It is good that kids know you have to do your own thing — just like they have to do theirs.

Nonetheless, Janet decided to provide more stability for her daughters, after Kelly came to her and said, "Mommy, my best friend has a new best friend." She immediately realized that it was time to cut back her travels. "She was trying to tell me we were moving around too much," Janet explained. "And I had to agree with her."[11]

10

New Horizons

When you are lucky, and I am lucky, I believe you've got to spread it around. — Janet Leigh

From 1969 to 1972 Janet tried her luck appearing as a guest star on several TV series and in pilots. This move was a choice made by many actresses her age who, unlike her, had to work for financial reasons. She played an attorney's wife in *The Monk*; a mysterious woman pursued by three gunmen in the wild west of *The Virginian*; and a love-starved neurotic wife in the melodramatic *House on Greenapple Road*, opposite Walter Pidgeon and Julie Harris. Other TV shows were canceled after only one episode, like *My Wives Jane*, a comedy about a daytime soap-opera star. "It was going to be on until the daytime soap people told the network: 'You can't make fun of such a lucrative audience,'" Janet explained.[1]

In addition to her work, Janet's busy schedule was now filled with raising two daughters, running her home, working for charities, playing tennis every day, skiing in Sun Valley and fishing in Wyoming. She also became involved with an in-depth study of Christian Science and the Unity movement. Brought up a Presbyterian, singing in the choir and regularly attending the Christian Endeavor meetings, Janet always kept private about her religious side, yet she expressed some of her spiritual ideas in an interview in 1971, saying, "The church is ceremonial and ritualistic. Jesus Christ was a martyr. There is *something* beyond — I don't know what. One's religion is really an inside thing. It's a mystery how nature is so intricately and perfectly balanced. But I think the pivot of life should be purity of the spirit."[2]

Janet became an avid reader of the *Daily Word* of the Unity Church, sending her daughters clippings of passages she found comforting. When she traveled, she always bade farewell with "Isten veled," a Hungarian phrase meaning, "God be with you," — something she had probably picked up from

Tony's father. As Jamie Lee confirmed years later, her mother's "deep sense of spirituality balanced out her toughness."[3]

In the early 1970s, Janet and Bob bought a condominium in Bear Valley, California. To promote the winter sport resort, Janet came up with the brilliant idea of sponsoring a ski race: the Janet Leigh, Benson and Hedges Celebrity Pro-AM Ski Classic. The first tournament took place in March 1971 when Janet entered herself in the competition and won.

"I realize I shouldn't have won," she said to the *New York Times* while holding the silver trophy cup. "I feel like a hostess getting the best steak at her own dinner party. But I'll bet Bing [Crosby] wouldn't turn down the cup if he won it in his tournament."[4] The celebrities in the race included Natalie Wood and her husband, producer Richard Gregson, Clint Eastwood, Hugh O'Brien, Ron Ely, Adam West, and Desi Arnaz, Jr. The purpose of the tournament was to raise money for the United States Deaf Ski Team, coached by Jimmy Heuga. Whereas the event boasted more comedy than talent on the slopes, the final result in fundraising was extremely satisfactory.

The race was so successful that it became one of the most fashionable annual events of the ski season. The following year the number of celebrity participants doubled, along with funds raised. Among those Janet invited was Lloyd Bridges, her recent co-star in the ABC TV movie *The Deadly Dream*. Bridges, a beginning skier, enjoyed the competition so much that he became a regular at the resort, where he later bought property.

Over the years Janet had spent an average of four hours per day — about 28 hours a week — working for charity. Her amazing efforts received some well-deserved recognition in 1972 with a plaque commemorating her 15 years of work with SHARE, as a chairman of the board and as one of the backbones of the annual variety show — a fundraiser that raised $200,000 each spring for emotionally disturbed children suffering from intellectual disabilities. "Those [plaques] [she had received a previous one in 1968] are worth more to me than any award for acting ever could be" she proudly admitted. "Working on behalf of retarded children has given me more inner satisfaction than I could ever describe. I feel very lucky that I found a profession which I could enjoy as much as I do acting and which puts me in a position to help others."[5]

That same year Janet returned to MGM to work in two mediocre films: *One Is a Lonely Number* and *The Night of the Lepus*.

After their recent success with *Willy Wonka and the Chocolate Factory*, producer Stan Margulies and director Mel Stuart once again teamed together on *One Is a Lonely Number*. The picture starred Academy Award winner Melvyn Douglas and the beautiful Trish Van Devere. Janet portrayed the sec-

With Trish Van Devere and Jane Elliott in *One Is a Lonely Number* (1972).

ondary role of Gert Meredith, a tough-talking man-hater, and president of the Divorcees League of Marine County.

Since the story showed life from the point of view of women deserted by their husbands, most of the critics dismissed it after negatively labeling it "a so-called woman's picture." Yet *Variety* lauded the superior script by David Seltzer, as well as Mel Stuart's direction, and classified *One Is a Lonely Number* as "a top-class woman's picture." Siding with *Variety* was the *New York Times*, which characterized Janet's performance as "excellent." Sadly, the two reviews were not enough to save the film from flopping at the box office.

Janet had only a few weeks to rest before flying to Tucson, Arizona, where *The Night of the Lepus* was to be filmed. Hoping to repeat the smashing success of a round of animal horror films that were extremely popular in that period — *Willard* and *Ben* (rats), *Frogs* (amphibians and insects), *Stanley* (snakes) — MGM decided to produce *The Night of the Lepus*, a story of a horde of mutant killer wild hares (the picture's original title was *Rabbits*; lepus is the Latin word for rabbit). The plot was based on *The Year of the Angry Rabbit*, which was a science fiction novel written in 1964 by Australian author Russell Braddon.

"The script was quite good," Janet said to justify what probably was the worst movie of her career. "The only thing that nobody had the foresight to see was that even if you make a rabbit six feet tall, he's still an Easter Bunny. You just want to burst out laughing because you have this herd of giant rabbits that are supposed to be menacing, and they're *bunny rabbits*. There was nothing we could do to make them frightening."[6]

A man in a bunny suit with ketchup coming out of its mouth was used in several scenes; not unexpectedly, the results were grotesque and ludicrous. The pseudo sci-fi suspense thriller also starred Stuart Whitman and Rory Calhoun. "It took about four or five days before we realized that perhaps we didn't have the ideal director," Janet explained. "That was disheartening. And then it was not until the first scene with the big bunnies that we all realized that it was hopeless."[7]

During the long and arduous two-and-a-half months of filmmaking in Arizona, Janet found time to appear in the "Follies" for the Junior League of Tucson, visit the Tucson Girls Club and make sixty spot announcements for POW-MIA. Asked by a local reporter how she could give so freely of her time, Janet quickly replied, "When you are lucky, and I am lucky, I believe you've got to spread it around." One of the reasons she accepted the film assignment was that it was made not too far from her home, allowing her to return on weekends or have Bob and the girls visit on the set. Nonetheless, she objected to having Kelly and Jamie Lee play minor roles in the picture, as she did not want them to see or be part of any type of horror film — something that now sounds awfully ironic, since the early success of Jamie Lee Curtis' career as an actress would be achieved years later thanks to two major horror movies.

"Hare-brained idea," "[Reminiscent of] every B-grade sci-fi picture from the '50s — but worse," "Dull and predictable," "At least it is not being released at Easter," — these were the puns and cracks made by the critics reviewing *The Night of the Lepus*. Despite being widely panned and entering into the annals of worst films ever made, the movie gained cult status years later for its unintentional campiness. "I've forgotten as much as I could about that picture," were Janet's words when she was asked about it by film scholar Tom Weaver years later.[8]

In the summer of 1972, Tony, who had been remarried twice and now had three children, invited Kelly and Jamie Lee to spend the holidays with him. Since their divorce, Tony had not been the best of fathers. He often justified his behavior by blaming his ex-wife for having turned the girls against him. Janet was mostly annoyed by his erratic behavior, which often caused him to disappear for long periods from their daughters' lives, followed by sudden demands of impromptu visits at their house.

With their mother's consent, Kelly and Jamie Lee, now sixteen and fourteen, flew to London, where Tony was completing the shooting of the TV series *The Persuaders*, opposite Roger Moore. As soon as the last take was done, Tony took them to Sardinia, where they spent six relaxing weeks in a beautiful house by the sea. For the first time in their lives, Kelly and Jamie felt very close to their father, who, when the holiday was over, wanted them to keep living with him.

"Kelly was a young teenager, a very difficult age," Janet told the British newspaper *Mail on Sunday*. "Bob and I were the parents, the disciplinarians, the ones who said you can't stay out after a certain time, or that's not exactly a good way to dress. And Tony offered a free life. There was no discipline; it was: do what you want. A teenager's dreamboat. And I couldn't compete with that."[9]

At the end of the summer Kelly decided not to go back home and stayed with Tony, his wife Leslie, her stepbrother Nicholas, and her two stepsisters Alexandra and Allegra (by Tony's marriage to Christine Kaufmann). Heavyhearted, Janet was worried by her leaving, but she accepted her daughter's decision. Five months later, in January 1973, Tony sought custody of Kelly in a Santa Monica court suit which named Janet as defendant. The following month he was awarded Kelly's custody after her mother consented to the change.

A devastated Janet was consoled by the advice of a close friend who explained that the roles had just reversed between Tony and her. "[He told me] that life may be appealing now," said Janet, "but, at some point, he's got to say no to something. You, on the other hand, are the one who can take her to lunch, shopping, be the friend." So Janet approached Kelly's decision wisely, and her friend's advice proved to be sage. "Unfortunately, Kelly was the one who was hurt the most because eventually he tired of that role," Janet recalled.[10]

In June Tony petitioned for Jamie Lee's custody. In court he claimed that Janet's home was fraught with tension and was otherwise "an unwholesome medium for the emotional stability and welfare of Jamie Lee." He also stated that his visits had been restricted and accused Janet of misappropriating child support funds for her own use and for "unbelievable items." Tony's lawsuit ignited a court battle in which Janet countersued with allegations that he had failed to pay child support. The legal dispute ended on October 4 when Tony agreed to allow Jamie Lee to remain with her mother. Both Janet and Tony dismissed their petitions. He admitted being satisfied that the retention of Jamie's custody by Janet was proper and that the funds paid for Jamie's support had been utilized for that purpose.

The unpleasant events between their parents did not stop Jamie Lee from later forming a warped bond with Tony, based on a mutual use of drugs. Tony himself admitted that, having been absent for so much of her life, it was "one way we interrelated." Said Janet:

> He has to live with himself. [Jamie Lee] had no inkling of what was going on. I did not know any of it. I actually encouraged her to see Tony because it's a terrible thing to be denied your birth father. Afterwards I felt very badly about it. For one thing, she hadn't told me. We've always been very close. She called me the night she had lost her virginity, which I consider the highest compliment I could have as a mother. So the fact she didn't tell me about the drugs....[11]

Eventually Jamie Lee cleaned up — "She was stronger than he was" — and persuaded Tony to enter the Betty Ford Center in the spring of 1984. Janet also confessed to smoking marijuana with Tony once; however, while her then-husband enjoyed the experience and later moved on to hard drugs, she had fallen asleep and had forgotten the event.

In August 1974 Helen Morrison passed away. Janet was very distraught by the death of her mother, who had not been the same since her husband's suicide.

From 1973 to 1975 Janet disappeared from the big screen and made only a few select appearances on TV. A memorable one came in 1975 as a guest star on the popular crime series *Columbo*, starring Peter Falk as the famous homicide detective Frank Columbo. In the episode "The Forgotten Lady," Janet played Grace Wheeler Willis, an aging musical movie and stage star who lived for the past and in a dream world where her fictional characters were real people. Desperate to recapture her glory days, she resorts to murder in the hope that the publicity will revive her Broadway career. In the episode Grace watches herself in one of her old films, which happened to be *Walking My Baby Back Home*. Although the character played by Janet in the 1953 picture was called Chris, Grace refers to her role as Rosie.

Peter Falk and Janet had previously worked together in 1966 in "Dear Deductible," a 60-minute episode of *Bob Hope Presents the Chrysler Theatre*. The episode was a lightweight romantic comedy about a songwriter and a penniless socialite who are rushed into marriage by their accountant in hopes of solving their financial problems.

On several occasions Falk stated how pleasurable it was working with Janet, who he called "a true lady." He also considered that *Columbo* episode one of his favorites and a real rarity in the series since the murderer gets away with it.

In 1975, the adult men's magazine *Oui* offered Peter Lawford $10,000 to pose nude along with one of his MGM co-stars, such as Janet or Esther Williams. Forty-eight-year-old Janet was amused and flattered by the odd offer, but she turned it down. Lawford told the press that the lady he would pose with would probably have to be younger than he was.[12]

Always ready to face a new challenge, Janet accepted her first role in a play. Ever since she saw *Life with Father* in 1948 she had hoped that one day she'd be on stage. "But I didn't know if I could, or if I'd have the courage to try," she said in an interview in 1975.[13]

Throughout the years of her career, Broadway producers had often asked her to appear in shows. Several of the plays she could have been in wound up big hits, with other actresses playing what would have been her parts. But, without regret, Janet turned them all down, feeling unready for such a big step.

In June 1975 she finally agreed to star in *Duplex*, a murder mystery play written by Bob Barry and directed by British director Val May, who had staged the hits *A Severed Head* and *The Killing of Sister George* in London's West End.

Before her Broadway debut in December 1975, Janet said:

I flew to London to meet him, and he is not intimidated by the fact that I've never done it. I'm nervous but not bad-nervous. I feel that if you know your craft, the medium doesn't matter. I recently did a *Columbo* that I'm quite proud of, and when Peter Falk heard about it, he told me: "You must do it and you will." I've told Val: "Make me whatever you want." I think if we stayed safe in our cocoons and never tried anything, life wouldn't be worth living.[14]

After meeting May in England, Janet signed her contract with producers Tyler Gatchell and Peter Neufeld for the lead in Bob Barry's play, scheduled for a brief tryout at the Shubert Theatre in New Heaven, Connecticut, followed by 12 performances at the New Locust Street Theatre in Philadelphia, prior to the Broadway unveiling at the Biltmore Theater. The intricate plot of *Duplex*, whose name was later changed to *Murder Among Friends*, involved murder and blackmail in the lives of a celebrated actor, played by Jack Cassidy, his wealthy wife, played by Janet, and his agent and producer, played by Lewis Arlt.

Rehearsals started in New York on November 2. In spite of her busy schedule, Janet found the time to be part of a fundraising event on behalf of the National Multiple Sclerosis Society, of which she was national chairman of the society's MS Read-a-thon program.

Four weeks later, ready for her stage debut, Janet boarded on a train to New Haven for a week of tryouts. A few moments before going on stage, while she was in the dressing room applying makeup, Janet felt the adrenaline begin pumping. She sat bolt upright and asked herself what she was doing there. That short moment of stage fright disappeared a few moments later when she was called onstage, where she performed impeccably.

As planned, the show moved for its official run to Philadelphia, where Janet took a suite at the Bellevue-Stratford Hotel. From December 8 to December 20, 1975, *Murder Among Friends* drew packed audiences in Philadelphia keen to see Janet's debut. The local press disliked the show. Some of the critics claimed that the plot badly paralleled the John S. Knight III murder case, and the play had premiered the day after the newspaper heir's mysterious death.

On the day of her first matinee, Janet had to face a noisy drunk in the second row. "I felt like I should ask him, 'Excuse me, but are you in this play?' For a moment I lost my concentration, but I snapped right back."[15] The noisy spectator was quickly ushered out of the theater, and the show kept on going smoothly.

Almost at the end of the run, just before her Broadway debut, Janet suddenly collapsed with stomach pains and had to be hospitalized for a couple of days because she thought some ailment had knocked her out of commission. Her understudy had to go on for her. She found out the cause of her mysterious sickness only two months later. Recalled Janet:

> Right when I checked in, I told my daughter, there was a funny smell in the room. Something was leaking, I thought, from the radiator pipes. Ordinarily, I'm not the one who gets sick, or misses work, and the doctors were never able to discover my stomach problem. A couple of months after we left Philadelphia we heard about the Legionnaire's disease, and how it had hit visitors at that hotel. I believe I had a form of it.

Before the New York premiere on December 28, the producers, along with the director, decided to make some radical changes to the plot. Yet the reviews of *Murder Among Friends* remained mixed. Janet, who was a Hollywood star, a category notoriously snubbed by theater critics, was treated surprisingly well by the press. The *New York Times* spared her a few kind words: "Miss Leigh ... lacks something in stage technique and energy, but she is charming and resourceful and remembers to keep out of the shower." *Variety*'s Hobe Morrison loved her performance: "Janet Leigh, making her Broadway stage debut, is effective as the unsavory wife who evidently hasn't been lavishing her wealth on overeating."[16]

Nonetheless, *Murder Among Friends* had its final curtain lowered on January 10, 1976. Janet's stoic reaction to the early closing of the show was upbeat: "I found out I could do it and I did it. I want to do it again."[17] She did regret the closing, but it turned out to be for the best since her husband could not stay in New York for a long run.

Janet continued to prefer working on TV shows, since they made it convenient for her to be at home in Beverly Hills. "I have never liked to be away from my family and that has always dictated my career,"[18] she said. Janet appeared in three TV movies: *Murder at the World Series, Telethon* and *Mirror, Mirror.* The latter was a film about plastic surgery and the pressure prompting three different women to opt for cosmetic surgery. Janet portrayed a lonely widow who engages in a rivalry with her college-aged daughter. "I have no hang-ups about it," was Janet's comment on that subject.

> I think it's a wonderful thing and everyone should look as good as they can, but I've never been able to make up my mind to do it myself. I'm Danish and I have good bone structure. I have some lines, but I like them. I'm 52 ... no point lying about it. I've loved every minute of it, but there are more important things in life than pretending you're something you're not.[19]

Janet loved her performance in *Mirror, Mirror,* considering it one of the best things she had ever done for television.

In July of 1978 Janet and Jamie Lee played mother-and-daughter roles on the popular TV series *The Love Boat.* The episode, called "Locked Away," marked their first appearance together on television. "We were a little nervous at first," Janet recalled. "But it was great fun. I didn't know whether I should be acting like a mother or like a fellow actress. After the first few lines I realized that Jamie knew exactly what she was doing, and we both relaxed as professional performers working together, in tandem."

After finishing high school, Jamie Lee, then nineteen, decided to follow Janet's footsteps and pursue an acting career. Said Janet:

> I think I knew ever since Jamie was born that she was going to be an actress. You might say she came out singing. And she was always acting, staging little shows with the kids of our neighbors or friends who came over to play tennis. I don't feel that the parent has a great deal to say — or should — about what their children want to do with their lives. There's guidance, of course, and you can be there as a sounding board.[20]

Jamie appeared on TV in several small roles before landing the part of Lieutenant Barbara Duran on the TV series *Petticoat Affair,* based on Blake Edwards' 1959 film *Operation Petticoat* (in which Tony had played the lead opposite Cary Grant).

During the spring of 1978, Janet received a script titled *Boardwalk* from director Steve Verona, who had made *The Lords of Flatbush* in 1974, casting a couple of unknowns named Sylvester Stallone and Henry Winkler. Janet read it and immediately loved the idea of playing a real woman and an average person. "It's not the biggest role in the picture, but I don't care about that," she said to Rex Reed. "I saw Florence when I read it and I wanted to play her."[21]

Boardwalk was a partially autobiographical script for Verona. The director was born in Brighton Beach, Brooklyn, where the film was going to be shot. His grandfather used to own a coffee shop — just like the main character in the picture. He also claimed that his mother, at certain times, looked like Janet. Shelley Winters campaigned for the part of Florence, but the director found her too harsh and preferred Janet, who was his first choice all along.

Filming began in Brighton Beach at the beginning of August. *Boardwalk* marked the first time Janet made a film in New York. It was her return to "movie-movies" after appearing exclusively on television for five years. The picture chronicled the uneasy battle on Coney Island between an elderly Jewish couple, the Rosens (played by 83-year-old Ruth Gordon and 78-year-old Lee Strasberg), against a violent teenage gang. The Rosens run a cafeteria where their daughter Florence works at the cash register. Florence is a widow for whom money and security are first priorities. Explaining her complex character, Janet said:

> [She] represents the missing link in this family structure. She married for love, and she married a bum. Then she blamed everything…. I didn't try to play her as a Jewish mother at all. I'm not Jewish and that would have been silly. I've known a lot of women like that, who marry a dashing kind of handsome man who's really very irresponsible and selfish. Then, when he splits and runs away, she digs in — like Flo — and tries to elevate herself. Moves to a different neighborhood because she thinks that will help. And ends up in a second marriage — which has taken a long time — to a man who is comfortable, kind, gentle, steady. Not demanding. Meanwhile, she'd become more and more withdrawn and bitter, alienated from her son. But the second husband's kindness will finally rub off on Florence, and will eventually mellow her. But she won't settle down. She'll find another job. She'll push her new husband the next step up the ladder. She'll keep trying to save more money for her son, who doesn't really want it.[22]

For the most part, the shooting schedule required Janet, who had taken a penthouse at the Middletowne Hotel in Manhattan's East Side, to be ready for makeup as early as 4 A.M. On the set she met veteran actress Ruth Gordon for the first time. "She is so tiny I wanted her to pick up and cradle her," she recalled.[23]

Working with Gordon in a scene in which the old actress dies of a sudden heart attack proved very challenging for Janet. "It took so much out of me," she explained, "that I left the set that evening in a daze, headed back to my Manhattan hotel, got dressed for the theater to see *Annie*, and, in the taxicab, noticed that I had forgotten to put on underpants."[24] When she was not expected too early on the set, Janet indulged in her favorite activity of watching plays and musicals on Broadway.

She returned to New York a year later, when in November of 1979 *Board-walk* opened with a charity premiere to benefit Lee Strasberg's new museum of Marilyn Monroe memorabilia (a project that was later aborted). Despite *Boardwalk* being acclaimed by some critics (it was successfully screened at the Cannes Film Festival), in America the picture had a very short and limited release, since the distributor went bankrupt as it came out in theaters.

For the role of Florence, Janet received many flattering reviews. *Films in Review* wrote, "Janet Leigh [was] in her best role in years." Vincent Canby praised her performance in a *New York Times* editorial, stating, "[Janet Leigh] creates a character who is vastly more complex, interesting and believable than the movie that surrounds her like urban blight."[25]

Janet and her daughter Jamie Lee Curtis.

Just when Janet finished her work for *Boardwalk*, Jamie Lee appeared on the American screen in her first lead role — in John Carpenter's horror *Halloween*. The movie's success was unbelievable, grossing $50 million around the world. Jamie Lee became an overnight star, and the movie spawned a long line of sequels. After watching the film, Janet was impressed not only by her daughter's skill but also by the quality of the production, which was made on an extremely low budget. Anxious to know Carpenter, she finally met him and became friends. The following year the director, who had long admired Janet, wrote a part for her in *The Fog*, starring Jamie Lee. Janet accepted it, liking the idea of being exposed to Carpenter's stimulating talent.

Following *Halloween*, *The Fog* marked the second creative collaboration of writer-director John Carpenter with writer-producer Debra Hill. The picture was shot outside San Francisco, near Point Reyes Lighthouse and Sir Drake Bay. It was a perfect location, since that area has what meteorologists consider one of densest and therefore most dangerous fogs in the country.

"I found some wonderful things that Carpenter has in common with Hitchcock," said Janet in the movie's press materials.

> Hitchcock, as is well known, has a movie all laid out in his mind before he starts actually shooting. So does John Carpenter. Also, John likes to find ways to shoot a scene that he doesn't have to constantly intercut between one thing and another. That's the way Hitchcock works too. But on the other hand, he's not

one of these young directors who are obsessed with making movies similar to Hitchcock's films.

She expressed her excitement at working on *The Fog*, saying, "I've done every kind of movie, comedy, drama, Western, period pictures, musical you name it! Now I look for parts that offer me some kind of challenge, because the part is something off the beaten path for me as an actress. In *The Fog* I play a warm, loving woman, but she's a little bit scatterbrained. I loved the part and I loved making the film."

Although Jamie Lee was happy to work with Janet, after the brief experience on the episode of *The Love Boat*, she expressed her concern at becoming part of an on-going package deal, playing mother and daughter. She was very pleased to learn, when she was offered a starring role in the film, that she and Janet had not been cast as mother and daughter.

Though not as big a hit as *Halloween*, *The Fog* was a commercial success, garnering mixed critiques. Carpenter was dissatisfied with the final product due to re-shoots and low production values. Janet found the film "done well … maybe just a little far-fetched."[26]

In October 1982 Janet flew to New York to appear arm in arm with Anthony Perkins on the stage of Radio City Music Hall in the TV special *Night of 100 Stars* in a segment about "famous couples." Perkins had just completed *Psycho II*, for which Jamie Lee had turned down the leading role. Janet profoundly disliked the sequel. In her opinion, the plot left nothing to the imagination, imagination that she firmly believed was the basis of the success of the original *Psycho* since very little was allowed to be shown.

When in 1986 *Psycho III* was released, Janet expressed her intent to see it because it was directed by Perkins, but she never got around to it. However, she found time to watch in 1990 *Psycho IV: The Beginning*, a TV movie written by Joseph Stefano, screenwriter of the original *Psycho*, and starring Perkins and Henry Thomas (as young Norman Bates). Janet found interesting the idea of a prequel that told the story of Norman's childhood. She agreed to host a brief introduction to the film the night it broadcast on the cable network Showtime.

Janet's appearances on the big and small screen decreased in the 1980s to a mere handful. She regretted that she and Jamie Lee did not find out soon enough about the making of *Terms of Endearment* because it could have been the right vehicle for both of them. She experienced a similar disappointment a few years later with *Postcards from the Edge*, which featured another mother and daughter tandem she believed they would have been right for.

"I don't get thought of for great things like those," she complained in an interview with Stephen Rebello in 1991. "I find it very difficult to sell myself. I am not an aggressive person, for myself. Jamie Lee, Bob and Kelly —

everybody — gets furious with me about this. Maybe it is that old fear of rejection."[27] Janet admitted, although never with regret, that self-doubt had often kept her from pursuing roles for which she would have been perfect, like parts in *Quo Vadis* in 1951 and *The Robe* in 1953.

In the spring of 1991 Janet was reunited, this time on stage, with Van Johnson, her favorite onscreen partner, in a performance of A.R. Gurney's Pulitzer Prize–nominated play *Love Letters*. The show ran at the Canon Theatre in Beverly Hills, where every week the cast, consisting of only two celebrity performers, read before a packed audience the letters two lovers exchanged during their separated lives.

"I loved doing that and loved Van in the role," said Janet to Johnson's biographer. "He is so funny." Janet recalled a curious incident after the intermission when, with Johnson, she was trying to return to the stage from the dressing room in total darkness. Neither of them could see while they were walking up the stairs. Johnson, who was hearing-impaired, all of a sudden exclaimed loudly, "Where the fuck is the flashlight?" When they appeared onstage the audience was still laughing, having heard his cursing.[28]

While Janet's screen appearances became fewer, she became involved in the new challenging activity of writing her autobiography, *There Really Was a Hollywood*, successfully published in 1984. This was followed by *Psycho: Behind the Scenes of the Classic Thriller* and her first novel, *House of Destiny*, both published in 1995. "I've always been able to express myself well," Janet explained on the occasion of the *Psycho* book release:

> People would always come to me and say, "Janet, would you write this letter for me?" I never thought of doing a novel or anything like that. I had an idea, and I like writing so much. I just plunged in. Sometimes they say ignorance is bliss. In this case it definitely was. I didn't know the number of manuscripts that are submitted and the number that are actually published each year. Knowing those statistics, I don't know whether I would have had the guts to start. I think I would have been frightened away![29]

Psycho: Behind the Scenes of the Classic Thriller was written in collaboration with biographer Christopher Nickens. Janet realized that after 35 years, Hitchcock's masterpiece was still a phenomenon that made a tremendous impact on each new generation. Hence she decided to tell her side of the story, setting the record straight on many myths and misconceptions about the making of the classic thriller.

House of Destiny, Janet's first novel, appeared in American bookstores in September 1995, becoming an instant bestseller. It was the story of a friendship between a Spanish bellboy and a movie star, who together discover and transform romance in Hollywood.

In March 1996 Janet toured Europe to promote the two books. She was first in France, where she was welcomed warmly. A Parisian bookstore organized a screening of *Psycho* after a signing event. Janet was very amused at watching herself onscreen speaking fluent French, since the movie was fully dubbed.

In Dublin a large group of fans lined up to have their books signed. Janet told the Irish press that even if she never received any literary prize, she fulfilled her ambition to write "a family saga, including all the things that families are: happy, sad, greedy, jealous."[30]

In June she returned to New York to attend a special evening organized by the Players Club to commemorate the 50th anniversary of her first movie contract. In a "Pipe Night" (as labeled by the club's members), Janet was celebrated by many of her closest friends and colleagues, including Van Johnson, Arlene Dahl, Gloria DeHaven, John Springer, Barry Nelson and Margaret Whiting. During the gala dinner, some of the guests took the podium and shared personal stories about Janet. Kelly had some moving words for her mother, while Jamie Lee appeared in a video message telling funny anecdotes and parodying all Janet's film titles. After a few clips from her movies were shown on a screen, Janet finally appeared on the podium, where she received an engraved silver tray as a memento of the celebration. It was an unforgettable and emotional moment. Janet could not hold back her tears of joy. Her thank-you speech, for the most part impromptu, reflected graciousness, humbleness and the wit of a true star.

Nineteen ninety-eight was a very busy year. Janet promoted the theatrical release of the re-edited version of *Touch of Evil*, going in May to the Cannes Film Festival to attend a screening that was eventually canceled due to a legal battle with Welles' daughter.

In August, she appeared on the big screen in a interesting cameo in *Halloween H20: Twenty Years Later*, starring Jamie Lee. The picture was the seventh installment in the slasher series and was Janet's first feature film since John Carpenter's *The Fog* eighteen years earlier. Jamie Lee came up with the concept to set the movie twenty years after the original *Halloween*, choosing the clever name *H20*, and pitched it successfully to Miramax.

Janet played Norma, a bumbling school secretary who drives the same car Marion Crane does in *Psycho*. In one brief scene, marked with levity, Janet addresses Jamie Lee: "If I could be maternal for a moment.... We've all had bad things happen to us...." The sequence ends with Janet entering her car as a brief yet recognizable portion of *Psycho*'s score plays on the soundtrack.

On the day Janet walked onto the set of *H20* for the first time, the entire crew stood up and applauded. They were all honored to have her in the picture that marked the reappearance on the screen of two icons of the horror genre (the so-called "Scream Queens") who also happened to be mother and daughter. It was a very touching moment. Janet was also moved by the audience's wild reaction at the film premiere in Los Angeles when she materialized onscreen. Nobody had forgotten Janet Leigh; nobody had forgotten *Psycho*. To further confirm her recognition, Janet received a tremendous amount of fan mail. Many of her old movies were now available on video or shown on cable channels. As she explained, "Each generation of people seems to rediscover some of these films. When people list their favorite movies of mine in their letters to me, number one isn't always *Psycho*, but it is always on the list. So is *Touch of Evil, Manchurian Candidate, Bye Bye Birdie, Scaramouche* and *The Naked Spur*. It's just that *Psycho* is on every list."[31]

In December Gus Van Sant directed a remake of *Psycho* with Vince Vaughn assuming the Norman Bates role and Anne Heche stepping into Janet's shower. Critics and fans of the original picture from all over the world were shocked by Van Sant's decision to remake the classic. The film was 90 percent homage to the Hitchcock movie, identically filmed scene for scene. When she was asked her opinion of that needless remake, Janet's sole reaction was to wish the filmmakers luck. Yet she refused to watch it. Needless to say, the film was a flop.

In April 1999 Janet traveled to France, where she received a cultural medal and the title *Chevalier* for her contributions to the art and entertainment world with her film career. "It was so nice, I was very moved," was her only comment to the press when she returned to the States.[32]

As she approached her 75th birthday, Janet remained extremely busy and active. She worked with American Movie Classics and the Library of Congress Film Registry to preserve film and television archives. She also continued serving on the board of the Motion Picture and Television Fund in Woodland Hills, a position she had held for more than fifteen years, raising funds for the retirement community for members of the entertainment industry.

In 2000 she starred in a small but pivotal role, with Christopher Lloyd, in *A Fate Totally Worse Than Death*, a silly movie for teenagers released straight to DVD in 2005 (with the new title *Bad Girls from Valley High*).

Janet's second novel, *The Dream Factory*, was published by Mira Books in 2002. The book was based on stories she had heard or experienced during her career in Hollywood. Once again Janet embarked on a promotional tour, patiently answering questions and signing copies for the hordes of fans attending the events.

When in an interview she was asked if she was ready to retire, Janet smiled and replied:

Retire? I don't think so. There is so much to do. I am a consultant in my husband's business. Since he's not been strong, I have incorporated my travels and travel for him as well. I have two children, two grandchildren and four-legged children [referring to her beloved dogs] that I take care of, so it's a busy time. I am also putting my own archive together — I realized no one else can do it.[33]

She hoped that a proposed documentary based on her autobiography, *There Really Was a Hollywood*, would be produced. Some producers had shown an interest in making a TV documentary in which Janet would have introduced the audience to Hollywood the same way she saw it when she first arrived, and take them through the years. The idea was tied to the possible release of an updated edition of her biography; unfortunately, the project remained unrealized.

In spite of an active and fairly healthy lifestyle, Janet was struggling with bulimia, a condition she had hidden for years but that became more evident as she aged. She was preoccupied with maintaining her slim figure, causing her to look frail and emaciated. Her public appearances became very rare. Yet she looked radiant and elegantly dressed at Liza Minnelli's fourth wedding extravaganza in New York in March 2002.

By the end of 2003 Janet's health had deteriorated. She was suffering from a vascular disease which rendered her right hand permanently disabled; gangrene later developed. Those hands Janet had constantly clenched into fists every time she became tense.

Jamie Lee nearly had to cancel an appearance at the British premiere of her latest film, *Freaky Friday*, to remain near her mother. Jamie Lee flew from Los Angeles to London for only a brief twenty-four hour period in order to be away from her mother as short a time as possible.

In spite of being in a wheelchair in May 2004, Janet traveled to Stockton to proudly accept an honorary Doctorate of Fine Arts degree from the University of the Pacific, her alma mater, where she never completed her studies in psychology and music. At the ceremony she delivered a remarkable speech about the importance of education and the value she placed upon her memories of her time in school. It was her last public appearance.

A few months later she was diagnosed with vasculitis, an inflammation of the blood vessels, to which she succumbed on Sunday, October 3, 2004. She passed away peacefully at her Beverly Hills home, surrounded by her caring, affectionate husband and loving daughters. Being "the world's greatest organizer," as Jamie Lee defined her, Janet had everything impeccably planned. Her spokeswoman, Heidi Schaeffer, who announced to the world her departure, stated that Janet had requested donations be made to the Motion Picture and Television Fund in lieu of flowers. After her remains were cremated, a private service was held at the Westwood Village Memorial Park in Los Angeles, where her ashes were buried.

Kelly and Jamie Lee organized a moving memorial with friends and family who gathered to pay a last tribute. As Janet specifically wrote in her will, the memorial began with an opening line delivered by Jamie Lee: "Well, I bet she tripped on her way through the pearly gates," a reference to her clumsiness and a last proof of her great sense of humor. People shared memories and personal stories, while some of her photographs appeared on a screen followed by a clip from *Bye Bye Birdie* in which Janet and Dick Van Dyke sang and danced to "Put on a Happy Face."

Jamie Lee recalled that at the memorial the most moving and profound words came from her seventeen-year-old daughter Annie, who thought that with her peaceful death her grandmother was finally able to let go of her controlled life. In that moment Janet achieved the greatest accomplishment of her life, being able to trust her family in those final moments and leaving them without any worries.[34]

In 2006 Kelly and Jamie Lee returned to Stockton for the posthumous naming of the Janet Leigh Plaza in front of a new theater complex, where a plaque was placed to honor their mother's name. As per Janet's wish, the University of the Pacific received a vast collection of material that decorated her home, including photographs, movie posters, correspondence, advertisements, magazine covers, and recognitions and awards, which later became the Janet Leigh collection, partially on view at the institution.

In September 2009 Bob Brandt, Janet's husband for forty-two years, passed away after a long battle with Alzheimer's Disease. His ashes were buried next to Janet's in Westwood Village Memorial Park Cemetery.

More than forty years after *Psycho*'s first release, Janet continues to be primarily remembered as Marion Crane and associated with the shower scene. In early 2012 twenty-seven-year-old actress Scarlett Johansson was announced to play the role of Janet in the film *Hitchcock* on Alfred Hitchcock and the making of *Psycho*, based on Steven Rebello's book.

As Janet kept repeating in all her interviews, "*Psycho* was not a curse at all to me, it was a blessing." She explained, "Laurence Olivier said that if an actor is privileged to play a role that leaves a definite strong impression on an audience, if he's remembered for that one role, then he is a lucky actor indeed. I feel the same way."[35]

"I love the way I live," Janet once said. "I'd do it all again. Yes, 100 times. It's like the story of the man who was angry because he only had one shirt ... until he saw a man who only had one arm."[36]

Filmography

Studio; Production Company (when applicable); Format; Running Time; Month and Year of Release; Production Credits; Cast; Plot; Film Reviews; Janet Leigh Reviews; Notes

The Romance of Rosy Ridge

MGM; Loew's Inc.; B&W; 105 minutes; Released: August 1947

CREDITS: *Producer*: Jack Cummings; *Director*: Roy Rowland; *Screenplay*: Lester Cole; based on a story by MacKinlay Kantor; *Photography*: Sidney Wagner; *Art Direction*: Richard Duce, Cedric Gibbons, Eddie Imazu; *Set Decoration*: Edwin B. Willis, Elliot Morgan; *Costumes*: Irene, Walles; *Music*: George Bassman; *Songs*: Earl Robinson, Lewis Allan; *Special Effects*: Warren Newcombe; *Film Editing*: Ralph E. Winters; *Makeup*: Jack Dawn.

CAST: Van Johnson (Henry Carson); Janet Leigh (Lissy Anne MacBean); Thomas Mitchell (Gill MacBean); Marshall Thompson (Ben MacBean); Selena Royle (Sairy MacBean); Charles Dingle (John Dessark); Dean Stockwell (Andrew MacBean); Guy Kibbee (Cal Baggett); Elisabeth Risdon (Emily Baggett); Jim Davis (Badge Dessark); Russell Simpson (Dan Yeary); O. Z. Whitehead (Ninny Nat); James Bell (John Willhart); Joyce Arling (Mrs. Willhart); William Bishop (Ad Buchanan); Paul Langton (Tom Yeary).

PLOT: In the years following the American Civil War, the worn, tired soldiers are struggling back through the Ozark region, one by one, to their long neglected farms. For several months the valleys surrounding Rosy Ridge have been ravaged by barn-burning night raiders. The hooded raiders take no sides — barns of Northerners, as well as those of the Southern sympathizers, have been laid waste. Bitterness between the two factions is stronger than ever, since each blames the other for the destruction. Gill MacBean has not been spared. After fighting with the Confederate Army, he has returned to his impoverished home. His teenage son Ben went to war after him and has not been heard from since. Now the family consists of Gill, his faithful wife Sairy, his lovely eighteen-year-old daughter Lissy Anne, and his twelve-year-old son Andrew.

One night the MacBeans give food and shelter to a handsome, husky twenty-year-old man named Henry Carson. Shortly the family falls under the spell of Henry's easy charm and winning manner. When the young man announces he intends to stay with the MacBeans until their barn is rebuilt, the family is overwhelmed. All except Gill, whose efforts to determine on which side Henry fought remain unsuccessful. Weeks pass and Henry is now one of the family, as he and Lissy Anne are madly in love. Suspecting that Henry is a Northerner, Gill refuses to allow Henry to return to his home. Lissy Anne, heartbroken by her father's decision, leaves Rosy Ridge with Henry. Vowing to bring his daughter home, Gill sets out with his rifle and bloodhounds to find them. He brings the two lovers home, after which Henry confesses that he fought alongside Ben. Henry tells the MacBeans that Ben, who was fatally wounded on the battlefield and died in his arms, made him promise that he would go to Rosy Ridge and help his family work the farm. Gill, moved to tears by Henry's revelation, invites the young man to stay and gives his blessing to marry Lissy Anne.

REVIEWS FOR *The Romance of Rosy Ridge*:

"It's all just too pat and contrived to carry any conviction. But the scenery is very beautiful."—*New York Times*

"*Rosy Ridge* attempts to base its romance on authentic and charming Americana. The job requires more than prettiness and benevolent patriotism. Faces, hands, clothes and postures need to suggest hard work, real life and certain tension of character rather than mere magazine illustration. Most of *Rosy Ridge*'s pleasant details are little more than mere magazine illustration."—*Time*

"*The Romance of Rosy Ridge* is a good screen entertainment."—*Variety*

REVIEWS FOR JANET LEIGH:

"Janet Leigh is as fresh and pretty as a daisy in the spring. This is Miss Leigh's first picture and it must be said that she is a welcome addition to the ranks of leading ladies. Time and a few more pictures will tell the full extent of her talent, for in *The Romance of Rosy Ridge*, Metro-Goldwin-Mayer has carefully avoided making heavy demands upon Miss Leigh."—*New York Times*

"A debut of unusual merit is staged by Janet Leigh, a fresh and lovely personality in the first acting she has ever attempted anywhere. It may be remembered that she was a discovery of Norma Sherer."—*Hollywood Reporter*

"*Rosy Ridge* introduces a charming discovery in Janet Leigh, an attractive young woman said to be Stockton born. She has a sympathetic understanding of the role of the young girl with divided love."—*San Francisco Evening News*

NOTE: *The Romance of Rosie Ridge* had three alternative titles before its release: *The Night Raiders*, *The Yankee* and *Missouri Story*.

If Winter Comes

MGM; Loew's Inc.; B&W; 97 minutes; Released: December 1947

CREDITS: *Producer:* Pandro S. Berman; *Director:* Victor Saville; *Screenplay:* Marguerite Roberts, Arthur Wimperis; based on a novel by A.S.M. Hutchinson; *Photography:* George Folsey; *Art Direction:* Cedric Gibbons, Hans Peters; *Set Decoration:* Edwin B. Willis; *Costumes:* Irene; *Music:* Herbert Stothart; *Special Effects:* Warren Newcombe; *Film Editing:* Cedric Gibbons; *Makeup:* Jack Dawn.

CAST: Walter Pidgeon (Mark Sabre); Deborah Kerr (Nona Tybar); Angela Lansbury (Mabel Sabre); Binnie Barnes (Natalie Bagshaw); Janet Leigh (Effie Bright); Dame May Whitty (Mrs. Perch); Rhys Williams (Mr. Bright); Reginald Owen (Mr. Fortune); John Abbott (Mr. Twyning); Rene Ray (Sarah, "Low Jinks"); Virginia Kelley (Rebecca, "High Jinks"); Hugh French (Tony Tybar); Dennis Hoey (Tiny Wilson); Halliwell Hobbes (the Coroner); Victor Wood (Mr. Fargus); Hugh Green (Freddie Perch); James Wethered (Harold Twyning); Owen McGiveney ("Uncle" Fouraker).

PLOT: Mark Sabre, writer of school text books for a publishing house, is a sentimental idealist. He lives a quiet, uninteresting life with his wife Mabel in a small English village. When his first love, Nona Tybar, now married to the aristocratic playboy Tony Tybar, returns to the village to live, they realize that they still love each other. As war clouds gather over England, Mark and Nona decide to run off together, but when Tony leaves to join his regiment, Nona realizes she cannot divorce him now. Rejected by the army because of a heart ailment, Mark throws himself into various types of war work. When his young friend, Freddie Perch, leaves to join the R. A. F., Mark arranges for Effie Bright, the attractive young daughter of one of the men in the publishing firm, to become the companion to Freddie's invalid mother. A series of incidents, although completely innocent, create the false impression that Effie and Mark are having an affair. When the girl's father discovers that she is pregnant and throws her out of the house, she goes to Mark for help, thus apparently confirming the growing gossip. Furious, Mabel leaves Mark. Effie, cited as co-respondent in the divorce proceedings that follow, commits suicide, and Mark finds himself pilloried in the Coroner's Court, where the jury returns a verdict of suicide but cautions him on his behavior. Mark finds a letter from the dead girl naming the father of her child, but as he has been killed in action, Mark and Nona (now a widower) decide to burn it and face life together.

REVIEWS FOR *If Winter Comes*:

If Winter Comes* is artificial from the word go and its entertainment potential is extremely small." — *New York Times*

"At times the story has a tendency to become overly-melodramatic, but it never gets out of hand because of the good direction and the competent acting." — *Harrison's Report*

"*If Winter Comes* shows its age. Pandro S. Berman has given it the usual Metro production polish but results will depend on value of cast names, which will give it some initial momentum." — *Variety*

REVIEWS FOR JANET LEIGH:

"Janet Leigh continues to show promise as the young girl who gets herself in trouble." — *Variety*

"Janet Leigh, as the unfortunate young girl who causes Mr. Pidgeon his greatest anguish is fetching and competent...." — *New York Times*

"Janet Leigh's moving performance as Effie should not go unmentioned." — *Monthly Film Bulletin*

NOTE: *If Winter Comes* was previously filmed a silent movie in 1923 by Harry F. Millarde. The role of Effie Bright was played by Gladys Leslie.

Hills of Home

MGM; Loew's Inc.; Technicolor; 97 minutes; Released: November 1948

CREDITS: *Producer:* Robert Sisk; *Director:* Fred M. Wilcox; *Screenplay:* William Ludwig; suggested by the Ian MacLaren sketches *Doctor of the Old School; Photography:* Charles Schoenbaum; *Art Direction:* Cedric Gibbons, Eddie Imazu; *Set Decoration:* Edwin B. Willis; *Costumes:* Walles; *Music:* Herbert Stothart; *Special Effects:* Warren Newcombe; *Film Editing:* Ralph E. Winters; *Makeup:* Jack Dawn.

CAST: Edmund Gwenn (Dr. Willam MacLure); Donald Crisp (Drumsheugh); Tom Drake (Tammas Milton); Janet Leigh (Margit Mitchell); Rys Williams (Mr. Milton);

Reginald Owen (Hoppa); Edmond Breon (Jaimie Soutar); Alan Napier (Sir George); Hugh Green (Geordie); Lumsden Hare (Lord Kilspindle); Eileen Erskine (Belle Saunders); Victor Wood (David Mitchell); David Thursky (Burnbrae); Frederick Worlock (Dr. Wesston); and the dog Pal as Lassie.

PLOT: Lassie, failing to become an efficient sheep dog, is adopted by Dr. MacLure, who saves her from being shot by her cruel master. Aided by his young friend Tammas Milton, MacLure trains Lassie to carry his bag and act as a messenger, but cannot overcome the animal's fear of water. When Tammas is stricken by appendicitis, the physician enlists Lassie's aid to test a new anesthetic: chloroform. Dr. MacLure successfully operates on Tammas, who, encouraged by his girlfriend Margit Mitchell, decides to study medicine.

During a blizzard, Dr. MacLure answers an emergency call and gets injured. Lassie's devotion to him rises triumphant, and she plunges into a raging torrent to summon neighbors to help. The doctor dies as the result of the ordeal, but not before passing on Lassie's ownership to Tammas and Margit.

REVIEWS FOR *Hills of Home*:

"A tender and sentimental story ... it's a film in the best tradition of inspirational romance.... Sincere and simple and unhurried, it is refreshing to have around." — *New York Times*

"This richly entertaining tearjerker rises above being just another Lassie film." — *Variety*

"M-G-M has framed this holiday confection in pretty mountain backgrounds attractively daubed in Technicolor. Occasionally the talk of the characters has a tangy humor that seems more authentic than the variety of burrs in which it is spoken. But the tang cannot hold out for long against the heavy flavor of molasses." — *Time*

REVIEWS FOR JANET LEIGH:

"Janet Leigh, only young femme in the picture, does well enough as the young student doctor's sweetheart." — *Variety*

NOTE: The film was released in the United Kingdom as *Master of Lassie*.

Words and Music

MGM; Lowe's Inc.; Technicolor; 120 minutes; Released: December 1948

CREDITS: *Producer:* Arthur Freed; *Director:* Norman Taurog; *Screenplay:* Fred Finklahoffe, based on a story by Guy Bolton and Jean Holloway; *Photography:* Charles Rosher, Harry Stradling, Sr.; *Art Direction:* Cedric Gibbons, Jack Martin Smith; *Set Decoration:* Richard Pefferle, Edwin B. Willis; *Costumes:* Helen Rose Walles; *Musical Direction:* Lennie Hayton; *Orchestration:* Conrad Salinger; *Vocal Arrangements:* Robert Tucker; *Choreographer:* Robert Alton; *Special Effects:* Warren Newcombe; *Film Editing:* Albert Akst, Ferris Webster; *Makeup:* Jack Dawn.

CAST: Tom Drake (Richard "Dick" Rodgers); Mickey Rooney (Lorenz "Larry" Hart); Ann Sothern (Joyce Harmon); Janet Leigh (Dorothy Feiner Rodgers); Perry Como (Eddie Lorrison Anders); Betty Garrett (Peggy Lorgan McNeil); Marshall Thompson (Herbert Fields); Jeanette Nolan (Mrs. Hart); Richard Quine (Ben Feiner, Jr.); Clinton Sunderberg (Shoe Clerk); Harry Antrim (Dr. Rodgers); Ilka Gruning (Mrs. Rodgers); Emory Parnell (Mr. Feiner); Helen Sprinf (Mrs. Feiner); Edward Earle (James Fernby Kelly); June Allyson, Judy Garland, Gene Kelly, Lena Horne, Cyd Charisse, Dee Turnell; the Blackburn Twins; Mel Tormé, Vera-Ellen (Guest Stars).

PLOT: The friendship of Richard (Dick) Rodgers and Lorenz (Larry) Hart resulted in one of American's greatest composing teams. It is in Larry's home that they first meet. Larry greets his visitor exuberantly, shows Dick to the piano and promptly forgets him. Dick halfheartedly strums a tune. When he is about to give up, Larry pops back into the room, singing a lyric that fits Dick's tune like a glove. They call the resulting song *Manhattan*. This kind of collaboration goes on for two years, but music publishers disregard their work. Dick, discouraged, finally decides to give up music for a business career. Larry gives a farewell party and, during it, meets Peggy McNeil; he falls madly in love with her. Before the party is over, the Theatre Guild telephones an offer to Dick and Larry to put on a one-show benefit performance. Their *Garrick Gaieties* is such a hit that they are back in business again, with an offer from a Broadway producer. Hit upon hit follows for the composing team, with Joyce Harmon and Eddie Anders as stars. Dick experiences a serious crush on Joyce, while Larry spends most of the time following Peggy on the road. In Detroit he proposes to her, but she turns him down. In an attempt to make Larry forget Peggy, Dick persuades him to go to London for a show. When they return for one of their greatest Broadway triumphs, *Connecticut Yankee*, they meet Ben Feiner, Jr., and his young sister Dorothy, Dick's friend since childhood. Suddenly they fall in love and marry. Dick and Larry turn their talents to writing for Hollywood, although Larry's sudden trips, on which he disappears for weeks at a time, don't make their work easy. After another disappearance, Larry returns home very ill. Despite a raging storm outside, he leaves his hospital room to attend the opening revival of *Connecticut Yankee*. During the intermission he wander off into the storm, with fatal results.

REVIEWS FOR *Words and Music*:

"It is a sumptuous production, employing a number of M-G-M acting notables in richly festooned settings.... *Words and Music* gives a slight hint of the wandering minstrel who should have been the focal point of an engrossing story accompaniment to great songs. The songs save it from ennui."—*New York Herald Tribune*

"*Words and Music* is a good show when it sticks to the business implied in its title."—*Newsweek*

"[The film] is a patently juvenile specimen of musical biography, as far from the facts in its reporting as it is standard in its sentimental plot."—*New York Times*

REVIEWS FOR JANET LEIGH:

"Janet Leigh turns in a pleasing job as the eventual Mrs. R."—*Variety*

"Janet Leigh's cooing as his [Mr. Rodger's] love-bird merits no more than his feeble singing of 'With a Song in My Heart.'"

NOTE: Songs included in *Word and Music* are: "Manhattan"; "There's a Small Hotel, Way Out West"; "With a Song in My Heart"; "Spring Is Here, on Your Toes"; "This Can't Be Love"; "The Girl Friend"; "Blue Room"; "Mountain Greenery"; "A Tree in the Park"; "Where's That Rainbow?"; "A Little Birdie Told Me So"; "Thou Swell"; "Someone Should Tell Them"; "Where or When"; "The Lady Is a Tramp"; "I Wish I Were in Love Again"; "Johnny One Note"; "Blue Moon"; "Slaughter on 10th Avenue"; "My Heart Stood Still."

Act of Violence

MGM; Lowe's Inc.; B&W; 82 minutes; Released: December 1948

CREDITS: *Producer:* William H. Wright; *Director:* Fred Zinnemann; *Screenplay:*

Robert L. Richards; based on a story by Collier Young; *Photography*: Robert Surtees; *Art Direction*: Cedric Gibbons, Hans Peters; *Set Decoration*: Edwin B. Willis, Henry W. Grace; *Costumes*: Helen Rose; *Music*: Bronislau Kaper; *Film Editing*: Conrad A. Nervig; *Makeup*: Jack Dawn.

CAST: Robert Ryan (Joe Parkson); Van Heflin (Frank R. Enley); Janet Leigh (Edith Enley); Mary Astor (Pat); Phyllis Thaxter (Ann Sturges); Berry Kroeger (Johnny); Taylor Holmes (Gavery); Harry Antrim (Fred Finney); Connie Gilchrist (Martha Finney); Will Wright (Pop).

PLOT: Ever since he came back from the war, Frank R. Enley has been haunted by the memory of a cowardly act, fleeing from the one man who knew about the act and who sought to avenge it. Frank has built a respected place for himself in Santa Lisa, a small town in California, and has kept his fear hidden from his wife, Edith, and their two-year-old son. Then, suddenly, he finds his nemesis has located him and, forced to make some explanation to his wife for his evident fear, he tells her a half-truth. It is from the pursuer, Joe Parkson, that Edith learns the whole truth. While her husband's entire aircrew were in a Nazi prison they planned an escape, but Frank, their captain, betrayed them. All the other men, except Joe, died from torture. Joe himself is badly crippled. When Edith follows Frank to Los Angeles and warns him that Joe means to kill him, Frank admits the truth. He had pretended to himself that he believed the Nazis' promises to treat the men decently, but he knows in his heart that he did it to save himself. Frank flees from Joe and gets involved with Pat, who introduces him to Johnny, a professional killer. Johnny offers to kill Joe for a price, and Frank, exhausted and befuddled, agrees to another betrayal. When he comes to his senses, he races back to Santa Lisa to stop the hired gunman from killing Joe. At the rendezvous at the train station, Frank sacrifices his life to take the shot aimed at Joe by the killer.

REVIEWS FOR *Act of Violence*:

"*Act of Violence* is a fine movie chase. The ending, while unconventional, is dramatically and morally satisfying." — *Time*

"'Unbearable suspense' is promised in *Act of Violence* and the promise is well kept." — *The Star* (London)

"Artistic skill of a rare order gives sharp effectiveness to this intensely motivated story of vengeance and cowardice." — *Motion Picture Herald*

REVIEWS FOR JANET LEIGH:

"Janet Leigh points up the role as Hefflin's worried but courageous wife." — *Variety*

"Mr. Zinnemann has also extracted a tortured performance from Janet Leigh as the fearful, confused and disillusioned wife of the haunted man." — *New York Times*

"A beautiful performance, too, comes from Janet Leigh as the wistful forlorn wife." — *Today's Cinema*

NOTE: All the credits except the title are at the end of the film, something very unusual for that time.

Little Women

MGM; Lowe's Inc.; Technicolor; 122 minutes; Released: April 1949

CREDITS: *Producer:* Mervyn LeRoy; *Director:* Mervyn LeRoy; *Screenplay:* Andrew Solt, Sarah Y. Mason, Victor Heerman, based on the novel by Louisa May Alcott;

Photography: Charles Schoenbaum, Robert Planck; *Art Direction*: Cedric Gibbons, Paul Groesse; *Set Decoration*: Edwin B. Willis, Jack D. Moore; *Costumes*: Walter Plunkett; *Music*: Adolph Deutsch; *Special Effects*: Warren Newcombe; *Film Editing*: Ralph E. Winters; *Makeup*: Jack Dawn.

CAST: June Allyson (Jo); Elizabeth Taylor (Amy); Peter Lawford (Laurie); Margaret O'Brien (Beth); Janet Leigh (Meg); Mary Astor (Marmee March); Lucile Watson (Aunt March); Leon Ames (Mr. March); Rossano Brazzi (Professor Bhaer); Sir C. Aubrey Smith (Mr. Lawrence); Elizabeth Patterson (Hannah); Harry Davenport (Dr. Barnes); Richard Stapley (John Brooke); Connie Gilchrist (Mrs. Kirke); Ellen Corby (Sophie); Will Wright (Mr. Grace, the Storekeeper); Harlan Briggs and Frank Darian (Croonies); Arthur Walsh (Young Man); Eloise Hardt (Sally Gardiner); Isabel Randholph (Mrs. Gardiner); Olin Howlin (Schoolteacher).

PLOT: The March family, living in a small New England town, is one closely knit by deep affection and loyalty. Bad investments have cost the family heavily, but Mrs. March and her four daughters accept their fate with good grace for the most part. Meg, the eldest girl, pretty and very feminine, patiently refashions their clothes and engages herself as governess to children of a wealthy family. Jo, the next oldest, full of energy and rebellion, and growing into a young lady, acts as companion to their wealthy Aunt March, meanwhile writing ceaselessly in hopes of becoming an author to supply her family with luxuries. Amy, the family beauty, ineffectually tries to cooperate. Beth, the youngest, is shy but musically gifted. When Jo becomes acquainted with the newly arrived Laurie, grandson of their rich neighbor, Mr. Lawrence, it leads to a match between Meg and Laurie's tutor, John Brooke, and the first break in the family. When Jo quarrels with Laurie, who believes he loves her, she goes to New York to try to focus on writing and meets Professor Bhaer, who gives her both sympathy and encouragement. Beth dies, Amy marries Laurie, and Jo, after having a novel accepted by a publisher, discovers that she can find a place in her life for both a career and marriage, and accepts Professor Bhaer's proposal. Thus the last of the "Little Women" flies from the nest.

REVIEWS FOR *Little Women*:

"Metro has not spared the pathos in bringing to the screen the sprightly and sentimental sisters of Luisa May Alcott's book. If anything, it has hauled back much too briskly on the strings of the heart and has strained a few muscles in the process. Its consequent agony shows."—*New York Times*

"Although the film has had the aid of three scenarists and is bright with Technicolor, it breaks into a series of tableaux, instead of being a warm and humorous recreation of family life in Concord at the time of the Civil War."—*New York Herald Tribune*

"There is not a faltering performance anywhere, and the famous characters come to life on the screen in all their fragile beauty and persuasive charm."—*The Hollywood Reporter*

REVIEWS FOR JANET LEIGH:

"Janet Leigh is saucy as the fairly substantial Meg."—*New York Times*

"Janet Leigh scores a personal success as Meg."—*Hollywood Reporter*

"Neither the Amy of Miss Taylor nor the Meg of Miss Janet Leigh makes any definite impression."—*The Times*

NOTE: Janet Leigh and Peter Lawford narrated the trailer for the film.

The Red Danube

MGM; Lowe's Inc.; B&W; 119 minutes; Released: September 1949

CREDITS: *Producer*: Carey Wilson; *Director*: George Sidney; *Screenplay*: Gina Kaus, Arthur Wimperis, based on the novel *Vespers in Vienna* by Bruce Marshall; *Photography*: Charles Rosher; *Art Direction*: Cedric Gibbons, Hans Peters; *Special Effects:* Warren Newcombe; *Set Decoration*: Edwin B. Willis; *Costumes*: Helen Rose; *Music*: Miklos Roska; *Film Editing*: James E. Newcom; *Makeup*: Jack Dawn.

CAST: Walter Pidgeon (Col. Michael "Hooky" Nicobar); Ethel Barrymore (Mother Superior); Peter Lawford (Major John "Twingo" McPhimister); Angela Lansbury (Audrey Quail); Janet Leigh (Maria Buhlen); Louis Calhern (Col. Piniev); Francis L. Sullivan (Col. Humprey "Blionker" Omicron); Melville Cooper (Private David Moonlight); Robert Coote (Brigadier C. M. V. Catlock); Alan Napier (the General); "Roman Toporow (2nd Lieut. Maxim Omansky); Kasia Orzazewski (Sister Kasimira); Tamara Shayne (Helena Nagard); Konstantin Shayne (Prof. Serge Bruloff); Janine Perreau ("Mickey Mouse"); David Hydes (Lt. Guedalia-Wood).

PLOT: In the summer of 1945, Colonel Nicobar of the British Army is transferred to Vienna to help in repatriating displaced persons. He is accompanied on the mission by his young assistant, Major Twingo McPhimister, and pretty senior subaltern Audrey Quail, who is unrequitedly in love with Twingo. When they are billeted in a convent headed by Mother Superior Auxilia, Twingo discovers Maria Buhlen, a lovely Russian-born ballet dancer who has taken refuge in the convent because she fears arrest by the Soviets. Meanwhile, Nicobar has received instructions to locate Maria for the Russians, and, when Soviet Colonel Piniev traces her to the convent, Nicobar is forced to surrender her. Later, however, disillusioned by the cruelty of the Russian repatriation policy, Nicobar and Mother Auxilia help Maria escape from a train and, together with Twingo, who had fallen deeply in love with her, arrange for the girl to be hidden in a mountain retreat. But now Nicobar is sent on a mission to Rome. While he is absent, a duty-blind officer, Colonel Omicron, enables the Russians once again to locate Maria. When Nicobar returns, the situation has reached a climax. His superior, Brigadier Catlock, insists he hand the girl over, but he refuses, at the risk of being relieved of his command. His humanity comes too late, however, for the terrified Maria commits suicide. It is now that some of the "miracles" promised by Mother Auxilia happen. The United Nations Council passes a ruling putting a stop to the forcible repatriation of displaced persons, and Nicobar, promoted to Brigadier, is given an assignment to "humanize" the Army.

REVIEWS FOR *The Red Danube*:

"In rapid succession the film veers from high tragedy to lowest comedy, from bitterly frank revelation of the high-level official double-dealing to an embarrassing parody of the military."—*Cue*

"The arguments are so weighted against the Soviets that, whatever your feelings in the matter may be, you may be inclined to root for the Reds."—*New York Herald Tribune*

"This is not precisely the sort of propaganda that Metro-Goldwyn-Mayer ... probably intend to pass around."—*The New Yorker*

REVIEWS FOR JANET LEIGH: "Janet Leigh is disarmingly pathetic as the tormented ballerina."—*New York Times*

"Janet Leigh is one of the best of the younger actresses, intelligent, delicate and perceptive." — *Picturegoer*

"As the ballerina, Janet Leigh gives a thin performance." — *New Yorker*

NOTE: *The Red Danube* was originally titled *Storm Over Vienna*. Irene Dunne, Spencer Tracy and Robert Taylor were set to star. It received an Academy Award Nomination for Best Black & White Art Direction–Set Decoration

The Doctor and the Girl

MGM; B&W; 98 minutes; Released: September 1949

CREDITS: *Producer:* Pandro S. Berman; *Director:* Curtis Bernhardt; *Screenplay:* Theodore Reeves, based on the novel *Bodies and Souls* by Maxence van der Meersch; *Photography:* Robert H. Planck; *Art Direction:* Cedric Gibbons, Preston Ames; *Set Decoration:* Edwin B. Willis, Arthur Krams; *Music:* Rudolph G. Kopp; *Film Editing:* Ferris Webster; *Makeup:* Jack Dawn.

CAST: Glenn Ford (Dr. Michael Corday); Charles Coburn (Dr. John Corday); Gloria De Haven (Fabienne); Janet Leigh (Evelyn Heldon); Bruce Bennett (Dr. Alfred Norton), Warner Anderson (Dr. George Esmond); Basil Ruysdael (Dr. Francis I. Garard); Nancy Davis (Marictte); Arthur Franz (Dr. Harvey L. Kenmore); Lisa Golm (Hetty): Joanne De Bergh (Child's Mother).

PLOT: The eminent Dr. John Corday plans an impressive future for his son Michael and urges him to take an impersonal attitude toward his medical carrier. Michael follows his father's advice until he falls in love with one of his patients, Evelyn Heldon. His marriage to Evelyn, who can offer her husband no social advantage, brings on a serious break between Michael and his father. But he finishes his training and sets up a practice in the poor quarters. Fabienne, Michael's younger sister, has also antagonized her father by falling in love with a married man. Against Michael's protests, she goes away with him. He deserts her, and she returns in dire trouble. Attempting to miscarriage, she brings about an untreatable hemorrhage. In desperation, she goes to Michael, who makes hospital arrangements for an emergency operation. Dr. Garard, an old friend of the family, operates at John Corday's pleading, but it is too late and Fabienne dies on the operating table. The tragedy brings John Corday and Michael together again, and once again the father tries to divert his son from general practice. But, while they argue, an emergency case is brought in. The father's mask of impersonality slips from him as he watches Michael at work, and he assures the patient's humble parents that they couldn't have come to a better man.

REVIEWS FOR *The Doctor and the Girl*:

"Here is a film done in the best tradition of the motion pictures, a film that makes one walk out with wonderful feeling of having seen a down-to-earth drama, a little heart-tugging, clever humor and a stirring story of conflicting emotions." — *Motion Picture Herald*

"All the suspense, drama and romance in the script is brought out to the fullest extent." — *Hollywood Reporter*

"Pungent, honest and moving drama with high caliber production, performances and direction." — *Film Daily*

REVIEWS FOR JANET LEIGH:

"Janet Leigh is winsome and bewitching as the little pre-operative case." — *New York Times*

"Coburn and Miss Leigh, both well cast, are excellent." — *Variety*

"[Janet Leigh] is among the lovelier as well as the more talented of Hollywood's younger stars." — *The Star* (London)

That Forsyte Woman

MGM; Loew's Inc.; Technicolor; 114 minutes; Released: November 1949

CREDITS: *Producer:* Leo Gordon; *Director:* Compton Bennett; *Screenplay:* Jan Lustig, Ivan Tors, James B. Williams, based on the novel *The Man of Property* (Book One of *The Forsyte Saga*) by John Galsworthy; *Photography:* Joseph Ruttemberg; *Art Direction:* Cedric Gibbons, Daniel B. Cathcart; *Set Decoration:* Edwin B. Willis, Jack D. Moore; *Music:* Bronislau Kaper; *Film Editing:* Frederick Y. Smith; Costumes: Walter Plunkett, Valles; *Makeup:* Jack Dawn.

CAST: Errol Flynn (Soames Forsyte); Greer Garson (Irene Heron Forsyte); Walter Pidgeon (Young Jolyon Forsyte); Robert Young (Philip Bosinney); Janet Leigh (June Forsyte); Harry Davemport (Old Jolyon Forsyte); Aubrey Mather (James Forsyte); Gerald Oliver Smith ((Beveridge); Lumsden Hare (Roger Forsyte); Stanley Logan (Swithun Forsyte); Hallywell Hobbs (Nicholas Forsyte); Matt Moore (Timothy Forsyte); Phyllis Morris (Julia Forsyte); Marjorie Eaton (Hoster Forsyte); Evelyn Beresford (Mrs. Taylor); Florence Auer (Ann Forsyte Hayman).

PLOT: Soames Forsyte, a self-centered and successful member of the Forsyte family, prides himself on getting the best bargain on anything he wants, and finds that he wants Irene Heron, a poor but beautiful piano teacher. Irene repeatedly refuses Soames on the ground she is not in love with him, but finally marries him for the security that he offers and on his promise to release her if their marriage proves a mistake. Two years prove their married life to be a complete failure, with Irene unable to give her husband the love he demands. But she has won the favor of a number of the Forsyte clan, among them the seventy-year-old patriarch Jolyon Forsyte, and pretty, young June Forsyte, whose father, Young Jolyon, has estranged himself from the family by running off with a nursery governess. The child, June, has been brought up by her grandfather. On the death of his second wife, Young Jolyon has returned to London. At an art gallery where one of his paintings is on exhibit, he meets Irene and falls completely under her spell. Meanwhile, June has fallen in love with the attractive but unsuccessful architect Philip Bossiney and persuades Irene to help her overcome family prejudice against him. In order to help the young architect, Irene convinces her husband to let Philip design a country house, and in the course of frequent meetings, she and Philip find themselves hopelessly in love. When June discovers their tryst, she informs Soames that his wife and Philip are having an affair. Soames accuses Irene of infidelity, and she leaves his house for good. At just this time Philip is killed in an accident which occurs in a fog. The tragic circumstances bring Irene and Young Jolyon together again, and when Soames later agrees to give Irene a divorce, she marries Young Joylon and finds happiness at last.

REVIEWS FOR *That Forsyte Woman*:

"There are moments of dramatic urgency in this M-G-M production, but they are too few and far between to sustain the translation of a celebrated novel." — *New York Herald Tribune*

"Metro has fashioned a long, elaborate and costly class feature out of John Galsworthy's writing about his Victorian family, the Forsytes." — *Variety*

REVIEWS FOR JANET LEIGH: "In addition to the four stars and Miss Leigh, whose role manages to ring truer than the others, there is some capable thespianing by the supporting players." — *Variety*

"Walter Pidgeon portrays with charm the part of the black sheep of the family, and Janet Leigh, ex-hotel receptionist from San Francisco, is very good as his daughter." — *The Mirror* (London)

NOTE: The film was released in the United Kingdom as *The Forsyte Saga*.

Holiday Affair

RKO Radio Pictures; B&W; 87 minutes; Released: November 1949

CREDITS: *Producer:* Don Hartman; *Director:* Don Hartman; *Screenplay:* Isobel Lennart, based on the story *The Man Who Played Santa Claus* by John D. Weaver; *Photography:* Milton R. Krasner; *Art Direction:* Albert S. D'Agostino, Carroll Clark; *Set Decoration:* Darrell Silvera, William Stevens; *Music:* Roy Webb; *Film Editing:* Harry Marker; *Costumes:* Howard Greer; *Makeup:* James House.

CAST: Robert Mitchum (Steve Mason); Janet Leigh (Connie Davis); Wendell Corey (Carl Davis); Gordon Gerbert (Timmy Ennis); Griff Barnett (Mr. Ennis); Esther Dale (Mrs. Ennis); Henry O'Neill (Mr. Crowley); Henry Morgan (Police Lieutenant); Larry J. Blake (Johnson, plainclothes officer); James Griffith (Floor Walker); Helen Brown (Emily); Frances Morris (Mary, housekeeper); Allen Mathews (Mr. Gow); Frank Johnson (Santa Claus).

PLOT: Connie Ennis is a young war widow working as a comparison shopper for a department store chain, selecting items to check on prices and quality. She buys an expensive electric train set from a rival store, although the salesman, Steve Mason, suspects the real purpose. When she returns it the following day, he refunds her money and is fired for failing to report her to his superiors. Far from being resentful, Steve treats Connie to lunch in Central Park and helps her in her comparison shopping, but loses her in a subway rush. At her apartment later Connie meets her young son Timmy and her fiancé Carl Davis, a pompous attorney. While the couple is trimming the Christmas tree, Steve shows up at her home, where Carl storms out after a disturbance with Timmy. Steve tries to mend matters between Connie and her boyfriend. The next morning Timmy finds the electric train returned to him, but Connie realizes that Steve has been the donor, and that he cannot afford it. He refuses to be reimbursed and announces that he is about to go to California. Baffled but intrigued, Connie returns home to prepare Christmas dinner for Carl and her in-laws. Meanwhile, Steve has been arrested on a petty charge. With Carl's help, Connie clears him and brings him home to share the holiday meal. At the table, Carl proudly announces that Connie has agreed to marry him. Steve stuns the assemblage by proposing to Connie herself, along with some kind words for his dismayed rival. Angrily, Connie sends Steve away, much to the disappointment of Timmy. The next morning the lad goes to the department store and gets back the value of the train for Steve, who, he has decided, needs the money. Carl, Connie and the boy seek out Steve. On the way, Carl realizes that Steve will make a better husband for Connie and leaves. Connie and Timmy accompany Steve to California.

REVIEWS FOR *Holiday Affair*:

"A slick and appropriate holiday film." — *New York Herald Tribune*

"A mildly pleasant and generally innocuous tale." — *Cue*

"*Holiday Affair* is a warm Christmas offering."—*Variety*

REVIEWS FOR JANET LEIGH:

"Miss Leigh covers up with pouts and dimples a peculiar shallow selfish dame."—*New York Times*

"Janet Leigh's artful underplaying of the girl gives the role sympathy and understanding."—*Hollywood Reporter*

"Miss Leigh, whose beautiful moulded features form Leicester Square's most frequently encountered film face at the moment ... is a delightful though not often very merry widow."—*The Star* (London)

NOTE: The film was originally advertised as *Christmas Gift*.

Strictly Dishonorable

MGM; B&W; 94 minutes; Released: July 1951

CREDITS: *Producers:* Melvin Frank, Norman Panama *Directors*: Melvin Frank, Norman Panama; *Screenplay*: Melvin Frank, Norman Panama, based on a play by Preston Sturges; *Photography*: Ray June; *Art Direction*: Cedric Gibbons, Hans Peters; *Set Decoration*: Edwin B. Willis, Hugh Hunt; *Music*: Lenny Hayton; *Film Editing*: Cotton Warburton; *Costumes*: Helen Rose; *Makeup*: William Tuttle.

CAST: Ezio Pinza (Augustino "Gus" Caraffa); Janet Leigh (Isabelle Perry); Millard Mitchell (Bill Dempsey); Gale Robbins (Marie Donnelly); Maria Palmer (Countess Lili Szadvany); Esther Minciotti (Mme. Maria Caraffa); Silvio Minciotti (Uncle Nito); Arthur Franz (Henry Greene); Sandro Giglio (Tomasso); Hugh Sanders (Harry Donnelly); Mario Siletti (Luigi).

PLOT: Augustino Caraffa is an opera singer known not only for his talent but also for being a heartthrob. During a fight with publisher Harry Donnelly (because Caraffa has axed the singing efforts of wife Marie), the opera singer meets Isabelle Perry. Perry, a wide-eye innocent girl straight off a Mississippi farm, has long been infatuated with him. Caraffa resists her charms, however, circumstance causes the singer to marry her for convenience. Isabelle really wants to make it an ideal marriage, despite the conniving efforts of the lush Countess Szadvany, who once was an old flame of Caraffa's. All problems are resolved by the finale.

REVIEWS FOR *Strictly Dishonorable*:

"An amusing celluloid treatment of the loves and life of a romantic opera star."—*Variety*

"*Strictly Dishonorable* is not without flaws. There could have been more music and more action. The running time is somewhat long, made by the overdone romantic passages."—*Hollywood Reporter*

"Despite the exigencies of the plot, the film has many genuinely funny moments...."—*Monthly Film Bulletin*

REVIEWS FOR JANET LEIGH:

"Janet Leigh is pretty and appealing with the purified material she has."—*New York Times*

"Miss Leigh is easy to take as the southern girl, adding charm to the footage even though she has trouble maintaining her mushmouth drawl."—*Variety*

"Janet Leigh is engaging as the Southern belle who takes up with a courtly rake in a Manhattan speakeasy."—*Time*

NOTE: *Strictly Dishonorable* was previously filmed in 1931 by John M. Stahl and produced by Universal Pictures. The role of Isabelle Perry was played by Sidney Fox.

Angels in the Outfield

MGM; B&W; 99 minutes; Released: October 1951

CREDITS: *Producer:* Clarence Brown; *Director:* Clarence Brown; *Screenplay:* Dorothy Kingsley, George Welles, based on a story by Richard Colin; *Photography:* Paul C. Vogel; *Art Direction:* Cedric Gibbons, Edward Carfagno; *Set Decoration:* Edwin B. Willis, Hugh Hunt; *Music:* Daniele Amfitheatrof; *Film Editing:* Robert Kern; *Special Effects:* A. Arnold Gillespie, Warren Newcombe; *Makeup:* William Tuttle.

CAST: Paul Douglas (Guffy McGovern); Janet Leigh (Jennifer Paige); Keenan Wynn (Fred Bayles); Donna Corcoran (Bridget White); Lewis Stone (Arnold P. Hapgood); Spring Byington (Sister Edwitha); Bruce Bennett (Saul Hellman); Marvin Kaplan (Timothy Durney); Ellen Corby (Sister Veronica); Jeff Richards (Dave Rothenberg); John Gallaudet (Joe Reynolds); King Donovan (Mack McGee); Don Haggerty (Rube Ronson); Paul Salata (Tony Minelli); Fred Graham ("Chunck," coach); John McKee (Bill Baxter); Patrick J. Molyneaux (Patrick J. Finley); Joe DiMaggio (Himself); Bing Crosby (Himself); Ty Cobb (Himself); Harry Ruby (Himself).

PLOT: Guffy McGovern is the bad-tempered, foul-mouthed manager of the Pittsburgh Pirates, an unsuccessful baseball team. One night, after another disastrous game, an angel offers to help the Pirates if Guffy will learn to moderate his language and his temper. The manager accepts the challenge, and his team makes a sudden remarkable recovery.

When reporter Jennifer Paige, who is assigned to cover the Pirates' season from a new perspective, writes a story about an eight-year-old orphan, Bridget White, who swears she has seen angels during a match at Forbes Field while on an orphanage field trip, she causes a frenzy in the world of baseball. Soon Jennifer and Guffy become involved, and little Bridget works herself into Guffy's heart. When Guffy is hit in the head by a line drive and admits to the press that indeed angels have been helping the team, the baseball commissioner thinks he has gone nuts and starts an investigation into the manager's sanity. Nevertheless, the Pirates go on playing and win the pennant.

REVIEWS FOR *Angels in the Outfield:*

"Clarence Brown, skipping nimbly the theological soft spots in his plot, takes a firm stand against the forces of the Evil." — *Time*

"*Angels in the Outfield* is strictly a pipedream but a very pleasant one." — *New York Times*

"*Angels in the Outfield* doesn't take long to get bogged down in the worst kind of corn, involving nuns, miracles and a heavenly ball team." — *Saturday Review of Literature*

REVIEWS FOR JANET LEIGH:

"Janet Leigh is as attractive a newshawk as you could wish." — *Hollywood Reporter*

"Janet Leigh is pretty although improbable as the 'household hints' reporter." — *New York Times*

"Miss Leigh foils cleverly." — *Variety*

NOTE: Interviewed during his presidency, Dwight Eisenhower named *Angels in the Outfield* his favorite film. He personally worn out three copies. The picture was released in the United Kingdom as *Angels and the Pirates*.

It's a Big Country
MGM; B&W; 88 minutes; Released: November 1951

CREDITS: *Producer:* Robert Sisk, Norman Panama; *Directors:* Clarence Brown, Don Hartman, John Sturges, Richard Thorpe, Charles Vidor, Don Weis, William A. Wellman; *Screenplay:* Melvin Frank, Norman Panama, based on a play by Preston Sturges; *Photography:* John Alton, Ray June, Willam C. Mellor, Joseph Rottemberg; *Art Direction:* Cedric Gibbons, Malcolm Brown, William Ferrari, Eddie Omazu, Arthur Lonergan, Gabriel Scognamillo; *Set Decoration:* Jack Bonar, Ralph S. Hurst, Arthur Krams, Fred M. MacLean, Alfred E. Spencer, Edwin. B. Willis; *Music:* John Green; *Film Editing:* Ben Lewis; Fredrick Y. Smith; *Special Effects:* A. Arnold Gillespie, Warren Newcombe; *Makeup:* William Tuttle.

CAST: Ethel Barrymore (Mrs. Brian Patrick Riordan); Keefe Brasselle (Sgt. Maxie Klein); Nancy Davis (Miss Coleman); Van Johnson (Adam Burch); Gene Kelly (Icarus Xenophon); Janet Leigh (Rosa Szabo); Marjorie Main (Mrs. Wrenley); Fredric March (Papa Esposito); George Murphy (Mr. Callaghan); William Powell (Professor); S. Z. Sakall (Stefan Szabo); Lewis Stone (Church Sexton); James Whitmore (Mr. Stacey); Keenan Wynn (Michael Fisher); Leon Ames (Secret Service Man) Angela Clarke (Mama Esposito); Bobby Hyatt (Joseph Esposito); Sharon McManus (Sam Szabo); Gary Cooper (Texas Cowboy).

PLOT: This is an eight-episode American anthology dealing with life in this country. Directed by Charles Vidor, Janet Leigh appears in the fourth episode, "Rosika, the Rose." Stefan Szabo, a jovial Hungarian immigrant, lives with his five unmarried daughters. The difficulty is not a lack of suitors for his beautiful girls but the lack of Hungarians. They are the only ones, according to him, good enough to marry them. Although he shudders at the thought of his daughters marrying non–Hungarians, he absolutely trembles when it occurs to him that they might even marry Greeks, whom Szabo, with his Old-World prejudices, regards as inferior. So it is with good reason that Rosika, his eldest and most beautiful daughter, conceals the fact that she has fallen in love with Icarus Xenophon, a successful young owner of an ice-cream parlor, and a Greek. Rosika, as far as the family knows, is merely working for Icarus, to which Stefan does not object since she assures him that her boss is married. Only Sam, Rosika's youngest sister, suspects that there is more going on after seeing Icarus kissing Rosika. The infuriated Stefan, with all his daughters in tow, storms into the ice-cream parlor. To the sound of breaking glasses, aid is summoned from the young Greek athletic club across the street. When, in the ensuing confusion, Stefan learns that Icarus and Rosika have been secretly married, and he sees the handsome young Greeks from across the street receiving anything but disinterested attention from his other daughters, his distress knows no bounds. Icarus tries to calm him down by offering a cup of coffee, but he is rebuffed. Never will Stefan drink Greek coffee, but when Icarus reaches under the counter and brings up a can of George Washington brand coffee, the old man looks at it for a moment, sees the light and slowly begins to sip it.

REVIEWS FOR *It's a Big Country:*

"[The picture] is a drum-beating, Fourth of July speech-making tribute to God's Own Country, with seven episodes geared mostly to sentiment or to whimsical comedy."—*Sight & Sound*

"A cheery, sentimental estimation of life in these United States, warmly wrapped up in the sort of optimism most familiar to Hollywood."—*New York Times*

"It is a frank pro–U.S. pitch, sometimes interesting but far from socko."—*Variety*
REVIEWS FOR JANET LEIGH:
"Gene Kelly, Van Johnson, Nancy Davis, Keefe Brasselle, Janet Leigh.... They all work hard, and like the U.S. itself, will undoubtedly survive this soapbox opera."—*Time*
"Gene Kelly and Janet Leigh are appealing as the Greek and the Hungarian lovers."—*Hollywood Reporter*
NOTE: A ninth episode, titled *Load*, directed by Anthony Mann, with Ann Harding and Jean Hersholt, was filmed but deleted.

Two Tickets to Broadway

RKO Radio Pictures; Technicolor; 106 minutes; Released: November 1951

CREDITS: *Producer*: Norman Krasna, Jerry Wald; *Director*: James V. Kern; *Screenplay*: Sid Silvers, Hal Kanter, based on a story by Sammy Cahn; *Photography*: Edward Cronjager, Harry J. Wild; *Art Direction*: Albert D'Agostino, Carroll Clark; *Set Decoration*: Darrell Silvera, Harley Miller; *Music*: Walter Scharf; *Choreography*: Busby Berkeley; *Film Editing*: Harry Marker; *Costumes*: Michael Woulfe, *Makeup*: Mel Berns.

CAST: Tony Martin (Dan Carter); Janet Leigh (Nancy Peterson); Eddie Bracken (Lew Conway); Ann Miller (Joyce Campbell); Barbara Lawrence (S. F. Rogers); Joe Smith (Harry, Palace Deli); Charles Dale (Leo, Palace Deli); Bob Crosby (Himself); Taylor Holmes (Villard Glendon); Buddy Baer (Sailor); The Charlivels (Themselves); Vera Miles (Showgirl, uncredited), George Nader (Sound Technician, uncredited).

PLOT: Through a mix-up in suitcases, Dan Carter and Nancy Peterson meet in a New York bus station. Dan is about to go home to Denver after two years of vainly trying to break into show business as a singer. Nancy has just arrived from a small town with high hopes of quick success on the Broadway stage. On the bus she has made friends with three girls on their way to New York after their show had bombed on a showboat. When Don returns the suitcase to Nancy, they fall in love. Dan's agent, Lew Conway, tells Nancy and her three girlfriends, now sharing an apartment together, that he has a spot for them on a TV show hosted by Bob Crosby. But at the very last moment the shady agent manages to put off the promised audition with Crosby, even after Dan and the girls score a big hit in a benefit show. After the ruse is uncovered, Nancy, heartbroken and thinking that Dan is involved, decides to give up her dreams of a show business career and go home. Soon after, Crosby learns about the hoax attached to his name and he decides to give Dan's act a chance, allowing him to perform that very evening. Frantically, Dan starts reviving the act while Conway looks for Nancy. The con agent finds her boarding a bus for her hometown and convinces her that he, not Dan, had orchestrated the hoax. Running against time through the crowded streets, Nancy arrives at the studio with seconds left in which to kiss Dan before going onstage for the triumphant finale.

REVIEWS FOR *Two Tickets to Broadway*:
"[The picture] is merely conventional in plot, brisk in pace, heavily freighted with song and light in comedy."—*New York Times*
"[The picture is] a breezy Technicolor musical replete with shapely gals and catchy tunes."—*Variety*
"*Two Tickets to Broadway* is an enchanting Technicolor musical, somewhat overlong in its present form, but otherwise an entertainment delight packed with bouncing

good humor and an array of specialties encompassing virtually everything in the revue book." — *Hollywood Reporter*

REVIEWS FOR JANET LEIGH:

"Janet Leigh is adequate as the heroine." — *Monthly Film Bulletin*

"Janet Leigh ... implements her fresh beauty with provocative singing and dancing ability." — *Hollywood Reporter*

NOTE: Viewers can spot actress Vera Miles in a bit part as a showgirl. In 1960 she would co-star with Leigh in Hitchcock's *Psycho*. Songs included in *Two Tickets to Broadway* are: "Let the Worry Bird Worry for You"; "Pagliacci"; "There's No Tomorrow"; "Manhattan"; "Big Chief Hole in the Ground"; "The Closer You Are"; "Baby, You'll Never Be Sorry"; "Pelican Falls High"; "It Began in Yucatan"; "Are You a Beautiful Dream?"; "Let's Make Comparison."

John Aalberg was nominated for an Academy Award for Best Sound Recording.

Just This Once

MGM; B&W; 90 minutes; Released: March 1952

CREDITS: *Producer*: Henry Berman; *Director*: Don Weis; *Screenplay*: Sidney Sheldon, based on a story by Max Trell; *Photography*: Ray June; *Art Direction*: Cedric Gibbons, James Basevi; *Set Decoration*: Edwin B. Willis, Keogh Gleason; *Music*: David Rose; *Film Editing*: Fredrick Y. Smith; *Makeup*: William Tuttle.

CAST: Janet Leigh (Lucy Duncan); Peter Lawford (Mark MacLene); Lewis Stone (Judge Samuel Coulter); Marilyn Erskine (Gertrude Crome); Richard Anderson (Tom Winters); Douglas Fowley (Frank Pirosh); Hanley Stafford (Mr. Blackwell); Henry Slate (Jeff Parma); Jerry Hausner (Stanley Worth); Benny Rubin (Herbert Engel); Charles Watts (Adam Backwith).

PLOT: Lucy Duncan, an obstinately efficient but attractive woman lawyer, is appointed by a judge as financial guardian to a spendthrift young millionaire, Mark MacLene. When she forbids him to spend money and allows him only a very inadequate weekly allowance, he decides that the most economical way to live is to move in to her apartment, proving his right to be there by a point of law that says he must be cared for, fed and housed. This causes friction between Lucy and her dull and frugal fiancé, Tom Winters. Mark even pretends to go to work to please Lucy. He gives her a taste of what it is like when a husband talks constantly about his work. Lucy comes to realize that there is more to life than money, that the rich have their point of view too. After falling in love with Mark, she finally agrees to marry him on his own terms: If someone inherits money it is sensible to spend it in the way which brings the owner the most enjoyment.

REVIEWS FOR *Just This Once*:

"Patrons below the age of 20 and above, let us say, 15 may find some remote amusement." — *New York Times*

"A gay, pleasantly-paced round of comedy is offered by *Just This Once*. Film has a youthful spirit." — *Variety*

"An amusing comedy, made with pace and some witty, if rather theatrical, dialogue." — *Monthly Film Bulletin*

REVIEWS FOR JANET LEIGH:

"Janet Leigh's bouncy, vivacious personality is put to good use in this attractive role." — *Hollywood Reporter*

"Miss Leigh is nice to look upon."—*New York Times*

NOTE: The script of *Just This Once* was written by Sidney Sheldon, who would later become a prolific bestselling novelist, with more than 300 million copies of his books sold worldwide.

Scaramouche

MGM; Lowe's Inc.; Technicolor; 115 minutes; Released: May 1952

CREDITS: *Producer:* Carey Wilson; *Director:* George Sidney; *Screenplay:* Ronald Millar, George Froeschel, based on the novel by Rafael Sabatini; *Photography:* Charles Rosher; *Art Direction:* Cedric Gibbons, Hans Peters; *Special Effects:* Warren Newcombe, A. Arnold Gillespie, Irving G. Ries; *Set Decoration:* Edwin B. Willis, Richard Pefferle; *Costumes:* Gile Steele; *Music:* Victor Young; *Film Editing:* James E. Newcom; *Makeup:* William Tuttle.

CAST: Stewart Granger (Andre Moreau / Scaramouche); Eleanor Parker (Lenore); Mel Ferrer (Noel, Marquis de Maynes); Janet Leigh (Aline de Gravillac); Henry Wilcoxon (Chevalier de Chabrillaine); Lewis Stone (Georges de Valmorin); Nina Foch (Marie Antoinette); Richard Anderson (Philippe de Valmorin); Robert Coote (Gaston Binet); Elizabeth Risdon (Isabelle de Valmorin); Howard Freeman (Michael Vanneau); Curtis Cooksey (Fabian); John Dehner (Doutreval); John Litel (Dr. Dubuque); Johonathan Cott (Sergeant); Dan Foster (Pierrot); Owen McGiveney (Punchinello); Hope Landing (M.M. Frying Pan); Frank Mitchell (Harlequin); Carol Hughes (Pierrette); Richard Hale (Perigore); Henry Corden (Scaramouche, the Dinker); John Elderidge (Clerk); Mitchell Lewis (Major Domo); Ottola Nesmith (Lady-in-Waiting); Dorothy Patrick (Dorie); John Sheffield (Flunky); Douglas Dumbrille (President); Frank Wilcox (De Crillon); Anthony Marsh (Capelier); John Crawford (Vignon); Bert LeBaron (Fencing Opponent).

PLOT: Andre Moreau, a vivid, resourceful character who is the illegitimate son of a French nobleman, becomes involved in Revolutionary affairs through his friend Philippe de Valmorine. Philippe is a young reformer who has written a pamphlet called "Liberty, Equality and Fraternity," for which the King's men are after him. Andre endeavors to help him escape from inevitable arrest. During their journey he and Philippe pass a coach with a broken wheel. Nearby, helpless, there languishes a young and beautiful girl. With engaging impudence, Andre orders Philippe to help mend the wheel; and when it is done, Andre rides with the girl in the coach to her home, falling in love with her on the way. He learns that her name is Aline de Gavrillac; and the Count de Gravillac, as he has recently discovered, is his father. Aline, therefore, is his half-sister. When they arrive at the seat of the Gavrillacs, the Count is found dead. Later, Andre joins Philippe at an inn. Here Philippe is arrested by the King's men and is provoked into a duel by the Marquis de Maynes, who, as the best swordsman in France, has promised Queen Marie Antoinette that he will pursue and personally destroy the author of the pamphlet "Liberty, Equality and Fraternity." Andre attempts to save Philippe from the duel but is held at sword-point by de Maynes's friend. Philippe is killed. Andre breaks away and, after vowing to avenge his friend, makes his escape. He is pursued but avoids capture when he takes refuge with a traveling company of actors. One of the troupe is an old sweetheart, Leonore. In the guise of Scaramouche, a clown, he takes part in the show, which is a success. Andre escapes recognition when the King's men search the theater and is accepted by the troupe. It is during this time that, with the object of fulfilling his vow, he takes secret fencing lessons from de Maynes's personal instructor. However, when De Maynes makes a surprise visit to his instructor and discovers him tutoring Andre, he challenges Andre to a duel. Andre is saved by Aline's intervention, who is unaware that Andre is her half-brother and is still deeply in love with him; but she has been chosen by Marie Antoinette to be de Maynes' bride. With Andre still playing Scaramouche, the troupe moves to Paris. And it is when de Maynes and Aline attend their show that Scaramouche reveals his identity, and from the stage provokes de Maynes into a duel. Andre is unable, however, to deliver the final thrust. He is then informed that de Maynes is indeed his half-brother. The fact not only reunites the two brothers but also frees Andre to marry Aline, whom he now knows is not his sister.

REVIEWS FOR *Scaramouche*:

"For solid entertainment, swashbuckling action and delightful, tongue-in-cheek humor *Scaramouche* must take its place among MGM's top epics." — *Hollywood Reporter*

"Lavishly produced and beautifully designed." — *Cue*

"More affected than exciting." — *New York Herald Tribune*

REVIEWS FOR JANET LEIGH:

"In the low gowns-powdered wigs department, Janet Leigh looks mighty good as the Bourbon Doll." — *New York Times*

"Miss Leigh is just an ingénue and not much more can be said. She plays the part that Alice Terry had in the original." — *Variety*

"Janet Leigh is a delight to look at in the romantic lead." — *Hollywood Reporter*

NOTE: MGM previously produced a silent version in 1923, directed by Rex Ingram and starring Ramon Novarro as Scaramouche. The role of Aline was played by Alice Terry.

Fearless Fagan

MGM; B&W; 78 minutes; Released: July 1952

CREDITS: *Producer:* Edwin H. Knopf; *Director:* Stanley Donen; *Screenplay:* Charles Lederer, from an adaptation by Fredrick Hazlitt Brennan, based on a story by Sidney Franklin, Jr., and Eldon W. Griffiths; *Photography:* Harold Lipstein; *Art Direction:* Cedric Gibbons, Leonid Vasian; *Set Decoration:* Edwin B. Willis, Fred M. MacLean; *Music:* Rudolph G. Kopp; *Special Effects:* A. Arnold Gillespie; *Film Editing:* George White; *Makeup:* William Tuttle.

CAST: Janet Leigh (Abby Ames); Carleton Carpenter (Pvt. Floyd Hilston of Company J); Keenan Wynn (Sgt. Kellwin of Company J); Richard Anderson (Capt. Daniels of Company J); Ellen Corby (Mrs. Ardley); Barbara Ruick (Nurse); John Call (Mr. Ardley); Robert Burton (Owen Gillman); Wilton Graff (Col. Horne); Parley Baer (Emil Tauchnitz); Jonathan Cott (Cpl. Geft of Company J).

PLOT: Floyd Hilston's career with a small traveling circus, in which he does an act with an unusual four-year-old, 400-pound lion, Fearless Fagan, is interrupted when he is drafted into the U.S. Army. Refusing to leave the lion behind because he is the only person who can handle him, Floyd hides him in the forest in an outlying section of the Army post. But Fagan is accidentally discovered by a Hollywood star, Abby Ames, who has come to the post to entertain the troops; and when she gives Floyd's secret away, his tough sergeant, Kellwin, orders him to find another home for the lion. But no one will have him — until the publicity results in an offer from a farm couple who consent to board him. Fagan, however, escapes from his cage on the farm to return to his master, and this time Floyd's commanding officer insists that he sell the lion to his former circus. Dissuaded by Abby from running away with Fagan, he finally submits, but when the circus animal trainer, Emil Tauchnitz, comes for Fagan and attempts to handle him with a whip, the lion attacks him and is wounded by a shot from Kellwin's gun. Floyd pursues Fagan into the woods, and when he catches up with him the frightened lion springs at him. But Fagan is subsequently subdued by Floyd and enticed into his cage by Abby, just as Fagan would have been put down. Abby comes to Floyd with the joyful news that she has interested a Hollywood producer in his story. Fagan is going to be a movie star, and Floyd and Abby are going to live romantically ever after.

REVIEWS FOR *Fearless Fagan*:

"A funny comedy ... Stanley Donen deserves laurels for his skillful integration of animal scenes with a moving story." — *Variety*

"The film starts with quite a nice little idea but mixes the comedy with boringly inflated sentiments." — *Monthly Film Bulletin*

"*Fearless Fagan* is a merry little romp, with the lion's share of the acting honors going to Fagan." — *Time*

REVIEWS FOR JANET LEIGH:

"Janet Leigh supplies the feminine charm in most satisfactory fashion, also getting over several hearty laughs with some delicate comedy touches." — *Hollywood Reporter*

NOTE: The song "The Loveliest Night of the Year," which is used to sooth Fagan throughout the film, was featured in *The Great Caruso* (Richard Thorpe, 1951), with Mario Lanza. The uncredited song "What Do You Think I Am?," performed by Janet Leigh to entertain the troops, was taken from *Best Foot Forward* (Edward Buzzell, 1943).

The Naked Spur

MGM; Technicolor; 91 minutes; Released: March 1953

CREDITS: *Producer:* William H. Wright; *Director:* Anthony Mann; *Screenplay:* Sam Rolfe, Harold Jack Bloom; *Photography:* William Mellor; *Art Direction:* Cedric Gibbons, Malcolm Brown; *Set Decoration:* Edwin B. Willis; *Music:* Bronislau Kaper; *Special Effects:* Warren Newcombe; *Film Editing:* George White; *Makeup:* William Tuttle.

CAST: James Stewart (Howard Kemp); Janet Leigh (Lina Patch); Robert Ryan (Ben Vandergroat), Millard Mitchell (Jesse Tate); Ralph Meeker (Roy Anderson).

PLOT: Howard Kemp, tempted by a "dead or alive" $5,000 reward, pursues killer Ben Vandergroat into the mountain country and, aided by Jesse Tate, an old prospector, catches up with his quarry on a high cliff. The sound of gunfire as Kemp shoots at Ben attracts young Roy Anderson, en route home after a dishonorable discharge from the U.S. Cavalry; and it is Roy who climbs the cliff to trap Ben. He finds him with Lina Patch, a homeless girl whom Ben has taken under his wing. As Kemp prepares to start back to Kansas with his prisoner, Tate and Roy demand to come along; and Ben slyly begins to play each man against the other. When they spot a band of Blackfeet Indians following them, Roy admits that the Indians have been trailing him, bent on revenge for a past incident with the tribe. When Kemp and Tate refuse to protect him, Roy rides on alone, then doubles back and opens fire on the Indians.

In the gun battle that follows, the Blackfeet are overcome, but Kemp is wounded in the leg. Lina nurses him, and he is out of danger by morning. But the delay has enabled a storm to catch them before they reach an already swollen river, and they take refuge in a cave. During the night Ben causes a cave-in by kicking a rock from its position and attempts to escape, but is overtaken by Kemp. Tension mounts higher when they reach the river and find it impassable. When Roy insists on swimming it, with Ben in tow, he and Kemp come to blows, with Kemp the victor. Now Ben makes a deal with Tate in which he will tell him of the whereabouts of a gold mine in return for his release. But after Ben, Tate and Lina get away, Ben suddenly turns on Tate and kills the old man. Taking cover overlooking the trail, he waits for Kemp and Roy to arrive. As the latter come upon Tate's body, Ben takes aim, but before he can fire, Lina tackles him. He knocks her aside and continues firing but is finally cut down by shots from Roy's gun, and his body topples into the river. Determined not to lose their valuable prize, Roy swims the river and gets a rope around Ben, but is struck by an uprooted tree and swept out of sight. Kemp pulls Ben's body to shore to tell Lina he's taking him back for the reward, despite her plea to bury him and forget the money. But Lina's love wins him over. Placing Ben's body next to Tate, he begins to dig. Life ahead with Lina brings the promise of a bright beginning.

REVIEWS FOR *The Naked Spur*:

"[The picture] is economical with words, generous in deeds, both dastardly and noble, and swiftly paced in settings that are superb and seemingly just created for Technicolor."—*New York Times*.

"The forthright story-telling ... has excellent performances from its five stars."—*Variety*

"*The Naked Spur* ambitiously tries to dig into the theme of human greed, but it is neither a *Greed* nor a *Treasure of the Sierra Madre*. Nonetheless, Director Anthony Mann has richly fleshed out the picture with the red meat of action."—*Time*

REVIEWS FOR JANET LEIGH:

"Miss Leigh is fiery and appealing as the girl and looks lovely, although her poodle-cut hairdo seems incongruous for the post–Civil War period."—*Hollywood Reporter*

"Janet Leigh, as Lina, makes a somewhat unlikely recruit to the ranks of the western wildcats."—*Monthly Film Bulletin*

"Ralph Meeker ... as well as Janet Leigh, a spitfire of a woman whose allegiance to her captive protector wanes as his character is exposed, contribute equally fine stints."—*New York Times*.

NOTE: The screenplay by Sam Rolfe and Harold Jack Bloom was nominated for an Academy Award; however, it lost out to the screenplay for *Titanic*.

Confidentially Connie

MGM; B&W; 71 minutes; Released: March 1953

CREDITS: *Producer*: Stephen Ames; *Director*: Edward Buzzell; *Screenplay*: Max Shulman, based on a story by Max Shulman and Herman Wouk; *Photography*: Harold Lipstein; *Art Direction*: Cedric Gibbons, Leonid Vasian; *Set Decoration*: Edwin B. Willis, Ralph S. Hurst; *Music*: Davide Rose; *Film Editing*: Fredrick Y. Smith.

CAST: Van Johnson (Joe Bedloe); Janet Leigh (Connie Bedloe); Louis Calhern (Opie Bedloe); Walter Slezak (Emil Spangenberg, butcher); Gene Lockhart (Dean Edward E. Magruder); Hayden Rorke (Professor Simmons); Robert Burton (Dr. Willis Shoop);

Marilyn Erskine (Phyllis Archibald); Kathleen Lockhart (Mrs. Martha Magruden); Arthur Space (Prof. Archie Archibald); Barbara Ruick / Barbara); June Whitley (Betty Simmons); Dick Sands (Moska).

PLOT: A wealthy Texan rancher, Opie Bedloe, visits his college instructor son, Joe, and his daughter-in-law Connie, in hopes of persuading Joe to give up his teaching career and take over the Texas ranch properties. When he finds out that Connie is expecting a baby and cannot have the steaks she yearns for because they are beyond her means, he arranges for her butcher, Spangenberg, to cut his price in half (with Opie covering the deficit), so Connie can have all the meat she desires. Spangenberg's reduced prices, however, lead to a price war between the town's butchers. Shocked that teachers cannot afford steak, Opie gives an endowment to the college to raise their salaries; he also tells the Dean that Joe will be returning to Texas and won't want a promotion. Joe is outraged at his father's machinations, but is finally persuaded of his good intentions and agrees to spend his summer vacations on the ranch. And when the baby is born, the family heads out for Texas, where Connie can get all the steaks she wants and a proud Opie looks upon his grandson as a future cattleman.

REVIEWS FOR *Confidentially Connie*:

"A fairly entertaining programmer."—*Hollywood Reporter*

"An entertaining, spiritedly domestic comedy."—*Variety*

"Although not in the first rank of MGM comedies, this is a film which can be enjoyed."—*Monthly Film Bulletin*

REVIEWS FOR JANET LEIGH: "Van Johnson, the professor, [and] Janet Leigh, as his wife ... are highly competent in their individual roles."—*Harrison's Report*

"Miss Leigh and Johnson team excellently."—*Variety*

"Performances by Johnson and Miss Leigh are charmingly competent."—*Hollywood Reporter*

NOTE: The working titles of this film were *A Steak for Connie* and *Connie*. The order of cast names in the opening credits differs slightly from the order of the end credits.

Houdini

Paramount Pictures; Technicolor; 106 minutes; Released: July 1953

CREDITS: *Producers:* George Pal, Frank Freeman, Jr.; *Director:* George Marshall; *Screenplay:* Philip Yordan, based on the book by Harold Kellock; *Photography:* Ernest Laszlo; *Art Direction:* Hal Pereira, Al Nozaki; *Special Effects:* Gordon Jennings; *Set Decoration:* Sam Corner, Ray Moyer; *Costumes:* Edith Head; *Music:* Roy Webb; *Film Editing:* George Tomasini; *Makeup:* Wally Westmore.

CAST: Tony Curtis (Harry Houdini); Janet Leigh (Bess Houdini); Angela Clarke (Mrs. Weiss); Torin Thatcher (Otto); Ian Wolfe (Fante); Stefan Schnabel (German Prosecuting Attorney); Sig Ruman (Schultz); Michael Pate (Dooley); Peter Baldwin (Fred), Connie Gilchrist (Mrs. Schultz); Douglas Spencer (Simms); Barry Bernard (Insp. Marlick); Malcom Lee Beggs (British Jail Warden); Frank Orth (Mr. Hunter); Mabel Paige (Medium); Lawrence Ryle (German Judge).

PLOT: Harry Houdini is a struggling twenty-one-year-old magician working in a New York dime museum as "Bruto the Wild Man." There he meets schoolgirl Bess, and after a quick courtship they are married. She becomes part of his magical acts but, discouraged by the rude treatment of the audiences, persuades him to leave his career and take a job in a safe and lock factory. Harry's new job allows him to learn the inner secrets of the devices, heightening his interest in escapology. One night Harry takes Bess to a magician's convention where he wins a round-trip ticket to Europe by freeing himself from a strait jacket. The couple travels to London, where Houdini wows audiences by escaping from a variety of supposedly "escape-proof" devices, including a jail. His fame spreads throughout Europe, and in Berlin he attempts to contact Von Schweger, an old magician who had perfected a trick of escaping from a large sealed bottle. Before they can meet, Von Schweger dies, but his assistant Otto agrees to return to America with the Houdinis. Back in his country Houdini is still relatively unknown and embarks on a series of death-defying stunts, determined to become a sensation. His dream is fulfilled; however, with the death of his beloved mother, Harry deserts the stage for over two years, turning all his attention to attempts to communicate with her through mediums. He only succeeds in exposing phony mediums. He eventually returns to the stage to perform an escape from a sealed tank of water while suspended head down and tied in a straight jacket. His appendix bursts while he is in the water, and when Bess screams, his assistant smashes the tank to free him, but he dies in his wife's arms.

REVIEWS FOR *Houdini*:

"A typical screen biography, presenting a rather fanciful version of Houdini's life, is contained in this lengthy Technicolor drama."—*Variety*

"With firmer direction, and with make-up that indicated ageing through more than powdered temples, Tony Curtis and Janet Leigh might well have been convincing."—*Monthly Film Bulletin*

"[The film] is hardly spellbinding ... not precisely cleaves to the truth and rarely breaks away from standard screen fiction."—*New York Times*

REVIEWS FOR JANET LEIGH:

"Curtis and Miss Leigh make a winning team, playing the love scenes with moving tenderness and performing many of the magic tricks themselves."—*Hollywood Reporter*

"As Houdini's wife and assistant, Janet Leigh (Mrs. Curtis in real life) is another cute trick."—*Time*

"As his wife, Janet Leigh is decorative but little else."—*The New Yorker*

NOTE: *Houdini* was the first film in which Janet and her husband Tony Curtis appeared together. Fifty-two costumes were exclusively designed for Janet's character by legendary Hollywood costume designer Edith Head.

Walking My Baby Back Home

Universal International Pictures; Technicolor;
95 minutes; Released: December 1953

CREDITS: *Producers*: Ted Richmond, Leonard Goldstein; *Director*: Lloyd Bacon; *Screenplay*: Don McGuire, Oscar Brodney; *Photography*: Irving Glassberg; *Art Direction*: Bernard Herzbrun, Emrich Nicholson; *Set Decoration*: Russell A. Gausman, Julia Heron; *Costumes*: Jay A. Morley, Jr.; *Music*: Henry Mancini; *Choreography*: Louis DaPron; *Film Editing*: Ted J. Kent; *Makeup*: Bud Westmore.

CAST: Donald O'Connor (Clarence "Jigger" Millard); Janet Leigh (Chris Hall); Buddy Hackett ("Blimp" Edwards); Lori Nelson (Claire Millard); "Scat Man" Crothers ("Smiley" Gordon); Kathleen Lockhart (Mrs. Millard); George Cleveland ("Colonel" Dan Wallace); John Hubbard (Rodney Millard); Norman Abbott (Doc); Phil Garris

(Hank); Walter Kingsford (Uncle Henry Hall); Sidney Miller (Walter Thomas); The Modernaires (Themselves); The Sportsmen (Themselves).

PLOT: After four years in the army, Private Jigger Millard is returned to the States and discharged. A clarinetist, he has organized an orchestra among his friends, with pretty Chris Hall, a W.A.C. sergeant, as the singer. Jigger's right-hand man is chubby pianist "Blimp" Edwards. They plan to continue the orchestra in civilian life — all except Chris, who has fallen in love with Jigger. She feels that he will never be in love with anything except his musical career. Accordingly, she goes to work with an uncle, "Colonel" Wallace, who runs a touring minstrel show. Jigger returns home to his rich Park Avenue family, only to be told that his grandfather, believing that Jigger had singing talent, left him a $5,000 fund for singing lessons. If Jigger makes good at a public concert, he inherits his grandfather's fortune. Jigger takes the $5,000, but instead of spending it on voice lessons, he uses it to form his band. He tries to get a band agent interested in the group, but the agent insists that their music is too symphonic. The band goes broke. One by one the members walk out on Jigger until only he and "Blimp" are left. As they work their way back to New York, they come across the "Colonel" Wallace minstrel troupe. Jigger and "Blimp" join the show, and Jigger and Chris are thrown together again. This time Jigger discovers he is in love with her. When the troupe finally disbands, Jigger persuades one of the members, Smiley, to form a new band with him. All the old group return and begin rehearsals, combining symphonic and jazz music. Jigger is desperate when his family informs him that they are in bad financial shape, and to assure that he inherit all of his late grandfather's money, they have arranged for his immediate singing debut. Hearing of the concert and believing that Jigger is double-crossing them, Chris and the other members of the band decide to pack up. Chris changes her mind, though, when she learns that Jigger is only going through with the concert in an attempt to save his family. On the night of the concert the band appears on stage at a last minute to rescue Jigger, who has lost his voice and is playback singing. The critics are so pleased with the new style of music that they proclaim Jigger a musical genius, thereby assuring him of his grandfather's inheritance.

REVIEWS FOR *Walking My Baby Back Home*:

"*Walking My Baby Back Home* is a musical with its brain and its feet." — *Time*

"The confused plot is not improved by feeble dialogue and rather indifferent jokes." — *Monthly Film Bulletin*

"*Walking My Baby Back Home* ... is one of those familiar medium budget musicals, filmed in vulgar colors, stuffed to bursting with slick song and dance sequences and impaled on an impossible and unbelievable story line." — *New York Time*

REVIEWS FOR JANET LEIGH:

"Miss Leigh is charming in the femme lead, managing to look cute and sexy at the same time in the eye popping Jay A. Morley, Jr., gowns and singing "The Glow Worm" with The Sportsmen and "South Rampart Street Parade" with The Modernaires in a small but pleasant voice. She also solos on "Camptown Races" and does some simple stepping, the choreography being skillfully designed by Louis DaPron to utilize her natural grace." — *Hollywood Reporter*

"Miss Leigh is made to look ridiculous in two of her musical numbers costumes by exaggerated aids to nature that are completely unnecessary in her case." — *Variety*

"With the production numbers enhanced by Miss Leigh, who presents an engaging

façade, dances quaintly and is decorative, this musical cornucopia is not a total loss."—
New York Times

NOTE: Songs included in *Walking My Baby Back Home* are: "The Glow Worm,"
"De Camptown Races," "South Rampart Street Parade," "Walkin' My Baby Back
Home," "Honeysuckle Rose," "Muskat Ramble," "Man's Gotta Eat!," "Liebestraum,"
"Hi Lee, Hi Low," and "Largo Al Factotum Della Città." Paula Kelly of the Moder-
naires dubbed Janet Leigh's voice for "De Camptown Races."

Prince Valiant

20th Century–Fox; Technicolor; 100 minutes; Released: April 1954

CREDITS: *Producer:* Robert L. Jacks; *Director:* Henry Hathaway; *Screenplay:* Dudley
Nichols, based on the comic strip by Harold R. Foster; *Photography:* Lucien Ballard;
Art Direction: Lyle Wheeler, Mark-Lee Kirk; *Set Decoration:* Stuart Reiss, Walter M.
Scott; *Costumes:* Charles le Maire; *Music:* Franz Waxman; *Film Editing:* Robert Simp-
son; *Makeup:* Ben Nye.

CAST: Robert Wagner (Prince Valiant); James Mason (Sir Brack); Janet Leigh (Aleta);
Debra Paget (Ilene); Sterling Hayden (Sir Gawain); Victor McLaglen (Boltar); Donald
Crisp (King Aguar); Brian Aherne (King Arthur); Barry Jones (King Luke); Mary
Philips (Queen); Howard Wendell (Morgan Todd); Tom Conway (Sir Kay); Sammy
Ogg (Small Page); Neville Brand (Viking Warrior Chief); Ben Wright (Seneschal);
Jarma Lewis (Queen Guinevere); Robert Adler (Sir Black's Man-at-Arms); Ray Spiker
(Gorlock); Primo Carnera (Sligon); Basil Ruysdael (Old Viking); Fortune Gordon
(Strangler); Percival Vivian (Doctor); Don Megowan (Sir Lancelot); Richard Webb
(Sir Galahad); John Dierkes (Sir Tristram); Otto Waldis (Patch Eye); John Davidson
(Patriarch).

PLOT: Prince Valiant, son of the exiled King Aguar of Scandia, comes to Camelot
to seek King Arthur's help against the usurper Sligon. On the way, he narrowly escapes
a mysterious Black Knight, whom he overhears plotting to deliver Aguar and his
family to Sligon in return for aid in overthrowing King Arthur. Valiant hurriedly
warns King Arthur, who subsequently rewards him by making him a squire to Sir
Gawain, although another Knight of the Round Table, Sir Brack, asks for Valiant's
services. As a pupil of Gawain, Valiant learns how to handle a sword and quickly
become a valuable asset to Camelot. Impressed with his derring-do, Princess Aleta
falls madly in love with him. Later Prince Valiant receives word from his father,
requesting his assistance, and quickly rides off to help. Along the way, however, he is
ambushed by the Black Knight, whom he discovers is Sir Brack in disguise. Together
with Princess Aleta, Valiant is taken to Scandia where Sligon throws him into a dun-
geon with his parents. Nevertheless, he gets help from Boltar and his loyal Viking fol-
lowers, who help him storm the castle. Aleta is rescued as Valiant burns down the
castle. On his safe return to Camelot, Valiant exposes Sir Brack as the villain and,
after an exciting duel, kills him. King Arthur rewards Prince Valiant by knighting
him and by giving him the hand of Princess Aleta.

REVIEWS FOR *Prince Valiant*:

"Splendidly photographed and costumed ... deliciously comic."— *The Star* (London)

"A good offering for those fans who dote on the fanciful derring-do of the Arthurian
period."— *Variety*

"A glorious tale of a thrillingly swashbuckling style that will delight the huge following of Harold Foster's King Feature comic strip." — *Hollywood Reporter*

REVIEWS FOR JANET LEIGH:

"Janet Leigh and Debra Paget flawlessly epitomize the traditional lovely princesses who inspire knights to mighty deeds." — *Hollywood Reporter*

"James Mason, Brian Aherne, Barry Jones, Janet Leigh, Debra Paget and Sterling Hayden ... they all struck me as very imparfit knights and ladies." — *The New Yorker*

"The acting — by a cast that includes James Mason, Victor McLaglen, Brian Aherne, Barry Jones, Donald Crisp, Robert Wagner, Janet Leigh and Debra Paget — is so absent-minded as to seem downright disinterested." — *Film Reviews*

NOTE: During the entire production of Prince Valiant, Robert Wagner had to join Janet Leigh and Debra Paget for his hair and make-up each morning.

Living It Up

Paramount Pictures; Technicolor; 94 minutes; Released: July 1954

CREDITS: *Producer:* Paul Jones; *Director:* Norman Taurog; *Screenplay:* Jack Rose, Melville Shavelson, based on the musical comedy *Hazel Flagg* by James Street, and on a story by James H. Street and a book by Ben Hecht; *Photography:* Daniel Fapp; *Art Direction:* Hal Pereira, Albert Nozaki; *Special Effects:* John P. Fulton; *Set Decoration:* Sam Comer, Emile Kuri; *Costumes:* Edith Head; *Music:* Walter Scharf; *Choreography:* Nick Castle; *Film Editing:* Archie Marshek.

CAST: Dean Martin (Dr. Steve Harris); Jerry Lewis (Homer Flagg); Janet Leigh (Wally Cook); Edward Arnold (Mayor of New York); Fred Clark (Oliver Stone); Sheree North (Jitterbug Dancer); Sammy White (Waiter); Sid Tomack (Master of Ceremonies); Sig Ruman (Dr. Emile Egelhofer); Richard Loo (Dr. Lee); Raymong Greenleaf (Conductor), Walter Baldwin (Isaiah Jackson).

PLOT: Homer Flagg, the station master of Desert Hole, New Mexico, yearns for a new life in New York. Attempting to run away, he steals an abandoned car, unaware that it has been used by the army for atomic research purposes. The story that Homer is dying of radioactive poisoning is broadcast throughout the nation. In New York, Wally Cook, a newspaper reporter, sells her publisher the idea of bringing Homer to New York for one last fling at life, a stunt that should boost the paper's circulation. She goes to Desert Hole to make the offer to Homer. He accepts, in spite of the fact that his doctor, Steve Harris, has found that he is *not* dying. Homer and Harris go to New York and they are celebrated at the airport, at the hotel, and at a jitterbug contest by the city officials. When Wally finds out that Homer is a fraud, she persuades him to write a fake suicide note and pretend to jump off a pier. When the news breaks, tons of New Yorkers converge on the pier to stop him. It all ends with a big public funeral for Homer, very much alive, watching with Steve the proceedings from the curbside. In the meantime, the Mayor secretly marries Wally and Steve and gives both Steve and Homer jobs as New York street cleaners.

REVIEWS FOR *Living It Up*:

"*Living It Up* is easily the best Martin and Lewis picture since *The Stooge*." — *Hollywood Reporter*

"It is the poorest Martin and Lewis comedy yet produced, for the comedy throughout is forced and ineffective." — *Harrison's Report*

"It is one of the best [Martin and Lewis] have had, a more amusing film than they have made since *That's My Boy*.... [It is] carefully mounted and employs some excellent supporting comic characters."—*Monthly Film Bulletin*

REVIEWS FOR JANET LEIGH:

"Miss Leigh is just plain adorable as the reporter, revealing a neat flair for comedy and also looking beautiful in some gorgeous Edith Head gowns."—*Hollywood Reporter*

"Miss Leigh is a pretty package to add looks to the comedy."—*Variety*

"Janet Leigh ... adds body to the fun but no flavor."—*Time*

NOTE: *Living It Up* is a remake of the screwball comedy *Nothing Sacred* (William A. Wellman, 1937), giving Jerry Lewis the part originally played by Carol Lombard, and Janet Leigh the part originally played by Fredric March.

The Black Shield of Falworth
Universal International Pictures; Technicolor; CinemaScope; 99 minutes; Released: September 1954

CREDITS: *Producers*: Robert Arthur, Melville Tucker; *Director*: Rudolph Maté; *Screenplay*: Oscar Brodney, based on the novel *Men of Iron* by Howard Pyle; *Photography*: Irving Glassberg; *Art Direction*: Alexander Golitzen, Richard H. Riedel; *Set Decoration*: Russell A. Gausman, Oliver Emert; *Costumes*: Rosemary Odell; *Music*: Joseph Gershenson; *Special Effects*; Fred Knoth; *Film Editing*: Ted J. Kent; *Makeup*: Bud Westmore.

CAST: Tony Curtis (Myles Falworth); Janet Leigh (Lady Anne); David Farrar (Gilbert Blunt, Earl of Alban); Barbara Rush (Meg Falworth); Herbert Marshall (William, Earl of Mackworth); Rhys Williams (Diccon Bowaman); Daniel O'Herlihy (Prince Hal); Torin Thatcher (Sir James); Ian Keith (King Henry IV); Patrick O'Neal (Walter Blunt); Craig Hill (Francis Guascoyne); Doris Lloyd (Dame Ellen); Leonard Mudie (Friar Edward); Charles Fitz Simons (Giles); Gary Montgomery (Peter); Claud Allister (Sir George); Robin Camp (Roger Ingoldsby).

PLOT: The throne of Henry IV, King of England, is threatened by the treachery of Gilbert Blunt, Earl of Alban, who has the complete confidence of the ailing King. The King believes his son and heir a drunkard and irresponsible. While Prince Hal, whose drunkenness is an act to fool Alban, is visiting the castle of William, Earl of Mackworth, who is loyal to the King, a peasant arrives with two charges whom he had raised from infancy. Their family name a secret, this brother and sister are known only as Myles and Meg. The two are taken into the Mackworth household where Myles receives the training of a squire. Here, too, he meets and falls in love with his host's lovely daughter, Lady Anne, and also runs afoul of Walter Blunt, brother of the Earl of Alban and ardent pursuer of the hand of Lady Anne. Mackworth soon orders that Myles be given arduous training for knighthood, for the boy's strength and skill convince him that here is the person to save the King from the scheming Alban. Myles is ready for his first test match in strength and skill, and is knighted by the King at Mackworth Castle before competing against a visiting French champion of the joust. It is at this knighting ceremony that the King and the Earl of Alban, and all present, learn of the true identity of Myles and Meg. They are children of the Earl of Falworth, who was unjustly accused of treason and murdered by Alban before he could plead his loyalty to the King. The entire family, with the exception of his two children, was put to death, and their property and titles confiscated. Alban immediately persuades the King to imprison Myles and his comrades as condemned traitors.

Myles, however, insists on his right as a knight to plead his case and to challenge Alban in combat. When it appears that Myles is the better of the two, Walter Blunt signals his brother's men to intervene. Myles duels with the traitorous Alban and slays him. At this point, Lady Anne and Meg, who earlier had fled for help, return with an army which rivals Alban's men. Finally the King is saved, the family name of Falworth redeemed, and Myles and Lady Anne reunited.

REVIEWS FOR *The Black Shield of Falworth*:

"[The film] has love, romance, movement and the staunch heroics that please mass audience."—*Motion Picture Herald*

"Film is shaped expertly ... there's enough good costume entertainment to give the picture appeal to all who want light, fast-moving filmfun in a fanciful vein."—*Variety*

"Rudolphe Maté maintains a brisk pace throughout, the fights are well-rehearsed, and he manages to pack the CinemaScope screen with more movement than has been noticeable in the past."—*Monthly Film Bulletin*

REVIEWS FOR JANET LEIGH:

"Janet Leigh occupies the same role that she did vis-à-vis with Prince Valiant. She plays it with equal élan."—*New York Times*

"Curtis, Miss Leigh and Miss Rush are exactly right as the young people."—*Hollywood Reporter*

"Janet Leigh and Barbara Rush are attractive heroines and provide the pleasing romantic interest."—*Harrison's Report*

NOTE: *The Black Shield of Falworth* is the first film produced in CinemaScope by Universal International Pictures.

Rogue Cop

MGM; B&W; 92 minutes; Released: September 1954

CREDITS: *Producer*: Nicholas Nayfack; *Director*: Roy Rowland; *Screenplay*: Sydney Boehm, based on the novel by William P. MacGivern; *Photography*: John Seitz; *Art Direction*: Cedric Gibbons, Hans Peters; *Special Effects*: Gordon Jennings; *Set Decoration*: Edwin B. Wills, Keogh Gleason; *Costumes*: Helen Rose; *Music*: Jeff Alexander; *Film Editing*: James E. Newcom; *Special Effects*: A. Arnold Gillespie; *Makeup*: William Tuttle.

CAST: Robert Taylor (Detective Sgt. Christopher Kelvaney); Janet Leigh (Karen Stephanson); George Raft (Dan Beaumonte); Steve Forrest (Eddie Kelvaney); Anne Francis (Nancy Corlane); Robert Ellenstein (Sidney Y. Myers); Robert F. Simon (Ackerman); Anthony Ross (Fathern Ahern); Alan Hale, Jr. (Johnny Stark); Peter Brocco (Georges "Wrinkles" Fallon); Vince Edwards (Joey Langley); Olive Carey (Selma); Roy Barcroft (Lt. Vince D. Bardeman); Dale Van Sickel (Manny); Ray Teal (Patrolman Mullins); Guy Prescott (Detective Ferrari); Dick Simmons (Detective Ralston); Phil Chambers (Detective Dirksen); Herbert Ellis (Bartender); Lillian Buyeff (Gertrude); Jimmy Ames (News Dealer); Joe Warning (Rivers); Paul Brinegar (Clerk); Robert Burton (Inspector Cassidy); Carleton Young (District Attorney); Jack Victor (Morgue Orderly).

PLOT: Christopher Kelvaney is a smart and handsome detective sergeant who has been for years on the payroll of the organized crime syndicate operated by Dan Beaumonte. His younger brother Eddie is also in the police force, but he is still an idealistic, honest rookie policeman. When Eddie is called upon to identify a minor crook, Chris is approached by Beaumonte, who suggests that it would be to Eddie's advantage not to identify the criminal. Eddie is stunned when Chris relays the proposition and indignantly refuses. Chris, knowing the underworld boss is deadly serious, now approaches Eddie's girlfriend Karen, a nightclub singer, and tries to persuade her to use her influence with Eddie to no avail. Playing for time, Chris tells Beaumonte and his associate Ackerman that Eddie has agreed to their plans, but the gang does not believe him. After a violent fight, Chris leaves to warn Eddie of the danger, but before he can find his brother, Eddie is murdered. Nancy, once Beaumonte's girl but now discarded by the gang leader, promises to help Chris, who is now wholeheartedly on the side of the law. Chris hides her in Karen's apartment and sets off on his investigation alone. His own shady reputation, however, brings demands for his resignation, but he promises to bring his key witness, Nancy, to the District Attorney. When he returns to Karen's apartment, however, he finds that Nancy too has been murdered. Setting off for a final showdown, Chris is arrested. Although he knows that it will incriminate himself, he persuades the detective to go with him. Together they find the gunman who killed Eddie, and in a furious shootout, both Beaumonte and Ackerman are killed. Chris is now ready to pay his debt to society.

REVIEWS FOR *Rogue Cop*:

"The satisfactory performance by all concerned almost bring the show off, and had the scripting been more logical the moral value would have had more point."—*Variety*

"*Rogue Cop* is not in itself a significant film, playing and direction are only mediocre."—*Monthly Film Bulletin*

"*Rogue Cop* is not so exceptional in its construction or performance that it is likely to cause surprise. But it is a well-done melodrama, produced and directed in a hard, crisp style."—*New York Times*

REVIEWS FOR JANET LEIGH:

"Miss Leigh's beauty and box-office following are a distinct asset. So is the variety and sureness of her acting."—*Hollywood Reporter*

"Janet Leigh as ... [Steve Forest's] girl and Anne Francis as Mr. Raft's cast-off mistress do well by their roles."—*New York Times*

"Anne Francis, as Raft's drink-sodden mistress, and Janet Leigh, as the murdered brother's sweetheart, are competent."—*Harrison's Reports*

NOTES: *Rogue Cop* was Janet Leigh's last film with MGM after an eight-year collaboration. It was directed by Roy Roland, the director who helmed her debut, *The Romance of Rosy Ridge*.

Pete Kelly's Blues

Warner Brothers; WarnerColor; CinemaScope; 95 minutes; Released: July 1955

CREDITS: *Producer*: Jack Webb; *Director*: Jack Webb; *Screenplay*: Richard L. Breen; *Photography*: Hal Rosson; *Art Direction*: Feild Gray; *Special Effects*: Gordon Jennings; *Set Decoration*: John Sturtevant; *Costumes*: Howard Shoup; *Music Arrangements*: Matty Matlock; *Film Editing*: Robert M. Leeds; *Makeup*: Gordon Bau, Stanley Campbell.

CAST: Jack Webb (Pete Kelly); Janet Leigh (Ivy Conrad); Edmond O'Brien (Fran McCarg); Lee Marvin (Al Gannaway); Peggy Lee (Rose Hopkins); Andy Devine (George Tenell); Ella Fitzgerald (Maggie Jackson); Martin Milner (Joey Firestone);

Jayne Mansfield (Cigarette Girl); Than Wyenn (Rudy Shulak); Herb Ellis (Bedido); John Dennis (Guy Bettenhouser); Mort Marshall (Cootie Jacobs); *Pete Kelley's Big Seven*: Dick Cathcart (Coronet), Matty Matlock (Clarinet), "Moe" Schneider (Trombone), Eddie Miller (Saxophone), George Van Eps (Guitar), Nick Fatool (Drums), Ray Sherman (Piano), Jud De Naut (Bass), and the Israelite Spiritual Church Choir of New Orleans.

PLOT: The scene is Kansas City in 1927, during Prohibition and the years of homemade gin, hot jazz and fevered parties. Pete Kelly is a cornet player and the leader of a jazz band which plays in a small, smoky speakeasy where the liquor comes out of tea urns and the champagne is manufactured on the premises. When gangster Fred McCarg moves in on the territory, organizing a protection racket and demanding a cut of the band's pay, the members of Kelly's Big Seven decide to resist. But after Joey Firestone, their courageous young drummer, is machine-gunned, Kelly loses his nerve and knuckles under to the mobster. He concentrates on his music and carries on a love affair with Ivy Conrad, a society girl who is pursuing him. McCarg brings along his protégé, Rose Hopkins, once a nightclub singer who now drinks heavily, and insists that she sings with the band. Rose, with Kelly's help, tries to regain her confidence. However, one night she gets so drunk she forgets the words of a song, and McCarg brutally beats her up, making her lose her sanity. This brutal treatment of Rose, together with the taunts of his friends, induce Kelly to make a stand against the blackmailer. He tries to obtain legal evidence by breaking into a dance hall where McCarg has an office and attempts to rob his safe of some papers that incriminate the gangster in Firestone's murder. There, he and Ivy are trapped and confronted by McCarg and two hoods, who initiate a gunfight. McCarg is killed, and Kelly, his self-respect regained and his drummer avenged, is able to ask Ivy to marry him.

REVIEWS FOR *Pete Kelly's Blues*:

"*Pete Kelly's Blues* is an incredible waste of tantalizing music and décor designed for the sole purpose of letting Jack Webb strut his stuff." —*New York Times*

"A melodramatic story that catches the mood of the Prohibition era." —*Variety*

"Fashionably serious in its approach to jazz and to the "twenties," *Pete Kelly's Blues* is concerned with striking attitudes and with establishing an atmosphere rather than with developing anything very coherent in the way of narrative." —*Monthly Film Bulletin*

REVIEWS FOR JANET LEIGH:

"Janet Leigh, as a society girl who lives recklessly and falls in love with Webb, is not given much of a chance in a comparatively minor role that is reminiscent of an F. Scott Fitzgerald characterization." —*Harrison's Report*

"An intelligent performance by Janet Leigh cannot obscure the rapturous absurdity of the final shooting match in a large empty dance hall." —*Sunday Times*

"Miss Leigh supplies the romantic angle, as an empty-headed Scott Fitzgerald species who chases the hero." —*New York Times*

NOTES: Actress Peggy Lee was nominated for an Academy Award for Best Supporting Actress. Although opening credits lists only two songs performed in the film ("He Needs Me" and "Sing a Rainbow"), according to the *Hollywood Reporter*, at least 38 musical numbers were at least partially featured in the picture including "I Never Knew," "Smiles," "Breezing Along with the Breeze," "Bye, Bye Blackbird," "After I Say I'm Sorry Sugar," "He Needs Me," "Somebody Loves Me," "Hard-Hearted-Hannah." Janet Leigh is dubbed when she sings "I'm Gonna Meet My Sweetie Now."

My Sister Eileen
Columbia Pictures; Technicolor CinemaScope;
107 minutes; Released: August 1955

CREDITS: *Producer*: Fred Kohlmar; *Director*: Richard Quine; *Screenplay*: Blake Edwards, Richard Quine, based on the play by Joseph Fields, adapted from the stories by Ruth McKenney; *Photography*: Charles Lowton, Jr.; *Art Direction*: Walter Holscher; *Set Decoration*: Willam Kiernan; *Costumes*: Jean Louis; *Music Arrangements*: George Duning; *Songs*: music by Jule Styne, lyrics by Leo Robin; *Choreography*: Robert Fosse; *Film Editing*: Charles Nelson; *Makeup*: Clay Campbell.

CAST: Janet Leigh (Eileen Sherwood); Betty Garrett (Ruth Sherwood); Jack Lemmon (Bob Baker); Kurt Kasznar ("Papa" Appopolous) Richard York (Ted "Wreck" Loomis), Robert Fosse (Frank Lippencott); Lucy Marlow (Helen); Tommy Rall (Chick Clark); Barbara Brown (Helen's Mother); Horace McMahon (Lonigan); Henry Slate (Drunk); Hal March (Drunk); Alberto Morin (Brazilian Consul); Queenie Smith (Alice); Richard Deacon (George); Ken Christy (Police Sergeant).

PLOT: Blond, beautiful Eileen Sherwood and her sister Ruth come to New York from Columbus, Ohio, to pursue careers as an actress and writer, respectively. Ruth attracts magazine editor Bob Baker by pretending she is the man-chased heroine of her hilarious *My Sister Eileen* stories. Eileen, hunting for a job, is helped by soda fountain manager Frank Lippencott and pursued by reporter Chick Clark. To get Eileen alone, Clark sends Ruth to Brooklyn to cover the arrival of a Brazilian cadet training ship. Ruth returns home, pursed by the cadets who initiate a gigantic conga line, which ends in a riot and jail. Bob admits his love for Ruth, and Frank proposes to Eileen. The Brazilian cadets arrive to apologize to the Sherwood sisters. Ruth inadvertently mentions the word "conga" and the dance riot starts again!

REVIEWS FOR *My Sister Eileen*:

"Catchy tunes, literate lyrics, excellent dancing and a pronounced lightless of spirit, all in the proper surroundings, make this version of a Broadway comedy hit one of the happier musicals that Hollywood has lately manufactured."—*Newsweek*

"Embellish by CinemaScope, Technicolor photography and musical routines, this is a highly amusing remake.... The production values are first rate."—*Harrison's Reports*

"The major virtues of Columbia's charming musical mounting of *My Sister Eileen* are the cheerfully melodic score by Jule Styne and Leo Robin, dance numbers by Bob Fosse which are simple, impish, underproduced tradition of the in-between numbers of the early Astaire-Rogers films.—*Saturday Review*

REVIEWS FOR JANET LEIGH:

"The always beautiful Miss Leigh does not play Eileen as a dumb blond as most of her predecessors have. She makes her a clean-minded, friendly, uncomplicated kid, whose very virtues invite wolves and trouble."—*Hollywood Reporter*

"Janet Leigh [is] very attractive as the little sister."—*Variety*

"Miss Leigh, as the prettier, guileless sister, is particularly nimble on her legs."—*New York Times*

NOTES: The musical numbers include: "Atmosphere" (Main Title)—Chorus; "As Soon as They See Eileen"—Betty Garrett; "I'm Great!"—Kurt Kasznar, Richard York, Betty Garrett, Janet Leigh; "No Room for Mr. Gloom," danced by Bob Fosse and Tommy Rall; "There's Nothing Like Love"—Janet Leigh; "Give Me a Band and My Baby"—Janet Leigh, Betty Garrett, Bob Fosse, Tommy Rall; "It's Bigger Than You and Me"—Jack Lemmon; "There's Nothing Like Love" (Reprise)—Bob Fosse; "Conga!," danced by Betty Garrett, Janet Leigh and Male Ensemble; "Finale" (*Conga!* reprise).

Safari
Columbia Pictures; Warwick Film Production Ltd.; Technicolor; 90 minutes; Released: June 1956

CREDITS: *Producers*: Irving Allen, Albert R. Broccoli, Adrian D. Worker; *Director*: Terence Young; *Screenplay*: Anthony Veiller, based on a story by Robert Buckner, adapted from the stories by Ruth McKenney; *Photography*: John Wilcox; *Art Direction*: Elliot Scott; *Costumes*: Olga Lehmann; *Music*: William Alwyn; *Film Editing*: Michael Gordon; *Makeup*: Fred Williamson.

CAST: Victor Mature (Ken Duffield); Janet Leigh (Linda Latham); Roland Culver (Sir Vincent Brampton); John Justin (Brian Sinden); Earl Cameron (Jeroge); Liam Redmond (Roy Shaw); Orland Martins (Jerusalem); Juma (Odongo); Lionel Ngakane (Kakora); Harry Quashie (O'Keefe); Slim Harris (Renegade); Cy Grant (Chief Massai); John Wynn (Charley); Arthur Lovegrove (Blake); Estelle Brody (Aunty May); Christopher Warbey (Kenny); John Harrison (Wambui); Glyn Lawson (Kikuyu); Frank Singuineau (African); Charles Hayes (Police Inspector); Bartholomew Sketch (Special Mau Mau); John Cook (District Commissioner); Bob Isaacs (Henderson).

PLOT: When his sister and his son are slaughtered by a Mau Mau gang led by Jeroge, Ken Duffield, a wild animal hunter, swears vengeance and determines to go after the gang alone. The District Commissioner considers his plan suicidal and thwarts him by withdrawing his hunting license. Ken spends his exile in Nairobi drinking and gathering information from his African friends in hopes of tracking down Jeroge. He gets his chance at revenge when he agrees to lead a safari for Sir Vincent Brampton, arrived in Nairobi with his fiancé Linda. During the safari Ken rescues Linda from a river infested with alligators. In the meantime, Brampton becomes obsessed to the point of madness with his desire to kill the famous lion Hatari, and he is seriously mauled in the attempt. In order to reach a doctor quickly, Ken risks taking the safari through dangerous territory where they run into the Mau Mau force led by Jeroge himself. Sir Vincent is shot before help arrives. Ken kills Jeroge. Linda, freed from a loveless engagement, and Ken, freed from his desire for revenge, prepare to start a new life together.

REVIEWS FOR *Safari*:

"This English-made African adventure melodrama ought to prove satisfactory with all types of audiences ... a good entertainment everywhere."—*Harrison's Reports*

"This Safari, someone sensibly declares at the sunset, spells 'trouble.' He couldn't have meant the location shots of elephants, crocodiles, giraffes and the lush scenery, all of which are lovely. It must have been the plot, after all."—*New York Times*

"One of the more trivial of the screen's African adventures."—*Monthly Film Bulletin*

REVIEWS FOR JANET LEIGH:

"Miss Leigh [is] acceptable as a blonde in a jungle setting."—*Variety*

"Miss Leigh makes the most of a desirable and somewhat hare-brained character."—*Hollywood Reporter*

"Miss Leigh ... seems out of her natural habitat, but she is a burnished blonde, who is cool and seductive enough in a variety of fancy costumes to turn a dour hunter's head." —*New York Times*

Jet Pilot

RKO Radio Pictures; Howard Hughes Productions;
Technicolor; 112 minutes; Released: September 1957

CREDITS: *Producer*: Jules Furthman; *Director*: Josef von Sternberg; *Screenplay*: Jules Furthman; *Photography*: Winton C. Hoch, Philip G. Cochran (as supervisor of aerial sequences); *Art Direction*: Albert S. D'Agostino, Field Gray; *Set Decoration*: Darrell Silvera, William Stevens; *Music*: Bronislau Kaper; *Film Editing*: Michael R. McAdam, Harry Marker, William H. Moore; *Costumes*: Michael Woulfe; *Makeup*: Mel Berns.

CAST: John Wayne (Colonel Jim Shannon); Janet Leigh (Anna Marladovna/Olga Orlief); Jay C. Flippen (Major General Black); Paul Fix (Major Redford); Richard Rober (FBI Agent George Rivers); Roland Winters (Colonel Sokolov); Hans Conried (Colonel Matoff); Ivan Triesault (General Langrad); Jon Bishop (Major Sinclair); Perdita Chandler (Georgia Redford); Denver Pyle (Mr. Simpson); Bill Erwin (Sergeant); Nelson Leigh (FBI agent); Sylvia Lewis (WAC Corporal); Bill Yeager (Captain).

PLOT: The radar screen at an air base on the northwest coast of America picks up an unidentified aircraft approaching from Siberia. Colonel Jim Shannon orders the interception of the craft, which is forced down on the air field. The plane is a Russian jet, piloted by Anna, who claims she is seeking political asylum. Her plane is impounded, and Anna is searched by Shannon and held to await the decision of higher authority. Major Black instructs Shannon to escort Anna wherever she wants to go in America, and, up to a point, to encourage her interest in American service equipment so that flaws and advances in the Russian counterparts can be gauged from her inquires. However, over the course of their tour and flights together, Shannon and Anna fall in love. Shannon now learns that Anna has been working as an agent for the Russians the whole time. He confronts her with this knowledge but declares that he is nevertheless still in love with her. When Anna bemoans what her fate will be, Shannon rushes her into marriage, hoping she will find protection as his wife. The authorities are furious when they learn of the union, but after lengthy considerations they decide Anna can remain in the States. Shannon is the first to be informed of this, but Shannon leads Anna to believe that the decision has gone against her. He tells her he has decided to fly back with her to Russia. When their flight is reported from the radar room, Major Black and his staff understand that Shannon has gone to work against the Soviets. Later, in Moscow, Anna realizes she really loves Shannon, and together they fly back to the U.S. in a stolen Soviet jet with a host of secret information. They finally settle down in Palm Springs, California, starting a normal matrimonial life.

REVIEWS FOR *Jet Pilot*:

"[The film] is a more than satisfactory action comedy, rather elementary in its approach to things but goodhearted and often amusing." —*Hollywood Reporter*

"Much of the production is a strange blend. It oscillates between light comedy, romance and melodrama with one not complementing the other." — *Variety*

"This is one of the most idiotic movies ever made." —*Saturday Review*

REVIEWS FOR JANET LEIGH: "Mr. Wayne and Miss Leigh play their quaint roles like a couple of fumbling kids." —*New York Times*

"Neither John Wayne, as the American pilot, nor Janet Leigh, as the Soviet ace, will win any acting honors for their portrayals, but they play their parts in amusing style and complement each other."—*Harrison's Report*

"Janet Leigh, hardly the most likely choice for a Russian lady pilot, tirelessly exploits a rather old-fashioned brand of sex appeal."—*Monthly Film Bulletin*

NOTES: *Jet Pilot* was the last film ever to bear the opening credit "Howard Hughes Presents." It took almost eight years to see release after its production began in December 1949.

Touch of Evil

Universal International; B&W; 96 minutes; Released: May 1958

CREDITS: *Producer*: Albert Zugsmith; *Director*: Orson Welles; *Screenplay*: Orson Welles, from a previous script by Paul Monash, based on the novel *Badge of Evil* by Whit Masterson; *Photography*: Russell Metty; *Art Direction:* Alexander Golitzen, Robert Clatworthy; *Set Decoration*: John P. Austin, Russell A. Gausman; *Music*: Henry Mancini; *Film Editing*: Virgil Ogle, Aaron Stell, Edward Curtiss; *Makeup*: Bud Westmore.

CAST: Charlton Heston (Ramon Miguel "Mike" Vargas); Orson Welles (Police Capt. Hank Quinlan); Janet Leigh (Susan "Susie" Vargas); Marlene Dietrich (Tanya); Joseph Calleia (Pete Menzies); Akim Tamiroff ("Uncle Joe" Grandi); Ray Collins (District Attorney Adair); Dennis Weaver (Motel Clerk); Joi Lansing (Zita); Zsa Zsa Gabor (Madame of Strip Joint); Valentin De Vargas (Pancho); Joanna Moore (Marcia Linnekar); Mort Mills (Schwartz); Victor Milan (Manolo Sanchez); Lalo Rio (Risto); Michael Sargent (Pretty Boy); Mercedes McCambridge (Gang Leader, the "Brunette"); Joseph Cotton (Coroner); Phil Harvey (Blaine); Harry Shannon (Police Chief Gould); Rusty Wescoatt (Casey); Gus Schilling (Eddie Farnham); Wayne Taylor (Gang Member); Ken Miller (Gang Member); Raymond Rodriguez (Gang Member); Arlene McQuade (Ginnie); Dominick Delgarde (Lackey); Eleanor Dorado (Lia); John Dierkes (Plainclothes Cop); Joe Basulto (Young Delinquent); William Tannen (Lawyer); Billy House (Construction Site Foreman).

PLOT: On their honeymoon in the Mexican town of Los Robles on the U.S.–Mexico border, Susan and "Mike" Vargas are appalled when a car crossed the frontier just ahead of them and then explodes in a blinding sheet of flame. Though Vargas is not a policeman but a special narcotics investigator for Mexico's Ministry of Justice, he feels it is duty to investigate. The time bomb explosion took place on the American side, but the car came from Mexico, and the incident might take on international significance. One victim is an obscure strip-tease dancer, but her companion, a man named Linnekar, virtually owned Los Robles. Vargas incurs the displeasure of the detective captain who takes charge of the case. Hank Quinlan, a bully and bigot, is a hero among American police, as he has never failed to get his man. Quinlan wants no Mexican interference in this case, but is forced, by orders from above, to cooperate with Vargas. As her husband talks to Quinlan over the torn bodies in the street, Susan is approached by a stranger with a note that piques her curiosity. She follows the man to a cheap hotel where she meets "Uncle" Joe Grandi, an underworld boss on both sides of the border. Grandi tries to browbeat Susan into persuading Vargas not to give evidence against Grandi's brother, who is facing a grave narcotics charge in Mexico City. Susan does not scare easily. She is more irked by her husband than frightened for his welfare when he gives the investigation priority over the honeymoon. She goes to wait for him in a lonely hotel on a deserted highway. Vargas discovers that Quinlan has planted evidence — dynamite of the type used to blow up Linnekar's car — in the apartment of a young Mexican named Sanchez, recently married to Linnekar's spoiled daughter, Marcia. The indignant and astounded Vargas probes Quinlan's past only to find that the police hero's arrests were usually made on false evidence. He has often framed the subject to ensure conviction. Incensed by Vargas' interference, Quinlan plots with Grandi, who also has good reason to blacken Vargas' name, to frame Susan. After proving to Quinlan's sergeant, Pete Menzies, that his boss is a criminal, Vargas enlists Menzies' aid to expose the corrupt police chief. They plan to trick Quinlan into tape-recording confessions through a microphone hidden in Menzies' clothes. Meanwhile, Quinlan has Susan drugged and brought to Grandi's hotel, where he places her, half-conscious and half-dressed, in a room with evidence of a narcotics orgy. Then, to eliminate the risk of blackmail, Quinlan chokes Grandi to death with Susan's stockings, leaving the dead man in her room. Vargas, frantically searching the town for his wife, finds Susan just as the vice squad, called by Quinlan, picks her up. In the room Menzies discovers the cane used by Quinlan, who has a game leg. This convinces the reluctant sergeant that he must go through with Vargas' plan to trap Quinlan. Outside the town Menzies meets his chief, who has been drinking heavily. As they stroll back, Vargas follows behind, recording the conversation in which Menzies draws an unwitting confession from Quinlan. When the astute Quinlan realizes what is happening, he shoots Menzies and goes after Vargas. But the dying sergeant shoots Quinlan before the captain can get Mike. As Quinlan's confession begins to unroll on the tape, word comes that the young Mexican suspect, Sanchez, has confessed to planting the time-bomb in the car to get the Linnekar inheritance for him and Marcia: Quinlan's intuition was right after all. Now with Quinlan dead, the Vargases are free to continue their honeymoon.

REVIEWS FOR *Touch of Evil*:

"This should have been a fine picture. But it isn't. [It's] a confusing mishmash." — *Hollywood Reporter*

"Sums up all the negative characteristics which appeal to Welles.... He must return to the moral values of America if he is ever to be the artist he could be." —*Films in Review*

"Nobody, and we mean nobody, will nap during *Touch of Evil*.... Where Orson Welles soundly succeeds is in generating enough sinister electricity for three such yarns and in generally staging it like a wild, murky nightmare." —*New York Times*

REVIEWS FOR JANET LEIGH:

"Miss Leigh, sexy as all get-out, switches from charm to fright with facility in a capable portrayal." — *Variety*

"Janet Leigh, as the American wife, is required to do so many unbelievable things that the most you can say for her is that she looks pretty and her lingerie fits like wallpaper." —*Hollywood Reporter*.

"Charlton Heston and Janet Leigh perform crisply and well." — *The Evening Standard*

NOTES: There are three principal versions of *Touch of Evil*. First, there is the 96-minute "theatrical" version that the public saw in 1958. Then there is a 109-minute "preview" version discovered at Universal in 1976, with additional material by Orson Welles and the studio; this eventually supplanted the first version. Finally, a newly edited 111-minute restored version was released in 1998 using material from the other two. This attempted to follow all the suggestions made in a lengthy memo written by Orson Welles to Universal, dated December 5, 1957, after viewing the studio's rough cut for the first time, which was similar but not identical to the "preview" version and no longer exists. The three versions were all released by Universal Pictures on DVD in 2008 to celebrate the film's 50th anniversary.

The Vikings

Bryna Productions; Technicolor; 114 minutes; Released: June 1958

CREDITS: *Producer*: Jerry Bresler; *Director*: Richard Fleischer; *Screenplay*: Calder Willingham, adapted by Dale Wasserman, based on the novel *The Viking* by Edison Marshall; *Photography*: Jack Cardiff; *Art Direction*: Harper Goff; *Set Decoration*: Harper Goff; *Music*: Mario Nascimbene; *Film Editing*: Elmo Williams; *Makeup*: John O'Gorman, Neville Smallwood

CAST: Kirk Douglas (Einar); Tony Curtis (Eric); Ernest Borgnine (King Ragnar); Janet Leigh (Princess Morgana); Alexander Knox (Father Godwin); Frank Thring (King Aella); James Donald (Lord Egbert); Maxine Audley (Enid); Eileen Way (Kitala); Edric Connor (Sandpiper); Dandy Nichols (Bridget); Per Buckhoj (Bjorn); Almut Berg (Pigtails); Kelly Curtis (Young Girl); Peter Douglas (Young Boy); Orson Welles (Narrator).

PLOT: At the height of the Dark Ages, Viking warriors, led by Ragnar, raid the English coast, raping and plundering. In one small kingdom he slays the king and rapes the queen, Enid, who later bears a child from the assault. Enid confesses to a young priest, Father Godwin, that her unborn child is the direct heir to the throne. Certain that Aella, the successor to the king, would murder anyone threatening his claim to the throne, Father Godwin sends the baby, Eric, aboard a pilgrim ship bound for Rome, where it will be raised by monks. During the journey the ship is seized by Vikings and the boy taken prisoner to grow up in slavery. Twenty years pass, and Eric, now a Viking slave who knows nothing about his parentage, dislikes Einar, King Ragnar's legitimate son. The two young men fight a duel, during which Eric's pet falcon claws out one of Einar's eyes. Enraged, the monocular Norseman orders the slave tossed into a pit of giant crabs kept for such occasions. Eric is saved when Lord Egebert, who was banned from England and was planning his return with the Vikings, recognizes the pommelstone of Northumbria's Sword around Eric's neck, which makes him realize that the slave must be Enid's rumored son. On another raid the Norsemen carry off Princess Morgana, the young daughter of the King of Wales, and Einar decides he wants her, although she has fallen in love with Eric. Morgana and Eric escape one night. When Einar and Ragnar chase them, the pursuing boat crashes on the rocks in the fjord and sinks. Ragnar is pulled aboard by Eric and taken to England as a gift for evil King Aella, who decides to kill Ragnar by pushing him into a pit of wolves. For defying Aella, Eric's left hand is severed by a sword, and he is cast adrift in a small boat with his companions, Kitala and Sandpiper. Now the head of the Viking village, Eric, after a grim sea journey, finds his way to Einar and informs him of his father's death. Einar roars for revenge, and the Viking fleet sets sail for England, guided by Eric. Aella's castle is the target, and the battle is long and furious, with the Vikings eventually gaining the upper hand. Einar kills Aella and frees Morgana, learning from her and Father Godwin about the pommelstone. He also realizes that the princess is in love with Eric. The fact that a slave is his half-brother does not stop him from challenging Eric to a battle to the death. After a furious fight, Einar is about to kill Eric; but he hesitates for a moment, apparently reluctant to kill his own kin. Eric, however, knows nothing about any blood ties and uses Einar's moment of indecision to drive his broken sword into him. Eric orders Einar's body cremated on a funeral ship with all the honors of a Viking king. As the burning ship glides off into the mist, Eric and Morgana stand arm in arm and watch it pass slowly from sight.

REVIEWS FOR *The Vikings*:

"*The Vikings* is a big, expensive, cornball, action spectacle ... [with a] childish screenplay." — *Hollywood Reporter*

"Superbly photographed in Technirama and Technicolor, and produced on a lavish and highly spectacular scale." — *Harrison's Report*

"An unashamedly romping epic ... lovingly photographed." — *Monthly Film Bulletin*

REVIEWS FOR JANET LEIGH:

"Janet Leigh plays the kidnapped Welsh princess with a conventional exaggeration of dread." — *New York Times*

"Miss Leigh would have benefitted from some emotional charging-up, what with a couple of armies fighting for her." — *Variety*

NOTES: The film inspired the 1959 TV series *Tales of the Vikings*, which utilized the movie's props, costumes and scale model ships.

The Perfect Furlough

Universal International Pictures; Color; CinemaScope;
93 minutes; Released: October 1958

CREDITS: *Producer*: Robert Arthur; *Director*: Blake Edwards; *Screenplay*: Stanley Shapiro; *Photography*: Philip Lathrop; *Art Direction*: Alexander Golitzen; *Set Decoration*: Russell A. Gausman, Oliver Emeret; *Costumes*: Bill Thomas; *Music*: Frank Skinner; *Film Editing*: Milton Carruth; *Makeup*: Bud Westmore.

CAST: Tony Curtis (Corporal Paul Hodges); Janet Leigh (Lt. Vicki Loren); Linda Cristal (Sandra Roca); Keenan Wynn (Harvey Franklyn); Elaine Stritch (Liz Baker); Marcel Dalio (Henri Valentine); King Donovan (Maj. Collins); Troy Donahue (Sgt. Nickels); Jay Novello (Rene Valentine); Les Tremayne (Col. Leland); Gordon Jones ("Sylvia," MP); Alvy Moore (Pvt. Marvin Brewer); Lilyan Chauvin (French Nurse); Dick Crockett (Hans, MP); Eugene Borden (French Doctor); Frankie Darro (Patient); James Lanphier (Assistant Hotel Manager).

PLOT: Morale at a polar Army base is low. The men, bachelors all, have been away from civilization — which means women too — for seven months. It will be another five months

before their job is done. In the Pentagon, Army psychologist Lt. Vicki Loren suggests, as a palliative, a plan to choose one of the men to take a "perfect leave." She reasons that the other men will share the leave vicariously. But at the base Corporal Paul Hodges wangles the selection. His idea of heavenly leave is three weeks in Paris with movie queen Sandra Roca. Sandra doesn't approve but is talked into it by her manager, Henry Franklin. The Pentagon, meanwhile, learns of Paul's record of love conquests and decrees that, as a safeguard, Vicki should go along on the trip. In Paris, all of Paul's attempts to make full use of his perfect furlough with Sandra are systematically spoiled by Vicki's presence. When Paul discovers that Sandra is secretly married — secretly because she didn't want to upset her studio and her manager — Paul behaves like a gentleman and later on withdraws from the contest. Meanwhile, Vicki has fallen in love with him herself. He is about to be sent back to the Arctic when she decides there is only one thing to do in order to keep him — pretend she is going to have a baby. The trick is successful, and Paul, not unwillingly, is forced to marry her.

REVIEWS FOR *The Perfect Furlough*:

"*Furlough* is a definitive encyclopedia of comic cliché."—*Time*

"There is nothing about *The Perfect Furlough* to warrant superlatives, but there's plenty to keep you giggling."—*New York Times*

"The plot ... is unashamedly divorced from reality, and the story allows the actors to romp from one hilarious scene to the next without pausing for too much explanation. A few moments of dragging pace are effectively balanced by the smartness and wit of dialogue in the best and most likeable transatlantic tradition."—*Monthly Film Bulletin*

REVIEWS FOR JANET LEIGH:

"Janet Leigh looking at once sweet and wholesome and sexy."—*Hollywood Reporter*.

"Tony Curtis ... Janet Leigh ... and Linda Cristal ... handle their roles in zestful style and make the most of what is basically thin and absurd material."—*Harrison's Report*

"Miss Leigh ... is the psychologist; this profession rarely yields such attractive practitioners."—*Variety*

NOTES: The film was released in the United Kingdom as *Strictly for Pleasure*. The original film poster promised the *The Perfect Furlough*'s audience "287 CERTIFIED LAUGHS"—certified in an audience test by Sindlinger & Co., Inc., Research Division, Ridley Park, Pennsylvania.

Who Was That Lady?

Columbia Pictures; B&W; 115 minutes; April 1960

CREDITS: *Producer*: Norman Krasna; *Director*: George Sidney; *Screenplay*: Norman Krasna, based on his play *Who Was That Lady That I Saw You With*, produced on the Broadway stage by Leland Hayward; *Photography*: Harry Stradling; *Art Direction*: Ted Haworth; *Set Decoration*: James M. Crowe; *Costumes*: Jean Louis; *Music*: Andre Previn; *Film Editing*: Viola Lawrence; *Makeup*: Ben Lane.

CAST: Tony Curtis (David Wilson); Dean Martin (Michael Haney); Janet Leigh (Ann Wilson); James Whitmore (Harry Powell); John McIntire (Bob Doyle); Barbara Nichols (Gloria Coogle); Larry Keating (Parker); Larry Storch (Orenov); Simon Oakland (Belka); Joi Lansing (Florence Coogle); Barbara Hines (Foreign Exchange Student); Marion Javits (Miss Mellish); Michael Lane (Glinka); Kam Tong (Lee Wong); William Newell (Schultz); Harry Jackson (Joe Bendix); Snub Pollard (Tattoo Artist); Jack Benny (Mr. Cosgrove); Alan Carney (Building Superintendent).

PLOT: When Ann Wilson catches her husband David, a Columbia University chemistry professor, being kissed by a pretty student, she threatens to leave for Reno to obtain a divorce. David enlists the help of Michael Haney, an imaginative TV writer, who convinces Ann that David is an undercover F.B.I. agent and that the girl in question was a possible spy. To augment his story, Michael makes use of the prop department at CBS, where David is provided with a service revolver and an identity card.

Ann believes the absurd story, and later protectively follows David and Michael to a Chinese restaurant where they are dining with two attractive blondes. Ann assumes these girls are more suspected subversives and attempts to pass her husband the "prop" gun he left behind at the apartment. She nearly creates a riot involving actual F.B.I. men, with a video news unit capturing the live action. When the story of David's undercover activities hits newspapers, real foreign agents assume David is linked to a top university project and kidnap the trio in order to extract information from them. The three captives are later taken to the sub-basement of the Empire State Building, where, under the effect of truth serum, David admits his deception. Ann gets free and storms out of the building. When David and Michael revive, they confusedly believe they are in an enemy submarine and decide to commit one final patriotic act — sink the submarine. They open all the valves in the basement. As the water rises to their knees, the F.B.I. arrives just in time to save them from their folly. Finally David reveals the full story. Ann overhears it and offers her forgiveness.

REVIEWS FOR *Who Was That Lady?*:

"A Film made without pretentions and thoroughly entertaining, there is some stylish playing with few sophisticated lines that all add up to a pleasant evening's entertainment." — *Films and Filming*

"A breezy free-wheeling little romantic farce [which takes] a nosedive after about half an hour." — *New York Times*

"A racy, explosively funny slapstick comedy." — *Cue*

REVIEWS FOR JANET LEIGH:

"The films upholds the high box-office standards of the Tony Curtis–Janet Leigh comedies. Both husband and wife season the farce with the infectious charm of their winning personalities. And in a couple of sincerely but lightly played scenes they make one feel they have an immense affection for each other." — *Hollywood Reporter*

"Miss Leigh is pretty and pert, what the role calls for." — *Variety*

"Janet Leigh is superb as the bubbly, effervescent wife who complicates the impersonation by becoming overenthusiastic about it." — *Harrison's Report*

NOTES: *Who Was That Lady?* was nominated for two Golden Globe Awards, for Best Comedy and Best Actor in a Comedy (Dean Martin).

Psycho

Universal International Pictures; B&W; 109 minutes; Released: June 1960

CREDITS: *Producer*: Alfred Hitchcock; *Director*: Alfred Hitchcock; *Screenplay*: Joseph Stefano, based on the novel by Robert Bloch; *Photography*: John L. Russell; *Art Direction*: Joseph Hurley, Robert Clatworthy; *Set Decoration*: George Milo; *Costumes*: Helen Colvig; *Music*: Bernard Herrmann; *Special Effects*: Clarence Champagne; *Film Editing*: George Tomasini; *Makeup*: Jack Barron, Robert Dawn; *Sound*: Waldon O. Watson, William Russell.

CAST: Anthony Perkins (Norman Bates); Vera Miles (Lila Crane); John Gavin (Sam Loomis); Janet Leigh (Marion Crane); Martin Balsam (Detective Milton Arbogast); John McIntire (Sheriff Al Chambers); Simon Oakland (Dr. Fred Richmond); Patricia Hitchcock (Caroline); Frank Albertson (Tom Cassidy); Vaughn Taylor (George Lowery); Lurene Tuttle (Mrs. Chambers); John Anderson (California Charlie); Mort Mills (Highway Patrol Officer); Sam Flint (County Sheriff); Francis De Sales (Deputy District Attorney Alan Deats); George Eldredge (Police Chief James Mitchell).

PLOT: Sam Loomis, a small-town businessman, and Marion Crane, a secretary, are having a lunch-hour tryst in a Phoenix, Arizona, hotel room. Sam can't marry Marion because he is paying off his father's debts and his former wife's alimony. At the real estate office where Marion works, her boss agrees to hold a large amount of cash, $40,000, given to him by a rich client. In a moment of weakness Marion drives off with the money, heading for Southern California. She falls asleep in her car at the side of the road, arousing the suspicion of a policeman in a patrol car who doesn't search her but follows her as far as a used car lot, where she trades in her car and $700 for another auto with California plates. In a heavy rain she spots a sign reading "Bates Motel" and pulls in, meeting Norman Bates, a sensitive young man who runs the motel with his old mother and spends the rest of his time stuffing birds. Marion hears Norman's mother scolding him harshly when he suggests he invite Marion to supper at their eerie Victorian mansion, which is adjacent to the motel cabins. Marion is the only visitor. That same night, while showering, she is murdered. Through the shower curtains we see a long-haired woman brandishing a big knife. Norman's finds Marion's body, puts it in the trunk of her car with all her belongings (including the stolen money), and pushes the auto into a deep swamp near the motel. Marion's worried sister, Lila, visits the town where Sam lives, which is near the motel, hoping he knows something about Marion's whereabouts. He doesn't. Arriving on the scene from Phoenix is a shrewd private detective, Milton Arbogast. Investigating the motel mansion, after calling Lila to tell her he saw Norman's mother in the window, Arbogast is also knifed to death and buried in his car like Marion. Lila and Sam go to the motel after the local sheriff says he saw no mother at the motel — the mother, in fact, has been dead for years. While Sam is detaining Norman and trying to rattle him with questions, Lila searches the big mansion. In a room in the cellar she sees the old lady sitting in a chair. It turns out to be Norman's mother — a preserved corpse. At that moment a woman appears with a big knife. It is Norman, wearing a wig and a dress. Sam overpowers him. Later at the police station, a psychiatrist explains how Norman, too attached to his mother, had killed her and the lover she found after his father's death. Norman unearthed her corpse and began playing two roles in life, his mother and himself. Gradually he became his mother, who was jealous of her son's interest in Marion. It turns out he had also killed some other young girls.

REVIEWS FOR *Psycho*:

"An unusual, good entertainment, indelibly Hitchcock." — *Variety*

"You better have a pretty strong stomach and be prepared for a couple of grisly shocks,.... There is not an abundance of subtlety or the lately familiar Hitchcock bent towards significant and colorful scenery in this obviously low-budget job." — *New York Times*

"The story is the sheerest rubbish, and it would be underrating Hitchcock's intelligence to suppose that he was not fully aware of this." — *Monthly Film Bulletin*

REVIEWS FOR JANET LEIGH:

"Miss Leigh is excellent as the young woman who steals $40,000 to buy-off her happiness and solve her boyfriend's money problems, only to be murdered at the motel." — *Hollywood Reporter*

"Mr. Perkins and Miss Leigh perform with verve." — *New York Times*

"Janet Leigh is exceptionally fine as the secretary who repents too late." — *Harrison's Report*

NOTES: Janet Leigh won a Golden Globe as Best Supporting Actress and was nominated for an Academy Award for Best Supporting Actress.

Pepe

Columbia Pictures; Color; 195 minutes; December 1960

CREDITS: *Producers*: George Sidney, Jacques Gelman; *Director*: George Sidney; *Screenplay*: Dorothy Kingsley, Claude Binyon, from a story by Leonard Spigelgass and Sonya Levien, based on the play *Broadway Zauber* by Ladislaus Bus-Fekete; *Photography*: Joe Mac Donald; *Art Direction*: Ted Haworth; *Set Decoration*: William Kiernan; *Costumes*: Edith Head; *Music*: John Green; *Film Editing*: Viola Lawrence, Al Clark; *Makeup*: Ben Lane.

CAST: Cantinflas (Pepe); Dan Dailey (Ted Holt); Shirley Jones (Susie Murphy); Carlos Montalban (Rodriguez); Vicki Trickett (Lupita); Susan Lloyd (Carmen); Joe Hyams (Charro); Hank Henry (Manager); Willam Demerest (Studio Guard); Matt Mattox (Dancer); Stephen Bekassy (Jeweler); Ernie Kovacs (Immigration Inspector); Judy Garland (Singing Voice). Special Guest Stars: Joey Bishop; Billy Burke; Michael Callan; Maurice Chevalier; Charles Coburn; Richard Conte; Bing Crosby; Tony Curtis; Bobby Darin; Sammy Davis, Jr.; Jimmy Durante; Zsa Zsa Gabor; Green Garson; Hedda Hopper; Peter Lawford; Janet Leigh; Jack Lemmon; Dean Martin; Kim Novak; Jay North; Andre Previn; Donna Reed; Debbie Reynolds; Edward G. Robinson; Cesar Romeo; Frank Sinatra.

PLOT: In Mexico, horse trainer Pepe adores his white stallion, Don Juan. When the horse is purchased at auction by Ted Holt, an American Hollywood producer, Pepe follows him to go to California. In Hollywood he meets many stars without realizing who they are. He sings with Bing Crosby and wrecks Jack Lemmon's car. He befriends Suzy Murphy, a disillusioned waitress and talented aspiring singer-dancer, who invites him to a nightclub to see her perform. At the venue Pepe gets involved in a series of accidents, costing Suzy her job at the club. Nevertheless, aided by his charm, Pepe wins enough money in Las Vegas casinos to back Ted's new film, in which Suzy gets a part. While on location in Acapulco, the production runs out of money. Ted decides to sell Don Juan to Edward G. Robinson in order to complete the shooting. Meanwhile, Suzie's attempts to befriend Pepe are mistaken by him as signs of romantic love. He buys her an engagement ring. But before he can ask Suzie to marry him, she becomes engaged to Ted. All ends happily when Ted's film is successful. The producer demands the horse back from Robinson and gives it to Pepe, who returns to Mexico.

REVIEWS FOR *Pepe*:

"George Sidney has produced and directed about as tastelessly as it could have been done."—*New York Time*

"The film has the shape of three Ed Sullivan shows end to end ... it is essentially a vaudeville show."—*New York Herald Tribune*

"A joyous production crammed with delightful entertainment ... studded with many of the most glittering names in filmland and adorned with beauty, exquisite color, popular vocalizing and expert dancing."—*New York Daily News*

REVIEWS FOR JANET LEIGH:

"Janet Leigh and Tony Curtis are amusing in a tiny part."—*Variety*

"The amount of space given the long list of guest stars is about equal, but some get more equal material than others. Standouts in the lengthy list are ... Janet Leigh holding her own in her comedy of misunderstanding with Cantiflas that also indicates Miss Leigh has been holding out, or been held out."—*Hollywood Reporter*

"Janet Leigh and Tony Curtis have good moments."—*Monthly Film Bulletin*

NOTES: Janet Leigh won the 1961 Laurel Award for Top Female Comedy Performance.

The musical numbers: "That's How It Went," All Right"— Bobby Darin; "The Rumble"— Andre Previn, danced by Michael Callan, Matt Mattox and Shirley Jones; "The Far Away Part of Town"— Judy Garland; "Hooray for Hollywood"— Sammy Davis, Jr.; "Fantasy Dance"— danced by Cantiflas and Debbie Reynolds; "Mimi" and "September Song"— Maurice Chevalier; "Mimi (reprise)"— Cantiflas, Dan Dailey; "Pepe"— Shirley Jones; "Lovely Day"— Shirley Jones.

The Manchurian Candidate

M. C. Production; United Artists; B&W; 126 minutes; October 1962

CREDITS: *Producers*: George Axelrod, John Frankenheimer; *Director*: John Frankenheimer; *Screenplay*: George Axelrod, based on a novel by Richard Condon; *Photography*: Lionel Lindon; *Art Direction*: Richard Sylbert; *Set Decoration*: George R. Nelson; *Costumes*: Moss Mabry; *Music*: David Amram; *Film Editing*: Ferris Webster; *Makeup*: Bernard Ponedel, Jack Freeman, Ron Berkeley.

CAST: Frank Sinatra (Major Bennett Marco); Laurence Harvey (Raymond Shaw); Janet Leigh (Eugenie Rose Chaney); Angela Lansbury (Mrs. Eleanor Shaw Iselin); Henry Silva (Chunjin); James Gregory (Senator John Yerkes Iselin); Leslie Parrish (Jocelyn Jordan); John McGiver (Senator Thomas Jordan); Khigh Dhiegh (Dr. Yen Lo); James Edwards (Corporal Allen Melvin); Douglas Henderson (Colonel Milt); Albert Paulsen (Zilkov); Madame Spivy (Berezovo's Lady Counterpart); Berry Kelley (Secretary of Defense); Joe Adams (Psychiatrist); Lloyd Corrigan (Holborn Gaines); Whit Bissell (Medical Officer); Mimi Dillard (Mrs. Melvin); Anton Van Stralen (Officer); John Lawrence (Grossfeld); Tom Lowell (Private Bobby Lembeck); Richard LePore (Private Ed Mavole); Nick Bolin (Berezovo); Nicky Blair (Silvers); William Thourlby (Little); Irving Steinberg (Freeman); John Francis (Hiken); Joe Gray (Soldier); Michael Masters (F.B.I. Agent).

PLOT: During the Korean War, a U.S. army platoon, led by Major Bennett Marco and Sergeant Raymond Shaw, is captured by the Communist enemies and taken to Manchuria, where they are brainwashed into believing that Shaw led a successful action against the Reds and is a hero. When Shaw comes back home, he receives a Congressional Medal of Honor for his action. The truth is that the Sergeant is a living time bomb and a programmed murderer. He is under the supervision of Communist agent Zilkov, who uses playing cards, specifically the queen of diamonds, to trigger Shaw's hypnotic obedience without memory of any action and consequently without any guilt. In the meantime, Major Marco, whose brainwashing has been only partially successful, is troubled by recurring nightmares in which he sees exactly what happened to the platoon. Although an army investigation gets underway, Marco decides to go to New York to see Shaw. On the train he is comforted by a young woman named Rosie. She helps him again after he visits Shaw's apartment and is attacked by Chunjin, Shaw's servant and formerly the patrol's Korean guide, who betrayed the platoon to the Communists. Finally Marco meets Shaw, who reveals that he hates his mother and stepfather, Senator John Inselin, for their right-wing political attacks. Marco convinces the Army that Shaw's mind is set to explode at a momentous time. With the help of a psychiatrist, Marco discovers the whole ordeal about the brainwashing. Subsequently he learns that Shaw's American contact is Shaw's mother, who intends to profit by his son's condition by making him shoot the presidential nominee during a rally at Madison Square Garden so that her reactionary husband, the vice presidential nominee, can take control. Marco attempts to stop Shaw, but the Sergeant seems to follow all his mother's instructions. At the very last moment, however, he turns the gun on his stepfather, his mother and then himself.

REVIEWS FOR *The Manchurian Candidate*:

"Many loud hurrahs for *The Manchurian Candidate*, a thriller guaranteed to raise all but the limpest hair.... The acting [is] all of high order." — *New Yorker*

"The picture is really fascinating despite its rather far-fetched premise and wholesale slaughter during later passages.... The cast is uniformly excellent." — *Los Angeles Times*

"Not since Hitchcock's heyday have we been privileged to see such high melodrama as *The Manchurian Candidate* ... through so compelling an eye." — *London Daily Herald*

REVIEWS FOR JANET LEIGH:

"Janet Leigh gives evidence of considerable enlargement of her screen personality, with more depth and legitimate sex than she has hitherto shown." — *Hollywood Reporter*

"A pleasant surprise is Janet Leigh as a sweet, swinging N.Y. career girl. The actress only has two or three scenes, but they count. One especially, on a ... train on which she picks up a semi-hysterical Sinatra, registers as one of the great love scenes since Bogart and Bacall first tossed non-sequiturs at one another in *To Have and Have Not*." — *Variety*

"With Frank Sinatra, Lawrence Harvey, Janet Leigh and Angela Lansbury all giving top performances." — *New York Times*

NOTES: Angela Lansbury won a Golden Globe for Best Supporting Actress and was nominated for an Academy Award for Best Supporting Actress. Ferris Webster was nominated for Best Film Editing. The picture was remade in 2004. The role of Eugenie Rose ("Rosie") was played by Kimberly Elise in the remake.

Bye Bye Birdie

Columbia Pictures; Technicolor; Panavision;
112 minutes; Released: April 1963

CREDITS: *Producer*: Fred Kohlmar; *Director*: George Sidney; *Screenplay*: Irving Brecher, based on the play by Michael Stewart produced on the Broadway stage by Edward Padula in association with L. Slade Brown; *Photography*: Joseph Biroc; *Art Direction*: Paul Groesse; *Set Decoration*: Arthur Krams; *Costumes*: Ed Ware, Marjorie B. Wahl, Pat Barto; *Music Arrangements*: Johnny Green; *Music Coordinator*: Fred Karger; *Music Orchestrator*: Johnny Green, Al Woodbury; *Choreography*: Onna White, Tommy Panko; *Film Editing*: Charles Nelson; *Makeup*: Ben Lane.

CAST: Janet Leigh (Rosie DeLeon); Dick Van Dyke (Albert Peterson); Ann-Margret (Kim McAfee); Maureen Stapleton (Mama Mae Peterson); Bobby Rydell (Hugo Peabody); Jesse Pearson (Conrad Birdie); Ed Sullivan (Himself); Paul Lynde (Harry McAfee); Mary LaRoche (Doris McAfee); Michael Evans (Claude Paisley); Robert Paige (Bob Precht); Gregory Morton (Maestro Borov); Bryan Russell (Randolph McAfee); Milton Frome (Mr. Maude); Ben Astar (Ballet Manager); Trudi Ames (Ursula); Cyril Delevanti (Mr. Nebbitt); Frank Albertson (Sam, the Mayor); Beverly Yates (Mayor's Wife); Frank Sully (Maude's Bartender); Bo Peep Karlin (Ursula's Mother); Melinda Marx (Teenager); Mel Turner (Shriner); Gill Lamb (Lanky Shriner);

Lee Aaker (Student Leader); Karel Shimoff (Prima Ballerina); Donald Lawton (Russian Consul); Yvonne White (Telephone Operator); Debbie Stern (Debbie); Sheila Dehner (Sheila); Pete Menefee (Harvey); George Spicer (Tommy); Dick Winslow (Leader, Fireman's Band); Hazel Shermet (Marge, Birdie's Secretary); Joe Gray (TV Director); John Daly (Himself).

PLOT: The news that Conrad Birdie, singing idol, is about to be drafted panics the girls of the nation and spells doom for Albert Peterson, a bankrupt songwriter who has written the title tune for the singer's next film. Peterson hoped the royalties would help him get away from his possessive mother, Mae, whose main purpose in life is to break up her son's romance with secretary Rosie DeLeon, Albert's long-time girlfriend. In an effort to make Albert rich and pry him away from his mom, Rosie schemes to have him write a special farewell tune for Birdie, "One Last Kiss, which the rock-and-roll star can sing while kissing a specially selected teenage fan, Kim McAfee, on the Ed Sullivan Sunday TV show. Albert, Rosie and Birdie travel to Sweet Apple, Ohio, home of Kim, to prepare the broadcast. Birdie's presence in the small town to rehearse the number with Kim precipitates a happy series of major romantic complications, especially for Kim's boyfriend, Hugo. Yet, just when everybody gets used to Birdie and his publicity, the producers decide to cut down his appearance, including axing Albert's song, in order to make space for a broadcast of a Russian ballet. Thanks to a cleaver scheme, Albert is able to restore his song; however, the Birdie appearance still ends in disaster when the jealous Hugo hits the singer — live on national television — for trying to kiss Kim. In the end, Albert's mother announces her plan to remarry and no longer interfere with her son's romance with Rosie, while Kim forgives Hugo for being so violently jealous.

REVIEWS FOR *Bye Bye Birdie*:

"Wit, inventiveness, and admirable verve have been lavished on the mountings of otherwise indifferent songs." — *Newsweek*

"Credit George Sidney with directing one of the better fun and frolic tune packages." — *Variety*

"George Sidney's *Bye Bye Birdie* is an alleged song and dance show, stiff with symptoms of whatever it was that killed the Hollywood musical." — *Sunday Telegraph*

REVIEWS FOR JANET LEIGH:

"Miss Leigh is called upon to play it straight, and does so attractively." — *Variety*

"The major loss, however, comes from the casting of Janet Leigh as Rosie. Miss Leigh makes a lovely-to-look-at blue eyed brunette, if not a fiery Latin of Chita Rivera's caliber, but a dancer of any caliber she's not and the show-stopping dance at the Shriner's meeting is a dud." — *New York Herald Tribune*

"Miss Leigh is attractive as the Mexican-born secretary to Van Dyke and also demonstrates some smart singing and dancing." — *Hollywood Reporter*

NOTES: *Bye Bye Birdie* received two Academy Award Nominations: Best Scoring of Music — Adaptation or Treatment, and Best Sound.

The songs: "The Telephone Hour" — Bobby Rydell, Ensemble; "How Lovely to Be a Woman" — Ann-Margret; "Put on a Happy Face" — Janet Leigh, Dick Van Dyke; "Bye Bye Birdie" — Ann-Margret, Paul Lynde, Mary LaRoche, Bryan Russell; "Honestly Sincere" — Jesse Pearson; "Sultan's Ballet" — Janet Leigh; "One Special Boy (Girl)" — Bobby Rydell, Ann-Margret, Janet Leigh; "Kids" — Dick Van Dyke, Paul Lynde, Maureen Stapleton, Bryan Russell; "Rosie" — Janet Leigh Dick Van Dyke; "A Lot of Livin' to Do" — Ann-Margret, Jesse Pearson, Bobby Rydell; "One Last Kiss" —

Ann-Margret, Bobby Rydell, Jesse Pearson; "We Love You, Conrad"— Ann-Margret, Ensemble

Wives and Lovers

Paramount Pictures; B&W; 103 minutes; Released: August 1963

CREDITS: *Producer*: Hall B. Wallis; *Director*: John Rich; *Screenplay*: Edward Anhalt, based on the play *The First Wife* by Jay Presson Allen; *Photography*: Lucien Ballard; *Art Direction*: Hal Pereira, Walter H. Tyler; *Special Effects*: Paul K. Lerpae; *Set Decoration*: Sam Comer, Arthur Krams; *Costumes*: Edith Head; *Music*: Lyn Murray; *Film Editing*: Warren Low; *Makeup*: Wally Westmore.

CAST: Janet Leigh (Bertie Austin); Van Johnson (Bill Austin); Shelley Winters (Fran Cabrell); Martha Hyer (Lucinda Ford); Ray Walston (Wylie Driberg); Jeremy Slate (Gar Aldrich); Claire Wilcox (Julie Austin); Lee Patrick (Mrs. Swanson); Dick Wessel (Mr. Liberti); Dave Willock (Dr. Leon Partridge); Jack Carr (Cab Driver); Eleanor Audley (Fan at Sardi's); Robert Carson (Sam, Diner at Sardi's); Fritz Feld (Waiter at Sardi's); Dabbs Greer (Waiter at Sardi's); Jerry Hausner (Waiter at Sardi's); Jeffrey Sayre (Diner at Sardi's).

PLOT: For three years Bill Austin has been staying home, writing the greatest American novel, while his wife Bertie has been working to support him. But their arguments become more and more frequent, and are not lost on their precocious daughter Julie. One night Bill's attractive literary agent, Lucinda, arrives at the Austins with a bottle of champagne and the good news that Bill's novel has been sold for publication, and will be a novel-of-the-month selection, a Theater Guild play and a Paramount movie. The "nouveaux riches" Austins leave their modest Brooklyn apartment and move into a fashionable home in Connecticut. Soon they become friendly with their next door neighbors— a divorcee named Fran Cabrell and her constant martini-mixing companion Wylie Driberg. Success brings problems to the Austin household. Bill is frequently in New York with Lucinda, working on the play. Young Julie misses having her daddy around, and Bertie feels her marriage is threatened by Lucinda. Gar Aldric, a handsome movie star scheduled to star in Bill's Broadway play, becomes smitten with Bertie. Bertie, suspecting that the relationship between Bill and Lucinda is not all business, decides to have a fling with Gar. Soon Bill is jealous of Gar— and Bertie is jealous of Lucinda. Although neither is really guilty of any wrong-doing, each suspects the worst, and their marriage seems to be floundering. After the successful opening of his play, Bill goes home to make marital peace with Bertie. Suddenly Gar arrives, causing Bill to lose his temper. Before Gar has a chance to speak, Bill punches and drags him outside. Bill storms back into the house to let Bertie know that nothing happened between him and Lucinda. Bertie, in turn, reveals that nothing happened between her and Gar. They both realize that their jealousy was foolish and decide to start acting like a happily married couple again.

REVIEWS FOR *Wives and Lovers*:

"*Wives and Lovers* is a triumph of script over plot. Working with a worn story line, producer Hal Wallis has managed to make a movie so amusing that it almost needs subtitles to catch the lines that gets away during the yaks." — *Time*

"It's incredible that a screenplay as hackneyed and witless as this one could get past first front-page reading in this rigid day and age, and it is pathetic that it should be directed as woodenly as this one by John Rich." — *New York Times*

"*Wives and Lovers* is a sophisticated marital farce ... well packed with laughs and romantic action." — *Hollywood Reporter*

REVIEWS FOR JANET LEIGH:

"Miss Leigh delivers her smoothest performance in some time." — *Variety*

"Janet Leigh ... is, as ever, delicious." — *The Times*

"Miss Leigh and Johnson handle their roles well." — *Hollywood Reporter*

NOTES: Costume designer, Edith Head was nominated for an Academy Award for Best Costume Design, Black and White.

Kid Rodelo

Paramount Pictures; B&W; 91 minutes; Released: January 1966

CREDITS: *Producers*: Jack O. Lamont, James J. Storrow, Jr.; *Director*: Richard Carlson; *Screenplay*: Jack Natterford, based on a novel by Louis L'Amour; *Photography*: Manuel Merino; *Art Direction*: Jaime Cubero, Jose Luis Galicia; *Sound*: Edgar Vetter, Maurice Askew; *Costumes*: Peris; *Music*: Johnny Douglas; *Film Editing*: Allan Morrison; *Makeup*: Fernando Martinez.

CAST: Don Murray (Kid Rodelo); Janet Leigh (Nora); Broderick Crawford (Joe Harbin); Richard Carlson (Link); Jose Nieto (Tomas Reese); Julio Peña (Balsa); Miguel Del Castillo (Chavas); Jose Villa Sante (Cavalry Hat); Alfonso San Felix (Gopher); Fernando Hilbeck (Perryman); Emilio Rodriguez (Warden); Roberto Rubenstein (Doctor); Billy Christmas (Guard).

PLOT: Kid Rodelo and Joe Harbin had been on the trail together. Harbin was sentenced to life in a Yuma jail for killing a former partner, while Rodelo's sentence was a year. Rodelo leaves prison, warned by the warden not to be bitter because his sentence may not have been justly imposed. The cowboy sets out on foot for the nearby town of Sheridan, where Harbin had $50,000 in golden hidden away. He is given a ride by two men, Link and Balsas, who are also after the gold and are traveling with Link's girl Nora. Meanwhile, Harbin breaks out of jail and heads the same way with two other convicts, Tomas and Gopher. Thinking they have found the gold, Balsas kills Link but is surprised by Harbin and his friends, and kills Tomas before making a bargain to share the money. Harbin agrees — only because he knows he will need Balsas' help until they reach the Mexican border to repel the attacks from a tribe of Indians who make their living hunting down escaped convicts for bounty money. Kid Rodelo, who knows the territory and acts as a guide, makes a similar bargain; and Nora, now falling in love with Kid, goes along. Desperately short of water, and pursued by the Indians, they struggle through the rocky desert. Then, thinking they are nearing safety, Harbin strands Rodelo without a horse and shoots Gopher and Balsas. But Rodelo survives, and catches up with Harbin and Nora just as the Indians attack and kill Harbin. Rodelo and Nora, the only survivors of the assault, ride away with the gold.

REVIEWS FOR *Kid Rodelo*:

"A cliché-ridden Western, which limps stolidly along in the wake of *Greed* and *Treasure of Sierra Madre*, with tired performances from the American leads and appalling ones from the dubbed Spanish players." — *Monthly Film Bulletin*

"A spavined Western ... [a] silly shivaree." — *New York Times*

"The Paramount release seems to be victim of bad editing. The story line is confused and sluggish ... [with] lack of pace and definition." — *Hollywood Reporter*

REVIEWS FOR JANET LEIGH:

"Miss Leigh looks continually startled." — *Variety*

"Murray and Miss Leigh don't register very effectively, their characters being less colorful than Crawford, so it is harder for them, and they don't have the scenes or the lines to help." — *Hollywood Reporter*

Harper

Warner Brothers; Technicolor; Panavision;
121 minutes; Released: February 1966

CREDITS: *Producers*: Jerry Gershwin, Elliott Kastner; *Director*: Jack Smight; *Screenplay*: William Goldman, based on the novel *The Moving Target* by Ross MacDonald; *Photography*: Conrad Hall; *Art Direction*: Alfred Sweeney; *Sound*: Stanley Jones; *Set Decoration*: Claude Carpenter; *Music*: Johnny Mandel; *Film Editing*: Stefan Arnsten; *Makeup*: Gordon Bau.

CAST: Paul Newman (Lew Harper); Lauren Bacall (Elaine Sampson); Julie Harris (Betty Fraley); Shelley Winters (Fay Estabrook); Robert Wagner (Allan Traggert); Janet Leigh (Susan Harper); Pamela Tiffin (Miranda Sampson); Arthur Hill (Albert Graves); Robert Webber (Dwight Troy); Harold Gould (Sheriff); Roy Jenson (Puddler); Strother Martin (Claude); Martin West (Deputy); Jacqueline de Wit (Mrs. Kronberg); Eugene Iglesias (Felix); Richard Carlyle (Fred Platt); Kathryn Janssen (Telephone Operator); China Lee (Dancer); Tom Steele (Eddie Fraley); Herbert Sullivan (Waiter).

PLOT: While his estranged wife Susan is planning divorce proceedings, private detective Lew Harper takes on a new case through the recommendation of a longtime friend, attorney Albert Graves. Harper's assignment is to investigate the disappearance of the millionaire husband of the crippled and acid-tongued Elaine Sampson. At the Sampson estate Harper meets Elaine's spoiled step-daughter, Miranda, and the Sampson's glamour-boy pilot, Alan Traggert. While searching the missing man's Los Angeles hotel suite, Harper finds a photograph of one-time starlet Fay Estabrook. He tracks down the now plump and alcoholic Fay, gets her drunk, takes her home and, while searching her apartment, intercepts an enigmatic phone call which leads him to The Piano Bar. There he meets Betty Fraley, a fading singer and drug addict. After being beaten up for asking too many questions, Harper visits a mountain top which Sampson gave to a religious fanatic, Claude, for the construction of a "Temple of the clouds." When Mrs. Sampson receives a kidnapping note, Harper drops off the ransom money as per instruction. But the money is intercepted by someone driving a white convertible. Aware that it was Betty Fraley, Harper accuses Traggert of being the singer's lover and of having planned the kidnapping. Traggert draws a gun on Harper but is shot down by Graves, who makes a timely appearance. Harper goes to Betty's and find her being tortured for the ransom money by Fay's husband, Troy, who is in league with Claude in smuggling Mexicans across the border. After killing Troy, Harper gets Betty to take him to the abandoned oil tanker where Sampson is held prisoner. There he meets Graves and the two men find the body of the murdered millionaire. Betty attempts to escape but is killed when her car plummets off a cliff. While returning to the Sampson estate, Harper tells his old friend that he knows he killed Sampson. Graves admits his guilt, his motivations being hatred for Sampson and love for young Miranda. He draws a gun but lowers his arm when Harper ignores him. And the two men disgustedly mutter, "Ah hell!"

REVIEWS FOR *Harper*:

"Warners has a smashing hit on its hands in *Harper*, a funny, exciting, off-beat love story in the form of a suspense mystery. Everything about *Harper* is just right, including one of the best casting in years."—*Variety*

"Given the script, the range of California exotic settings, and the cast, the film really ought to have fired on all cylinders. It isn't a bad try, but it never slips into overdrive."—*Monthly Film Bulletin*

"This is a hugely entertaining thriller that manages to come up with suspense and excitement and comedy and yet never goes out of hand."—*New York Journal-American*

REVIEWS FOR JANET LEIGH:

"Janet Leigh has never had a better role, and she demonstrates ability not always realized."—*Hollywood Reporter*

"Janet Leigh as Mr. Newman's helpless wife and Strother Martin as a fake religious healer are excellent for types and atmosphere."—*New York Times*

"Miss Leigh accounts for perhaps 10 minutes of screentime, yet the character does nothing for the plot."—*Variety*

NOTES: The film was released in the United Kingdom as *The Moving Target*, which is the title of Ross MacDonald's original novel.

Three on a Couch

Columbia Pictures; Color; 108 minutes; June 1966

CREDITS: *Producer*: Jerry Lewis; *Director*: Jerry Lewis; *Screenplay*: Bob Ross, Samuel A. Taylor, from a story by Arne Sultan and Marvin Worth; *Photography*: W. Wallace Kelly; *Art Direction*: Leo K. Kuter; *Set Decoration*: Howard Bristol; *Costumes*: Moss Mabry; *Music*: Louis Brown; *Sound*: Walter Goss; *Film Editing*: Russel Wiles; *Makeup*: Ben Lane, Jack Stone.

CAST: Jerry Lewis (Christopher Pride / Warren / Ringo / Rutherford / Heather); Janet Leigh (Dr. Elizabeth Acord); James Best (Dr. Ben Mizer); Mary Ann Mobley (Susan Manning); Gila Golan (Anna Jacque); Leslie Parrish (Mary Lou Mauve); Kathleen Freeman (Murphy); Buddy Lester (the Drunk); Renzo Cesana (the Ambassador); Fritz Field (the Attaché); Renie Riano (Green Stamps); Danny Costello (Ballroom Singer); Scatman Crothers (Party Guest); Pepper Curtis (Girl in the Carousel).

PLOT: An artist, Christopher Pride, wins $10,000 in an art mural competition, along with the commission to paint an important mural in Paris. Chris plans to honeymoon in Paris with his fianceé, Elizabeth, a psychiatrist who insists her patients needs her. Three of them are all man-haters because of unhappy love affairs — Mary Lou is a Southern belle now immersed in zoological studies; Anne Jacque has become infatuated with the Old West; and Susan Manning has turned to athletics. With the help of his friend Dr. Ben Mizer, Chris undertakes to cure all three girls by making love to them so Elizabeth can be free to wed him. So he masquerades in turn as Rutherford, a bugs-and-beetles addict, for Mary Lou; as Raintree Ringo, king of the cowboys, for Anne Jacque; and as Warren, a health fanatic practicing karate and judo, for Susan. Chris manages to keep the three girls apart, and to keep Elizabeth happy. When the three girls confide in their psychiatrist that they have each fallen in love with a new man, Elizabeth finally consents to go to Paris.

Before leaving she invites her now cured patients to meet Chris at a farewell party —

where Chris has to reveal his real identity. Nevertheless, the girls accept the deception in good grace and persuade Elizabeth to forgive Chris.

REVIEWS FOR *Three on a Couch*:

"Lewis is agreeable and sometimes funny in his various guises ... but the film itself is a long drag through stock situations."—*Monthly Film Bulletin*

"Jerry Lewis, functioning as his own director, disciplines his super natural gift in a way that others never could. He is proceeding more intelligently, more funnily than he has in years.... There are any number of first-class gags scattered throughout the movie."—*Life*

"Only the studio is new in this latest Jerry Lewis effort. Star, director, producer and to a large degree, the script, remain the same. That means fun for Lewis fans, profits for Columbia, and some disappointment for the few who believe the promise that this would be a 'more sophisticated approach to comedy.' It isn't, although most Lewis addicts couldn't care less."—*Variety*

REVIEWS FOR *Janet Leigh*:

"Janet Leigh, looking lean and weather-beaten, plays the psychiatrist."—*New York Times*

"Janet Leigh is sharp and pretty as [the] girlfriend."—*Hollywood Reporter*

"Janet Leigh, as interesting as ever with her cool, lively face, her sad eyes and her delicately sweet-and-sour lips, sometimes brings her thinly-written part to life."—*Films and Filming*

NOTES: *Three on a Couch* was Jerry Lewis' seventh film as director and marked the first time he did not have a screenwriting credit.

An American Dream

Warner Brothers; Technicolor; 103 minutes; Released August 1966

CREDITS: *Producer*: William Conrad; *Director*: Robert Gist; *Screenplay*: Mann Rubin, based on a novel by Norman Mailer; *Photography*: Sam Leavitt; *Art Direction*: LeRoy Deane; *Set Decoration*: Ralph S. Hurst; *Costumes*: Howard Shoup; *Music*: Johnny Mandell; *Film Editing*: George Rohrs; *Makeup*: Gordon Bau.

CAST: Stuart Whitman (Stephen Richard Rojack); Janet Leigh (Cherry McMahon); Eleanor Parker (Deborah Kelly Rojack); Barry Sullivan (Lt. G. Roberts); Lloyd Nolan (Barney Kelly); Murray Hamilton (Arthur Kabot); J. D. Cannon (Sgt. Walt Leznicki); Susan Denberg (Ruta); Les Crane (Nicky); Warren Stevens (Johnny Dell); Joe De Santis (Eddie Ganucci); Stacy Harris (Detective O'Brien); Paul Mantee (Shago Martin); Harold Gould (Ganucci's Lawyer); George Takei (Attorney Ord Long); Kelly Jean Peters (Freya Stephen's Secretary); James Nolan (Monsignor Jim); Jack Shea (Police Detective); Richard Derr (Jack Hale).

PLOT: After accusing the police of associating with a Mafia group led by Eddie Ganucci, Stephen Rojack, a successful television commentator, calls on his drunken and degenerate wife Deborah, determined to ask her for a divorce. Deborah chides him unmercifully and a fight develops, which leads to Stephen attempting to throttle her, after which he half-pushes her into the street 30—floors below. He identifies the body and is taken to police headquarters, where tough Lieutenant Roberts and Sergeant Leznicki try to force a confession of murder from him. Also at the station are Ganucci, his gangster nephew, Nicky, and the latter's girlfriend, Cherry MacMahon, a nightclub singer who reminds Stephen of their affair years earlier. Released by the police for lack of evidence, Stephen resumes his liaison with Cherry in her apartment. Barney, Deborah's father, arrives to investigate her death and needles Stephen into a confession, but leaves him to his own tormented conscience. Nicky decides that Stephen must die before he can disclose anything more, and persuades Cherry to reveal the whereabouts of her apartment in return for a new club contract. She meets Stephen on the roof and begs him to leave with her. But he has come to the end of the line; borrowing her revolver, he enters the apartment and is mown down by Nicky's gang.

REVIEWS FOR *An American Dream*:

"With four months still to go the year's worst movie may well turn out to be *An American Dream*. Like a tired, jaded, mire-splattered old turkey."—*New York Times*

"[The picture] is a compelling and absorbing attraction."—*Hollywood Reporter*

"There is little to be said in favour of this relentlessly sordid and over-heated melodrama."—*Monthly Film Bulletin*

REVIEWS FOR JANET LEIGH:

"Miss Leigh must play a tarnished charm worn with casual cruelty by her benefactor, a mob chieftain and still suggest some remnants of purity. Her situation is detailed with some silliness, but she gives it remarkable conviction."—*Hollywood Reporter*

"At any rate, nothing turns out right for this picture from the understandable confusion of Mr. Whitman to the weird wall-eyed utterances of Miss Leigh."—*New York Times*

"Whitman and Miss Leigh try hard to make their dialog believable, but their romantic dalliance flags the pace and makes the plot holes more noticeable. Miss Leigh's character undergoes an abrupt change as she sells out her lover, a climactic irony which would have been neat had she not managed to convince an audience that she was really in love with him again."—*Variety*

NOTES: *An American Dream* was released in the United Kingdom as *See You in Hell, Darling*. The picture received an Academy Award nomination for Best Original Song, "A Time for Love," written by Johnny Mandel and Paul Francis Webster, which Janet Leigh's character performs in a scene voiced by Jackie Ward).

Ad Ogni Costo

(In the U.S., Grand Slam)
Paramount Pictures; Technicolor; 121 minutes; Released February 1968

CREDITS: *Producers*: Harry Colombo, George Papi; *Director*: Giuliano Montaldo; *Screenplay*: Mino Roli, Augusto Caminito, Marcello Fondato, Marcello Coscia, Jose A. De La Loma: *Photography*: Antonio Macasoli; *Art Direction*: Alberto Boccianti, Juan Alnert Soler; *Costumes*: Giorgio Desideri, Enrique Carriga; *Music*: Ennio Morricone; *Special Effects*: Armando Grilli; *Film Editing*: Nino Baragli; *Makeup*: Mario Van Riel, Adrián Jaramillo.

CAST: Janet Leigh (Mary Ann); Robert Hoffmann (Jean Paul Audry); Klaus Kinski (Eric Weiss); Riccardo Cucciolla (Agostino Rossi); Adolfo Celi (Mark Milford); Edward G. Robinson (Prof. James Anders); Jussar (Setuaka); George Rigaud (Gregg); Jean Paul Audry (Robert Hoffman); Miguel Del Castillo (Manager); Fulvio Mingozzi (Milford's Thug).

PLOT: After teaching for thirty years at a convent school in Rio de Janeiro, Professor James Anders travels to New York to see Mark Milford, an old friend who is now a prominent racketeer. Anders explains to Milford a complicated plan for an elaborate heist at a diamond company whose building he overlooked from his classroom. Milford recruits four men to do the job, which they plan to execute during Carnival. The four men go to Rio: Eric Weiss, a former German army N.C.O. and the team leader; Gregg, an English butler and a safecracker; Agostino Rossi, an Italian toy maker, and an electronic expert; and Jean Paul Audry, a French playboy whose task is to seduce Mary Ann, secretary to the diamond company. Mary Ann, in fact, holds a special magnetic key to the vault. The day before Carnival, the diamond delivery is made, but the gang discovers that the "Grand Slam 70," a new and very sensitive alarm system, has been installed. After making an alternative plan, the gang executes the robbery successfully. But a small blunder by Jean Paul makes Mary Ann suspicious and, she alerts the police. The gang begins bickering, and two members are killed by the police. Jean Paul is murdered by Eric, who is shot by Milford (who planned to double cross them all). However, when Milford examines the briefcase containing the diamonds, it is empty. Later Mary Ann meets Professor Anders in Rome; she is about to hand over the gems when a young purse snatcher rides by on a motorcycle and grabs Mary Ann's handbag, unknowingly making off with millions of dollars in stolen diamonds.

REVIEWS FOR *Ad Ogni Costo*:

"[With] a fine, tight script ... *Grand Slam* is paced like a stirring horse race."—*Variety*

"The film is short on originality and minus one smidgen of humor. Yet with a blunt, dogged tenacity it burrows away to a simmering climax."—*New York Times*

"[*Grand Slam* is] a taunt, tense, meticulously detailed enactment of an international gem theft ... from [an] architecturally fine screenplay."—*Hollywood Reporter*

REVIEWS FOR JANET LEIGH:

"Janet Leigh, as the cold, repressed but not inhuman bank secretary, gives the picture's best and lowest-keyed performance."—*New York Times*

"Performances by Robinson, Miss Leigh, Robert Hoffman ... are all standout."—*Variety*

"Janet Leigh nearly walks off with the movie as well as the surprise ending."—*TV Guide*

NOTES: *Ad Ogni Costo* opened in Italy on September 28, 1967, five months earlier than its American release.

Hello Down There

Paramount Pictures; Color; 98 minutes; Released: March 1969

CREDITS: *Producer*: George Sherman; *Director*: Jack Arnold; *Screenplay*: John McGreevely, Frank Telford, based on a story by Ivan Tors and Art Arthur; *Photography*: Clifford Poland; *Art Direction*: Jack Collis; *Set Decoration*: Don Ivey; *Wardrobe*: Peggy Kunkle; *Music*: Jeff Barry; *Film Editing*: Erwin Dumbrille; *Makeup*: Guy Del Russo.

CAST: Tony Randall (Fred Miller); Janet Leigh (Vivian Miller); Jim Backus (T. R. Hollister); Roddy McDowall (Nate Ashbury); Ken Berry (Mel Cheever); Merv Griffin (Himself); Kay Cole (Lorrie Miller); Gary Tigerman (Tommie Miller); Richard Dreyfus (Harold Webster); Lou Wagner (Marvin Webster); Charlotte Rae (Myrtle Ruth); Bud Hoey (Mr. Webster); Frank Schuller (Alan Briggs); Lee Meredith (Dr. Cara Wells); Bruce Gordon (Admiral Sheridan); Harvey Lembeck (Sonarmar); Jay Laskay (Philo); Arnold Stang (Jonah); Lora Kaye (Secretary); Andy Jarrell (Radioman).

PLOT: Inventor Fred Miller has designed and built an underwater house he calls "the Green Onion." When his boss at Underseas Development Inc. refuses to believe the project will work, Miller puts his idea into practice, persuading his wife and family to come and live with him under the sea for thirty days. The undersea party consists of Mrs. Miller, Fred's son Tommie, his daughter Lorrie, Lorrie's fiancé Harold and all the members of the Hang-Ups, a rock group to which the teenagers belong. At first everything goes well under the sea. The ladies turn out exotic sea dishes. Fred keeps busy with his experiments. And the Hung-Ups experiment with new sound. Then Fred's rival at Underseas Development Inc., Mel, pursues his pet theory — an underwater mining machine — and also arrives on the ocean floor. When the mining machine, through mismanagement, runs out of air, Mel's assistant, appropriately named Jonah, siphons a tank full of air from one of the pylons supporting the Green Onion. With one of the pylons out of action, suddenly everything becomes more chaotic. Mrs. Miller becomes less understanding, quarreling with her husband and refusing to speak to him. Meanwhile, at a U.S. Naval Sonar Station, bewildered technicians begin to pick up rock music from under the sea. They decide the music is a sonar blocking device developed by the enemy and set out to investigate. But all's well that ends well. Inspired by the wild happenings in the Green Onion, the Hang-Ups come up with a new song which is immediately voted a hit by the most important and influential young tycoon in the music world, Nate Ashbury. Mel and Jonah's mining machine collapses. Fred rescues his rivals from a watery grave. And the investigating task force from the U.S. Navy discovers that the only thing they have to fear under the sea is the Green Onion. All the merits of Fred's house are finally acknowledged.

REVIEWS FOR *Hello Down There*:

"A pleasant, unsophisticated family film." — *Los Angeles Times*

"*Hello Down There* is a typical, routine family comedy for general audiences.... Surprisingly, the songs a rock and roll combo sing are pleasant.... The underwater photography is good.... The film is [a] light entertainment." — *New York Daily News*

"[The film] should definitely be ignored." — *New York Times*

REVIEWS FOR JANET LEIGH:

"[Miss Leigh] hit some fine moments with her controlled panic button during the action and looks as lovely as the view from her underwater window." — *Hollywood Reporter*

"Both Randall and Miss Leigh clown their way through the action." — *Variety*

"Janet Leigh is as fresh as ever." — *Monthly Film Bulletin*

NOTES: The film was re-released in 1974 under the name *Sub-a-Dub-Dub*.

One Is a Lonely Number

MGM; Color; 97 minutes; Released June 1972

CREDITS: *Producer*: Stan Margulies; *Director*: Mel Stuart; *Screenplay*: David Seltzer, based on the story "The Good Humor Man" by Rebecca Morris; *Photography*: Michael Hugo; *Art Direction*: Walter M. Simonds; *Set Decoration*: George Gaines; *Wardrobe*: Dina Joseph; *Music*: Michel Legrand; *Film Editing*: David Saxon; *Sound*: Bud Alper.

CAST: Trish Van Devere (Amy Brower); Monte Markham (Howard Carpenter); Janet Leigh (Gert Meredith); Melvyn Douglas (Joseph Provo); Jane Elliot (Madge Frazier); Jonathan Lippe (Sherman Cooke); Mark Bramhall (Morgue Attendant); Paul Jenkins (James Brower); A. Scott Beach (Frawley King); Henry Leff (Arnold Holzgang); Maurice Argent (Pool Manager); Thomas McNallan (Hardware Clerk); Joseph

Spano (Earl of Kent); Morgan Upton (Earl of Gloucester); Kim Allen (Ronnie Porter); Peter Fitzsimmons (Employment Office Clerk); Christopher Brooks (Marvin Friedlander).

PLOT: Amy Brower is in disbelief when, after four years of marriage, her husband walks out on her. A professor of English literature, James promptly disappears from his classes, from the city, and from her life. Amy's puzzled wait is broken by a letter stating his plans for divorce. During an evening of remedial carousing, a conversation with two friends reveals Amy's vulnerable unworldliness. Through an employment agency, Amy gets a job as a summer lifeguard at a municipal pool, but she is too frightened to give the required weekly high dive exhibitions. She feels lonely, but Mr. Provo, an elderly neighborhood grocer, can guess her story from her pitifully small purchases and her brave façade. The old man confides his own grief. After thirty-nine years of marriage, he cannot stop loving the memory of his wife — although he's learned, he warns Amy, it's not good for people to be alone too much. Amy survives a rather ugly assault by Sherman, a young man from the employment agency, but the summer progresses unevenly until she meets at a little party in an art gallery Howard, an attractive, fortyish guy who takes her to dinner and then back to his apartment. But Amy gets cold feet and awkwardly flees. At a birthday celebration, Amy accepts Mr. Provo's invitation to attend a performance in the park of *King Lear*. But the evening ends on a sad note when the twosome dissolve into tears, commiserating with each other on their mutual loneliness. Returning home, Amy finds Howard waiting, and now she embarks on her first post-marital affair. Her temporary state of happiness is jolted back to harsh reality when Howard confesses he is already married, and when she learns that her husband is living in Reno with a nineteen-year-old. Amy becomes vindictive and orders her lawyer to make James pay dearly for his freedom. Finally, on the day of her divorce hearing, she walks to the courthouse in a different state of mind and flatly states that all she wants, or needs, is her freedom. Once the legal procedures are over, Amy goes to the swimming pool, climbs to the top of the high board, no longer afraid, and executes a perfect dive.

REVIEWS FOR *One Is a Lonely Number*:

"What differentiates this from the traditional matinee weeper ... is a certain hardness around the edges, which is probably equally attributable to Mel Stuart's documentary-style direction and David Seltzer's straightforward, unadorned script."—*Hollywood Reporter*

"*One Is a Lonely Number* is a social satire, a judicious blend of wit and compassion and full of perceptive observations of contemporary mores. It also evokes the pain of loneliness yet affirms the preciousness of life."—*Los Angeles Times*

"The film ... is an odd mixture of true and false notes, wit and corn."—*The Village Voice*

REVIEWS FOR JANET LEIGH:

"Janet Leigh [is] excellent."—*New York Times*

"The supporting characters each get a chance to stand out in passing scenes: Miss Leigh, for example as a bitchy divorcee."—*Variety*

"Janet Leigh and Melvyn Douglas add some undeserved luster to the proceedings."—*Monthly Film Bulletin*

NOTES: Despite general good reviews, *One Is a Lonely Number* did not do well at the box office. MGM tried changing the title to *Two Is a Happy Number*, but it didn't help.

Trish Van Devere received a Golden Globe nomination for her performance.

The Night of the Lepus

MGM; Color; 88 minutes; Released October 1972

CREDITS: *Producer:* A. C. Lyles; *Director:* William F. Claxton; *Screenplay:* Don Holliday, Gene R. Kearney, based on the novel *The Year of the Angry Rabbit* by Russell Braddon; *Photography:* Ted Voigtlander; *Set Decoration:* William F. Calvert; *Wardrobe:* Norman Burza; *Music:* Jimmy Haskell; *Film Editing:* John McSweeney, Jr.; *Special Effects:* Howard A. Anderson Company; *Sound:* Jerry Host, Hal Watkins; *Makeup:* Wes Dawn.

CAST: Stuart Whitman (Roy Bennett); Janet Leigh (Gerry Bennett); Rory Calhoun (Cole Hillman); DeForest Kelley (Elgin Clark); Paul Fix (Sheriff Cody); Melanie Fullerton (Amanda Bennett); Chris Morrell (Jackie Hillman); Chuck Hayward (Jud); Henry Wills (Frank); Francesac Jarvis (Mildred); William Elliot (Dr. Leopold); Robert Hardy (Professor Dirkson); Richard Jacome (Deputy Jackson); Inez Perez (Housekeeper); G. Leroy Gaintner (Walker); Evans Thornton (Major White); I. Stanford Jolley (Dispatcher); Robert Gooden (Leslie); Walter Kelley (Truck Driver); Frank Kennedy (Doctor); Don Star (Cutler); Peter O'Crotty (Arlen); Phillip Avenetti (Officer Lopez); Russell Morrell (Priest).

PLOT: Cole Hillman, an Arizona rancher, finds that after getting rid of the coyotes that used to roam his land, he is faced with the problem of disposing of a profusion of hungry rabbits. He contacts his friend, Elgin Clark, at Porterville College, who sends him Roy and Gerry Bennett, scientists who are experimenting with pest control by natural means. They isolate a control group of rabbits at their laboratory and inject each with a different virus in an attempt to develop a contagious disease, but their daughter Amanda manages to switch control rabbit with an infected one and allow it to escape on Cole's land. Sometime later a truck breaks down near the Hillman ranch, and the driver gets out to repair the damage. Meanwhile, Amanda and her friend Jackie visit an old prospector at his mine, only to find his body being dragged into the tunnel by something huge and furry. Deputy Jason finds the truck driver's mangled corpse, which bears marks similar to those on the remains of the old miner. The significance of these killings slowly dawns on the horrified local inhabitants. The inoculations have resulted in a startling mutation — somewhere in the Arizona desert there is a hoard of carnivorous wolf-sized rabbits. Hillman tries to blow up their burrows, but the enormous explosion only serves to panic the rabbits, who, maddened by hunger, thunder forth to terrorize the farming community. The rabbits leave a trail of carnage and destruction before Hillman and his friends are able to find a means of halting this furry stampede forever.

REVIEWS FOR *Night of the Lepus*:

"The basic plot line of *Night of the Lepus* had the makings of a superior, timely, thought-provoking sci-fi exploitationer; however, inept dialog and worse direction reduce the A.C. Lyles production to a shambles." — *Variety*

"Technical laziness as much as the stupid story or the dumb direction ... leaves the film in a limbo and place it in neither one camp nor the other — neither with *Attack of the 50-Foot Woman* nor with Flopsy, Mopsy and Cottontail." — *New York Times*

"Dull and predictable ... at least it's not being released at Easter." — *Cue*

REVIEWS FOR JANET LEIGH:

"Whitman, Miss Leigh, and Calhoun moved through their roles with stoic uncertainty." — *Hollywood Reporter*

"Stuart Whitman, Janet Leigh, and Rory Calhoun are given no characterizations to enact other than to be normal, everyday people caught up in a crisis, and they react credibly and register pleasantly." —*Los Angeles Times*

NOTES: The original title was *Rabbits*, but MGM ultimately decided such a moniker didn't suit a horror film.

Boardwalk

Atlantic Releasing Corporation; Technicolor;
98 minutes; Released November 1979

CREDITS: *Producer*: George Willoughby; *Director*: Stephen Verona; *Screenplay*: Leigh Chapman, Stephen Verona; *Photography*: Billy Williams; *Art Direction*: Glenda Ganis; *Set Decoration*: Caryl Heller; *Costumes*: Betsy Jones; *Music*: William S. Fisher, Michael Kamen, Rob Mounsey, Coleridge-Taylor-Perkinson; *Film Editing*: Thorn Noble; *Special Effects*: Peter Kunz; *Makeup*: Elke Gordon.

CAST: Ruth Gordon (Becky Rosen); Lee Strasberg (David Rosen); Janet Leigh (Florence Cohen); Joe Silver (Leo Rosen); Eddie Barth (Eli Rosen); Merwin Goldsmith (Charley); Michael Ayr (Peter); Forbesey Russell (Marilyn); Chevi Colton (Vera Rosen); Teri Keane (Betty Rosen); Eli Mintz (Friedman); Rashel Novikoff (Sadie); Lillian Roth (Ruth); Kim Delgado (Strut); Ramon Franco (Pappy); Scoot Paco Coleman (Juan); Linda Manz (Girl Satan); Antonia Rey (Carmelita); Nat Polen (Dr. Rothbart); Sammy Cahn (Morris); Arnold Soboloff (Benny); Harold Gary (Morganstern); Altovise Davis (Mrs. Bell); Lloyd Hollar (Mr. Bell); Andrea Kessler (Hairdresser); Annette Miller (Mrs. Lerner); Mark Stephan Kondracki (Stuart Lerner); David R. Ellis (Bath Attendant); Gina DeAngelis (Mrs. Pompianno); Sam Rubinsky (Fruit Man); Zvee Scooler (Rabbi).

PLOT: The Brooklyn beach-front community in which David and Becky Rosen have spent a long, loving life together is disintegrating. Menacing street gangs have invaded the area, causing stores to close and neighbors to sell up and move away. But David refuses to be driven out. Strut, the arrogant leader of the Satan gang, attempts to provoke David on the boardwalk. David quietly yet firmly refuses to be drawn into a confrontation and leaves Strut seething. But now David has become a target, and Strut incites one of the gang to steal from David's cafeteria in which David, his two middle-aged sons and daughter Florence all work together. David's attempt to befriend the would-be thief is rejected, and the boy returns to the gang. The next night the gang pillages the home of Friedman, the local grocer, leaving the old couple in tears. A seemingly insurmountable generation gap exists between Florence and her rock musician son Peter. When Florence enters into a loveless marriage of convenience, a disapproving Peter avoids attending the ceremony. Florence, in turn, is shaken and angry when Peter brings Marilyn, the girl he is living with, to meet the family. Joyful, sympathetic Becky welcomes the young couple, but her peace of mind is disturbed when, after a sinister encounter with a gypsy fortune-teller, her failing health is confirmed by a doctor. Yet, even though she is further distressed by witnessing a fire-bomb attack by the gang on the cafeteria, she resolves to keep her secret and face her fate with courage. She attends her grandson's opening at a Manhattan nightclub and prepares for a 50th wedding anniversary. However, the celebration proves too much for her, and, after a last waltz together, she dies in David's arms. Strut steps up his reign of terror, again breaking into Friedman's home and threatening his wife with sexual abuse. It is the last straw. Two days later the bodies of the old couple are found in their gas-filled apartment. Peter breaks up with Marilyn and returns briefly to stay with his bereaved grandfather but soon takes to the road in pursuit of his musical career. Still out for revenge on David, who had kicked him in the jaw and broken his nose in an earlier encounter, Strut and his gang savagely vandalize the temple in which David worships and then attack his home, destroying his prized possession. An enraged David seeks out for the gang on the boardwalk. Strut draws a knife, but David knocks it from his hand and, now a man possessed, grabs Strut by the throat. The gang backs away as the life goes out of their leader. David lets go of Strut, and as the body falls to the boardwalk, the Satans disperse.

REVIEWS FOR *Boardwalk*:

"Despite its schematized structure, *Boardwalk* succeeds in evoking a palpable and authentic sense of character and environment." — *Variety*

"Verona ... while he does capture a sense of realism, he has been unable to create a sense of pace to the script, which is made up of short, mostly gloomy scenes. This structure is jerky and Verona's staging occasionally seems to be pretentiously arty." — *Hollywood Reporter*

"The sole distinction of this mawkish saga is that one would probably have to reach back as far as *Birth of a Nation* to find a more direct incitement of racial hatred." — *Monthly Film Bulletin*

REVIEWS FOR JANET LEIGH:

"Janet Leigh, in her best roles in years." — *Films in Review*

"A still stunning-looking Janet Leigh." — *Films and Filming*

"The only thing the movie has going for it is a cast of good actors Mr. Strasberg, Miss Gordon and Miss Leigh provide their roles with depths of feelings that come out of their own resources, certainly not the director's or the writers." — *New York Times*

The Fog

Avco Embassy Picture; Color; 91 minutes; Released February 1980

CREDITS: *Producer*: Debra Hill; *Director*: John Carpenter; *Screenplay*: John Carpenter, Debra Hill; *Photography*: Dean Cundey; *Art Direction*: Craig Stearns; *Production Design*: Tommy Lee Wallace; *Costumes*: Steven Loomis, Bill Whitten; *Music*: John Carpenter; *Film Editing*: Tommy Lee Wallace, Charles Bornstein; *Sound*: Craig Felburg; *Special Effects*: Richard Albain, Jr.; *Makeup*: Dante Palmiere, Ed Ternes, Erica Ueland.

CAST: Adrienne Barbeau (Stevie Wayne); Jamie Lee Curtis (Elizabeth Solley); Janet Leigh (Kathy Williams); Hal Holbrook Father Malone); Tom Atkins (Nick Castle); John Houseman (Mr. Machen); Nancy Loomis (Sandy Fadel); James Canning (Dick Baxter); Charles Cypher (Dan O'Bannon); Ty Mitchell (Andy); John Goff (Al Williams); George "Buck" Flower (Tommy Wallace); Regina Waldon (Mrs. Kobritz); Jim Haynie (Dockmaster); Darrow Igis (Mel); John Vic (Sheriff Simms); Jay Jacobs (Mayor); Fred Franklyn (Ashcroft); Ric Moreno (Ghost); Lee Sacks (Ghost); Bill Taylor (Bartender); Rob Bottin (Blake); Darwin Joston (Mr. Phibes); John Strobel (Grocery Clerk); John Carpenter (Bennett).

PLOT: Late one night an old fisherman, Machen, captivates a group of children with a ghost story of a shipwreck that occurred 100 years ago that very night on the shoals just off Antonio Bay, where the campfire burns brightly. The story tells of a treasure ship, the "Elizabeth Dane," deliberately misled by a false beacon light, and the eerie, supernatural fog which strangely enveloped the ship as it was wrecked. Local superstition has it that when the fog returns to Antonio Bay, the murdered mariners will rise from their watery graves and seek vengeance. This innocent retelling of an old legend becomes the prelude for a harrowing sequence of events. The transformation of this ancient tale into a real-life occurrence brings several characters in focus. Stevie Wayne, the local disc-jockey and radio station owner, is warned that night of an approaching fog bank. At the same time, Nick Castle and a young hitchhiker he has picked up, Elizabeth Solley, are stunned when all the glass in Nick's truck suddenly explodes into pieces. Father Malone, alone in his church, is startled when a section of stone slab falls from the wall of his study; and Kathy Williams, chairwoman of the town's anniversary celebration, is perplexed at the failure of her husband to return with the trawler "Sea Grass." The gaping hole in the wall of the old church reveals a journal, which in turn tells of a sinister plot to deliberately shipwreck the "Elizabeth Dane." Father Malone discovers that six of the founders of Antonio Bay were the culprits. Should the fog ever return, six people must die in atonement. Stevie Wayne, from her lighthouse radio station, gradually realizes that a strange evil power is creeping over the town of Antonio Bay as its centennial celebration progresses. She continuously tries to warn the town of the impeding danger, while she, herself, must make a lone stand against the supernatural fog. Nick and Elizabeth are the first to discover the mysterious deaths of the men on the "Sea Grass," and they are drawn deeper and deeper into the mystery. In the end they are effective in saving several lives, including that of Stevie's son, Andy, who becomes involved when he discovers a piece of driftwood bearing the name of the stricken ship, the "Dane." Kathy Williams, her assistant Sandy Fadel, Nick, Elizabeth, Andy Wayne and Father Malone are all drawn together as victims of the ghostly vengeance, and together they make a last stand against the supernatural terror at the church. Five people have died by the time Nick and Father Malone confront the ghostly predator with a cross made of treasure gold. In the ensuing struggle, the cross glows white hot, and the ghostly element disappears as the fog recedes. But the question remains — do five deaths atone for six crimes?

REVIEWS FOR *The Fog*:

"Well-made suspenser looks to be a good bet to equal or surpass the returns on Carpenter's sleeper hit *Halloween*."—*Variety*

"*The Fog* has its moments. Carpenter excels at building a sense of menace."—*Hollywood Reporter*

"*The Fog* is constructed of random diversions. There are too many story lines, which necessitate so much cross-cutting that no one sequence can ever build a decent climax. The movie looks quite pretty but prettiness of this sort is beside the point in such a film."—*New York Times*

REVIEWS FOR JANET LEIGH:

"Thesping is okay in all departments, although Leigh isn't given much to do, nor is daughter Curtis."—*Variety*

NOTES: *The Fog* is the first feature in which Janet Leigh and her daughter Jamie Leigh Curtis appear together.

Halloween H20: Twenty Years Later

Dimensions Film; Color; 86 minutes; Released August 1998

CREDITS: *Producer:* Debra Hill; *Director:* John Carpenter; *Screenplay:* John Carpenter, Debra Hill; *Photography:* Dean Cundey; *Art Direction:* Craig Stearns; *Production Design:* Tommy Lee Wallace; *Costumes:* Steven Loomis, Bill Whitten; *Music:* John Carpenter; *Film Editing:* Tommy Lee Wallace, Charles Bornstein; *Sound:* Craig Felburg; *Special Effects:* Richard Albain, Jr.; *Makeup:* Dante Palmiere, Ed Ternes, Erica Ueland.

CAST: Jamie Lee Curtis (Laurie Strode/Keri Tate); Josh Hartnett (John Tate); Adam Arkin (Will Brennan); Michelle Williams (Molly Cartwell); Adam Hann-Byrd (Charlie Deveraux); Jodi Lyn O'Keefe (Sarah Wainthrope); Janet Leigh (Norma Watson); Nancy Stephens (Marion Chambers Whittington); LL Cool J (Ronald "Ronny" Jones); Joseph Gordon-Levitt (Jimmy Howell); Lisa Gay Hamilton (Shirley "Shirl" Jones); Chris Durand (Michael Myers); Larisa Miller (Claudia); Emmalee Thompson (Casey); Tom Kane (Dr. Samuel Loomis); Matt Winston (Detective Matt Sampson); Branden William (Tony Allegre); Beau Billingslea (Detective Fitzsimmons).

PLOT: Twenty years after terrorizing his sister, Laurie Stode, Michael Myers is still on the loose. He murders Marion Wittington, former nurse of his late doctor Sam Loomis, and steals her file on Laurie. Having faked her death years ago, Laurie has changed her name to Keri Tate and is headmistress at a boarding school where John, her teenage son from a marriage that went bad, is a student. With Halloween approaching, Laurie has become skittish about the possibility of Michael returning, and her guidance counselor boyfriend, Will Brennan, tries to calm her frayed nerves. On Halloween day the students leave the school for a camping trip, but, unbeknownst to Laurie, John stays behind with his girlfriend Molly and their friends Charlie and Sarah. Michael does indeed return, and the fleeing John and Molly are rescued by Laurie and Will. As they try to escape, Will accidentally shoots security guard Ronny before Michael kills him. Laurie sends John and Molly off to safety before turning back to confront Michael. A lengthy battle ends with Laurie stabbing her brother and pitching him out a window. When the paramedics arrive, Laurie steals the coroner's van containing Michael's body, and when he revives she crashes the van and decapitates Michael with an ax.

REVIEWS FOR *Halloween H20:*

"For horror films devotees eager to know how this unseasonable visit from the darker spirit of autumn rates, frankly, it's more marketing trick than moviegoers treat."—*New York Times*

"While plot mechanics aren't wildly imaginative, pic nonetheless delivers requisite jolts in an above-average package."—*Variety*

"*Halloween H20* is engaging but unremarkable, far more sexually charged than the original and anything but scary. Instead of covering their eyes, audiences now smile knowingly."—*Daily Telegraph*

REVIEWS FOR JANET LEIGH: "Curtis's off-screen mom Janet Leigh, no minor horror icon herself, appears in a small role, garnering an appreciative laugh when she says to Curtis, "Allow me to be maternal for a moment."—*Hollywood Reporter*

"The appearance of Janet Leigh as a school secretary is thrill-pure and simple, Jamie Lee's mother, the star of *Psycho*! "If I can be maternal for a moment," she murmurs to Laurie, and then the camera pulls back to reveal the old woman's car—the Ford cruiser *Psycho*'s Marion Crane drove nearly four decades ago! Leigh's brief reunion with her heartily likable, resilient daughter carries more of a charge than any pileup of bloody bodies."—*Entertainment Weekly*

"*Halloween H20* has some fun by positioning Janet Leigh, Ms. Curtis's mother and the star of the terror classic *Psycho*, as one of the school staff, which gives her an opportunity to begin one conversation by saying, "If I could be maternal for a moment" and going on to observe, "We've both had bad things happen to us."—*New York Times*

NOTES: *Halloween: H20* is the seventh film in the series started in 1978 with *Halloween*, directed by John Carpenter and starring Jamie Lee Curtis.

Bad Girls from Valley High
Universal Home Entertainment; Color;
84 minutes; Released direct to DVD March 2005

CREDITS: *Producers*: Sid Sheinberg, Jon Sheinberg, Bill Sheinberg; *Director*: John T. Kretchmer; *Screenplay*: Andrew Lane, Robert Locash, based on the novel by Paul Fleischman; *Photography*: Suki Medencevic; *Art Direction*: Craig Stearns; *Production Manager*: Christina Toy; *Costumes*: Patricia L. Hargreaves; *Music*: Shawn K. Clement, Sean Murray; *Film Editing*: Ross Albert; *Sound*: Patrick Ramsay; *Makeup*: Tony Gardner.

CAST: Julie Benz (Danielle); Monica Keena (Brooke); Nicole Bilderback (Tiffany); Jonathan Brandis (Drew); Aaron Paul (Jonathan Wharton); Suzanna Urszuly (Katarina); Chris D'Elia (Gavin); Janet Leigh (Mrs. Witt); Christopher Lloyd (Mr. Chauncey); Terrance Morris (Track Athlete); Tanja Reichert (Charity Chase); Jennifer Anne Carmichael (Sales Girl), Bobby Jo Moore (Girl in Towel); Dolores Drake (Nurse Chambers); Luisa Cianni (Nicole).

PLOT: Danielle, Tiffany and Brooke are three teenage girlfriends who accidentally cause the death of Charity Chase, a fellow student, when a prank goes wrong. The unfortunate girl was dating Drew, an ex-jock who Danielle wanted for herself. One year later Katarina, a mysterious Romanian foreign exchange student, turns up and begins dating Drew. The three girls plot revenge, but soon all sorts of strange events start happening to them. Suddenly, they start to age rapidly, becoming gray-haired and tired. The three suspect Katarina of being the ghost of Charity seeking her revenge. They lure Drew to the same spot where Charity died and attempt to shoot him; however, in the commotion, Danielle and Tiffany get hurt and later end up dying. Brooke, thanks to her kindness and sense of self-control, is the only one to survive. In the meantime, lurking in the background is Mr. Chauncey, a clumsy teacher who suspects that the teenagers may have had something to do with each other's death. At the funeral the teacher forgives Brooke, who regrets what she has done with her girlfriends. Danielle and Tiffany, with their youth restored, wake up in Hell, where they are forced to endure for eternity the company of Jonathan, the most annoying nerd at the school, who had committed suicide just to be with them forever.

REVIEWS FOR *Bad Girls from Valley High*:

"The picture isn't great cinema by any means, but it's an occasionally amusing B-Movie."—*Current DVD*

"Very Bad. This lame excuse for a comedy/thriller fails at each level."—*Movieman's Guide to the Movies*

NOTES: The film was shot in 2000 with the title *A Fate Worse Than Death*, but it was released directly to DVD in 2005 as *Bad Girls from Valley High* just a few months after Janet Leigh's death.

Television Films

The Monk

Thomas-Spelling Productions; Color; 90 minutes; ABC 10/21/1969

CREDITS: *Producer*: Tony Barrett; *Director*: George McCowan; *Teleplay*: Blake Edwards, based on a story by Blake Edwards; *Photography*: Fleet Southcott; *Music*: Earle Hagen; *Film Editing*: Bob Lewis; *Art Direction*: Tracy Bousman.

CAST: George Maharis (Gus Monk); Janet Leigh (Janice Barnes); Jack Albertson (Tinker); Carl Betz (Danny Gouzenko); Raymond St. Jacques (Lieutenant Edward Heritage); Rick Jason (Wideman); William Smithers (Leo Barnes); Jack Soo (Hip Guy); Edward G. Robinson, Jr. (Trapp); Mary Wickes (Mrs. Medford); Jo Besser (Herbie); George Burrafato (Stranger); Walter Reed (Director); George Saurel (Sergeant Mawson); John Hancock (Charlie); Bob Nash (Doorman).

PLOT: Unlicensed private investigator Gus Monk is somewhat embarrassed after finding himself the prime suspect in the murder of an underworld lawyer who had hired him to guard a valuable envelope containing incriminating evidence on a mafia boss.

NOTES: *The Monk* was an unsuccessful pilot for a never-produced TV series developed by Blake Edwards.

Honeymoon with a Stranger

20th Century–Fox Television; Color; 90 minutes; ABC 12/23/1969

CREDITS: *Producer*: Robert L. Jacks; *Director*: John Peyser; *Teleplay*: David P. Harmon, Henry Slesar, based on the novel *Piege Pour un Homme Seul* by Robert Thomas; *Photography*: Rafael Pacheco de Usa; *Music*: Mark Bucci; *Film Editing*: Joe Gluck; *Art Direction*: Santiago Otanon Fernandez.

CAST: Janet Leigh (Sandra Lathman); Rossano Brazzi (Captain Sevilla); Joseph Lenzi (First Ernesto); Cesare Danova (Second Ernesto); Juan Elices (Juanito); Eric Braeden (Frederico Caprio); Barbara Steele (Carla); Sancho Garcia (Sergeant); Raul Anthony (Policeman).

PLOT: While honeymooning in Spain, a bride wakes up to discover her husband gone and an imposter in his place, but she cannot convince the police of the switch.

House on Greenapple Road

Quinn Martin Productions; Color; 135 minutes; ABC 1/11/1970

CREDITS: *Producer*: Adrian Samish; *Director*: Robert Day; *Teleplay*: George Eckstein, based on a novel by Harold R. Daniels; *Photography*: Robert Hoffman; *Music*: Duane Tatro; *Film Editing*: Thomas Ness; *Art Direction*: James D. Vance.

CAST: Christopher George (Lieutenant Dan August); Janet Leigh (Marian Ord); Julie Harris (Leona Miller); Tim O'Connor (George Ord); Walter Pidgeon (Mayor Jack Parker); Barry Sullivan (Chief Frank Untermyer); Keenan Wynn (Sergeant Charles Wilentz); Mark Richman (Sal Gilman); William Windom (Paul Durstine); Burr DeBenning (Bill Foley); Lynda Day (Lillian Crane); Joanne Linville (Connie Durstine);

Edward Asner (Sheriff Muntz); Eve Plumb (Margaret Ord); Laurence Dane; Ned Romero; Paul Fix; Alice Jubert; Paul Lukather; John Ward; Geoffrey Deuel; Tina Menard; Ress Vaugh; Olan Soule.

PLOT: A dogged detective investigates the murder of the promiscuous wife of a meek salesman, whose body cannot be found.

REVIEWS FOR JANET LEIGH:

"Miss Leigh is truly fine as Marion Ord.... Hers are some of the finest scenes of the evening." — *Hollywood Reporter*

NOTES: *The House on Greenapple Road* was originally made for theatrical release, but was trimmed of nearly 30 minutes and sent straight to ABC-TV.

The Deadly Dream

Universal Television; Color; 90 minutes; ABC 9/25/1971

CREDITS: *Producer*: Stan Shpetner; *Director*: Alf Kjellin; *Teleplay*: Barry Oringer; *Photography*: Jack Marta; *Music*: Dave Grusin; *Film Editing*: Robert L. Kimble; *Art Direction*: Lloyd S. Papez; *Costumes*: Grady Hunt.

CAST: Lloyd Bridges (Dr. Jim Hanley); Janet Leigh (Laurel Hanley); Carl Betz (Dr. Howard Geary); Leif Erickson (Dr. Harold Malcom); Don Stroud (Kagan); Richard Jaeckel (Delgreve); Phillip Pine (Dr. Farrow); Herbert Nelson (Dr. Goldman); Arlene Dahl (Connie); Salome Jens (Mary); Janet Lombard (Betty); Chuck Morrell (Ambulance Driver).

PLOT: A research scientist is driven to madness by a recurring dream that he is marked for murder by a mysterious tribunal, and that his wife and friends are part of the conspiracy. Soon he becomes unable to separate dreams from reality and vice versa.

NOTE: This was the first ABC-TV "Movie of the Weekend" feature presentation.

Murdock's Gang

Don Fedderson Productions; Color; 90 minutes; ABC 3/20/1973

CREDITS: *Producer*: Edward S. Feldman; *Director*: Charles S. Dubin; *Teleplay*: Edmund H. North; *Photography*: Michael Joyce; *Music*: Frank DeVol; *Film Editing*: Charles Van Enger; *Art Direction*: Perry Ferguson II.

CAST: Alex Dreier (Bartley James Murdock); Janet Leigh (Laura Talbot); Murray Hamilton (Harold Talbot); William Daniels (Roger Bates); Harold Gould (Dave Ryker); Don Knight (Glenn Dixon); Walter Burke (Bert Collins); Colby Chester (Larry DeVans); Donna Benz (Terry); Norman Alden (Red Harris); Ed Bernard (Ed Lyman); Charles Dierop (Denver Briggs); Dave Morick (Mickey Carr); Milton Selzer (Frank Winston); Frank Campanella (Barney Pirelli); Fred Sadoff (Dr. Barkis); Eddie Firestone (Hellstrom); William Fletcher (George); Larry McCormick (TV Reporter); Karen Arthur (Ryker's Secretary).

PLOT: Bartley James Murdock, a flamboyant attorney framed for a crime he never committed, is disbarred and incarcerated. Upon his release, he and his staff of ex-cons are hired by a multimillionaire to solve the disappearance of a trusted bookkeeper. The investigation uncovers a trail of murder, suicide, blackmail and double-dealing.

NOTES: *Murdock's Gang* was a TV pilot for a never produced TV series.

Murder at the World Series

ABC Circle Films; Color; 120 minutes; ABC 3/20/1977

CREDITS: *Producer*: Cy Chermak; *Director*: Andrew V. McLagen; *Teleplay*: Cy Chermak; *Photography*: Richard C. Glouner; *Music*: John Cacavas; *Film Editing*: John F. Link, Richard A. Harris; *Art Direction*: Elayne Barbara Ceder.

CAST: Lynda Day George (Margot Mannering); Murray Hamilton (Harvey Murkinson); Karen Valentine (Lois Marshall); Gerald S. O'Loughlin (Moe Gold); Michael Parks (Larry Marshall); Janet Leigh (Karen Weese); Hugh O'Brian (the Governor); Nancy Kelly (Alice Dakso); Johnny Seven (Severino); Tamara Dobson (Lisa); Joseph Wiseman (Sam Druckman); Bruce Boxleitner (Cisco); Larry Mahan (Gary Vawn); Cooper Huckabee (Frank Gresham); Maggie Wellman (Kathy); Cynthia Avila (Jane Torres); Monica Gayle (Barbara Gresham); Liasa Hartman (Stewardess); Bob Allen (Reporter); Dick Enberg (Radio Announcer).

PLOT: A troubled young man, bent on avenging the Houston Astros baseball team's rejection, plots a series of bizarre kidnappings during the final two games of the World Series in Houston and places the lives of five innocent women in jeopardy.

NOTES: The original title for this movie was *The Woman in Box 539*. Jamie Lee Curtis appears in the credits as "Dialogue Coach."

Telethon

ABC Circle Films; Color; 120 minutes; ABC 11/6/1977

CREDITS: *Producer*: Robert Lovenheim; *Director*: David Lowell Rich; *Teleplay*: Roger Wilton; *Photography*: James R. Marquette; *Music*: Peter Matz; *Film Editing*: Howard Epstein, Michael Karr; *Art Direction*: Bill Kenney.

CAST: Polly Bergen (Dorothy Goodwin); Lloyd Bridges (Matt Tallman); Red Buttons (Marty Rand); Edd Byrnes (Charlie Barton); Dick Clark (Irv Berman); Janet Leigh (Elaine Cotten); John Marley (Arnold Shagan); Kent McCord (Tom Galvin); Eve Plumb (Kim); David Selby (Roy Hansen); Jill St. John (Fran Sullivan); Randi Oakes (June); Sheila Sullivan (Lorna); Dave Burton (Himself); Jimmy Walker (Himself); Sugar Ray Robinson (Himself); Deborah Denomme (Jennifer); The Fercos (Themselves); Heather and David (Themselves); Norman Honath (Bus Driver); Jean Magowan (Jean); Peter Rich (Norm Fenton); Dawn Rowan (Sue Marie Atkins); Chad Schooley (Bobby); Billy Snyder (Pitt Boss); Carol Van Dyke (Mrs. Arkins).

PLOT: This is the behind-the-scenes story of a Telethon, a twenty-four-hour TV show held at the Dunes Hotel in Las Vegas with an all-star TV cast. The organizer of the show has to pay off the syndicate and relies on faded comedy star Marty Rand to help him.

Mirror, Mirror

Christiana Productions; Color; 120 minutes; NBC 10/10/1979

CREDITS: *Producer*: Jerry Adler; *Director*: Joanna Lee; *Teleplay*: Charles Dennis, Leah Appet; *Photography*: Ben Colman; *Music*: Jimmie Haskell; *Film Editing*: Carroll Sax; *Art Direction*: Kim Swados.

CAST: Janet Leigh (Millie Gorman); Lee Meriwether (Vanessa Wagner); Robert Vaughn (Michael Jacoby); Loretta Swift (Sandy McLaren); Peter Bonerz (Andrew

McLaren); Robin Mattson (Pamela Gorman); Walter Brooke (Dr. Samuel Shaw); McKee Anderson (Annie); Elizabeth Robinson (Paula Johnson); Chris Lemmon (Jonathan Shelton); Shelley Smith (Nola McGuire); Michael Hughes (Dr. Richards); Angus Duncan (Bud Stone); Ken Medlock (Ken, Coach); Chris Ciampa (Chris McLaren); José DeVega (Armando, the Chauffer); Regis Philbin (TV Host); Harold P. Pruett (Joey McLaren); Ernestine Barrier (Lillian Appleby); Scott Howard Pincus (Sam McLaren); Amanda Davies (Booking Coordinator).

PLOT: Millie Gorman, a wealthy widow; Sandy McLaren, a restless housewife; and Vanessa Wagner, a former model become casually acquainted at an exercise studio. They all seek to reshape themselves through cosmetic surgery. They all tell each other the real reasons behind their decision to undergo cosmetic surgery. Millie is in a rivalry with her college-aged daughter; Sandy is insecure about her flat chest; while Vanessa, who wishes to run her own model agency, wants surgery before a reunion with a lover she hasn't seen in ten years.

In My Sister's Shadow
Steinhart-Baer Pictures; CBS Entertainment Pictures;
Color; 120 minutes; CBS 1/5/1999

CREDITS: *Producer*: Sandra Saxon Brice, Kimberly Rubin; *Director*: Sandor Stern; *Teleplay*: Dan Vining, Ronni Kernd, based on a story by Rob Fresco; *Photography*: Ron Orieux; *Music*: Dennis McCarthy; *Film Editing*: Jere Huggins; *Production Designer*: Frederick C. Weiler.

CAST: Nancy McKeon (Joan Connor); Thomas McCarthy (Michael); Alexandra Wilson (Laurie Connor); Mark Dobies (Mark); Janet Leigh (Kay Connor); Scott Wilkinson (Detective Hunt); Christy Summerhays (Trish); Chelsey Rice (Young Joan); Billy Mondy (Mr. Connor); Monique Betty (Young Laurie); Brad Slocum (Bill); Jaime Rodriguez (Punk); Adam Smoot (Punk); Timothy Shoemaker (Flower Delivery Man); Jeff Olson (Building Superintendent); Joey Miyashima (Uniformed Cop); Rober Conder (Uniform Cop); Jim Holmes (SWAT Commander); Brenda Sue Cowley (Bartender); Luke Baird (Boy in the Fish Store); Jeff Rector (Man at Bar).

PLOT: Joan Connor, an average florist, becomes involved with Michael, her sister's ex-boyfriend, who begins stalking his ex and her new beau. Michael turns Joan against her sister, and soon she becomes caught up in a web of deadly revenge.

NOTES: *In My Sister's Shadow* was completed in 1997, but CBS didn't air it until January 1999.

Short Films

How to Smuggle a Hernia Across the Border
(1951)

CREDITS: *Producer*: Jerry Lewis; *Director*: Jerry Lewis; *Screenplay*: Jerry Lewis.
CAST: Jerry Lewis; Tony Curtis; Janet Leigh.
PLOT: In this farcical short, Jerry Lewis plays a dual role as a near-naked American Indian and as an effeminate Army recruiting officer.
NOTE: From 1951 on, Jerry Lewis directed a number of "home movies" shot in 16

mm. They were usually spoofs of current Hollywood films, sporting such titles as *A Streetcar Named Repulsive, Come Back, Little Shiksa, Watch on the Lime, A Spot in the Shade, Son of Lifeboat, Son of Spellbound, Melvin's Revenge, The Re-Enforcer* and *Fairfax Avenue* (a spoof of *Sunset Blvd.* in which Janet played Norma Desmond), and were made with many of his friend actors. Among others were Janet Leigh, Tony Curtis, Dean Martin, Sammy Davis, Jr., Shelley Winters, John Barrymore, Jr., and Jeff Chandler. Those films were intended for personal use and were never released; therefore it is impossible to catalogue them.

Appendices

A. Television Appearances

Some of Janet Leigh's appearances were cameos, such as when she talked for a few seconds at the world premiere of 1954's *A Star Is Born* or in the 1949 MGM documentary *Some of the Best: Twenty-Five Years of Motion Pictures Leadership*. Another rarity is the *Olympic Fund Telethon* hosted by Bob Hope and Bing Crosby. It broadcast live on two networks: NBC and CBS from June 21 at 8 P.M. to June 22 at 10:30 P.M., 1952.

Leigh's television appearances include:

The Colgate Comedy Hour, cameo, May 31, 1953, NBC
 Janet Leigh appears with Tony Curtis.

Today, 1954, NBC
 Janet Leigh appears in a segment from Atlantic City, along with host Jack Lescoulie and a bathing-beauty contestant.

What's My Line, mystery guest, April 5, 1954, CBS

Person to Person, guest, November 12, 1954, CBS
 Janet Leigh and Tony Curtis are interviewed at home by Ed Murrow.

What's My Line, panelist, January 9, 1955, CBS
 Tony Curtis is the mystery guest; Janet Leigh is one of the panelists.

The Colgate Comedy Hour, cameo, May 8, 1955, NBC
 Janet Leigh appears with Tony Curtis.

The Colgate Comedy Hour, guest, July 24, 1955, NBC

The Bob Crosby Show, guest, 1955, CBS
 Janet Leigh models one of the dresses she designed and answers questions from the audience.

The Rosemary Clooney Show, guest, July 10, 1956, syndicated
 A pregnant Janet Leigh performs a musical duet with Clooney.

Toast of the Town (a.k.a. *The Ed Sullivan Show*), guest, December 2, 1956, CBS
 Janet Leigh receives a special Modern Screen Award as Most Popular Cover Girl of 1956. She also gives a special Star of Tomorrow award to Victoria Shaw and to Anthony Perkins.

Schlitz Playhouse of the Stars: "Carriage from Britain," March 8, 1957, NBC
 This was Leigh's first appearance in a teleplay.

Playhouse 90: "Around the World in 90 minutes, Pt. 1," guest in the audience, October 17, 1957, CBS

Toast of the Town (a.k.a. *The Ed Sullivan Show*), guest, December 8, 1957, CBS
   Janet Leigh appears in a segment made on location in Munich, Germany, on the set of *The Vikings*.

30th Annual Academy Awards, performer, March 26, 1958, NBC

31st Annual Academy Awards, co-presenter — Best Animated Short Film and Best Live Action Short Film, April 6, 1959, NBC

Take a Good Look, guest, November 4, 1959, ABC
   Ernie Kovaks moderates, with panelists Janet Leigh and Cesar Romero.

This Is Your Life: "Mervyn LeRoy," guest, March 2, 1960, NBC

32nd Annual Academy Awards, co-presenter — Best Writing Awards, April 4, 1960, ABC

What's My Line, mystery guest, October 23, 1960, CBS

Mother's March, guest, January 24, 1960, syndicated
   Janet Leigh appears with her husband Tony Curtis.

Menschen, Hoffnungen, Medaillen, documentary in German on the 8th Olympic Winter Games in Squaw Valley, CA, 1960

33rd Annual Academy Awards, Nominee: Best Actress in a Supporting Role (*Psycho*), and co-presenter — Best Documentary Award, April 17, 1961, ABC

Here's Hollywood, May 1, 1961, NBC
   Interview with Janet Leigh in her home.

What's My Line, mystery guest, December 3, 1961, CBS

I've Got a Secret, guest, December 11, 1961, CBS

Meet Me at Disneyland: "Plaza Gardens," guest, June 16, 1962, KTTV

I've Got a Secret, guest, October, 1, 1962, CBS

The Tonight Show Starring Johnny Carson, guest, October 23, 1962, NBC

Art Linkletter's House Party, guest, 1962, CBS

Password, guest, March 25, 1963, CBS
   Guests are Janet Leigh and Peter Lawford.

The Tonight Show Starring Johnny Carson, guest, August 20, 1963, NBC

Celebrity Tennis, guest tennis player, August 25, 1963, CBS
   Rhoda Flemings and Pancho Segura vs. Janet Leigh and Pedro Gonzales, from Dean Martin's estate in Beverly Hills.

Talent Scouts, guest, August 27, 1963, CBS
   Host Merv Griffin welcomes Janet Leigh and other guests to present the talent hopefuls.

The Andy Williams Show, guest, September 24, 1963, NBC
   Janet Leigh, Art Carney and Andy Williams sing and dance.

Password, panelist, October 9, 1963, CBS
   Guests are Sammy Davis, Jr., Polly Bergen, Peter Lawford and Janet Leigh.

Bob Hope Special, guest, December 13, 1963, NBC
Janet Leigh plays in a sketch parodying a popular TV show, in which she performs the double role of Bob Hope's wife and girlfriend.

Hollywood Backstage, "Charity Fashion Show," 1963, syndicated
Behind-the-scenes look at a charity fashion show by Italian designer Emilio Pucci to benefit Cedars-Sinai Hospital in Los Angeles. Janet Leigh presents the event and models an outfit on the runway.

Alumni Fund, guest, January 5, 1964, CBS
Janet Leigh, along with Richard Pedersen of the U.N. and Darren McGavin, represents the University of the Pacific.

Bob Hope Special, special guest star, February 14, 1964, NBC
Janet Leigh appears in a madcap romp with Bob Hope.

The Andy Williams Show, guest, October 5, 1964, NBC
Janet Leigh performs a solo number, and a song and dance with Andy Williams.

Bob Hope Presents the Chrysler Theatre (a.k.a. *Theatre of Stars*): "Murder in the First," October 9, 1964, NBC.
Janet Leigh plays Carol Hartley in a teleplay directed by Sydney Pollack.

The Hollywood Palace, guest-host, November 27, 1965, ABC
Janet Leigh hosts the show. She also performs a duet with Allan Sherman on "Sarah Jackman."

Bob Hope Presents the Chrysler Theatre (a.k.a. *Theatre of Stars*): "Dear Deductable," November 9, 1966, NBC
Janet Leigh plays Virginia Ballard in a teleplay directed by Raphael Blau.

The Bob Hope Comedy Special Show, guest, December 15, 1965, NBC
Janet Leigh appears together with Nancy Wilson, Jack Benny and Bing Crosby.

The Man from U.N.C.L.E: "The Concrete Overcoat Affair, Part 1," November 25, 1966, NBC
Janet Leigh plays Mrs. Diketon in an episode directed by Joseph Sargent.

The Red Skelton Hour: "Jerk Be Nimble," November 29, 1966, CBS
Janet Leigh as Daisy June.

The Man from U.N.C.L.E: "The Concrete Overcoat Affair, Part 2," December 2, 1966, NBC
In 1967 the two *U.N.C.L.E.* episodes were combined and released in the U.K. and in other European theaters as a motion picture titled *The Spy in the Green Hat*.

Art Linkletter's House Party, guest, 1966, CBS

The Smothers Brothers Comedy Hour, guest, May 14, 1967, CBS
Janet Leigh plays in a sketch with Tom Smothers, set in a French restaurant.

The Smothers Brothers Comedy Hour, guest, September 10, 1967, CBS
Janet Leigh appears in a skit with Tom and Dick Smothers, parodying high school dropouts.

The Jerry Lewis Show, guest, October 3, 1967
Janet Leigh joins Jerry Lewis and Ben Gazzara in two comedy sketches.

The Dean Martin Show, guest, October 5, 1967, NBC

Janet Leigh sings and dances to "Big Spender" and "Put Your Arms Around Me, Honey," a duet with Dean Martin.

The Danny Thomas Hour: "One for My Baby," February 5, 1968, NBC
Janet Leigh plays Liza Merrick.

The Joey Bishop Show, guest, February 12, 1968, ABC

The Merv Griffin Show, guest, February 13, 1968, syndicated

Chrysler Presents Bob Hope: "For Love of $$$$," guest, April 12, 1968, NBC
Janet plays a socialite opposite Bob Hope, Fernando Lamas and Eddie Mayehoff.

The Joey Bishop Show, guest, May 7, 1968, ABC

Personality, 1968, NBC

Kraft Music Hall: "Alan King at the Movies," guest, October 9, 1968, NBC
Janet Leigh sings "Dear Hearts and Gentle People" with host Alan King and guest Paul Lynde, spoofing old-time movie gangsters.

The Bob Hope Special, guest, December 19, 1968, NBC

Andy Griffith Special: "Looking Back," guest, February 21, 1969, CBS
Janet Leigh performs two dance numbers in a dream sequence that evokes Fred Astaire and Ginger Rogers.

The Joey Bishop Show, guest, March 12, 1969, ABC

What's It All About, World?, guest, March 27, 1969, ABC
Janet Leigh performs a sketch with host/star Dean Jones, and sings a duet with him, "Oh, You Beautiful Doll," followed by a dance number with Kevin Carlisle.

The Tonight Show Starring Johnny Carson, guest, October 23, 1969, NBC

The Merv Griffin Show, guest, October 20, 1969, syndicated

The Red Skelton Hour: "It's Better to Have Loved and Lost — Much Better," December 2, 1969, CBS.
Janet Leigh plays Daisy June/Clara Appleby.

The Dick Cavett Show, guest, August 7, 1970, ABC
Janet Leigh and Anthony Perkins discuss *Psycho* on its 10th anniversary rerelease.

The Men from Shiloh (a.k.a. *The Virginian*): "Jenny," September 30, 1970, NBC
Janet Leigh plays Jenny Davis.

The Tim Conway Comedy Hour, guest, October 25, 1970, CBS

Bracken's World: "The Anonymous Star," November 13, 1970, NBC
Janet Leigh plays Maggie Moran.

The Merv Griffin Show, guest, November 23, 1970, syndicated

The Name of the Game: "The Man Who Killed the Ghost," January 29, 1971, NBC
Janet Leigh plays Gloria Bates in an episode that reunites with her *Prince Valiant* co-star Robert Wagner.

Hollywood Squares, guest, May 17–21, 1971, NBC

The Tonight Show Starring Johnny Carson, guest, May 19, 1971, NBC

Hollywood Squares, guest, June 28–July 2, 1971, NBC

Comedy Playhouse: "My Wives Jane," August 1, 1971, CBS
Janet Leigh plays Jane Franklin.

Hollywood Squares, guest, August 23–27, 1971, NBC

The Mike Douglas Show, co-host, September 13–17, 1971, syndicated
    Janet Leigh's daughter Jamie Lee Curtis appears as a guest at one point.

Hollywood Squares, guest, September 27–October 1, 1971, NBC

Rowan & Martin's Laugh-In, cameo, October 18, 1971, NBC

Hollywood Squares, guest, October 18–22, 1971, NBC

Rowan & Martin's Laugh-In, cameo, December 13, 1971, NBC

Hollywood Squares, guest, December 27–31, 1971, NBC

Hollywood Squares, guest, January 24–28, 1972, NBC

Hollywood Squares, guest, January 31–February 6, 1972, NBC

Hollywood Squares, guest, April 10–14, 1972, NBC

Hollywood Squares, guest, June 26–30, 1972, NBC

Camera Three: "The Illustrated Alfred Hitchcock," July 16, 1972, CBS

Dinah's Place, guest, 1972, NBC

Jerry Visits, interviewee, 1972, CBS

Rowan & Martin's Laugh-In, cameo, September 18, 1972, NBC

The Wacky World of Jonathan Winters, guest, September 30, 1972, syndicated

Circle of Fear (a.k.a. *Ghost Story*): "Death's Head," January 3, 1973, NBC
    Janet Leigh plays Carol.

Hollywood Squares, guest, March 12–16, 1973, NBC

Hollywood Squares, guest, June 13–17, 1973, NBC

The Wacky World of Jonathan Winters, guest, September 1, 1973, syndicated
    Janet Leigh plays in a sketch with Robert Clary.

The Mike Douglas Show, guest, September 28, 1973, syndicated

The Mike Douglas Show, guest, October 19, 1973, syndicated

Love Story: "Beginner's Luck," November 28, 1973, NBC
    Janet Leigh plays Leonie.

ABC's World of Entertainment: "That's Entertainment! 50 Years of MGM," May 29, 1974, ABC
    Janet Leigh appears at the premiere of the film *That's Entertainment!*

Celebrity Tennis, guest tennis player, June 30, 1974, CBS
    Ron Ely and Janet Leigh vs. Dabney Coleman and Barbara Luna.

Celebrity Tennis, guest tennis player, August 25, 1974, CBS
    Ann B. Davis and Janet Leigh vs. Joan Darling and Chelsea Brown.

The American Film Institute Salute to Orson Welles, guest, February 17, 1975, CBS

Movin' On: "Weddin' Bells," April 9, 1975, NBC
    Janet Leigh plays Nina Smith.

Bicentennial Minute, April 1975, CBS
    One-minute educational segment commemorating the bicentennial of the American Revolution.

Celebrity Tennis, guest tennis player, June 25, 1975, CBS
  Lloyd Bridges and Janet Leigh vs. Richard Roundtree and Cathy Lee Crosby.

Celebrity Tennis, guest tennis player, August 17, 1975, CBS
  Bert Convey and Janet Leigh vs. Gary Collins and Mary Ann Mobley.

Columbo, Season 5: "Forgotten Lady," September 14, 1975, NBC
  Janet Leigh plays Grace Wheeler Willis. A scene from *Walking My Baby Back Home* is shown in the episode.

Hollywood Squares: "The 1 Hour Special Weekday Show," guest, November 3–7, 1975, syndicated

Sammy and Company, guest, February 15, 1976, syndicated

Celebrity Tennis, guest tennis player, February 27, 1976, syndicated
  Gary Collins and Mary Ann Mobley vs. Bert Convy and Janet Leigh.

Celebrity Tennis, guest tennis player, May 27, 1976, syndicated
  Abby Dalton and Beau Bridges vs. Lloyd Bridges and Janet Leigh.

Hollywood Squares, guest, November 1–5, 1976, syndicated

Circus of the Stars, guest, January 10, 1977, CBS
  Janet Leigh performs an aerial ladder act with former Miss America Mary Ann Mobley and television actress Niki Dantine.

Dinah!, guest, October 25, 1977, CBS
  Janet Leigh's daughter Jamie Lee Curtis also appears as a guest.

Hollywood Squares, guest, October 24–28, 1977, syndicated

All-Star Tribute to Elizabeth Taylor, guest, December 1, 1977, CBS

Gene Kelly: An American in Pasadena, March 13, 1978, CBS

Dean Martin Celebrity Roast: "Jimmy Stewart," May 10, 1978, NBC

The Hollywood Greats: "Judy Garland," August 24, 1978, BBC (U.K.)
  Documentary series profiling various Hollywood stars. Janet Leigh talks about her friendship with Garland.

The Love Boat: "Till Death Do Us Apart"—Maybe/Chubs/Locked Away," November 11, 1978, ABC
  Janet Leigh plays Gail, the mother of a character played by her real-life daughter, Jamie Lee Curtis.

Over Easy, guest, November 17, 1978, PBS
  Janet Leigh is interviewed by Hugh Downs.

The Mike Douglas Show, guest, November 30, 1978, syndicated

Fantasy Island: "Birthday Party / Ghostbreaker," March 3, 1979, ABC
  Janet Leigh plays Carol Gates.

The American Film Institute Salute to Alfred Hitchcock, guest, March 7, 1979, CBS

Good Morning America, guest, February 20, 1980, ABC
  Janet Leigh's daughter Jamie Lee Curtis also appears as a guest.

Fear on Film: Inside "The Fog," 1980.
  In this 7-minute documentary to promote the film *The Fog*, Janet Leigh comments on the film.

The Tony Tennille Show, guest, September 14, 1980, syndicated

All-Star Salute to Mother's Day, guest, May 10, 1981, NBC
   In this TV special where celebrities honor Mother's Day, Jamie Lee Curtis also appeared among the many guests.

Bob Hope's Women I Love Beautiful but Funny, guest, February 28, 1982, NBC

Night of the 100 Stars, guest, March 8, 1982, ABC
   All-star variety show celebrating the Actor's Fund of America at Radio City Music Hall in New York.

Matt Houston: "Who Would Kill Ramona?" October 31, 1982, ABC
   Janet Leigh plays Ramona Launders.

Tales of the Unexpected: "Light Fingers," July 4, 1982, ITV (U.K.)
   Janet Leigh plays Joan Stackpole, a disenchanted housewife married to a glove manufacturer.

Fantasy Island: "Roller Derby / Thanks a Million," December 4, 1982, ABC
   Janet Leigh plays Suzanne King.

Dolce Cinema, February 21, 1984, RAI Uno (Italy)
   In the documentary about Hollywood stars in the Italian cinema, Janet Leigh talks about her experience with director Giuliano Montaldo in *Ad ogni costo*.

The Screen Actors Guild 50th Anniversary Celebration, guest, May 29, 1984, CBS

Tales of the Unexpected: "I Like It Here in Wilmington," cameo, November 8, 1984, ITV (U.K.)

The Love Boat: "Instinct" and "Unmade for Each Other — Bos," January 5, 1985, ABC
   Janet Leigh plays Joan Philipps.

Lifestyles of the Rich and Famous, interviewee, January 12, 1985, syndicated

Night of the 100 Stars II, guest, March 10, 1985, ABC
   All-star variety celebrating the Actor's Fund of America at Radio City Music Hall in New York.

On Our Way, June 24, 1985, CBS
   In this pilot for a never-produced TV series, Janet Leigh plays Kate Walsh.

Hitchcock: Il brivido del genio, July 16, 1985, RAI Uno (Italy)
   In a 3-part documentary on Hitchcock produced by the Italian national television network, Janet Leigh talks about her experience working with the director on *Psycho*.

Omnibus: "Hitchcock: Sex, Murder and Mayhem," October 3, 1986, BBC (U.K.)
   Two-part profile of Alfred Hitchcock combining home movies, clips from his films and interviews with people who knew him. Janet Leigh talks about *Psycho*.

Starman: "Society's Pet," November 28, 1986, ABC
   Janet Leigh plays Antonia Weyburn

Cinéma cinémas: "La douche," January 20, 1987, France 4 (France)
   Janet Leigh talks about the shower scene in *Psycho* for a French TV program.

Happy 100th Birthday, Hollywood, May 18, 1987, ABC
   This all-star show celebrates Hollywood's 100th anniversary at the L.A. Shrine Auditorium. Janet Leigh appears, tap-dancing with a group of other stars.

Hollywood the Golden Years: The RKO Story: "Howard's Way," August 7, 1987, BBC (U.K.)

A 6-episode documentary dedicated to RKO stories. This episode is on Howard Hughes. Janet Leigh discusses *Jet Pilot*.

Murder, She Wrote, fourth season: "Doom with a View," December 13, 1987, CBS

Janet Leigh plays Cornelia Montaigne Harper.

Talking Pictures, 1988, BBC 1 (U.K,)

This ten-part series charted the history of Hollywood, from its inception to modern day. Janet Leigh is one of the interviewees.

The American Film Institute Salute to Jack Lemmon, guest, May 30, 1988, CBS

The Twilight Zone: "Rendezvous in a Dark Place," March 12, 1989, syndicated

Janet Leigh plays Barbara LeMay.

Superstars and Their Moms, May 8, 1989, TBS

In this special featuring interviews with five mothers of well-known entertainers, Kelly Curtis and Jamie Lee Curtis discuss their relationship with mother Janet Leigh.

Good Morning America, guest, June 13, 1990, ABC

Janet Leigh and author Stephen Rebello discuss Rebello's new book, *Alfred Hitchcock and the Making of Psycho*.

Larry King Live, guest, June 14, 1990, CNN

Janet Leigh and Stephen Rebello discuss *Alfred Hitchcock and the Making of Psycho*.

The Joan Rivers Show, guest, June 18, 1990, syndicated

The Horror Hall of Fame, co-presenter, September 30, 1990, syndicated

The first of three annual celebrations of horror cinema. Janet Leigh appears among many others, including Anthony Perkins and Patricia Hitchcock.

The Thalians, 1991, TMC

A 15-minute special chronicling the history of "The Thalians," Hollywood's long-standing fundraising group. Janet Leigh is one of the speakers

The Phil Donahue Show, guest, March 22, 1992, syndicated

Janet Leigh's daughter Jamie Lee Curtis also appears as a guest.

One on One with John Tesh, guest, April 21, 1992, NBC

Vicky!, guest, September 7, 1992, syndicated

Janet Leigh is interviewed by Vicky Lawrence.

Okavango: The Wild Frontier, episode 48, 1993, syndicated

Janet Leigh plays Rachel Scofield.

The Story of Lassie, August 14, 1994, PBS

In this documentary on Lassie, Janet Leigh talks about *Hills of Home*.

Good Morning America, guest, May 23, 1995, ABC

The Late Show with Tom Snyder, guest, June 30, 1995, CBS

Le Club: "Janet Leigh," 1995

French TV-series dedicated to a different movie star each week.

Biggers and Summers, guest, 1995, LIFE Channel

Biography: "Charlton Heston," August 19, 1995, A&E TV

Inside the Dream Factory, November 1, 1995, TCM
  In this documentary that goes behind the scenes of Hollywood's legendary studio system, Janet Leigh comments on her contract with MGM.
Biography: "Jerry Lewis, the Last American Clown," September 1, 1996, A&E
  Janet Leigh talks about Lewis' home movies. Rare footage from *Come Back Little Shiksa* is shown, featuring Janet Leigh, Dean Martin and Patti Lewis.
Biography: "Jamie Lee Curtis," 1996, A&E
Lifetime Applauds: The Fight Against Cancer, guest, October 13, 1996, LIFE Channel
  Janet Leigh's daughter Kelly Curtis also appears as a guest.
Intimate Portrait: "Janet Leigh," October 20, 1996, Lifetime
  A documentary exploring Janet Leigh's life and career, featuring interviews (conducted by Carol Langer) with Jamie Lee Curtis, Kelly Curtis, Charlton Heston, Robert Mitchum, John Frankenheimer, Leonard Gershe and Lillian Burns Sidney.
The Daily Show, guest, October 24, 1996, Comedy Central
E! True Hollywood Story: "Anthony Perkins," October 26, 1997, E! TV
  In this profile of Anthony Perkins, Janet Leigh talks about her professional and personal relationship with the actor.
E! True Hollywood Story: "Grace, Caroline and Stephanie: The Curse of the Royal Family," September 7, 1997, E! TV
Touched by an Angel: "Charades," November 16, 1997, CBS
  Janet Leigh plays Vera Galser.
Crook & Chase, guest, October 1, 1998, syndicated
Clive Barker's A–Z of Horror, "American Psycho," October 2, 1997, BBC (U.K.)
  A six-part series. Janet Leigh talks about *Psycho*.
Close Up on James Stewart, December 20, 1997, BBC2 (U.K.)
  Daily series celebrating the career of James Stewart. Janet Leigh reminisces about *The Naked Spur*.
Celebrity Profiles: "Jamie Lee Curtis," 1998, E! TV
  Janet Leigh talks about her relationship with her daughter.
E! True Hollywood Story: "Frank Sinatra," May 14, 1998, E! TV
Biography: "Anthony Perkins: Life in the Shadow," January 11, 1999, A&E
  The life and career of Anthony Perkins. Janet Leigh talks about her friendship with the actor.
E! True Hollywood Story: "Dean Martin," January 24, 1999, E! TV
5th Annual Screen Actors Guild Awards, March 7, 1999, TNT
  Janet Leigh co-presented the Life Achievement Award to Kirk Douglas.
E! Mysteries & Scandals: "Orson Welles," March 22, 1999, E! TV
  Janet Leigh talks about Welles' *Touch of Evil*.
E! True Hollywood Story: "Anthony Perkins," 1999, E! TV
  Janet Leigh talks about her friendship with Tony Perkins.
Reputations: "Alfred Hitchcock," May 31, 1999, A&E
  Hitchcock's life and career are covered in a two-part documentary titled *Hitch: Alfred the Great Part 1* and *Hitch: Alfred the Auteur, Part 2*. Janet Leigh talks about her relationship with the director.

E! True Hollywood Story: "Alfred Hitchcock," August 8, 1999, E! TV

Saturday Night Live 25, guest, September 25, 1999, NBC
A TV special celebrating the 25th Anniversary of *Saturday Night Live*. Janet Leigh appears with her daughter Jamie Leigh Curtis.

Hitchcock: Shadow of a Genius, October 13, 1999, TMC
This documentary on Hitchcock was broadcast in the U.K. as *Dial H for Hitchcock: The Genius Behind the Showman*. Janet Leigh talks about *Psycho*.

Psycho IV—The Beginning, November 10, 1999, Showtime
Janet Leigh gave a short introduction before the showing of the film on cable.

The Century: America's Time: "Homefront 1941–1945," 1999, ABC
In episode 7 of this 15-part documentary, Janet Leigh talks about Frank Sinatra.

Biography: "The Rat Pack," 1999, A&E
In this four-part series which explores the careers of Frank Sinatra, Dean Martin, Peter Lawford and Sammy Davis, Jr., Janet Leigh talks on the subject.

Cubby Broccoli: The Man Behind Bond, 2000
In this short documentary about producer Albert Broccoli, Janet Leigh briefly comments about Broccoli as an independent producer. It was released on the James Bond Ultimate Edition DVD of *Diamonds Are Forever*.

Howard Hughes: His Women and His Films, June 27, 2000, TCM
In this biography of the billionaire producer, Janet Leigh talks about *Jet Pilot*.

E! Mysteries & Scandals: "Beverly Hills Babylon," September 29, 2000, E! TV
Janet Leigh talks about Beverly Hills and Zsa Zsa Gabor.

Intimate Portrait: "Jamie Lee Curtis," September 11, 2000, Lifetime
A documentary exploring Jamie Lee Curtis' life and career, featuring an interview with Janet Leigh.

Scene by Scene, December 16, 2000, BBC2 (U.K.)
Janet Leigh talks with Mark Cousins about her career.

Reconstructing Evil: The Making of Touch of Evil, December 17, 2000, BBC2 (U.K.)
A TV documentary about the making of Orson Welles's classic crime drama. Janet Leigh talks about her experience on the set.

Sinatra: Good Guy—Bad Guy, December 27, 2000, ITV (U.K.)
This documentary on the life of Frank Sinatra includes interviews with those who knew him.

AFI's 100 Years ... 100 Thrills: America's Most Heart-Pounding Movies, June 12, 2001, CBS
Hollywood's top people talk about their favorite thrilling films. *Psycho* ranks number one on the list.

Family Law: "The Quality of Mercy," February 5, 2001, CBS
Janet Leigh plays Mary Sawyer.

Howard Stern Radio Show, guest, May 5, 2001, syndicated

Howard Stern guest May 8, 2001, E! TV

E! 101: "Most Shocking Moments in Entertainment," interviewee, July 15, 2001, E! TV
Janet Leigh comments on the *Psycho* shower scene.

Michael Jackson: 30th Anniversary Celebration, guest, November 13, 2001, CBS
For Michael Jackson's special tribute at Madison Square Garden in New York, Janet Leigh is one of the 200 stars from the entertainment industry there to honor the singer.

Kings of Black Comedy: "A Funny Thing Happened to Sammy Davis, Jr.," February 23, 2002, Channel 4 (U.K.)
Friends and colleagues, including Janet Leigh, reminisce about the all-singing, all-dancing star.

Bookmark: "Fabulous After Fifty," April 11, 2002, KOCE-TV
Janet Leigh talks about her second novel, *House of Dreams.*

The Hollywood Greats: "Tony Curtis," April 16, 2002, BBC (U.K.)
In this documentary profiling Tony Curtis' life and career, Janet Leigh talks about her marriage with Curtis.

Autograph, interviewee, May 1, 2002, syndicated
An in-depth 30-minute interview with Janet Leigh.

E! True Hollywood Story: "Liza Minnelli," July 21, 2002, E! TV

Revealed with Jules Asner, October 9, 2002, E! TV
Jamie Leigh Curtis talks about her life. Janet Leigh appears in clips and photographs.

Intimate Portrait: "Elizabeth Taylor," December 2, 2002, Lifetime
A documentary exploring Elizabeth Taylor's life and career featuring an interview with Janet Leigh.

Biography: "Elizabeth Taylor: Facets," March 16, 2003, A&E
In this exploration of the life and career of Elizabeth Taylor, Janet Leigh talks about *Little Women.*

E! True Hollywood Story: "Jerry Lewis," May 18, 2003, E! TV

AFI's 100 Years ... 100 Heroes & Villains, June 3, 2003, CBS
Hollywood's top people talk about their favorite heroes and villains in films. Norman Bates from *Psycho* ranks number two on the list of the villains.

E! True Hollywood Story: "Scream Queens," October 31, 2004, E! TV
Janet Leigh and Jamie Lee Curtis both appear in this tribute to horror movie heroines.

Larry King Live, guest, August 25, 2003, CNN
Guests Janet Leigh, Eve Marie Saint, Tippi Hedren and Patricia Hitchcock reminisce about Alfred Hitchcock.

The 100 Greatest Scary Moments, October 25, 2003, Channel 4 (U.K.)
A countdown of the scariest moments on film and TV, as voted by the viewers. Janet Leigh is included with *Psycho.*

Biography: "Janet Leigh," October 27, 2003, A&E
Janet Leigh, with friends, family and colleagues, talks about her life and career.

Love Hollywood Style, February 14, 2004, FOX-TV

Biography: "Ava Gardner: Another Touch of Venus," December 12, 2004, A&E

Sinatra: Dark Star, August 3, 2005, BBC (U.K.)
A biography of Frank Sinatra.

B. Documentaries

The Fantasy Film Worlds of George Pal, Arnold Leibovit Entertainment, 1985
   A documentary about Academy Award–winning producer-director George Pal. Janet Leigh talks about *Houdini*, which Pal produced.

Stephen Verona: Self Portrait, Hatchwell Productions, 1991
   A 75-minute documentary featuring the many facets of director-producer-artist Stephen Verona. Janet Leigh talks about *Boardwalk*.

The Making of "Psycho," Universal, 1997
   A retrospective on the entire movie, with interviews with many members of the cast and crew. It was featured on the Collector's Edition DVD of *Psycho* released in 2005 by Universal Video.

Mary Pickford: A Life on Film, Milestone Films, 1997
   A biography of the silent screen star Mary Pickford. Janet Leigh comments on the actress's life and career.

Unmasking the Horror, Buena Vista Video, 1998
   A short documentary included among the extras on the *Halloween H20* DVD. Janet Leigh talks about the "homages" to *Psycho* in *Halloween H20*.

Tales from the Mist: Inside "The Fog," Automat Pictures, 2002
   In this 28-minute documentary presented as an extra on the 2002 special edition DVD of *The Fog*, Janet Leigh comments on the film.

LIFE: Great Romance, Volume Four, Madacy Home Video, 2003
   In this documentary on twenty famous couples, Tony Curtis and Janet Leigh's love story is analyzed, with footage from films and personal interviews.

Bringing Evil to Life, Universal Studios, 2008
   Retrospective documentary on the production of *Touch of Evil*, featuring interviews with the cast, crew members and film historians. It was included the 50th Anniversary Edition DVD of *Touch of Evil*.

C. Archive Footage Appearances

Television

Camera Three: "The Illustrated Alfred Hitchcock, Part I," July 16, 1972, CBS
   A montage of scenes from Hitchcock's most popular films are shown, including *Psycho*.

The Horror Show, February 6, 1979, CBS
   Anthony Perkins hosts a 90-minute documentary made up of clips from horror films. *Psycho* is included.

Hollywood Out-Takes and Rare Footage (a.k.a. *Hollywood Graffiti*), February 27, 1983
   Outtakes, promotional shorts, public service pleas, newsreel footage, documentary material, etc. from Hollywood's Golden Age. Janet Leigh and Tony Curtis appear in a segment from the 1954 world premiere of *A Star Is Born*.

Alfred Hitchcock: The Art of Making Movies, Universal Studios, Orlando, FL, 1990
   This part-3-D film, part-live action show was presented as an attraction at the

Universal Studios, Florida, theme park. The film part was narrated by Anthony Perkins and included a clip from *Psycho*. The attraction opened in June 1990 and closed in January 2003. Janet Leigh was listed in the credits as creative consultant.

The Best of Hollywood (a.k.a. *50 Years: The Best of Hollywood*), 1998
Tab Hunter narrates a collection of clips from classic films, including *Psycho*, in this television documentary.

Biography: "Tony Curtis: Tony of the Movies," May 25, 2001, A&E
A biography focused on Tony Curtis' career.

101 Biggest Celebrity Oops, March 2, 2004, E!TV
Gus Van Sant's 1998 remake of *Psycho* is on the list. Scenes from the original *Psycho* are shown in the segment.

11th Annual Screen Actors Guild Awards, February 5, 2005, TNT
Archive footage of Janet Leigh appears in a memorial tribute.

77th Academy Awards, February 27, 2005, ABC
Janet Leigh is remembered with a brief sequence from the *Psycho* shower scene during the "in memoriam" segment.

How Art Made the World, May 9, 2005, BBC (U.K.)
The *Psycho* shower scene is shown during this five-episode documentary.

A Life in Words and Music, New Wave Entertainment, July 24, 2007
This 20-minute documentary celebrating the work by Richard Rodgers and Lorenz Hart was included on the *Words and Music* DVD. Janet Leigh appears in a photograph taken on the set of *Words and Music*.

A Night at the Movies: "The Suspenseful World of Thrillers," October 2, 2009, TCM
A special dedicated to the genre of thrillers. *Psycho* is included.

82nd Academy Awards, March 7, 2010, ABC
The *Psycho* shower scene is included in a tribute to horror films.

A History of Horror with Mark Gatiss: "The American Scream," October 25, 2010, BBC 4 (U.K.)
A three-part documentary series exploring the history of horror films. Host Mark Gatiss visits the Bates Motel, the set location for Hitchcock's *Psycho*. The *Psycho* shower scene is shown.

Edición Especial Coleccionista: "Comparativa Psicosis," April 12, 2011, Cinemaverick (Spain)
A Spanish TV program dedicated to the analysis of DVDs. In this episode two different DVD versions of *Psycho* are compared.

A Night at the Movies: "Merry Christmas!," December 6, 2011, Turner Classic Movies
Actors and filmmakers reveal the secret of great holiday classics. Footage from *Little Women* and *Holiday Affair* is shown.

Films

Terror in the Aisle (a.k.a. *Time for Terror*), directed by Andrew J. Kuehn, October 26, 1984
A compilation of trailers and scenes from crime, horror and sci-fi films. *Psycho* is included.

The Best of Film Noir, released straight to video, 1999
Collection of clips and interviews on over 30 films in the film noir genre. Scenes from *Touch of Evil* are included.

Going to Pieces: The Rise and Fall of the Slasher Film, ThinkFilm 2006
A critical and historical look at slasher films, which includes scenes from *Psycho*.

Double Take, directed by Johan Grimonprez, 2009
A Belgian-Dutch-German documentary which intercuts clips and interviews of Alfred Hitchcock with archive footage from his films, including *Psycho*.

Rock Hudson: Dark and Handsome Stranger, directed by Andrew Davies and André Schafer, 2010
A documentary on Rock Hudson, twenty-five years after his tragic death.

The Psycho Legacy, directed by Robert V. Galluzzo
Released straight to DVD in 2010, this documentary examines the history of the *Psycho* films saga. Janet Leigh appears in archival footage from the original *Psycho*.

Tony Curtis, Driven to Stardom, directed by Ian Ayres, French Connection Films, 2011
This French-produced documentary in English is an intimate journey into Tony Curtis' life and career. Janet Leigh appears in newsreels and in clips from the films in which she co-starred with her former husband.

D. Newsreels and Other Appearances

"Harvey" Six-Foot Rabbit Makes Movie Debut, Universal-International News, October 1950
Voice: Court Benson. Stars entering the Carthay Circle Theatre in Hollywood to attend the preview premiere of *Harvey*. Janet Leigh is escorted by Tony Curtis.

Bright Victory Premiere, Universal-International News, July 23, 1951
Voice: Ed Herlihy. Gala scenes from Hollywood to celebrate the premiere of *Bright Victory*. Janet Leigh and Tony Curtis pose at the microphone.

News in Brief: Pennsylvania, Variety Club Event, Newsreel, 1952
The Variety Club celebrates its silver anniversary. Janet Leigh and Tony Curtis are among the guests.

"Thunder Bay" Ushers in Era of Wide Screen Movies, Universal-International News, July 23, 1953
Voice: Maggie McNellis. The gala world premiere of *Thunder Bay* in Times Square. Janet Leigh and Tony Curtis are shown arriving at the event.

"Prince Valiant" Scores Triumphs in East and West, Movietone News, April 2, 1954
Voice: Joe King. Hollywood and New York premieres of *Prince Valiant*. Janet Leigh appears alongside her co-stars Robert Wagner and Debra Paget.

Fall Fashion Finery, Universal-International News, September 6, 1954
Voice: Ed Herlihy. From Universal City, California, Janet Leigh and Barbara Rush, along with professional models, display a clothing line inspired by the film *The Black Shield of Falworth*.

"Living It Up" in Atlantic City, Paramount News, 1954
Dean Martin, Jerry Lewis and Janet Leigh at the premiere of *Living It Up* in Atlantic City.

"6 Bridges to Cross" Premiere, Newsreel, January 20, 1955.
Premiere of the film *6 Bridges to Cross* in Boston, Massachusetts. Janet Leigh and Tony Curtis arrive at the event, welcomed by a crowd of fans.

Night of Stars: 5 U-I Names Among World Film Favorites, Universal-International News, March 9, 1959
Voice: Ed Herlihy. At the Hollywood Foreign Press Awards Ceremony, Janet Leigh and Tony Curtis are among the guests introduced as the stars of *The Perfect Furlong*.

News in Brief, Universal-International News, April 1959
Voice: Fred Maness. Clips from the 31st Academy Awards in Hollywood. Janet Leigh and Tony Curtis appear on the red carpet.

Academy Awards, Universal-International News, April 1960
Voice: Fred Maness. Clips from the 32nd Academy Awards in Hollywood. Janet Leigh and Tony Curtis are co-presenters.

18th Golden Globes Awards, newsreel, March 16, 1961
Janet Leigh and Tony Curtis celebrate Leigh's award as Best Supporting Actress for *Psycho* at the Beverly Hills Hotel.

Spartacus Takes Four Awards, Universal-International News, April 1961
Voice: Ed Herlihy. Clips from the 33rd Academy Awards in Hollywood. Janet Leigh and Tony Curtis appear on the red carpet.

Chinese Fete: "Flower Drum Song" Has Exotic Showing, Universal-International Newsreel, December 4, 1961
Voice: Ed Herlihy. The premiere of Universal's film *Flower Drum Song* in Los Angeles. Janet Leigh is among the stars in attendance.

Happy Birthday: Universal Pictures' Golden Anniversary, Universal-International Newsreel, 1962
Voice: Ed Herlihy. A newsreel celebrating Universal's 50th anniversary. Janet Leigh and Tony Curtis are seen attending the 1960 *Spartacus* premiere.

World Premiere of "It's a Mad, Mad, Mad, Mad World," Hollywood Star Newsreel, November 7, 1963
Voice: John Willis. Janet Leigh arrives at the premiere of *It's a Mad, Mad, Mad, Mad World* as lead sponsor for the Cedars-Sinai Hospital charity event.

American Heritage Foundation, "Advertising Council Exhibition: In the Public Interest," October 22, 1964
In this 20-second public service announcement on behalf of the American Heritage Foundation, Janet Leigh reminds viewers of their civic responsibility to vote in the upcoming presidential election.

Meet Maggie Mulligan (a.k.a. *This Is Maggie Mulligan*), 1965, CBS
Unsold sitcom pilot which concerned the adventures of an artist living in New York City. It was produced and directed by Don McGuire.

Man in Motion, 1966
A Columbia featurette that goes behind the scenes on Jerry Lewis' *Three on a Couch*.

Das Ei (a.k.a. *Janet Leigh ist das Ei*), Kurzfilm, Germany, 1993
A 3-minute black-and-white short made by Hans Georg Andres. *Das Ei* (*The Egg*)

is a spoof of the *Psycho* shower scene. Janet Leigh's voice, along with Bernard Herrmann's original score, is matched with images of an egg shown as the victim.

E. Stage Appearances
Plays

Murder Among Friends
A play in two acts (four scenes), written by Bob Barry
Biltmore Theater, New York
Preview: December 23, 1975; Opening:
December 28, 1975; Closing: January 10, 1976

CREDITS: *Director*: Val May; *Producers*: R. Tyler Gatchell, Jr., Peter Neufeld, in association with Barnard S. Straus; *Associate Producers*: Erv Tullman, Barry Potashnick; *Setting*: Santo Loquasto; *Costumes*: Joseph G. Aulisi; *Lightning*: Jennifer Tipton; *Makeup & Hairstyle* for Miss Leigh: Mr. Vincent at Enrico Caruso

CAST: Janet Leigh (Angela Forrester); Lewis Arlt (Ted Cotton); Jack Cassidy (Palmer Forrester); Jane Hoffman (Gertrude Saidenberg); Richard Woods (Marshall Saidenberg); Michael Durrell (Larry).

PLOT: Angela Forrest, one of the richest women in the world, is married to Palmer, an egotistical actor. She plans to kill him, with the help of her lover Ted Cotton, who happens to be Palmer's agent and his former lover. The plan, which is set to go off in the couple's Manhattan duplex apartment on New Year's Eve, is quite ingenious; however, not everything goes as smoothly as intended.

REVIEWS FOR *Murder Among Friends*:

"[The play] aims at nothing more than an evening's entertainment, and for most of the time is pretty much on target.... Mr. Barry keeps his surprises going pretty well during the evening and fires off a few good cracks." — *New York Times*

"A laboriously concocted comedy-melodrama." — *Variety*

REVIEWS FOR JANET LEIGH:

"Miss Leigh ... lacks something in stage technique and energy, but she is charming and resourceful and remembers to keep out of the shower." — *New York Times*

"Janet Leigh, making her Broadway stage debut, is effective as the unsavory wife who evidently hasn't been lavishing her wealth on overeating." — *Variety*

NOTES: Before opening on Broadway, *Murder Among Friends* had a tryout at the Shubert Theatre in New Haven, Connecticut, from November 29 to December 6, 1975, followed by 12 performances at the New Locust Street Theatre in Philadelphia, from December 8 to December 20, 1975.

Love Letters
A play in two parts, written by A. R. Guerney
The Canon Theatre, Beverly Hills, CA; April 3, 1991

CREDITS: *Director*: Ted Weiant; *Producers*: Susan Dietz, Joan Stein, in association with Elizabeth Williams; *Casting Director*: Steven Fertig

CAST: Janet Leigh (Melissa Gardner); Van Johnson (Andrew Makepeace Ladd III).

PLOT: The play is based upon the epistolary communication between Andrew Makepeace Ladd III and Melissa Gardner over the last fifty years. Andy and Melissa, both born to wealth and position, are childhood friends whose lifelong correspondence begins with birthday party thank-you notes and summer camp postcards. Platonically involved, they continue to exchange letters through the boarding school and college years. While Andy is off at war as a naval officer, Melissa gets married, but she continues to keep in touch with Andy as he marries, becomes a lawyer, gets involved in politics and eventually is elected to the U.S. Senate. Meanwhile, Melissa's marriage is a shambles. Eventually she and Andy become involved in a brief affair, but it is really too late for both of them. However, Andy's last letter, written to her mother after Melissa's premature death, makes it clear how much they really meant to each other — even if physically apart, they were always spiritually close.

NOTES: The original production of *Love Letters* debuted at the Long Wharf Theatre in New Haven, CT, in 1988 after a run at the off–Broadway Promenade Theatre. It opened on Broadway on October 31, 1989, at the Edison Theatre, where it ran for 96 performances, changing its cast weekly.

Other Stage Appearances

Variety Show
London Coliseum, London; December 10, 1951

Midnight gala to aid the British National Playing Fields Association, sponsored by the International Variety Club. Janet performed in a musical sketch with Tony Curtis, and sung solo a medley of tunes by composer Jimmy McHugh.

F. Radio Programs

The Cresta Blanca Hollywood Players
"All Through the House," 12/24/1946, CBS
A young woman brings peace to her three feuding brothers just as the New Year begins.
CAST: Joseph Cotten (Joseph, the Butler); John Garfield (John); Gene Kelly (Gene); Janet Leigh (Janet); Gregory Peck (Gregory).
COMMERCIAL: Cresta Blanca and Roma Wines.

Lux Radio Theater
"Three Wise Fools," 9/1/1947, CBS
Based on the 1946 Warner Bros. film, in turn based on a story by Karel Benes.
CAST: Margaret O'Brien (Sheila O'Monohan); Lionel Barrymore (Richard Gaunt); Lewis Stone (James Trumbull); Edward Arnold (Theodore Findlay); Bill Johnstone (Terence O'Davern); Janet Scott (Sister Mary); Earle Ross (Judge Watson); Ira Grossel (Johnson); Eddie Marr (Quimbly); Norman Field (Butler); Clarke Gordon (Reporter); George Neise (Young Trumbull).
INTERMISSION GUEST: Janet Leigh, MGM starlet.

Lux Radio Theater
"The High Wall," 11/7/1949, CBS
Based on the 1947 MGM film, in turn based on a story by Alan Clark and Bradbury Foote.
CAST: Van Heflin (Steve Kenet); Janet Leigh (Dr. Ann Lorrison); Donald Randolph (Whitcomb); Raymond Largay (Dr. Dunlap); and Gerald Mohr, Herbert Ellis, Leo Cleary, Joan Banks, Bill Johnstone, Jay Novello, Shepard Menken, Cliff Clark, Gwenn Delano, Bob Griffin, Ruth Perrott, Lon Krugman, Alan Reed, Jr., and Eddie Marr.

INTERMISSION GUEST: Sheilah Graham, Hollywood columnist and radio commentator.

The Screen Guild Theater
"The Romance of Rosy Ridge," 11/23/1950, ABC
Based on the 1947 MGM film, in turn based on a novel by Mackinlay Kantor.
CAST: Ida Lupino (Sairy MacBean); Janet Leigh (Lissy Anne MacBean).

Lux Radio Theater
"Little Women," 3/13/1950, CBS
Based on the 1949 MGM film, in turn based on the novel by Louisa May Alcott.
CAST: June Allyson (Jo); Peter Lawford (Laurie); Margaret O'Brien (Beth); Janet Leigh (Meg); Betty Lou Gerson (Marmee March); Rhonda Williams (Amy); Eleanor Audley (Aunt March); Robert Boon (Professor Bhaer); Herbert Butterfield (Mr. Lawrence); Noreen Gammill (Hannah); Rye Billsbury (Jorn); William Johnston (Young Man in Act 2); Marissa O'Brian (Sally Gardiner); Janet Scott (Mrs. Gardiner); Eddie Marr (Man in Act 3); Dirk Davis (Soloist).
INTERMISSION GUEST: Benay Ventura, MGM actress.

Lux Radio Theater
"The Red Danube," 3/19/1951, CBS
Based on the 1949 MGM film, in turn based on the novel *Vespers in Vienna* by Bruce Marshall.
CAST: Walter Pidgeon (Col. Michael "Hooky" Nicobar); Hellen Van Tuy (the Mother Superior); Peter Lawford (Major John "Twingo" McPhimister); Constance Cavendish (Audrey Quail); Janet Leigh (Maria Buhlen); Ed Begley (Col. Piniev); Bill Conrad; Bill Johnstone; Ben Wright; Herb Butterfield; Eric Snowden; Paul Dubov; Eddie Marr; Gladys Holland.
INTERMISSION GUEST: Phyllis Kirk, MGM starlet.

Stars in the Air
"Model Wife," 2/14/1952, CBS
Based on the 1941 Universal Pictures film.
CAST: Tony Curtis (Fred Chambers); Janet Leigh (Joan Keating Chambers).

Lux Radio Theater
"Strictly Dishonorable," 12/8/1952
Based on the 1951 MGM film, in turn based on a play by Preston Sturges.
CAST: Fernando Lamas (Gus Karana); Janet Leigh (Isabelle Perry); Ted de Corsia (Bill Dempscy); Gale Robbins (Marie Donnelly); Maria Palmer (Countess Lili Szadvany); Jay Novello (Luigi); Barney Phillips (Harry Donnelly); Jonathan Hole (Henry Greene); Jeanette Nolan (Mrs. Peccatori); Stephen Dunne (the Reporter); Herbert Butterfield (Uncle Nito); Hellen Van Tuy (Mama); William Johnstone (the Lawyer); Dorothy Fay (Marie); Robert Griffin (Charlie); Eddie Marr (the Stage Manager).
INTERMISSION GUEST: Annette Kellerman, former professional swimmer and motion picture actress.

Hollywood Star Playhouse
"Encore," 1/25/1953, NBC
CAST: Janet Leigh

Lux Radio Theater
"The People Against O'Hara," 3/9/1953, CBS

Based on the 1951 MGM film, in turn based on the novel by Eleazar Lipsky.

CAST: Walter Pidgeon (Jim); Janet Leigh (Ginny); Tom Brown (Johnny O'Hara); Jack Moyles (Barra); William Conrad (Ricks); Nestor Pavia (Lanzetta); William Tracy (Jeff); Diane Abbott (Theresa); Ann Morrison (Mrs. O'Hara); Peter Rankin (Kovac); William Jonstone (Judge/Doctor); Eddie Marr (Jailer/Newsboy); Joe Du Val; Charlie Seel; Shep Menken; Herb Rawlinson.

INTERMISSION GUEST: Frances Scully, MGM publicist.

Lux Radio Theater
"Angels in the Outfield," 4/6/1953, CBS
Based on the 1951 MGM film, in turned based on a story by Richard Colin.

CAST: George Murphy (Guffy McGovern); Janet Leigh (Jennifer Paige); Joseph Kearns (the Angel); Donna Corcoran (Bridget White); Dan Riss ("Chunck," coach); Shep Menken (the Umpire); Helen Kleeb (Sister Edwitha);Lawrence Dobkin (the Rabbi); Herb Ellis (Saul); Stephene Dunne (Baulis); Yvonne Peatie (Sister Veronica); Fred MacKaye (Dr. Blane); William Johnstone (Patrick J. Finley); Herb Butterfield (Father O'Hollihan); Eddie Marr (Al); Tony Barrett, Bob Griffin, Eddie Firestone, Herb Rawlinson, Ralph Montgomery.

INTERMISSION GUEST: Frances Scully, MGM publicist.

The Martin and Lewis Show
1/20/1953 NBC
SPECIAL GUEST: Janet Leigh
Highlights of this program include the following segments: Jerry Lewis attempts to come across as a man of the world as he tries to impress Janet Leigh; Jerry Lewis, Dean Martin and Janet Leigh perform in a sketch about Henry VIII in which Lewis portrays the King, Martin is the Prime Minister, and Leigh plays Henry's final wife.

CAST: Dean Martin; Jerry Lewis; George Fenneman (Announcer).

Philip Morris Playhouse on Broadway
"The Miracle of Morgan's Creek," 5/20/1953, CBS
Based on the 1944 Paramount film, based on a screenplay by Preston Sturges.
CAST: Janet Leigh (Trudy Kockenlocker).

Bud's Bandwagon
Record show with DJ Bud Widom program number 210, 1954, AFRST
The first record is, "Real Gone Mambo" by the Bill Doggett Trio. Bud interviews Janet Leigh.

Bud's Bandwagon
Record show with DJ Bud Widom, program number 419, 1954, AFRST
The first record is "Skokian," by Prez Prado and His Orchestra. Bud interviews Tony Curtis and Janet Leigh, who promote their latest picture, *The Black Shield of Falworth*.

Bud's Bandwagon
Record show with DJ Bud Widom, Program number 611, 1955, AFRST
The first record is "Huckleberry Pie," by the Paris Sisters. From the set of *Pete Kelly's Blues* on the Warner Brothers lot, Bud interviews Janet Leigh.

Sunday Evening with Mitch Miller
6/5/1958, CBS
SPECIAL GUESTS: Janet Leigh, Theodore Bikel, Erroll Garner, Milton Kamin, Bob Merrill.

Casper Citron Program
6/29/1996, W0R
Special Guest: Janet Leigh.

Janet Leigh Discusses "Psycho"
3/10/1999, WHYY
Leigh talks about working on Alfred Hitchcock's *Psycho* on National Public Radio.

G. Literary Works

There Really Was Hollywood, Garden City, NY: Doubleday, 1984.
Janet Leigh Autobiography.

Psycho: Behind the Scenes of the Classic Thriller, written with Christopher Nickens, New York Harmony Books, 1995.
Leigh's closer look at the Hitchcock masterpiece.
REVIEWS: "What is fresh about Ms. Leigh's memoirs are the sections about her own experience with the famous movie ... this book serves the useful purpose of throwing greater light on Hitchcock's meticulousness as a director."—*New York Times*

House of Destiny, Ontario, Canada: Mira Books, 1995.
Leigh's first novel, set in the late '30s, is about a friendship between a Spanish bellboy and a movie star who together transform and discover romance in Hollywood.
REVIEWS: "Her characters are too rich, noble and wise to be believed, but her settings ring with authenticity. Ms Leigh writes about beachfront real estate and celebrity weddings with the authority of one who has been there."—*New York Times Book Reviews*

The Dream Factory, New York: Mira Books, 2002.
Leigh's second novel is also set in Hollywood. Hired by a studio to find talented actors and make them into stars, Eve Handel quickly becomes one of the most powerful women in the industry. As she influences the careers of many Hollywood stars, her uncanny ability to listen makes her the confidante of their secrets and scandals.
REVIEWS: "Sadly, Leigh's campy, jejune second take on Tinseltown is more *Pollyanna* than *All About Eve*, as the author barely scratches the surface of what could have been a veritable gold mine of trashy behind-the-scenes melodrama."—*Publishers Weekly*

H. Recordings

ALBUMS:

Bye Bye Birdie; Original soundtrack, RCA, New York, 1963
Songs included: "Overture (Bye Bye Birdie — Main Title)"—Ann-Margret, Johnny Green and the Columbia Studio Orchestra; "How Lovely to Be a Woman"—Ann-Margret; "The Telephone Hour"—Bobby Rydell and the Sweet Apple Teenagers; "Put on a Happy Face"—Janet Leigh, Dick Van Dyke; "Honestly Sincere"—Jesse Pearson; "Hymn for a Sunday Evening"—Ann-Margret, Paul Lynde, Mary La Roche, Bryan Russell; "One Last Kiss"—Jesse Pearson; "One Boy"—Ann-Margret, Janet Leigh, Bobby Rydell; "Kids"—Dick Van Dyke, Paul Lynde, Maureen Stapleton, Bryan Russell; "A Lot of Livin' to Do"—Ann-Margret, Jesse Pearson, Bobby Rydell; "Rosie and Bye Bye Birdie"—Janet Leigh Dick Van Dyke; "We Love You, Conrad"—Ann-Margret, Janet Leigh, Dick Van Dyke, Bobby Rydell

The Sounds of Christmas (a.k.a. *Salvation Army Presents The Sound of Christmas*); Ranchos Palos Verdes, CA, 1990s
  Music provided by Julie Andrews, Tony Bennett, Voices of Liberty, and special guest Janet Leigh. A compilation of popular Christmas songs.

I. Awards and Honors

Key to the City of Stockton, California, January 15, 1950

Golden Apple: Most Cooperative Actress, 1952

Golden Nugget Award, for *The Naked Spur*, 1953

Modern Screen Popularity Award, for achievement in motion picture industry, one of top ten, 1956

Certificate of Award by *Photoplay* magazine, as one of the most popular actresses of 1956

Golden Apple: Most Cooperative Actress, 1960 (shared with Nanette Fabray)

Star on the Walk of Fame and *Walk of Fame Plaque*, February 8, 1960

The Most Perfect Figure in the World, April 13, 1960
  A trophy awarded in Hollywood by Jantzen Swimsuit Company

Golden Globe: Best Supporting Actress, for *Psycho* (1960), 1961

Academy Award Nomination: Best Supporting Actress, for *Psycho* (1960), 1961

Golden Laurel: Top Female Supporting Performance, 2nd place, for *Psycho* (1960), 1961

Golden Laurel: Top Female Comedy Performance, for *Pepe* (1960), 1961

University of Pacific Alumni Fun Silver Bowl, 1964

SHARE Inc., 1968

Caritas Society Award, October 13, 1971

First Bear Valley Celebrity Pro-Am Ski Classic Tournament, Bear Valley, CA, March 1971

Proclamation of Janet Leigh Day, Office of Mayor, Stockton, CA, September 28, 1972

Appreciation for Outstanding Service, National Association for Retarded Citizens, 1974

The Lloyd Bridges Celebrity Tennis Trophy, 1975

SHARE Inc., Member of the Year, 1975

National Film Award, 1978

Certificate of Honor as a founding member of the Professional Guild of the American Film Institute, 1983

Harriett and Alan Lederman Hope for Multiple Sclerosis Award, 1983

Outstanding Mother's Award, conferred by the National Mother's Day Committee, New York, April 22, 1986

The American Film Institute Tribute to Jack Lemmon Award, May 1988

Merit of Achievement Award, Italy 1992

MGM Girls' Reunion Plaque, Beverly Hills, August 1992

The Joel McCrea Merit of Achievement Award, Beverly Hills, February 1994

Premiere Magazine Lifetime Achievement Trophy, 1995

The Florida Film Festival Ezian Award, Orlando, FL, June 1995

Cinecon Society for the Cinephiles Award, 1995

Cinema Arts Centre Distinguished Artistic Achievement Award, 1996

Pipe Night at the Players Club, New York, June 23, 1996
    An engraved tray was given to Janet Leigh as a tribute to her 50th career anniversary

AMC Promenade Theaters Lifetime Achievement Award, 1996

The Arthur Award, University of Arizona, 1996

Outstanding Mother of the Year, bestowed by Cedars-Sinai Medical Center's Helping Hands Organization for her philanthropic work through SHARE and the Women's Guild of Cedars-Sinai, May 2, 1997

The Harvey Award, Indiana, Pennsylvania, 1997
    Awarded by the Jimmy Stewart Museum to a distinguished celebrity tied to James Stewart's spirit of humanitarism.

Pantheon of the Arts, University of the Pacific, 1998

Eyegore Award, 1998

Recognition of Performance in Psycho *as number 18 of America's 100 Greatest Movies*, American Film Institute, 1998

Recognition of Performance in The Manchurian Candidate *as number 67 of America's 100 Greatest Movies*, American Film Institute, 1998

The Carl Laemmle Award, Washington, DC, 2000

Lake Tahoe Achievement Award, Lake Tahoe, CA, 2000

Certificate of Appreciation in Recognition of 15 Years of Distinguished Service, Board of Trustees, Motion Picture and Television Fund, 2002

The Augusta Curtis Cultural Center Award, Meriden, CT, 2002

Honorary Doctor of Fine Arts Degree, University of the Pacific, Stockton, California, May 14, 2004

Janet Leigh Plaza— the city of Stockton renamed and dedicated a downtown movie theater and plaza to Janet Leigh, 2006

Janet Leigh Theatre— the University of the Pacific renamed and dedicated the campus movie theater to Janet Leigh, June 2010
    NOTE: Most of Janet Leigh's awards and trophies have been donated by the family to the University of the Pacific in Stockton, California. They are now on exhibit at the Janet Leigh Theatre on campus and in the Holt-Atherton Special Collections reading room.

Chapter Notes

Chapter 1

1. Helen Morrison, "She's Magic," *Photoplay*, February 1949, p. 59.
2. *Projection 7: A Forum for Film-Makers on Film-Making* (London: Faber & Faber, 1997), p. 117.
3. Morrison, "She's Magic," p. 90.
4. *Ibid.*
5. Janet Leigh, "Love Comes More Than Once," *Photoplay*, February 1950, p. 78.
6. *Projection 7: A Forum for Film-Makers on Film-Making*, p. 90.
7. *Ibid.*, pp. 113–114.
8. John K. Newnham, "Dame Fortune Presents Janet Leigh," *Picturegoer*, October 15, 1949, p. 11.
9. Morrison, "She's Magic," p. 91.
10. J.E.A. Bawden, "Janet Leigh," *Films in Review*, January 1979, p. 2.
11. "Girl's First Screen Role Is Opposite Van Johnson," *The New York Times*, August 22, 1946.
12. Wilson D'Arne, "Norma Shearer–Talent Scout!," *Picturegoer*, November 8, 1947, p. 9.
13. Bawden, "Janet Leigh," p. 2.
14. *Projection 7: A Forum for Film-Makers on Film-Making*, p. 115.
15. Ronald L. Davis, *Van Johnson: MGM's Golden Boy* (Jackson: University Press of Mississippi, 2001), p. 107.
16. *Ibid.*
17. Walter Pidgeon, "Naive Is the Word," *Silver Screen*, May 1948, p. 63.
18. *Projection 7: A Forum for Film-Makers on Film-Making*, p. 115.

Chapter 2

1. Thomas M. Pryor, *The New York Times*, September 12, 1947, sec. 3, p. 18.
2. Pidgeon, "Naive Is the Word," p. 64.
3. Leo Verswijver, *Movies Were Always Magical* (Jefferson, NC: McFarland, 2003), p. 95.
4. Janet Leigh, *There Really Was a Hollywood* (Garden City, NY: Doubleday, 1984), p. 68.
5. Pidgeon, "Naive Is the Word," p. 37.
6. Bawden, "Janet Leigh," p. 3.
7. Morgan Hudgins, "Cinderella Herself," *The New York Times*, August 10, 1947, p. X3.
8. Doug McClelland, *Forties Film Talk: Oral Histories of Hollywood* (Jefferson, NC: McFarland, 1992), p. 111.
9. *Ibid.*
10. Thomas S. Hischack, *The Rodgers and Hammerstein Encyclopedia* (Westport, CT: Greenwood Press, 2007), p. 317.
11. Bawden, "Janet Leigh," p. 3.
12. Fred Zinnemann, *An Autobiography* (New York: Scribner's, 1992), p. 74.
13. Gabriel Miller, *Fred Zinnemann Interviews* (Jackson: University Press of Mississippi), 2004, p. 116.
14. Robert Surtees, "Act of Violence," *American Cinematographer*, August 1948, p. 282.
15. McClelland, *Forties Film Talk*, p. 111.

16. Bosley Crowther, *The New York Times*, January 24, 1949, p. 16.

17. Ray Nielsen, "Janet Leigh and 'Little Women,'" *Classic Images*, August 1986, p. 34.

18. Mervyn LeRoy and Dick Kleiner, *Mervyn LeRoy: Take One* (New York: Hawthorne, 1974), p. 166.

19. Ray Nielsen, "Janet Leigh and *Little Women*," p. 34.

20. McClelland, *Forties Film Talk*, pp. 111–112.

21. June Allyson and Frances Spatz Leighton, *June Allyson* (New York: Putnam, 1982), p. 123.

22. *Projection 7: A Forum for Film-Makers on Film-Making*, p. 90.

23. McClelland, *Forties Film Talk*, p. 112.

24. Leigh, "Love Comes More Than Once," p. 78.

25. *Ibid.*

26. McClelland, *Forties Film Talk*, p. 112.

27. James Spada, *Peter Lawford: The Man Who Kept the Secrets* (London: Bantam, 1991), pp. 130–131.

28. Eric Monder, *George Sidney: A Bio-Bibliography* (Westport, CT: Greenwood Press, 1994), p. 164.

29. Patricia Seton Lawford, *Peter Lawford: Hollywood, the Kennedys, the Rat Pack and the Whole Damn Crowd* (London: Sidwick & Jackson, 1988), p. 37.

30. Spada, *Peter Lawford: The Man Who Kept the Secrets*, p. 131.

31. Mary Kiersch, *Curtis Bernhardt* (Metuchen, NJ: Scarecrow Press, 1986), p. 144.

32. Peter Ford, *Glenn Ford: A Life* (Madison: University of Wisconsin Press, 2011), p. 104.

33. *Variety*, September 14, 1949.

34. *Projection 7: A Forum for Film-Makers on Film-Making*, pp. 119–120.

35. *Ibid.*

36. Lee Server, *Robert Mitchum: Baby, I Don't Care* (New York: St. Martin Press, 2001), p. 244.

37. *Ibid.*, pp. 244–245.

38. Thomas F. Brady, "Janet Leigh Gets 2 RKO Film Leads," *The New York Times*, July 1, 1949, p. 14.

39. Doug McClelland, *Forties Film Talk*, pp. 112–113.

40. *Intimate Portrait*, "Janet Leigh," October 20, 1996, Lifetime.

41. John Baxter, *The Cinema of Josef von Sternberg* (New York: A.S. Barnes, 1971), pp. 165–166.

42. Bawden, "Janet Leigh," p. 4.

43. Anita Colby, "She's Younger Than Springtime," *Photoplay*, November 1949, p. 59.

44. *Projection 7: A Forum for Film-Makers on Film-Making*, pp. 121–122.

45. John Anthony Gilvey, *Before the Parade Passes By: Gower Champion and the Glorious American Musical* (New York: St. Martin's Press, 2005), pp. 40–41.

46. Ray Nielsen, "Janet Leigh and Two Tickets to Broadway," *Classic Images*, March 1986, p. 51.

Chapter 3

1. Janet Leigh, *There Really Was a Hollywood*, p. 115.

2. Tony Curtis and Barry Paris, *Tony Curtis: The Autobiography* (London: Heinemann, 1994), p. 109.

3. *Ibid.*, p. 110.

4. Tony Curtis, "Across a Crowded Room," *Photoplay*, February 1951, pp. 95–96.

5. *Ibid.*, p. 97.

6. Curtis and Paris, *Tony Curtis*, p. 110.

7. Piper Laurie, *Learning to Live Out and Loud: A Memoir* (New York: Crown Archetype, 2011), p. 96.

8. Janet Leigh, "And So We Were Married," *Silver Screen*, October 1951, p. 39.

9. Jamie Lee Curtis, "Memories of Mother," *More*, May 2010.

10. Tony Curtis, *American Prince* (New York: Harmony Books, 2008), p. 134.

11. Jerry Lewis, "I'm in Love with My Best Friend's Wife," *Photoplay*, August 1952, p. 88.

12. Shawn Levy, *King of the Comedy. The Life and Art of Jerry Lewis* (New York: St. Martin Press, 1996), p. 151.

13. Pete Martin, "The Perils of Being a Young Movie Star," *The Saturday Evening Standard*, February 9, 1952, p. 78.

14. Doug McClelland, *Eleanor Parker: A Woman of Thousand Faces* (Metuchen, NJ: Scarecrow Press, 1989), p. 72.

15. Michael Munn, *Tony Curtis: Nobody's Perfect* (London: JR Books, 2011), p. 79.

Chapter 4

1. Stephen M. Silverman, *Dancing on the Ceiling. Stanley Donen and His Movies* (New York: Knopf, 1996), p. 172.

2. *Ibid.*

3. Bawden, "Janet Leigh," pp. 5–6.

4. Donald Dewey, *James Stewart: A Biography* (Boston: Little Brown, 1996), p. 494.

5. *Ibid.*, pp. 351–352.

6. Davis, *Van Johnson*, p. 152.

7. Tom Weaver, *Science Fiction and Horror Heroes: Interviews with Actors, Directors, Producers and Writers of the 1940s through 1960s* (Jefferson, NC: McFarland, 1991), p. 277.

8. Ibid., p. 279.

9. Janet Leigh, "People Are Wonderful," *The Film Show Annual*, 1952, p. 56.

10. James Mason, *Before I Forget* (London: Hamish Hamilton, 1981), p. 243.

11. Tony Curtis, *American Prince*, pp. 150–151.

12. Pauline Swanson, "No Sad Songs," *Photoplay*, October 1953, p. 86.

13. Munn, *Tony Curtis*, p. 93.

14. Bawden, "Janet Leigh," p. 5.

15. Levy, *King of Comedy*, p. 177.

16. William Schoell, *Martini Man: The Life of Dean Martin* (Dallas: Taylor, 1994), p. 89.

17. Rosemary Clooney, *Girl Singer: An Autobiography* (New York: Doubleday, 1999), pp. 112–113.

18. Curtis and Paris, *Tony Curtis*, p. 100.

19. Bawden, "Janet Leigh," p. 6.

20. "Janet Leigh's Marriage Secrets," *Silver Screen*, July 1954, p. 70.

21. Tony Curtis, *American Prince*, p. 158.

22. Bawden, "Janet Leigh," p. 6.

23. Martin Gottfried, *All His Jazz: The Life & Death of Bob Fosse* (New York: Bantam, 1990), p. 86.

24. Michael Freedland, *Jack Lemmon* (London: Weidenfeld and Nicolson, 1985), p. 38.

25. Gottfried, *All His Jazz*, p. 87.

Chapter 5

1. "Some Like It Dark: Tony Curtis Talks to Jamie Lee Curtis," *Projection 5* (London: Faber & Faber, 1996), pp. 18–19.

2. Ronnie Maasz, *A Cast of Shadows* (Lanham, MD: Scarecrow Press, 2004), pp. 39–40.

3. Bob Monkhouse, *Crying with Laughter* (London: Arrow, 1994), pp. 296–297.

4. Louella Parsons, "A New Home for Baby," *Pictorial TView, New York Journal American*, March 11, 1956, p. 3.

5. Michael Musto, "La Dolce Musto," *The Village Voice*, September 22, 1998, p. 12.

6. Aljean Meltsir, "Once Upon a Time...," *Photoplay*, December 1956, p. 74.

Chapter 6

1. *Projection 7: A Forum for Film-Makers on Film-Making*, pp. 131.

2. Bawden, "Janet Leigh," p. 7.

3. *Ibid.*

4. Charlton Heston, *In the Arena* (New York: HarperCollins, 1995), p. 156.

5. Peter Bogdanovich, *This Is Orson Welles* (New York: DaCapo Press, 1998), p. 314.

6. Heston, *In the Arena*, p. 176.

7. Dalya Alberge, "Welles Premiere Is Cut Short by Legal Threat," *The Times*, May 22, 1998, p. 13.

8. Ernest Borgnine, *Ernie: The Autobiography* (New York: Citadel Press, 2008), p. 128.

9. Curtis and Paris, *Tony Curtis*, p. 139.

10. Hazel K. Johnson, "Curtises Break Up Duo Act," *New York World-Telegram*, January 17, 1958.

11. Jean Francois Hauduroy, "Sophisticated Naturalism: Interview with Blake Edwards," *Cahiers du Cinéma in English* 3, 1966, p. 23.

12. Tony Curtis, *American Prince*, p. 188.

13. Florabel Muir, "Janet Leigh in Crash; Sinatra Calls Cops," *Daily News*, August 25, 1958, p. 8.

14. Mike Connolly, "We Are One of the Happiest Families in Hollywood," *Screen Stories*, October 1959, p. 56.

15. *Intimate Portrait*, "Janet Leigh."

16. "Motherhood Puts Curves on Janet," *New York Journal-American*, August 5, 1959.

17. "Film Clips," *Sight & Sound*, Spring 1968, p. 99.

18. "Who Was That Lady?," *Harrison's Report*, December 26, 1959, p. 206.

Chapter 7

1. Stephen Rebello, *Alfred Hitchcock and the Making of Psycho* (New York: St. Martin's Griffin, 1998), p. 60.
2. Janet Leigh and Christopher Nickens, *Behind the Scenes of Psycho* (New York: Harmony Book, 1995), p. 42.
3. Rebello, *Alfred Hitchcock*, p. 61.
4. James W. Merrick, "Hitchcock Regimen for 'Psycho,'" *The New York Times*, December 27, 1959.
5. Simon Bround, "Inside the Head of Psycho," *Empire*, August 1998, p. 90.
6. Leigh and Nickens, *Behind the Scenes of Psycho*, p. 76.
7. Robert Graysmith, *The Girl in the Alfred Hitchcock's Shower* (London: Titan, 2010), pp. 66–67.
8. Peter Bogdanovich, *Who the Devil Made It* (New York: Knopf, 1977), p. 477.
9. Merrick, "Hitchcock Regimen for 'Psycho.'"
10. Dermot Purgavie, "I Have No Intention of Taking a Shower Ever Again," *Mail on Sunday*, August 27, 1995, p. 43.
11. "Psycho in Threat to 'Psycho' Star," *New York Journal-American*, October 21, 1960.

Chapter 8

1. Erskine Johnson, "That Girl Next Door? Not Janet," *New York World-Telegram*, April 12, 1961.
2. Tony Curtis, *American Prince*, p. 227.
3. *Biography*, "Janet Leigh," October 27, 2003, A&E.
4. James Robert Parish and Don E. Stanke, *The Swashbucklers* (New Rochelle, NY: Arlington House, 1976), p. 612.
5. Weaver, *Science Fiction Stars*, pp. 283–284.
6. Eugene Archer, "Spotlight on Garden Main Event," *The New York Times*, February 22, 1962.
7. *Projection 7: A Forum for Film-Makers on Film-Making*, p. 122.
8. Weaver, *Science Fiction Stars*, p. 284.
9. Vincent Canby, "The Manchurian Candidate," *Variety*, October 17, 1962.
10. Jamie Lee Curtis, "Memories of Mother," *More*, May 2010.
11. *Projection 7: A Forum for Film-Makers on Film-Making*, p. 125.
12. Ralph Blumenstein, "Janet Leigh Puts in a Small Claim," *New York Post*, June 17, 1962, p. 3.
13. "Janet, the Belle of the Brawl...," *Life*, August 10, 1962, p. 41.
14. Dick Van Dyke, *My Lucky Life In and Out of Show Business: A Memoir* (New York: Crown Archetype, 2011), p. 100.
15. Stephen Rebello, "Janet Leigh on Surviving Hollywood with Style and Grace," *Movieline*, January 1, 1991, p. 85.

Chapter 9

1. Louella O. Parsons, "Janet Leigh: Her New Leading Man," *Pictorial TView*, November 4, 1962, p. 3.
2. John Rich, *Warm Up the Snake* (Ann Arbor: University of Michigan Press, 2006), p. 65.
3. *Ibid.*, pp. 66–67.
4. Martha Hyer, *Finding My Way: A Hollywood Memoir* (San Francisco: HarperSanFrancisco, 1990), pp. 78–79.
5. Jack Thompson, "Janet's Waiting to Become 'House' Wife," *New York Mirror*, August 27, 1963.
6. Sally Hammond, "Janet Leigh Taping Andy Williams Show," *New York Post*, August 18, 1964.
7. Joe Morella and Edward Epstein, *Paul and Joanne: A Biography of Paul Newman and Joanne Woodward* (New York: Delacorte Press, 1988), p. 111.
8. Levy, *King of Comedy*, p. 337.
9. Alberto Crespi, *Dal Polo all'Equatore: I film e le avventure di Giuliano Montaldo* (Venezia: Marsilio, 2005), p. 74.
10. Howard Thompson, *The New York Times*, February 21, 1968, sec. 4, p. 60.
11. Bawden, "Janet Leigh," p. 9.

Chapter 10

1. Rebello, "Janet Leigh on Surviving Hollywood...," p. 86.

2. Marian Christy, "Janet Dresses in Pink for Luck," *Daily Mirror*, September 13, 1971.

3. Jamie Lee Curtis, "Memories of My Mother."

4. "Hollywood Society: Some Stay Home or Golf, No One Has Tea," *The New York Times*, March 16, 1971, p. 43.

5. Albert Ashton, "Janet Leigh Says Working for Retarded Children Is More Satisfying Than Acting," *National Enquirer*, 1972.

6. "Profile Janet Leigh," *Premiere UK*, June 1996, p. 29.

7. Weaver, *Science Fiction*, pp. 285–286.

8. Ibid.

9. Louette Harding, "I Only Wanted to Play Mother," *Mail on Sunday*, January 14, 1996, p. 30.

10. Ibid.

11. Ibid., pp. 30–32.

12. Spada, *Peter Lawford: The Man Who Kept Secrets*, p. 424.

13. Sidney Fields, "Only Human," *Daily News*, p. 41.

14. "Whodunit Janet?," *New York Sunday News*, September 14, 1975, p. 3.

15. Fields, "Only Human," p. 41.

16. Hobe Morrison, "Shows on Broadway," *Variety*, December 31, 1975, p. 43.

17. Earl Wilson, "Bonos Reuniting — but Only in TV," *The Milwaukee Sentinel*, January 16, 1976, p. 15.

18. Lawrence Van Gelder, "Janet Leigh: Happily at Work in Brooklyn," *The New York Daily Metro*, September 14, 1978, p. 48.

19. Rex Reed, "The Starlet Grows Up," *New York Sunday News*, November 18, 1979, p. 19.

20. Rob Baker, "Beyond Showers and Peach and Cream," *Soho Weekly News*, November 22, 1979, p. 37.

21. Reed, "The Starlet Grows Up," p. 3.

22. Baker, "Beyond Showers and Peach and Cream," p. 37.

23. Rebecca Morehouse, "Janet Leigh Remembers Her Athletic Courtship," *The Star-Ledger*, September 28, 1978, p. 42.

24. Arthur Bell, "Bell Tells," *The Village Voice*, September 11, 1978, p. 50.

25. Vincent Canby, "Some Small Pleasure in a So-So Season," *The New York Times*, December 2, 1977.

26. Weaver, *Science Fiction*, p. 286.

27. Rebello, "Janet Leigh on Surviving Hollywood...," p. 87.

28. Davis, *Van Johnson*, pp. 223–224.

29. Michael Ankerich, "Psyched Up for Psycho," *Classic Images*, September 1995, p. 32.

30. Mick Brown, "Out of the Shower and into Print," *Daily Telegraph*, November 16, 1996, p. 17.

31. Ian Spelling, "The Original Marion," *Fangoria*, January 199, p. 29.

32. Marilyn Beck, "Janet Leigh Showered with Honors," *Daily News*, April 7, 1999, p. 38.

33. Verswijver, *Movies Were Magical*, p. 100.

34. Jamie Lee Curtis, "Memories of My Mother."

35. Ankerich, "Psyched Up for Psycho," p. C4.

36. William Ottorburn-Hall, "Janet Leigh at 43: Pragmatic Polyanna," *Louisville Courier-Journal*, March 29, 1970, p. E 2.

Bibliography

Allyson, June, and Spatz Leighton Frances. *June Allyson*. New York: Putnam, 1982.

Astor, Mary. *A Life in Film*. New York: Delacorte Press, 1971.

_____. *My Story: An Autobiography*. Garden City, NY: Doubleday, 1959.

Baltake, Joe. *The Films of Jack Lemmon*. Secaucus, NJ: Citadel Press, 1977.

_____. *Jack Lemmon: His Film and His Career*. London: Columbus Books, 1986.

Basinger, Janine. *Anthony Mann*. Middletown, CT: Wesleyan University Press, 2007.

_____. *Gene Kelly*. New York: Pyramid Books, 1976.

Basten, Fred E., and Paul A. Kaufman. *Max Factor's Hollywood: Glamour Movies Make-Up*. Santa Monica: General Publishing Group, 1995.

Baxter, John. *The Cinema of Josef von Sternberg*. New York: A.S. Barnes, 1978.

Beck, Robert. *The Edward G. Robinson Encyclopedia*. Jefferson, NC: McFarland, 2002.

Belton, John. *Robert Mitchum*. New York: Pyramid Books, 1976.

Berg, Chuck, and Thomas L. Erskine. *The Encyclopedia of Orson Welles*. New York: Facts on File, 2003.

Bergan, Ronald. *Anthony Perkins: A Haunted Life*. London: Little, Brown, 1995.

Berni, Oriano. *Stewart Granger. Un divo in calzamaglia*. Corazzano, Pisa, Italy: Titivillus, 2009.

Bogdanovich, Peter. *This Is Orson Welles*. New York: DaCapo Press, 1998.

_____. *Who the Devil Made It*. New York: Knopf, 1997.

Borgnine, Ernest. *Ernie: The Autobiography*. New York: Citadel Press, 2008.

Boswell, John, and David Jay. *Duke: The John Wayne Album*. New York: Ballantine, 1979.

Brady, Frank. *Citizen Welles: A Biography of Orson Welles*. New York: Scribner's, 1989.

Bret, David. *Errol Flynn: Satan's Angel*. London: Robson, 2004.

Bride, Douglas. *Lost Films of the Fifties*. Secaucus, NJ: Citadel Press, 1988.

Brion, Patrick. *Hitchcock: Biographie, filmographie illustrée, analyse critique*. Paris: Édition de la Martinière, 2000.

Bubbeo, Daniel. *The Women of Warner Brothers*. Jefferson, NC: McFarland, 2002.

Burkart, Jeff, and Bruce Stuart. *Hollywood's First Choices*. New York: Crown Trade, 1994.

Capua, Michelangelo. *Anthony Perkins: Prigioniero della paura*. Torino, Italy: Lindau, 2004.

_____. *Deborah Kerr: A Biography*. Jefferson, NC: McFarland, 2010.

Casper, Joseph Andrew. *Stanley Donen*. Metuchen, NJ: Scarecrow Press,1983.

Champlin, Charles. *John Frankenheimer: A Conversation with Charles Champlin*. Burbank: Riverwood Press, 1995.

Clooney, Rosemary. *Girl Singer: An Autobiography*. New York: Doubleday, 1999.

Cole, Lester. *Hollywood Red: The Autobiography of Lester Cole*. Palo Alto: Rampant Press, 1981.

Collins, Ace. *Lassie: A Dog's Life. The First Fifty Years*. Rutherford, NJ: Penguin, 1993.

Crespi, Alberto. *Dal Polo all'Equatore: I film e le avventure di Giuliano Montaldo*. Venezia: Marsilio, 2005.

Crowther, Bruce. *Charlton Heston: The Epic Presence*. London: Columbus Books, 1986.

_____. *Mitchum: The Film Career of Robert Mitchum*. London: Robert Hale, 1991.

Culver, Roland. *Not Quite a Gentleman*. London: William Klein, 1979.

Curtis, Tony. *American Prince*. New York: Harmony Books, 2008.

_____, and Barry Paris. *Tony Curtis: The Autobiography*. London: Heinemann, 1994.

Davis, Ronald L. *Van Johnson: MGM's Golden Boy*. Jackson: University Press of Mississippi, 2001.

Dewey, Donald. *James Stewart: A Biography*. Atlanta: Turner, 1996.

Douglas, Kirk. *The Ragman's Son: An Autobiography*. New York: Simon & Schuster, 1998.

Edelman, Rob, and Audrey E. Kupferberg. *Angela Lansbury. A Life on Stage and Screen*. New York: Birch Lane Press, 1996.

Fishgall, Gary. *Pieces of Time: The Life of James Stewart*. New York: Scribner's, 1997.

Ford, Peter. *Glenn Ford: A Life*. Madison: The University of Wisconsin Press, 2011.

Freedland, Michael. *Dean Martin: King of the Road*. London: Robson Books, 2004.

_____. *Jack Lemmon*. New York: St. Martin's Press, 1985.

Fujiwara, Chris. *Jerry Lewis*. Champaign: University Press of Illinois, 2009.

Gerosa, Mario. *Il cinema di Terence Young*. Piombino, Livorno, Italy: Edizioni Il Foglio, 2009.

Gilvey, John Anthony. *Before the Parade Passes By: Gower Champion and the Glorious American Musical*. New York: St. Martin's Press, 2005.

Goldman, William. *Adventure in the Screen Trade*. London: Macdonald, 1983.

Gottesman, Ronald. *Focus on Orson Welles*. Englewood Cliffs, NJ: Prentice-Hall, 1976.

Gottfried, Martin. *All His Jazz: The Life & Death of Bob Fosse*. New York: Bantam, 1990.

Gottlieb, Sidney. *Alfred Hitchcock Interviews*. Jackson: University Press of Mississippi, 2003.

Granger, Stewart. *Sparks Fly Upward*. London: Granada, 1981.

Graysmith, Robert. *The Girl in Alfred Hitchcock's Shower*. London: Titan Books, 2010.

Grubb Boyd, Kevin. *Razzle Dazzle: The Life and Work of Bob Fosse*. New York: St. Martin Press, 1989.

Harvey, James. *Movie Love in the Fifties*. New York: Da Capo Press, 2001.

Heston, Charlton. *In the Arena: An Autobiography*. New York: Simon & Schuster, 1995.

Hickey, Des, and Gus Smith. *The Prince: Being the Public and Private Life of Larushka Mischa Skikne, A Jewish Lithuanian Vagabond Player, Otherwise Known as Laurence Harvey*. London: Leslie Frewin, 1975.

Higham, Charles. *The Films of Orson Welles*. Berkley: University of California, 1970.

_____. *Merchant of Dreams: Louis B. Mayer, M.G.M., and the Secret Hollywood*. New York: Donald I. Fine, 1993.

Hirschhorn, Clive. *The Films of James Mason*. London: LSP Books, 1975.

Hischack, Thomas S. *The Rodgers and Hammerstein Encyclopedia*. Westport, CT: Greenwood Press, 2007.

Hunter, Allan. *Tony Curtis: The Man and His Movies*. New York: St. Martin Press, 1985.

Jacobs, Jack, and Myron Brown. *The Films of Norma Shearer*. Cranbury, NJ: A. S. Barnes, 1976.

Jarlett, Franklin. *Robert Ryan: A Biography and Critical Filmography*. Jefferson, NC: McFarland, 1990.

Karney, Robyn. *Hollywood Love Stories*. London: Octopus Books 1987.

Keaney, Michael. *Film Noir Guide: 745 Films of the Classic Era, 1940–1959*. Jefferson, NC: McFarland, 2003.

Kelley, Kitty. *Elizabeth Taylor: The Last Star*. London: Michael Joseph, 1981.

Kiersch, Mary. *Curtis Bernhardt*. Metuchen, NJ: Scarecrow Press, 1986.

Lambert, Gavin. *Norma Shearer: A Life.* London: Hodder & Stoughton, 1990.

Laurie, Piper. *Learning to Live Out and Loud: A Memoir.* New York: Crown Archetype, 2011.

Lawford Seaton, Patricia. *Peter Lawford: Hollywood, The Kennedys, The Rat Pack and the Whole Damn Crowd.* London: Sidwick & Jackson, 1988.

Lee, Peggy. *Miss Peggy Lee: An Autobiography.* New York: Donald I. Fine, 1989.

Lehman, Peter, and William Luhr. *Blake Edwards.* Athens: Ohio University Press, 1981.

Leigh, Janet. *There Really Was a Hollywood.* Garden City, NY: Doubleday, 1984.

_____, and Christopher Nickens. *Psycho: Behind the Scenes of the Classic Thriller.* New York: Harmony Books, 1995.

Lentz, Robert J. *Lee Marvin: His Films and Career.* Jefferson, NC: McFarland, 2000.

LeRoy, Mervyn, and Dick Kleiner. *Mervyn LeRoy: Take One.* New York: Hawthorne Book, 1974.

Levy, Shawn. *King of the Comedy: The Life and Art of Jerry Lewis.* New York: St. Martin Press, 1996.

Lewis, Jerry, and Herb Gluck. *Jerry Lewis in Person.* New York: Atheneum, 1982.

Maasz, Ronnie. *A Cast of Shadows.* Lanham, MD: The Scarecrow Press, 2004.

Margret, Ann, and Gold Todd. *Ann Margret: My Story.* New York: Putnam, 1994.

Marill, Alvin H. *The Complete Films of Edward G. Robinson.* Seacacus, NJ: Carol, 1990.

_____. *Movies Made for Television, 1964–2004.* Lanham, MD: Scarecrow Press, 2005.

_____. *Robert Mitchum on the Screen.* London: Barnes, 1978.

Martin, Mart. *Did He or Didn't He?* New York: Citadel Press, 2000.

Marx, Arthur. *Everybody Loves Somebody Sometime: The Story of Dean Martin and Jerry Lewis.* New York: Hawthorn Books, 1974.

_____. *The Nine Lives of Mickey Rooney.* New York: Stein and Day, 1986.

Mason, James. *Before I Forget.* London: Hamish Hamilton, 1985.

McBride, John. *Orson Welles.* London: BFI, 1972.

McClelland, Doug. *Eleanor Parker: A Woman of Thousand Faces.* Metuchen, NJ: Scarecrow Press, 1989.

_____. *Forties Film Talk: Oral Histories of Hollywood.* Jefferson, NC: McFarland, 1992.

Miller, Gabriel. *Fred Zinnemann Interviews.* Jackson: University Press of Mississippi, 2004.

Mogg, Ken. *The Alfred Hitchcock Story.* Dallas: Taylor, 1999.

Molyneaux, Gerard. *James Stewart: A Bio-Bibliography.* Westport, CT: Greenwood Press, 1992.

Monder, Eric. *George Sidney: A Bio-Bibliography.* Westport, CT: Greenwood Press, 1994.

Monkhouse, Bob. *Crying with Laughter.* London: Arrow Books, 1994,

Morella, Joe, and Edward Epstein. *Judy: The Films and Career of Judy Garland.* London: Leslie Frewin, 1969.

_____, and _____. *Paul and Joanne: A Biography of Paul Newman and Joanne Woodward.* New York: Delacorte Press, 1988.

Moseley, Roy. *Evergreen: Victor Saville in His Own Words.* Carbondale: Southern Illinois University Press, 2000.

Munn, Michael. *Charlton Heston.* New York: St. Martin Press 1986.

_____. *Kid from the Bronx: A Biography of Tony Curtis.* London: W.H. Allen, 1984.

_____. *Kirk Douglas.* London: Robson Book, 1985.

_____. *Tony Curtis: Nobody's Perfect.* London: JR Books, 2011.

Parish, James Robert. *The Best of MGM: The Golden Years 1928–1959.* Westport, CT: Greenwood Press, 1981.

_____. *The George Raft File: The Unauthorized Biography.* New York: Drake, 1973.

_____. *Hollywood Great Love Teams.* Carlstadt, NJ: Rainbow Books, 1974.

_____, and Ronald L. Bowers. *The MGM Stock Company: The Golden Era.* New Rochelle, NY: Arlington House, 1973.

_____, and Don E. Stanke. *The Swashbucklers*. New Rochelle, NY: Arlington House, 1976.

Pickard, Roy. *Frank Sinatra at the Movies*. London: Robert Hale, 1994.

Porter, Darwin. *Merv Griffin: A Life in the Closet*. New York: Blue Moon Productions 2009.

Pratley, Gerald. *The Films of John Frankenheimer*. London: Cygnus Art, 1998.

Quirk, Lawrence. *The Films of Paul Newman*. Secaucus, NJ: Citadel Press, 1971.

_____. *The Films of Robert Taylor*. Secaucus, NJ: Citadel Press, 1975.

Rebello, Stephen. *Alfred Hitchcock and the Making of Psycho*. New York: St. Martin's Griffin, 1998.

Reemes, Dana M. *Directed by Jack Arnold*. Jefferson, NC: McFarland, 1998.

Reynolds, Debbie, and David Patrick Columbia. *Debbie Reynolds: My Life*. London: Sidgwick & Jackson, 1989.

Ricci, Mark, and Boris Zmijewsky and Steve Zmijewsky. *The Films of John Wayne*. New York: Citadel Press, 1970.

Rich, John. *Warm Up the Snake: A Hollywood Memoir*. Ann Arbor: The University Press of Michigan, 2006.

Richmond, Peter. *Fever: The Life and Music of Miss Peggy Lee*. New York: Henry Holt, 2006.

Ringgold, Gene, and Clifford McCarty. *The Films of Frank Sinatra*. Secaucus, NJ: Citadel Press, 1971.

Roberts, Jerry. *Robert Mitchum: A Bio-Bibliography*. Westport, CT: Greenwood Press, 1992.

Rovin, Jeff. *The Films of Charlton Heston*. Secaucus, NJ: Citadel Press, 1977.

Saline, Carol, and Sharon J. Wohlmuth. *Mothers & Daughters*. New York: Doubleday, 1997.

Santopietro, Tom. *Sinatra in Hollywood*. New York: Thomas Dunne Books, 2008.

Sarris, Andrew. *The Films of Josef Von Sternberg*. New York: Museum of Modern Art, 1966.

Schoell, William. *Martini Man. The Life of Dean Martin*. Dallas: Taylor, 1999.

Server, Lee. *Robert Mitchum: Baby, I Don't Care*. New York: St. Martin Press, 2001.

Sheppard, Dick. *Elizabeth: The Life and Career of Elizabeth Taylor*. London: W.H. Allen, 1975.

Silver, Alain, and Ward Elizabeth. *Film Noir*. Woodstock, NY: Overlook Press, 1992.

Silverman, Stephen M. *Dancing on the Ceiling: Stanley Donen and His Movies*. New York: Knopf, 1996.

Sinai, Anne. *Reaching the Top: The Turbulent Life of Laurence Harvey*. Lanham, MD: Scarecrow Press, 2003.

Skerry, Philip J. *Psycho in the Shower: The History of Cinema's Most Famous Scene*. New York: Continuum, 2009.

Spada, James. *Peter Lawford: The Man Who Kept the Secrets*. London: Bantam Press, 1991.

Spoto, Donald. *The Dark Side of a Genius. The Life of Alfred Hitchcock*, New York: Da Capo Press, 1999.

_____. *Spellbound by Beauty*. New York: Harmony Books, 2009.

Summers, Anthony. *Sinatra. The Life*. New York: Knopf, 2005.

Tavernier, Bertrand. *Amis américains*. Paris: Institute Lumiere/Actes Sud, 1993.

Thomas, Tony. *Films of Gene Kelly*. Secaucus, NJ: Citadel Press, 1975.

_____. *The Films of Kirk Douglas*. Secaucus, NJ: Citadel Press, 1972.

_____. *Howard Hughes in Hollywood*. Secaucus, NJ: Citadel Press, 1985.

_____. *A Wonderful Life. The Films and Career of James Stewart*. New York: Citadel Press, 1998.

_____, and Clifford McCarthy. *Films of Errol Flynn*. Secaucus, NJ: Citadel Press, 1969.

Tosches, Nick. *Dino: Living High in the Dirty Business of Dreams*. New York: Doubleday, 1992.

Troyan, Michael. *A Rose for Mrs. Miniver: The Life of Green Garson*. Lexington: University Press of Kentucky, 1999.

Van Dyke, Dick. *My Lucky Life In and Out of Show Business: A Memoir.* New York: Crown Archetype, 2011.

Vermilye, Jerry, and Mark Ricci. *The Films of Elizabeth Taylor.* Secaucus, NJ: Citadel Press, 1985.

Verswijver, Leo. *Movies Were Always Magical.* Jefferson, NC: McFarland, 2003.

Wagner, Robert J. *Piece of My Heart: A Life.* London: Hutchinson, 2009.

Walker, Alexander. *Elizabeth.* London: Weidenfeld and Nicolson, 1990.

Wallis Hyer, Martha. *Finding My Way: A Hollywood Memoir.* San Francisco: HarperSanFrancisco, 1990.

Wander Bonanno, Margaret. *Angela Lansbury: A Biography.* New York: St. Martin Press, 1987.

Wasson, Sam. *A Splurch in the Kisser: The Movies of Blake Edwards.* Middletown, CT: Wesleyan University Press, 2009.

Wayne, Jane Ellen. *Robert Taylor.* London: Robson Books, 1991.

Weaver, Tom. *Science Fiction and Horror Heroes: Interviews with Actors, Directors, Producers and Writers of the 1940s through 1960s.* Jefferson, NC: McFarland, 1991.

Wilcoxon, Henry, and Katherine Orrison. *Lionheart in Hollywood: The Autobiography of Henry Wilcoxon.* Metuchen, NJ: Scarecrow Press, 1991.

Winecoff, Charles. *Split Image: The Life of Anthony Perkins.* New York: Dutton, 1996.

Yudkoff, Alvin. *Gene Kelly: A Life of Dance and Dreams.* New York: Back Stage Books, 1999.

Zinnemann, Fred. *Fred Zinnemann: A Life into the Movies.* New York: Scribner's, 1992.

Index